D1439065

LATIN AMERICAN DEVELOPMENT AND PUBLIC POLICY

Latin American Development and Public Policy

Edited by

Stuart S. Nagel
Professor of Political Science
University of Illinois at Urbana-Champaign

St. Martin's Press

First published in Great Britain 1994 by
THE MACMILLAN PRESS LTD
Houndmills, Basingstoke, Hampshire RG21 2XS
and London
Companies and representatives
throughout the world

This book is published in the *Policy Studies Organization Series*
General Editor: Stuart S. Nagel

A catalogue record for this book is available
from the British Library.

ISBN 0–333–58733–2

Printed in Great Britain by
Ipswich Book Co Ltd
Ipswich, Suffolk

First published in the United States of America 1994 by
Scholarly and Reference Division,
ST. MARTIN'S PRESS, INC.,
175 Fifth Avenue,
New York, N.Y. 10010

ISBN 0–312–10650–5

Library of Congress Cataloging-in-Publication Data
Latin American development and public policy / edited by Stuart S.
Nagel.
p. cm.
Includes index.
ISBN 0–312–10650–5
1. Latin America—Economic policy. 2. Latin America—Social
policy. 3. Latin America—Politics and government—1980–
I. Nagel, Stuart S., 1934– .
HC125.L3465 1994
338.98—dc20   93–31948
                                               CIP

Dedicated to improving public policy and its administration in Latin America

Contents

Notes on the Contributors   ix

Introduction   xi

PART I   ECONOMIC POLICY

1   The Crisis of the Welfare State and its Influence
    on Latin America in North–South Relations
    Ernesto Aragón, Claudia Dorado, Javier Benavente,
    Verónica Marcelino and María Teresa Piñero de Ruiz   3

2   Assessing Public Policy in the Andean Pact
    Gordon Mace   20

PART II   SOCIAL POLICY

3   Social Policy and Political Dynamics in
    Latin America
    Ernesto Aldo Isuani   55

4   Dilemmas and Solutions in the Implementation of
    Social Policies in Latin America
    Bernardo Kliksberg   71

PART III   TECHNOLOGY AND ENVIRONMENTAL POLICY

5   Administering Electronics: The Experience of
    India and Brazil
    Jørgen D. Pedersen   91

6   Bureaucrats as Technology Policy Partners
    Elisa P. Reis   122

7 Ecotourism: Toward a Policy of Economic
Development and Environmental Balance in
Latin America
Michele Zebich-Knos 140

PART IV POLITICAL POLICY

8 Beyond the Party List: Electoral Reform in
Venezuela
José Molina 165

9 Contagion of Democracy in Latin America:
The Case of Paraguay
Mikael Bostrom 186

10 Post-Marxism, the Left and Democracy in
Latin America
Ronald H. Chilcote 214

11 The Legacy of Authoritarianism in Democratic
Brazil
Paulo Sérgio Pinheiro 237

PART V CONSTITUTIONAL POLICY

12 From Coparticipation to Coalition: The Problems
of Presidentialism in the Uruguayan Case, 1984–90
María Ester Mancebo 257

13 Chile and the Prosecution of Military Officials
for Human Rights Violations: A Comparative
Approach
Allan Metz 282

PART VI PUBLIC POLICY ANALYSIS

14 Political Science in Mexico in the Cold War and
Post-Cold War Context
Enrique Suárez-Iñiguez 303

Index 313

Notes on the Contributors

Ernesto Aragón, Political Science Department, National University of Cordoba, Cordoba, Argentina.

Javier Benavente, Political Science Department, National University of Cordoba, Cordoba, Argentina.

Mikael Bostrom, Political Science Department, University of Umea, Umea, Sweden.

Ronald H. Chilcote, Political Science Department, University of California at Riverside, Riverside, California, USA.

Claudia Dorado, Political Science Department, National University of Cordoba, Cordoba, Argentina.

Ernesto Aldo Isuani, Centro Interdisciplinario para el Estudio de Politicas Publicas, Buenos Aires, Argentina.

Bernardo Kliksberg, Director, United Nations Regional Project for Modernization of Organization and State Management, Caracas, Venezuela.

Gordon Mace, International Relations Center and Political Science Department, Laval University, Quebec City, Quebec, Canada.

María Ester Mancebo, Political Science Institute, University of the Republic, Montevideo, Uruguay.

Verónica Marcelino, Political Science Department, National University of Cordoba, Cordoba, Argentina.

Allan Metz, Drury College, Springfield, Missouri, USA.

José Molina, Center of Investigation and Study of Politics and Administration, University of Zulia, Maracaibo, Venezuela.

Stuart S. Nagel, Political Science Department, University of Illinois, Urbana, Illinois, USA.

Jørgen D. Pedersen, Political Science Institute, University of Aarhus, Aarhus, Denmark.

Paulo Sérgio Pinheiro, Center for the Study of Violence, Political Science Department, University of São Paulo, Sao Paulo, Brazil.

Elisa P. Reis, IUPERJ, Rio de Janeiro, Brazil.

María Teresa Piñero de Ruiz, Political Science Department, National University of Cordoba, Cordoba, Argentina.

Enrique Suárez-Iñiguez, Political Science Department, National University of Mexico (UNAM), Mexico City, Mexico.

Michele Zebich-Knos, Political Science Department, Kennesaw State College, Marietta, Georgia, USA.

Introduction

This book contains updated versions of the most relevant papers that were presented at the 1991 Buenos Aires conference of the International Political Science Association (IPSA). Other papers were also contributed through the Latin America network of the Policy Studies Organization.

The book analyzes various important aspects of methodology and substance regarding economic, social and political policy in Latin America directed toward achieving more effective, efficient and equitable societal institutions. The chapters are written by experts from within Latin America and also from Latin America research institutes elsewhere. The book combines practical policy significance with insightful causal and prescriptive generalizations. The emphasis is on the role of governmental decision making and the important (but secondary) role of the market-place, social groups and engineering.

Part I, on economic policy, considers the crisis in the welfare state and consensus building in developing international economic communities. Part II emphasizes problems of the poor, especially the provision of health care, and aspects of poverty and ethnic groups. Part III deals with developing electronics for export and for internal consumption, with an emphasis on the role of government and technologists as policy partners. Part IV comprises four chapters dealing with electoral reform, the spread of democracy, post-Marxism and the legacy of authoritarianism. Part V examines the role of coparticipation, and the prosecution of human rights violations. The book ends with an analysis of the development of political science in Mexico and Latin America.

The need for better policy analysis in Latin America and elsewhere can be illustrated by the problem of presidential versus parliamentary government for Argentina, as shown in Table I.1. The analysis was developed at the Buenos Aires IPSA conference. The conservative position is generally to support presidential government because it gives greater stability, which conservatives like. The liberal position is to support parliamentary government, largely because it is more responsive and liberals have traditionally been more interested in responsiveness, at least with regard to economic issues (although not necessarily with regard to civil liberties issues). The neutral position is to try to find a middle position, which is not so easy. One can make it easier to remove

Table I.1 Presidential versus parliamentary government

Criteria / Alternatives	C Goal Continuity	L Goal Responsiveness	N Total (neutral weights)	L Total (liberal weights)	C Total (conservative weights)
C Alternative Presidential government	4	2	12	10	14*
L Alternative Parliamentary government	2	4	12	14*	10
N Alternative Compromise	3	3	12	12	12
S Alternative Right to continuous economic growth and right to upgraded work	5	5	20	20**	20**

Notes:

SOS tables in general:

1. Symbols in these tables include: C = conservative; L = liberal; N = neutral; S = super-optimum; #1 = group 1; #2 = group 2.
2. The 1–5 scores showing relations between alternatives and goals have the following meanings: 5 = the alternative is highly conducive to the goal; 4 = mildly conducive; 3 = neither conducive nor adverse; 2 = mildly adverse; 1 = highly adverse.
3. The 1–3 scores showing the relative weights or multipliers for each goal have the following meanings: 3 = this goal has relatively high importance to a certain ideological group; 2 = relatively middling importance; 1 = relatively low but positive importance.
4. A single asterisk shows the winning alternative on this column before considering the SOS alternative. A double asterisk shows the alternative that simultaneously does better than the conservative alternative on the conservative totals, and better than the liberal alternative on the liberal totals.

Presidential parliamentary table:

1. Presidential government serves for a fixed number of years. This provides for smoother continuity than a government that can be thrown out of office at almost any time. The continuity appeals to conservatives.

2. Parliamentary government serves only until there is a vote of no confidence in the parliament or until about five years has passed. This provides for a more responsive government. The responsiveness appeals to liberals.
3. Presidential and parliamentary government are equally desirable unless continuity is more heavily weighted than responsiveness, or vice versa.
4. Another alternative is to redefine continuity to mean expansion at a nearly continuous rate of growth, especially economic growth, rather than stability or predictability.
5. Responsiveness can also be redefined in a modern way to mean that the government is responsive to the need of the people to constantly have their skills upgraded.
6. To better assure upward economic growth and the upgrading of skills, these should be made modern constitutional rights. The constitution can also specify the establishment of institutions to assure the achievement of these goals, for example institutions such as the Ministry of International Trade and Industry of Japan.
7. By providing for expanded continuity and expanded responsiveness, the SOS alternative should exceed the best expectations of conservatives and liberals regardless of the less important issues of government structure.

---

the president through impeachment, but that has never been done in the US. One can try to give parliamentary government more stability by saying that it takes a two-thirds vote to bring down the prime minister rather than a mere majority vote, but that has never been done. One can have a presidential government with short terms and no provision for re-election in order to get more responsiveness. One can likewise have long terms for members of parliament in order to gain more stability.

The conservative goal should be referred to as continuity, not as stability. Stability sounds like stagnation. Continuity implies growth, but smooth rather than jerky growth. Continuity can imply change, but change in accordance with some kind of predictability based on previously developed trends. The key liberal goal is responsiveness, which is broad enough to include more than just electoral responsiveness. This could be an example of raising one's goals so as to broaden the concept of responsiveness and also broadening the concept of continuity.

An object of the analysis might be to find an alternative whereby conservatives, liberals and holders of other major viewpoints can all come out ahead of their best initial expectations simultaneously. For example, conservatives receive 80 units when they only ask for 70, and liberals receive 90 units when they only ask for 85. Such an alternative is referred to as a super-optimum solution (SOS) since it is better than both the conservative and liberal best using their goals and weights. One way of arriving at a super-optimum solution in this context is to find an alternative that does well on both continuity and responsiveness, rather than well on one and not so well on the other.

The government structure, that is whether the chief executive is chosen directly by the people or indirectly by the people through the parliament, is thus not especially important. What is needed is a constitutional or statutory commitment on the part of the chief executive and the government in general to significant responsiveness and continuous growth. Responsiveness should go beyond merely reading the public opinion polls in order to get reelected. Responsiveness in the traditional political context has meant that it is easy to throw the government out of power. That is more a process designed to bring about responsiveness, rather than responsiveness in itself. Responsiveness should mean such things as that the government is sensitive to people who are displaced as a result of new technologies or reduced tariffs; that is, the government is responsive to their need for new jobs. A government is more responsive if it sees to it that displaced workers find new jobs. That is partly true even though the president is a president for life and cannot be thrown out of office, as contrasted to a government in which the prime minister can be replaced by 51 per cent of the parliament saying they want to get rid of him. Responsiveness should mean that, when people are suffering, the government does something about it other than changing prime ministers.

On the matter of stability, we do not want stability. We want continuity. We want continuous growth. Growth is change, not stability. We want statutes and constitutional provisions that will require the government, regardless of whether it consists of Republicans or Democrats, to engage in policies that guarantee about 6 per cent growth per year. The US has a 1946 Employment Act and a 1970 Humphrey-Hawkins Act that say unemployment should not get above 3 per cent, or that inflation should not get above 3 per cent. Such laws mean nothing because they embody no provision for enforcement. Worse, they provide no mechanism to achieve those goals. They are the same kind of fiat as King Canute's asking the waves to stop: they can be stopped by the Army Corps of Engineers building appropriate dams, but not simply by issuing a vacuous statement.

The SOS would thus be a set of statutes or a pair of statutes (or better yet, a pair of constitutional provisions). One provision would require 6 per cent a year continuous growth. There is nothing wrong with doing better than that, even if progress is jerky, with one year 10 per cent, another year 6 per cent, another year 12 per cent. That sounds very unstable, but neither conservatives nor liberals would object to that kind of instability. Nobody is likely to object to having highly unstable income if it is $1 million one year and $20 million the next. When people talk about instability they mean jumping from positive to negative, or positive to zero, but not from very high positive to positive and back.

The second statute or constitutional right is an obligation for displaced workers to be retrained and relocated. This is like two new constitutional rights. Traditionally constitutional rights have related to free speech, equal protection and due process. Modern constitutional rights relate to social security, a minimum wage, a safe workplace and, more recently, clean air. What is being proposed is a constitutional right to economic growth and to be relocated if one is a displaced worker. The word 'relocated' sounds too much like moving a person from one city to another. We are also talking about upgrading skills so one can get a better job without moving to another city. Instead of talking about the right to relocation, we should talk about the right to upgraded work. It is not the 'right to work', a phrase which has been ruined by people who use it to mean the right not to be in a union. A problem with the concept of the right to upgraded work is that there is nothing in that concept that confines it to displaced workers, although that is not necessarily bad. Perhaps all workers should have a right to upgraded work, but it is especially the case for those who have no work at all as a result of technological change or tariff reductions. If there were really a meaningful right to economic growth and upgraded work, that kind of SOS would score high on continuity. To emphasize that, we need to talk about continuous economic growth. The right to have periodic retraining at government expense in order to upgrade one's working skills especially relates to the idea of responsiveness by the government.

A key point is that rights are not made meaningful by merely being stated in statutes or constitutions. Nor are they made especially meaningful by saying that someone who feels he has been denied a particular right can sue parliament or the president. They are made meaningful by establishing institutions like the Ministry of International Trade and Industry that has a mandate, a budget, personnel and sub-units that are meaningfully relevant to promoting continuous economic growth. One could establish a separate government agency to enforce the right to upgraded work. The rights become meaningful when you have institutions in place to enforce them, not just words in place in a statute or a constitution. The courts cannot enforce them. It requires specialized administrative agencies. The courts can enforce due process by reversing convictions that violate due process. The courts can enforce free speech and equal protection by issuing injunctions ordering the police to cease interfering with speakers or marchers, or by ordering schools to cease operating segregated classrooms. The courts have no power to award well-directed subsidies or tax credits which are needed for economic growth and upgraded work. That requires appropriate administrative agencies. An example would be a 1 per cent payroll tax on all business firms that is refundable if they use the money to upgrade worker skills.

The important point of this example is that systematic policy analysis is needed to supplement or replace ideological, technocratic and spending approaches, although they can also be useful. Systematic policy analysis emphasizes the processing of goals to be achieved, alternatives available for achieving them and relations between goals and alternatives in order to arrive at the best alternative, combination, allocation, predictive decision rule or super-optimum solution whereby all major positions can simultaneously come out ahead of their best initial expectations.

It is the purpose of this book to apply related policy analysis ideas to public policy problems in Latin America that deal with economic, social, technological and political problems. The book is a key volume in a four-volume set. The other three volumes deal with Africa, Eastern Europe and Asia. It is hoped that the full set will help the development of those regions through better policy analysis and better public policy.

Part I
Economic Policy

1 The Crisis of the Welfare State and its Influence on Latin America in North–South Relations

Ernesto Aragón, Claudia Dorado,
Javier Benavente, Verónica Marcelino and
María Teresa Piñero de Ruiz

INTRODUCTION

The 'welfare state' in the past two decades has gone through a critical turning-point which has forced structural changes in politics and policies throughout Latin America, creating considerable modifications in power relations within the nations themselves and, from an international perspective, setting new trends in the relations between North and South.

A number of factors have influenced the decline of the welfare state, which began to develop in the post-Second World War era in response to social and economic demands. A state which lacked a firm theoretical genesis, and adopted indiscriminate policies of intervention to meet social demands, not foreseeing it was destined to overdimension. Our goal is to analyze the causes that led to this critical stage, not only from the classical economic standpoint, but also from a theoretical sociopolitical perspective which we believe was highly relevant to the welfare state's downfall. The analysis will focus on the objective of demonstrating how current trends, which aim to restructure the state, influence a re-vised concept of colonialism and dependency from a Latin American perspective, concentrating on Argentina and its possibility of reinsertion.

The evolution of the capitalist state in the twentieth century is well known, particularly so when we refer to the aftermath of the 1930s crisis and, following the Second World War, to the process of change from the laissez-faire (liberal state in Latin America) to the welfare state model. From the nineteenth-century laissez-faire state, defined

3

by Marx as a 'superstructure', an ideological entity separated from
and above society, there was a move to the welfare state, where the
situation was reversed, with the expansion of the state and its greater
intervention in society.

At this point it becomes necessary to offer a brief description of the
main characteristics of the laissez-faire state, in order to better understand the rise of the welfare state as a consequence of a new reality
experienced in society and within the context of the state.

THE LAISSEZ-FAIRE STATE

The laissez-faire state flourished after the French Revolution, supported
by a bourgeoisie eager to expand its sphere of economic influence,
without the cumbersome intrusion of government authority. Its goals
and values included the protection of individual freedom, private property,
collective security and peaceful coexistence, as well as the efficient
delivery of public services.

The main idea was to generate maximum protection of individual
freedom, limiting government action through a system of checks and
balances. Hence the concept of a 'hands-off' state, whose role was to
watch and moderate the evolution of the different forces within society.
The legal system served to guarantee individual rights so that the ideological dimension of *legitimacy* would be in accordance with its sociological dimension. Therefore there was a correspondence between the
concept of a laissez-faire legal system and the interest of the bourgeoisie who, for historical reasons, were the only ones to dictate the
law. The system's legitimacy derived from its legal justification. Traditional capitalism was based on the accumulation of wealth needed
to increase production at the expense of the needs of the majority of
the population: that is, at the expense of wages, which led to the exploitation of the working masses by the capitalist minority.

While it is true that a bourgeoisie cannot develop without a certain
amount of cultural upward mobility on the part of the working classes,
it is also true that the workers' participation in the cultural process is
always limited, if not almost non-existent. The workers, as in the past
the peasants and artisans, were the economic pillars of the system but
they did not participate in the cultural process, for there is no possibility of gaining access to education if there are no material means or
free time to do so. To this should be added that the dominant class's
defensive strategy requires that the dissemination of culture be lim-

ited and reduced to a minimum, for all cultural advancement on the part of the workers is a step towards the acquisition of power. The development of Marxist theory in the first decades of this century, together with the economic crisis of the 1930s, brought about the downfall of the laissez-faire state in theory and in practice.

THE WELFARE STATE

In general terms, the welfare state meant the attempt of the traditional state to adapt itself to the social conditions of the Industrial Revolution which brought about new and complex problems, as well as new economic and organizational possibilities. At the end of the nineteenth century a trend towards the implementation of 'social policies' began in the more developed countries, with the purpose of improving the very low standard of living among the more deprived sectors of the population. These sectors were already moving towards social revolution, which became possible only after the people achieved a certain degree of education and became aware of their situation. The solution at that point was not to do away with the laissez-faire state, but to provide it with more socially oriented institutions.

The shift from the laissez-faire to the welfare state meant the real implementation of the principles of freedom and equality and the realization on the part of the classes in power that without social and economic rights for everyone (and the real possibility of enjoying them) those principles became a mere illusion. In the first half of the twentieth century, several constitutions, such as those of Mexico (1917) the Weimar Republic (1919) and Spain (1941) adopted this new social ideology, which became even more prevalent after 1945. According to Offe, the welfare state came into being to ease the tension between 'mass democracy', understood as the universal right to vote under a presidential or parliamentary type of government, and 'laissez-faire democracy', understood as the bourgeoisie's concept of freedom. Furthermore, according to the same author, the coexistence of democracy and capitalism was only made possible through the action of two intermediaries: mass political parties on the one hand, and Keynes's welfare state on the other. This new concept of the state was the one borrowed after the 1930s crisis to regulate the economy and to begin a new stage of capitalism. Again, in the case of center nations, we find that the first responses to the crisis of the laissez-faire state came under pressure of circumstances. Political leaders were trying to give a new impulse to economic activity in order to restore demand and increase employment. The state, as a new social regulator, was seen as a force that could and should stimulate the badly pressed economy.

But none of these efforts was coherent or systematic enough to give new strength to the system. Opposition on the part of some social forces in some cases, and the predominant persistence of the old paradigms in others, created enough obstacles to invalidate most efforts at revitalization and the outcome was a 'war economy'. The Second World War created conditions equivalent to those of a social revolution and it opened the way to the more dynamic forces in each nation. A series of socioeconomic reforms in Europe and Japan, together with the infusion of US financial aid, gave new impulse to postwar economies. The resulting development was not the consequence of a new theoretical model, but of a specific evolution with new power interplay between the different socioeconomic groups, which adopted as their own the Keynesian 'mixed economy model'.

The experiment did not last very long. Some subtle changes began to affect the system and weakened governments' capacity to regulate the economy, which brought to an end the basic version of the Keynesian model. The whole system was neutralized from within by counteracting forces that eliminated any future possibilities. This is how the welfare state lost its basis for legitimacy.

CRISIS OF THE WELFARE STATE

In post-industrial Western nations the welfare state came under attack from neo-liberal rightist groups, as well as neo-Marxist forces. Both based their criticism on some very real contradictory aspects of the socially oriented state. The left called attention to the lack of genuine citizen participation in the political process and the right emphasized the deficiencies of the economic model. According to the left, the institutional link that made possible the political coexistence of capitalism and democracy in developed countries was dissolving in the midst of intrinsic contradictions. The problem revolved around the struggle between those who are subject to power (participation crisis) and around the way in which those in power turn their class interests into 'values' for the society as a whole (cultural hegemony).

In more recent times, with the arrival of the 'new right' and the beginning of the Reagan era in the US, the left suffered a serious setback in most parts of the Western hemisphere. In some countries, such as Germany and Sweden, social democratic parties lost the elections even if the social benefits obtained still remained. In other countries, such as Italy, everything was called into question, and in others, like Great Britain, there was a sharp diversion from the Keynesian model.

The fall of the dollar, the stock exchange crash, the gradual impoverishment of the middle classes all over the world, together with the failure to control public expenditures, to reduce the fiscal deficit and to repay foreign debt, brought new hope for progressive forces who tried to regain their former historical role. Thus we see the neo-reform groups picking up the remains of Marxist ideologies, bringing together the anti-nuclear and 'green' advocacies and even permeating some sectors of the traditional right. They denounce the possibility of doing away with the welfare state and maintain that its objectives are as valid today as they were before, only accepting the need for some changes to ensure its viability. They do not discard all criticism coming from the right, but they do believe it is a matter of reform and not of total rejection of the welfare state. The criticism from the right focused more on the deficiencies of the Keynes model than on the political or cultural problems of the socially oriented state.

Until the oil crisis in the early 1970s, and the electoral victories of Ronald Reagan and Margaret Thatcher, the welfare state was generally accepted in many Western nations, regardless of the party in government. This welfare state solved to a considerable degree the problem of stabilizing demand in macroeconomic terms, but could not offer the proper solution to under-production and worker exploitation. Also the need for capital pushed national budgets into unprecedented deficits and huge foreign debts.

The right's main objections to Keynes's welfare state are that (a) by easing or solving a crisis, the state neutralizes its positive function as a 'destruction force' (as it works in a capitalist system); (b) it takes away incentives to work and to invest; (c) it has no market control that could allow regulation of social policies and eliminate self-defeating contradictions; and (d) the public sector becomes a burden to the private sector, which brings as a consequence a chronic lack of investment capital.

In addition, the middle class is angered by high inflation and heavy taxes. Bureaucrats, whose function should be to solve problems, seem to be interested in perpetuating them as a means of securing their source of employment. Laissez-faire formulas to correct this situation are well known and are nowadays being tried everywhere: reduction of public expenditure, deregulation, privatization, lowering of interest rates, cutbacks in industrial subsidies and so on. Political consequences of the welfare state crisis are now unpredictable. In the last few years we have seen its undesirable effects which, besides causing economic instability, have a negative impact on the political system.

At this point, it would be useful to quote Mexican author Carlos Fuentes (1990), who wrote:

> this is the dynamic reality of our time, it translates into new paradigms never imagined by Adam Smith or Karl Marx, which allow us to go beyond the debate about the end of socialism or the triumph of capitalism. Let's stop whipping 19th-century dead horses and start looking at the 21st century. We are facing a dynamic capitalism because it knew how to recognize its mistakes and at the same time we are facing a stagnant socialism because it lacked self-criticism. There is no pure capitalism in the world and, wherever it accepted criticism, it grew. But where it refused it, it paid a very high price: deficits, social turmoil, lowering of educational standards, decline in competitiveness and so on.
>
> Therefore the present danger for capitalism is to stop recognizing its mistakes, for this will affect not only the United States, but also Europe and Latin America.[1]

THE WELFARE STATE IN LATIN AMERICA

Historically, laissez-faire formulas have not been alien to Latin America reality. As a matter of fact, in the case of Argentina they were the basis for the country's early framework of development. Until the late 1930s or the late 1940s, two economic systems coexisted: one of clear laissez-faire thinking, applied to commerce and industry, and another of mercantilist extraction, applied to agriculture, land ownership and labor relations.

After the Second World War, the influence of European socialist ideologies became apparent in many Latin American countries, which adapted those ideologies to their particular circumstances. That is why the welfare state in Latin America presents its own characteristics, slightly different from the European model. Social policies on the western side of the Atlantic were not the result of 'social pacts', as in many center nations, but they came as a consequence of the over-extended power of a given social group in the overall decision-making process (that is, labor unions in Argentina, grouped under the powerful CGT – General Confederation of Labor).

There was not one welfare state model applicable to all Latin American countries. Each of them implemented its social policies according to its own economic and political circumstances at a given time. Nor was there a 'pure' example of welfare state in the different national experiences, but rather a 'hybrid' combination that sometimes went together with democratically elected governments and sometimes went hand-in-hand with military dictatorships (Velasco Alvarado in Peru, Perón in Argentina, Getulio Vargas in Brazil, and so on). Another factor that contributed to this lack of uniformity was the influence of foreign models, some of which translated the very moderate US experience, while others followed the more advanced European version.

Besides the agreement between social groups in center nations, that brought about an extraordinary economic development, was only possible, according to Philippe Schmitter, at the expense of the third world countries, whose situation worsens as a consequence of unfair trade conditions which tend to favor all the industrial products from a recently reconstructed Europe. That situation is reverted after the 1973 oil crisis, as we will analyze in detail when we discuss North–South relations, based on the Brandt, Palme and Brundtland reports. An appropriate analysis of Latin American reality requires a prior study of the existing social structures from two perspectives: urban or rural and class status. In order to apply this analysis to any given country, we must ask ourselves the following questions:

(1) Which are the principal social classes?
(2) Which are the most powerful?
(3) Which groups are allied with which?
(4) How autonomous is the state? Is it controlled by one of these classes?
(5) What are the predominant factors in the international scene?

This approach is almost inevitable because the history of Latin America and its political future derive to a great extent from its social structure (national perspective) and this structure derives largely from each country's position in the world economy (foreign perspective). For this reason a comparative analysis of these conditions will help greatly to understand the social and political variables in each country. Because our analysis is focused mainly on Argentina, the following national perspective will relate to that country.

NATIONAL PERSPECTIVE

Starting in 1945, after the Peronist party inaugurated its first period in government, we saw the beginning of what could be considered one of the closest experiments to a welfare state in Latin America (which has survived to a certain extent until today). It was a hybrid-type state that included some aspects of the European welfare state model, institutionalized through a corporatist state structure.

From a constitutional and political point of view, the system was a legitimate democracy for it derived its mandate from popular election and majority vote. But that majority considered itself (and the government it elected) the only representative of the people's will and therefore rejected any opposing political expression as a disturbing element in a unified 'national project'. The reason for denying other political options was supposedly the need to avoid the 'social conflict' that would arise from the opposition of minority groups to the 'national project'. This political behavior by popular sectors in a so-called 'democracy' is not casual but stems from the way they became actors in the political arena.

During the first Peronist regime, the antinomies people–people's enemy, and nation imperialism, were intrinsic to the context of this new concept of mass participation, which pushed for redistribution of wealth and more protection of the worker' social rights. As a result, mass equality from an economic point of view and the granting of 'social rights' to the nation's workers were achieved in Argentina at the expense of traditional rights and political pluralism.

The European welfare state's legitimacy was based on its capacity successfully to solve social conflict through economic reform policies in which all classes participated. This is how, in the center nations, labor unions went from permanent confrontation to a labor–capital compromise, articulated through agreements with the government and capital owners. In Europe this model propelled an amazing economic development, to which other factors, such as postwar US aid, also contributed, but in Argentina, even though the idea of a social pact was introduced in 1945, the achievements were meager, since no permanent structural changes were obtained, owing to the system's inability to achieve sustained economic development, which would have translated into a sound redistribution of wealth. In addition Argentina's recurrent political instability worked against any coherent development.

According to O'Donnell:

a way of shifting alliances is at the start of the economic and political cycles in Argentina (1965–1976). On the one hand, we find the alliance of the oligarchic factions of the urban and rural bourgeoisie, a pendular alliance that took place in times of balance of payment crisis, fostering the great urban and rural bourgeoisie's common interests and starting 'stabilization programs' of recessive consequences, that worked against the interests of the working class and of the weakest urban bourgeois sectors.[2]

On the other hand, there was a 'defensive alliance' between the working class and weaker bourgeoisie that supported a nationalist and 'socially just' development model, but did not fully realize the vastly oligopolic and international structure of the capitalist system, of which they were the weakest part.

The always temporary triumphs and defeats of each alliance created a spiralling cycle in which, at each turn, the winner would reverse the existing development model and ransack the already shattering state structure. All these shifts evidently prevented the effectiveness of any political or economic agreement that tended to achieve sustained economic growth.

FOREIGN PERSPECTIVE

In order to fully understand present reality in Latin America and in Argentina, it is imperative to analyze the main development in international politics from 1970 on, with particular emphasis on North–South relations. This will allow us to evaluate the possibility of development for Latin America within the present global context. To that end we quote the opening paragraph of Michael Hoffman's (1988) doctoral thesis on North–South relations: 'I refer to the Brandt, Palme and Brundtland report whose proposals are normative and programmatic for the 1990s. They clearly point out global risks and dangers and give each a name which (in truth) is something that has to be done.'[3]

At the beginning of the 1970s it seemed that developing countries could turn global economic conditions in their favor. The elites in these countries showed self-confidence which resulted from (a) their successful efforts in organizing primary goods producers' associations (such as OPEC) and the uncertainty in the North about long-term primary goods supply; (b) the fact that their growth rate was undoubtedly above that of industrialized countries; and (c) the industrial advances made in the Far East and Latin America and the growing concern in industrialized countries, especially within the labor force, about new competitors attracting business. In the Group of 8 and in the 'non-aligned' bloc, the so-called 'Third World' countries agreed on a series of demands aiming to achieve a new world order. Some degree of success was achieved in the UN committee voting, but not in changing the world economic order because the primary goods producers' associations turned out to be no more than paper tigers. This allowed industrial nations effectively to oppose Third World demands, bringing the North–South dialogue to a halt, for it became obvious that the South did not have the political power or the economic strength to set the rules of the game in the international arena.

In recent years the North–South dialogue has been confined to the back burner and any hope of spectacular results in that area soon vanished because (a) the US, a key player in that dialogue, rejected it within the UN context (this position was eased later on, in agreement with other industrialized countries); and (b) most industrialized countries concentrated on an effort to improve their competitiveness on world markets. The increasing tensions and disparities within the OECD are proof of the stiff competition in world markets. New technological advances have determined important changes in the production structure and from now on competition will be encouraged through government-supported programs. The Brundtland report deals with the advantages and dangers of applying these new technologies, especially as regards developing countries and world ecology.

In a few years, trade, investment and technological exchange between OECD countries intensified to an unprecedented extent, with a consequent loss of interest among those countries in looking for new commercial partners from the developing world:

- those developing countries with more political and economic potential preferred individual agreements instead of collective negotiation with the industrially developed nations;
- the Soviet Union maintained its traditional position of making the Western world responsible for all developing nations' problems;
- the US, Japan and Western Europe are still applying neo-mercantilism' in the economic and technological areas, following their own short- and medium-term interest *vis-à-vis* Third World countries, which are becoming increasingly skeptical in their reactions.

Promises to do away with protectionism and trade barriers, as well as to ensure resource transfer were not fulfilled by OECD countries. At the same time they demanded more efforts from developing countries and, through the International Monetary Fund (IMF) and the World Bank, imposed economic policy corrections which were not always the best solution to Third World countries' problems. After two years of testing, it became evident that the Baker plan (structural adjustment with growth through fresh money loans) was not the appropriate tool to buy time for developing countries because, far from obtaining any relief, they only wasted more time. The economic crisis in many Third World countries was a consequence not only of global structural changes but also of serious mistakes at the national and international levels. The North was responsible for granting unlimited loans to the South as a means of averting the crisis, and the South was responsible for accepting them without discrimination. Many still refuse to accept that unwise global behavior (recycling instead of adjustment and restructuring) made the crisis everybody's responsibility. Industrialized countries tend to forget that the rise in interest rates in the US sent many developing countries into a blind-alley and encouraged capital flight. For their part, third world countries have been slow to recognize negligent or corrupt government polices that led to the dilapidation of resources and the misuse of foreign loans.

The debt crisis and the changes in global economic structures have altered North–South relations in a number of ways:

- A slower growth rate in industrial countries has decreased demand for Third World products as well as reduced technology transfer opportunities.
- Owing to the amazing speed of technological development in the North, developing countries have been cut off from the top, meaning that primary goods have been increasingly replaced by other products and that cheaper labor, one of the last Third World advantages, is not enough by itself to ensure competitiveness in the global market.
- Primary goods prices have reached their lowest level since the Second World War, as a consequence of which North–South trade terms have changed dramatically. Nevertheless the majority of developing countries are still dependent on their primary goods exports because more than 80 per cent of manufactured products come from Taiwan, South Korea, Singapore, Hong Kong, Brazil, Mexico and the People's Republic of China.

- Since the early 1980s, direct investment in developing countries has decreased steadily except in the case of East and South-East Asian countries. Technology transfer is concentrated only among a few countries that have already developed industrial infrastructure and human resources, which allows them active participation in global production.

The balance of payments works in favor of industrialized countries, which get more money from developing countries (in interest and principal amortization together) than they disburse for new loans. As a result of their generally narrow financial margin, a vicious cycle of under-development is the fate of most Third World countries: because of a lack of foreign exchange they are forced to restrict their imports, sometimes even those of basic spare parts, which reduces their productive capacity; the constant loss of purchasing power leads to deindustrialization and excessive exploitation of natural resources; an ever-growing 'informal sector' of the economy is a disguised form of increasing unemployment. It is difficult to find any positive aspect to this crisis, with all the human suffering it entails, but we should point out that many developing countries are starting to evaluate their possibilities in a more realistic light and are ready to try some reforms. They are more cautious, for example, in accepting new loans from industrial countries and, at the same time, they are more strict in their demands. This is why many lenders, including the World Bank, are having trouble in allocating their loans, since most developing countries now take into serious consideration the cost of any new project and the terms and obligations to which they would be subject. As a consequence, all lending institutions have been forced to make their loans more flexible.

All over the Third World there is an increasing number of non-governmental organizations which promote cooperative and self-help projects in their own countries and at the international level. This lends a human face to the threatening ghost of adjustment. The 1980s crisis revealed the basic weakness of developing countries, regardless of their economic system or their form of government: their lack of flexibility to react fast and efficiently to a new global reality and to the changing needs of their own economic structures.

There have been, of course, different patterns of reaction in different countries and continents. These are due, not to their different levels of economic development, but rather to the present condition of their social structures, their geographical location and their governments' powers of enforcement.

CONCLUSION

In the face of this very difficult outlook, the younger generation in Latin America must not surrender hope, but find new ways to change its future. Our proposal is to build a new state model, which would identify neither with the welfare state, a concept outgrown by new political–economic developments, nor with the traditional laissez-faire state, which created international dependence, through policies of submission to center nations.

This state is our own Utopia, understood as a new scale of political values that goes beyond present reality. It is a set of new parameters that would help constitute the 'ideal' state for Argentina and maybe other countries in the same hemisphere. The first prerequisite to any new political formulation is to fully assume our dependent and peripheral condition in relation to those center nations that at the present time hold the 'key to the kingdom of wealth'.

The present structure of the world economy implies a high interdependency of transnational, regional and national economies that move according to the political rulers of the center (the US, the EEC and Japan). The globalization of price value, as a consequence of the present production system, means that labor is given the same value everywhere in the international market. Nevertheless labor has different prices in different countries. Without trying to analyze in detail the correspondence between global market values and prices, we can estimate that, under present conditions, the value transfer from the periphery to the center is of the order of $400 billion. It is an invisible transfer because it is hidden within the world price structure itself.

This is one of the many aspects of the adjustment to which we are subject. Perhaps in a few years Argentina will be part of what Samir Amin calls the 'Fourth World'; that is, a group of totally deprived countries, which have become completely unimportant through having exhausted their adjustment capacity. Thus the only possibility of recovery for Latin American countries is to strengthen their systems, assert their autonomies and reform their institutions, to make them serve better their political and social needs.

We are not proposing a theory of confrontation between Latin America and the developed world. We are proposing the implementation of domestic policies that would allow a certain degree of autonomy to Latin American countries, while making their economies more efficient within a framework of true social justice, based on political agreement. We are not talking of cutting ourselves off from the global market,

we are talking about an autonomy of decision, that would make possible the creation of a competitive state structure, that will have an
active role within the new world order, and will no longer be a passive
spectator, subject to the decisions of the world industrial powers.

To achieve this purpose, we have to think of a two-level project,
the levels coordinated in order to reach a common goal. The first
level is *political and economic agreement between Latin American
nations to form a regional bloc*. These nations must assume their dependent condition and work together on that factual basis. They must
develop a common strategy to avoid the negative consequences of
adjustment and form a regional common market. The second level is
political and economic agreement within each nation. The adjustment
process in the periphery economies, such as Argentina's, compels the
state to play an active role as a moderator between different forces
within society. The state, in order to respond to the international pressures
regulating the adjustment, is forced to drastically reduce public expenditure as well as to implement policies of fiscal restriction, deregulation, privatization, decentralization and so on. All these measures
have a negative impact on the more deprived social sectors.

When the state takes it upon itself to guarantee and coordinate the
social pact, agreement becomes possible and, when all sectors in society
feel duly represented, they also take responsibility for the success of
any common project.

According to Maria Scandogliero (1990):

in this case, concertation becomes important to achieve the goal of
a common objective. Through a mechanism of negotiation and compromise between the different political and socio-economic sectors, moderated by the state, we would obtain a social recomposition where the
political and the economic would be included, through agreement
and articulation of the different actors, interests and projects, aiming
at a desirable new order with a minimum of legitimacy at the base.[4]

Within this context, the state must carry out a political program where
it becomes a mediating force between organized political and social
groups, securing at the same time the participation of non-organized
sectors of society.

The state must also become directly responsible for the implementation of the social pact, by making available its enforcement structure and follow-up capability. This would mean an actual sharing in
policy-making responsibility between the government and different social

groups, which 'would not deteriorate the system's formal government process, as long as there is a self-imposed limit on demands, in exchange for institutional guarantees of a successful and increasingly equitable development.

Nevertheless this transformation is unthinkable without a change in the behavior of the different political actors. First of all, it would be necessary to decentralize state policies, to allow the participation of grass root organizations, which would mean a new, 'peculiar' form of representation as a means of ensuring democracy. Secondly, in the case of political parties, they must change their traditional dynamics within Latin American societies in order to become efficient instruments for channeling social demands. They must place less emphasis on ideological contents in favor of a more pragmatic approach to political representation.

Agreement is also important from the standpoint of ensuring a transition period for a revitalized democracy in Latin America. We must be aware that this democratization process might be endangered by the withdrawal of popular support for those government policies aiming at adjustment. This situation might foster the action of non-democratic groups which pose a threat to the system, groups that otherwise would and should be isolated from society.

In conclusion we quote Professor María Pinero (1989):

> when we manage to achieve a different political structure, where a new social logic is negotiated, that is when we will achieve a new project for democratic stability. At this point is where concertation appears as an adequate means of starting a new political scene, that is of becoming the focal point for meaningful redemocratization. Common accord is the only basis for positive achievements society.[5]

Notes

1. Carlos Fuentes, 'El Mundo de los Años '90', *La Nación*, special supplement, 1990, p. 14.
2. Guillermo O'Donnell, 'Estado y Alianzas en la Argentina 1956–1975', *Social Science Magazine*, no. 64, March 1977.
3. Michel Hoffman, 'Tésis de la relacion Norte – Sur' (Fundación Freiderich Ebert, 1988).

4. Maria Susana Bonetto de Scandogliero, 'Concertación y Consolidación Democrática', Cordoba, 1990.
5. Piñero, 'Concertacion y Consolidacion Democratica – obra antedicha (1990).

References

AGUILERA DE PRATT, CESAREO M., 'Problemas de la Democracia de los partidos políticos', *Revista de Estudios Políticos – Nueva Epoca* (Ene–Marzo 1990) no. 67.

AQUILES, GAY, La Tecnología, el Ingeniero y la Cultura – Ed. TEC 1991 – Publicación del Centro de Cultura Technológica – Bv de las Heras 480 – Cba.

BONETTO DE SCANDOGLIERO, MARIA SUSANA and PATRICIA SERVAIO – 'El Estado Social de Derecho: Un Modelo Agotado en Argentina?'.

BONETTO DE SCANDOGLIERO, M.T. and JUAREZ CENTENO, C y otros – 'Concertación y consolidación democrática' – Ed. Advocatus – Cba – 1990.

CALDERON, FERNANDO and MARIO DOS SANTOS, 'Hacia un Nuevo Order Estatal en America Latina – Veinte tesis sociopolíticas y un corolario de cierre – Conferencia Regional PNUD – CLACSO – UNESCO – BS AS – Abril 1990.

CUADERNOS DE LA REFORMA – Programa General – Serie Decentralización – Minist. de La Función Publica y de la Reforma Administrativa' – Gob. de Cba.

DIARIO LA VOZ DEL INTERIOR – 'La Próxima Crisis Económica: Japón Vs EE.UU' – 123/01/91.

DIARIO LA VOZ DEL INTERIOR – 'Rompiendo las cadenas del estancamiento' – (Mercosur) – 17/03/91.

DIARIO SINTESIS – Semanal de Noticias – 'Hay que integrarse a la región para que la Argentina avance – 13/04/91 – Sintesis Ed. SRL – Antonio del Viso 691 – Cba.

GARCIA PELAYO – 'Las Transfromaciones del Estado Contemporáneo' – Alianza – Madrid – 1982.

GRACIARENA, JORGE – 'El Estado Latinoamericano en Perspectivas' – Figuras, Crisis, Prospectiva.

HOFFMAN, MICHEL – 'Tesis de la Relación Norte – Sur' – Fundación Friederich Ebert – Stiltuno – (FES) – 1988.

JUNTO LOPEZ, AVARIO – 'Introducción a los Estados Políticos'.

PIÑERO RUIZ, M.T. – 'Algunas disertaciones sobre concertación política y concertación económica y social – 1989.

PORRAS, NODALES, A.J. – 'La Función del Gobierno: Su ubicación en un Emergente Modelo de Estado Postsocial – *Revista de Estudios Políticos – Nueva Epoca* (June 1987) no. 56.

REVISTA LA NACION: El Mundo de los años '90 – Número extraordinario – Dec. 1990 – Arg.

REVISTA SOCIEDAD RURAL DE JESUS MARIA – No. 46 – Cba – Arg – 1990.

SAMIR AMIN – 'El Eurocentrismo'.
SCHARZER, JORGE – 'El Estado y su Mecanismo de Regulación frente a diferentes situaciones Macroeconómicas' – CISEA.
SERVATO, PATRICIA – 'Tendencias Políticas Contemporáneas' – 'El Neomarxismo' – 1990.

2 Assessing Public Policy in the Andean Pact

Gordon Mace

INTRODUCTION

At the end of the 1980s people formerly associated with the Andean pact lamented the fact that the integration process had not been able to achieve its original objectives. From their point of view the future of the Pact was very bleak indeed considering the misfortunes of the preceding 15 years and the difficulty in overcoming the obstacles. Today some people are putting forward the idea that a new form of integration has developed in the region quite different from past experiences of regional integration. This new concept of integration appeared as a response to the profound changes that characterized the world economy during the 1980s. It implies a more limited form of integration restricted mainly to technical aspects of free trade and customs union. The 'new integration' implies also a significant reduction of the powers previously held by community institutions, and more open relations with the rest of the world.[1]

In order to assess the eventual success of this new form of integration in the Andean region, one has to understand the reasons explaining the limited success of the previous experiment at regional integration in the framework of the Andean Pact. This public policy evaluation is the only way to bring forward insights on what has happened in the region in terms of regional integration and on what lies ahead in this regard. Public policy studies have been defined as 'the study of the nature, causes and effects of governmental decisions for dealing with social problems'.[2] This implies an analysis of policy formation, causation, implementation and optimization. Applied to a regional integration scheme, public policy evaluation supposes an examination of the original goals of the integration process, a brief description of its main institutions and policy mechanisms, an analysis of major policy decisions and of the reasons explaining the success or failure of these decisions and, finally, an overall evaluation of the experiment and what this implies for future developments.

Consequently this chapter will attempt three things: (1) a brief presentation of the initial objectives of the Andean Pact and of its main institutions and policy instruments; (2) an analysis of the success or failure of three main policy decisions; and (3) an overall evaluation of the Andean integration experiment up to the mid-1980s with, on this basis, an assessment of the latest developments to have occurred.

THE ANDEAN PACT: OBJECTIVES, INSTITUTIONS, MECHANISM

The Andean Group was launched officially in May 1969 but the idea for a sub-regional scheme had in fact been circulating in the region since the middle of the 1960s. From a more abstract point of view, it can be fairly stated that the Andean integration process was in many ways related to the movement for a new world economic order. Part and parcel of the emergence of Third World countries on the international scene, it was believed that regional integration should be used as a major collective instrument for development purposes and an ideal mechanism available to Third World countries who wanted to negotiate a better deal in the current world system.

On a more concrete basis, though, the idea of a sub-regional integration scheme was directly related to the failure of the Latin American Free Trade Association (LAFTA). That failure had become immediately clear in 1962, only two years after the beginning of LAFTA. At that time it was very clear, particularly for the intermediate-level member countries, that the two major mechanisms of LAFTA, the free trade measures and the complementary agreements, would benefit mainly Brazil, Mexico and Argentina. Therefore LAFTA would fail the member countries that needed it most and, in so doing, would increase the existing gap between the 'Big Three' and the rest of the countries of the region. For the Andean countries, such a result would have the effect of adding a new dependency relationship to the one already existing with the industrialized countries of the North and especially with the US.[3]

Objectives

This is why the heads of states of the Andean region decided to launch an integration process which would not be in opposition to LAFTA but would be a distinct endeavor more suited to the needs of the Andean countries. The process started in 1966 with the Conference of the Five Nations, which was held in Bogota at the invitation of Presidents Frei of Chile and Lleras Restrepo of Colombia. The conference ended with the adoption of two major documents which were the direct result of a political negotiation.[4] These contained the major orientations that were to guide the integration process afterwards. Among the basic principles established at that time were the idea that the Andean Group would not develop in opposition to LAFTA but would be a different means to strengthen the unity movement in Latin America. It was also an accepted idea that one of the major goals of the integration process would be to favor the development of its member countries on an equal basis. This would imply the need for strong community institutions along with the necessity of establishing an economic union and favoring a high level of policy harmonization, including the area of foreign investment.

However the policy orientations established at Bogota needed to be made operational and transformed into concrete integration mechanisms. That was done during the meetings of the Comision Mixta, which held six meetings from June 1967 to May 1969. That two-year period was a very exciting one, with moments of great tension due to the fact that the stakes were high for all the member countries on a collective as well as on an individual basis. After several months of hard negotiations, an agreement was finally achieved. The Carthagena Agreement was signed on 26 May 1969 by the representatives of Bolivia, Colombia, Chile, Ecuador and Peru. The Venezuelan government had to make a last-minute withdrawal owing to internal pressures, particularly from the Fedecamaras.

The main objectives of the Andean integration process appear in the first chapter of the Carthagena Agreement.[5] These objectives were (a) to encourage harmonious and balanced development between member countries, (b) to facilitate participation of the Andean countries in LAFTA and encourage an eventual transformation of LAFTA into a common market with the ultimate goal of improving the welfare of the Andean population; and (c) to arrive at an equitable distribution of the benefits of the integration scheme for all members concerned. Underlying this formal statement of objectives was also the political will of the governments involved to use the integration scheme as an instrument to obtain a better deal in negotiations with multinational enterprises and, more generally, with industrialized countries. This vision of relations with the outside world was a particular product of the times and fitted also very well with the philosophy that would be at the heart at the Third World position in the discussions concerning the establishment of a new international economic order.

Institutions

The Andean Group has been qualified as a unique experience in economic integration among developing countries.[6] This statement is a totally adequate qualification which has also been made by several observers of the Andean integration experiment. A succinct overview of the institutions and mechanisms of the Andean Group will suffice to demonstrate how original and far-reaching was the original integration project compared to other similar experiments elsewhere in the world.

The institutional structure of the Andean Group was similar in many ways to the one established by the European Economic Community. The major decision-making body is the Commission, which is composed of representatives of each member country.[7] The Commission acts on all major aspects of the integration process by way of decisions adopted in the course of ordinary and extraordinary sessions. The decisions are adopted with a vote of two-thirds of the member countries, except for very important aspects of the integration process, like the adoption of the sectoral programs or modifications to the initial treaty, which need a unanimous vote, and these decisions are binding for each participating country. This binding character of community decisions was a major handicap for the integration process until the establishment of an Andean Tribunal in the 1980s.[8]

The most innovative institution of the Andean Group and the one most responsible for the progress made by the integration process is the Council of Junta.[9] Similar to the EEC Commission, this body is composed of three members selected from the nationals of the member countries or other countries in Latin America. These members are the chief executives of the junta, which acts as the technical secretariat of the Andean Group. Although the junta members have been nationals of the member countries until now, the record shows that their loyalty went to the integration process before anything else. The junta has the responsibility of initiating and implementing community policies while acting as general supervisor for all aspects pertaining to personnel, budget and day-to-day functioning of the integration process. Although it does not hold any supranational powers, the Junta can act in a fashion similar to supranational institutions in matters of a technical nature. It then proceeds by way of resolutions.

The most interesting aspect of the functioning of the Junta has to do with the community decision-making process. As said earlier, the Junta has the responsibility of initiating policy and its success in this matter had a lot to do with the consultation mechanisms established by the Carthagena Agreement. The policy consultation process normally proceeds according to the following pattern: (1) the junta prepares at the start a first draft of a policy proposal to be submitted ultimately to the Commission; (2) this draft is submitted for comments to the national secretariats for integration, to the Consultative Committee, which is composed of representatives of each member country whose role is to keep close contacts with the junta and, eventually, to the Economic and Social Committee, which is composed of representatives of labor and business of each member country; (3) this part of the process enables the junta to have a clear understanding of the reactions in each member country which it will use to modify its initial proposal; (4) the new draft is resubmitted for consultation; (5) following this consultation the junta makes final amendments; and (6) it presents the proposal for adoption by the Commission.

The Commission, the junta, the Consultative Committee, the Economic and Social Committee and the national secretariats for integration therefore constitute the institutional backbone of the Andean integration process.[10] Alongside these central institutions, we also find the Andean Development Bank (Corporacion Andina de Fomento) which was the first exclusively Latin-American financial international organization.[11] Located in Caracas, the bank's major role is to support regional development, especially by offering financial and technical assistance in the field of industrial development.[12] Completing the Carthagena Agreement institutional structure are the particular institutions related to the Andres Bello Agreement, the Hipolito Unanue Agreement and the Simon Rodriguez Agreement. These agreements constitute instruments of policy coordination in the respective fields of education and culture, health, and employment and labor relations. Each agreement has its own specific institutions which, all together, constitute the institutional basis of the Andean integration system.

Policy Instruments

From the point of view of its policy instruments, the Andean integration process can be conceived as a three-level-structure.[13] This particular configuration was the direct result of the failures of the other integration schemes in Latin America. Benefiting from the experiences of LAFTA and the Central American Common Market (CACM), the architects of the Andean Group designed a particularly bold and imaginative structure whose ultimate goal was to foster a balanced development of the countries of the region.

The main mechanism of the first level of integration is trade liberalization. In the Andean Group, the liberalization process covers all the items produced in the region except those reserved for the sectoral programs and those included in each country's exception list (valid on a temporary basis only). Some of the items were immediately free of tariffs while the rest were submitted to the liberalization process. Unlike what was the case in LAFTA, the interesting feature here was the automaticity of the process. Instead of negotiating a reduction of tariffs on a yearly basis, the Carthagena Agreement stipulated an annual reduction in tariffs of 10 per cent during a 10-year period.[14] Although the member countries had to extend the period for trade liberalization, this mechanism has undoubtly been the most successful of the policy instruments of the Andean integration scheme.[15]

The other important policy instrument at this level is the common external tariff (CET). This a strategic element in an integration process because it not only helps to foster regional trade but, more importantly, it can be used by member governments to influence economic development by encouraging or making it more difficult for a particular sector of production to survive. Because of the complex structure of external tariffs existing in the region, it was felt that it would not have been feasible to adopt a common external tariff at the start of the integration process. It was decided to proceed therefore in a progressive manner. The more developed countries of the region would immediately put in place a minimum common external tariff applicable to 175 items included in the first common list of LAFTA. (This measure was in effect in 1970.) Then the member countries would start discussions concerning the application of the CET with a deadline for adoption in 1980.[16] At the start of the 1990s the CET has not yet been adopted, but it is still included in the Quito Protocol which modified the Carthagena Agreement in 1987.[17]

As demonstrated by the experience of LAFTA, an integration scheme based only on a free trade area has a very good chance of benefiting mainly its more developed members, with the overall effect of increasing the existing gap between them and the less developed members of the integration process. This is why policy instruments of a second level are needed to contain or overcome the negative effects of the liberalization process. In the Andean Group the three most salient mechanisms at this level are industrial programming, harmonization of economic policies and special treatment for less-developed countries. The preferential treatment for less-developed countries is a major feature of the Andean Group and is much more developed than anything similar elsewhere in Third World integration schemes.[18] It contains a set of measures included in different policy instruments of the integration process designed to help Bolivia and Ecuador to benefit more from the integration scheme. Special measures of this kind have been adopted in the liberalization process and in sectoral programming but problems of compliance by other member countries have been noted and a special program of support for Bolivia had to be put in place in 1977.[19]

As to what pertains to harmonization of policies, a distinction was made between commercial and economic policies. In the commercial sector, harmonization measures have been adopted in the fields of tariffs, export financing and in what pertains to trade distortion policies and rules of origin. Harmonization of economic policies has not proceeded very far but some progress has been made in the agricultural sector.[20] Clearly the major policy instrument of the Andean strategy of development is industrial programming, which covers the twin sectors of industrial rationalization and sectoral programming. Industrial rationalization deals with existing industries which were to be the object of a rationalization process covering the whole of the region. This mechanism did not receive a lot of attention in the first years of the integration process but it became more important when the difficulties in adopting the sectoral programs were more pronounced.[21]

Sectoral programming is the most innovative instrument developed in the framework of the Andean integration process. It is an instrument by means of which the member governments jointly plan the industrial development of the region by assigning resources to specific industrial sectors.[21] Sectoral programming covers the same seven industrial sectors that are the object of industrial rationalization but in this case the program deals with the establishment of future industries. It is a policy instrument in which the member states decide who is going to produce what but leave to the private sector basic economic decisions concerning costing, rate of production and so on. To the present day, four sectoral programs have been adopted (metal-working, automobile, petrochemical and fertilizers) but progress in this field has been more and more difficult. For this reason, sectoral programming was profoundly changed in 1983 and again in 1987 to become a much less binding mechanism than the original version.[23]

As shown by the experience of the Central American Common Market,[24] a regional strategy of development, particularly in the case of industrial programming, has good chances of advantaging foreign enterprises over local ones in the absence of controlling devices of foreign investment. The result in this instance is to favor the more developed countries of an integration scheme which are in a better position to take advantage of foreign investment. A more important effect, as shown by the CACM, is the creation of a protected market for foreign enterprises involved in the region, with the ultimate result that the integration process, instead of reducing dependence, makes it more profound. To reduce this possible danger, the member governments of the Andean Group decided to develop a third level of integration specifically aimed at reducing dependency. The most important mechanism at this level was of course the much-publicized Andean Investment Code. This code was enacted through Decision 24, adopted in 1970.[25] Decision 24 contained a host of measures to regulate foreign investment, ranging from rules concerning profit reinvestment and profit remittance to measures concerning divestment of ownership. These rules were not at all designed to exclude altogether foreign investment from the region.[26] Instead, their objective was to provide a general framework for foreign investment in the region while at the same time establishing a more equal basis for negotiation between the Andean countries and multinational corporations. The regulations concerning foreign investment were modified in 1977 and again in the 1980s. Finally the Andean Investment Code was completely abandoned with the adoption of the Quito Protocol.

The policy instruments discussed in the preceding pages were the most important mechanisms of the Andean integration process. Taken as a whole, they represented the most innovative experiment of regional integration in the Third World. All of them have been changed, severely curtailed or completely abandoned and the Andean Group today is only a pale imitation of the original project. It is nevertheless a fascinating experiment whose lessons are still worth reflecting upon. In the next section of the chapter we will therefore examine three of the most salient policy instruments of the Andean Pact: the common external tariff, sectoral programming and the rules concerning foreign investment. We will try to identify the main decisions adopted in the framework of each instrument and we will attempt also to explain how member countries have reacted to these decisions and why. For clarity of presentation, each policy instrument will not be discussed separately but we will deal with all of them at three specific periods:

the early years (1969–72); the first crisis (1974–8); and the second crisis (1981–3).

DECISION MAKING RELATED TO EXTERNAL TARIFF, SECTORAL PROGRAMMING AND FOREIGN INVESTMENT

The Early Years (1969–72)

The first period of the Andean integration process was without doubt the most successful and the most rewarding of all. Many reasons can be found to explain the initial success of the Andean Group. First of all, one has to look at the international system, which was characterized in the 1960 and early 1970s by the appearance of new actors, as a result of the decolonization process, and by a changing world agenda resulting from the demands formulated by Third World countries. The 'Bandung Spirit', concerning the status of Third World countries in the international system, the emergence of the Non-aligned Movement and the creation of the United Nations Conference on Trade and Development (UNCTAD) all contributed to putting at the head of the world agenda the problem of North–South relations embedded in the demands for a new international economic order.[27] This contesting of the old world order generated a process of economic nationalism closely related to what was happening in Latin America at that time.

This period was also characterized by the progressive termination of the Cold War era and by emerging trends of transformation in the industrialized world, with the ascendt of Japan and the Federal Republic of Germany accompanied by the perception of a relative decline in overall US power. The US involvement in Vietnam and the Nixon shock of August 1971, which imposed a surface on imports to the US and ended the fixed parity of the dollar in relation to gold, were seen as demonstrations that the US had lost some of her previous imperial status, while the Nixon measures served to demonstrate to Latin American governments that whatever special relationship they had with Washington would now be ended.

These elements created a general context favorable to the Andean experiment, but, more than that, the success of the first years of the Andean integration process was due mainly to events occurring in Latin America itself. First of all, the relative economic progress of the region in the 1960s contributed to the creation of a climate of confidence which caused local governments to believe that progress lay ahead if only they could put their act together. More importantly, the situation in Peru, in Chile and, to a lesser extent, in Bolivia was particularly supportive of an integration process oriented towards economic nationalism. In Peru, the military government of Juan Velasco Alvarado, which had seized power in October 1968, had embarked on a course of harsh economic nationalism. The government had immediately nationalized the assets of the International Petroleum Company, which set the course for a tough policy of control of foreign investment. The General Law of Industries established a distinction between three sectors of the economy.[28] The most important sector comprised all basic and services industries, in which no foreign investment would be tolerated in the future. This sector would progressively lose its importance to the benefit of the social property sector, whose enterprises would be wholly owned by the workers and which was to become the main engine for economic growth. The third sector, the industrial communities, was to be composed of enterprises partly owned by workers and private capital of which a part could be of foreign origin.[29]

This restructuring of the economy was accompanied by massive nationalizations and expropriations in many sectors of the local economy, including banking, mines, fisheries and services. The government also took important measures with respect to agrarian reform, export diversification and workers' participation in the political process, although these last two measures were less successful.[30] Nevertheless it is not difficult to understand that with what was going on in Peru itself the Peruvian government had no problem whatsoever in supporting the measures of economic nationalism contained in the integration process. Peru was at that time the most supportive member of the Andean Group because the measures adopted at home were going a lot further than the ones adopted in the integration scheme.

Much the same can be said concerning Chile, after the election victory of the Popular Unity, although integration affairs were not as salient in the governmental agenda, owing to the fact that a good deal of the government's attention had to be constantly focused on its own survival. But the economic strategy of the Allende government was every bit as nationalist and state-oriented as the one in Peru and it went even farther in the case of agrarian reform. Furthermore mass mobilization and popular participation in the political process were much more developed in Chile than in Peru, while workers' involvement in the management of enterprises was also more accentuated.[31] It was therefore only natural that Chile should side with Peru in supporting the economic nationalism of the integration process. They both acted as leaders of the Andean Group in which they worked to have adopted policy instruments such as sectoral planning and Decision 24. The only difference in behavior was that the Peruvian government itself was more involved in the community decision-making process, while in Chile the secretariat for integration was more left to itself, although benefiting none the less from the government's confidence. But it was clear that the head of Chile's secretariat for integration, Juan Somavia, had for greater room for manoeuvre than his counterparts at the Andean Commission.[32]

Bolivia and Ecuador, although less important actors during this period, were also supportive of the objectives of economic nationalism reflected by the policy instruments of the integration process. Ecuador was the least active of the member governments in the early 1970s because President Velasco Ibarra was mostly concerned with the survival of his presidency. The military coup of 1972 launched the military regime of Guillermo Rodriguez Lara, who favored a strategy of economic nationalism which, however, was a much paler version of the one pursued in Chile and Peru.[33] But from 1972 to 1974 it was clear that the nationalist orientations of the Rodriguez government influenced the Ecuadorian position in the sense of supporting the major mechanisms of the Andean Group.

As for Bolivia, the everlasting tumultuous political situation of that country made it difficult for its government to play a major role in the integration process at the start of the 1970s. From 1969 to 1971, Bolivia was governed by three military regimes of different socioeconomic orientations. The moderately nationalist regime of Ovando Candia was replaced in October 1970 by another military regime led by Juan Jose Torres. Seen at the start as a continuation of the Ovando regime, the Torres government rapidly came under fire and had to choose between opposing factions. The new regime began to radicalize itself by launching a new wave of nationalizations and encouraging popular participation in the political process.[34] With policies similar to the ones adopted in Peru and Chile at that time, the Bolivian government had no problem in supporting the orientations favored by these two countries in the integration process. The military coup of August 1971 was not to change that situation very much since the new Banzer government was more preoccupied with establishing its regime on a sound basis than with integration affairs. However it is true that in early 1972 the Banzer government started to adopt more liberal measures concerning foreign investment; the other member governments chose to ignore the fact and consider it as part of the special treatment for Bolivia. Consequently for most of this period Bolivia was very supportive of the Andean integration process, mostly because of her faith in industrial programming and the perceived positive effects of this mechanism on the future development of the country.

That left Colombia, which was never a major supporter of industrial programming and community regulations concerning foreign investment. But Colombia was, with Chile, the main initiator of the Carthagena Agreement and still felt in the early 1970s that the integration process could generate substantial commercial dividends for the country. Therefore the Colombian government was willing to compromise on what seemed to it less interesting community policy instruments in order to maintain the momentum of an integration process which could still succeed in establishing a concrete free trade area of which Colombia, because of her diversified economy, would be the main beneficiary. Furthermore there were still many members of the Colombian political elite who had been involved in the negotiations to establish the Andean Group and who would have seen their political stature diminish were the integration process to fail.[35] Consequently Colombia's position in the early years of the Andean Group was to push consistently for trade liberalization while not opposing openly industrial programming and Decision 24, which she was very slow to implement. All in all, Colombia's position from the start was to work quietly but consistently to orient the integration process along the lines of the earlier commercialist strategy contained in the Bogota Declaration of 1966 but modified in the Carthagena Agreement.

Two other elements can be added to the previous development as contributing factors in the success of the Andean Group's early period. The first arose from the fact that this was the easy period of the integration process. If we except the application of Decision 24 and the progressive implementation of the metal working sectoral program (adopted in 1972), no major and potentially costly compliance behavior was asked of the member countries during this period. Consequently the potential for conflict was kept at a very low level. The second contributing factor was related to the very special climate of complicity and comradeship that had developed between the first representatives of the member countries participating in the works of the Commission. Peru's representative, Luis Barandiaran, was particularly effective in this sense in building a personal relationship with Juan Somavia, Jorge Valencia and the others whom he invited occasionally to his home in Lima and for whom he organized excursions to Cuzco and Macchu Picchu. These close personal relationships were not unimportant in erasing divergencies and setting problems. This very special climate among Andean negotiators did not survive after 1973.

We may sum up the analysis of this first period of the Andean Group by concluding that the early success of the integration scheme was due to a combination of local and international factors. In the international system, the events of the 1960s, mentioned earlier, clearly created a favorable environment not only for the launching of the Andean integration process but also for the early success of the scheme. However the most salient determinants of success were located at the local level. First among these was certainly the compatibility of the national strategies of economic development with the one pursued at the regional level. This was particularly true for Peru, Chile and, to a lesser extent, Bolivia and Ecuador. Second in importance would be the close working relationship established by the representatives of the member countries at the Commission. These people, animated by a common faith with regard to the idea of integration, not only worked very closely with the junta but also acted sometimes as defenders of the integration process inside their own governments. Finally the small cost of participating in the integration process, along with potential expected benefits, also serves to explain the support by the member countries of the integration scheme and the success of the early years of the Andean Group.

The First Crisis (1974–8)

By the middle of the 1970s the situation had changed dramatically for the Andean Group. The international environment was much more difficult for Third World integration schemes than it was only a few years earlier. The period 1974–7 was of course the high point of the North–South dialogue but it was then clearly evident that whatever progress was made in favor of Third World countries would be on a scale much smaller than what was expected at the start of UNCTAD. More importantly the oil shock of 1973 would, very rapidly, severely affect Third World non-producing countries, starting a period of increasing foreign indebtedness that would reduce the borrowers' margin for manoeuvre and pave the way for the debt squeeze of the 1980s. In Latin America, the rise in prices of petroleum products would have particularly adverse effects on economic growth.

On a local level, the first major crisis of the Andean Group would be triggered by the deadlines established by the Carthagena Agreement for the adoption of the sectoral programs and for the start of the discussions leading to the adoption of the common external tariff. More importantly and somewhat ironically the crisis would be brought about also by the entry of Venezuela in the Andean Group which, by making necessary a redistribution of the member countries' allocations in the framework of the metalworking program, would serve as an excuse to discuss again the basic rules governing product allocations in sectoral programming.

As for Venezuela, the decision to join the Andean Group after refusing to do so in 1969 can be explained by a combination of factors. First of all, the early success of the integration scheme was a decisive element for a country which finally saw that it would be more costly not to join an integration process which apparently had some chance of success: the more so when it became apparent with the Nixon measures of August 1971, that Venezuela's commercial treaty with the US would not bring particularly easy access to the US market. Thirdly, rising petroleum revenues would make it easier for Venezuela to take advantage of sectoral programming which necessitated huge inflows of cash and which the Venezuelan government always considered an important asset in its efforts at restructuring the economy. Finally the increasing political importance of Carlos Andres Perez, an outspoken supporter of Andean integration, and the concessions earned in pre-entry negotiations also loomed large in the decision to finally join the Andean Group.[36]

The crisis of the mid-1970s started of course with Chile, but not immediately after the coup of September 1973. The first months in power of General Pinochet's military government were used to crush the opposition to the regime and it was only in March 1974 that the new Chilean government finally managed to adopt clear policy orientations. The program made public at that time proposed an economic model that completely reversed the course followed previously by the Popular Unity government. The social economy market model emphasized productivity and competition, private property and an important reduction in the role of the state in economic affairs.[37] The program was soon followed by drastic reduction in tariffs, with a maximum effective rate of 60 per cent foreseen for 1977,[38] and the government eased the rules for investment by foreign corporations with the adoption of Decree Law 600 which was a clear breach of the rules established by Decision 24.[39]

The military junta also suspended the agrarian reform process, sold many of the former state-owned companies and concluded settlements with resources-based foreign companies previously nationalized by the Allende government.[40] These companies were then given back their former titles of property. Therefore the military government's economic program was not only a reversal of the economic development strategy pursued by the Allende government but, more than that, it sought to erase completely all the achievements of the Popular Unity in the economic and social sectors of Chilean society. Consequently it was easy to foresee that such an approach to economic development would bring the Chilean government into conflict with other member countries of the Andean Group on particular community policy instruments. The crisis started with Chile's demand for important changes in the rules governing foreign investment in the region. Its own policy in this respect was no more compatible with community regulations since Decree Law 600 contained specific clauses contrary to the ones included in Decision 24. For example, the Chilean legislation exempted foreign corporations from becoming national or mixed companies if they were not involved in production for the regional market. Also the government ended the special treatment reserved for local enterprises in terms of access to credit, and reinvestment of profits without authorization was permitted up to 10 per cent of the initial investment, while the limit established by Decision 24 was 5 per cent.[41] There were other inconsistencies in Decree Law 600 compared with Decision 24 which, globally, implied a completely different and opposing approach to foreign investment from the one pursued at the community level.

On the opposite side, Venezuela was the staunchest supporter of Decision 24 in its original form. Throughout the 1970s, Venezuela was to be the member country whose compliance with the community regulations concerning foreign investment was the strictest.[42] The Venezuelan position was easy to understand since the country was now receiving huge amounts of petroleum revenues which made foreign investment less important. Furthermore the new government of Carlos Andrès Perez had embarked on a course of economic nationalism, with nationalization of the petroleum and iron ore industries, that, although penalizing the country for a short period in terms of foreign investment, did not undermine the position of Venezuela in this respect during the 1970s. At the end of the 1970s, in effect, Venezuela was still receiving 45 per cent of all foreign investment going to the Andean region.[43]

Ecuador, also an OPEC member, supported the Venezuelan position, while Bolivia was more sympathetic to Chile's position. Bolivia's position on this aspect has to be understood in the light of its internal situation at that time. The Banzer government had by then secured its position on the domestic front and was progressively embarking on a market-oriented economic strategy which, however, did not go as far as the one adopted in Chile. The Bolivian rationale was also that, if the integration scheme could assure Bolivia of fair treatment in sectoral programming it should permit easier access for the country to foreign investment. But the Bolivian government was not ready to go as far as Chile in its criticism of Decision 24.

That left Peru and Colombia, which had in-between positions concerning Decision 24. As said before, Colombia had never been the most fervent supporter of Decision 24 but the Colombian government complied with community regulations because of the benefits foreseen in the trade area. During the 1974–8 crisis, Colombia was therefore in favor of a downgrading of Decision 24 regulations, but she was also ready to compromise on this point in order to prevent the collapse of the integration process.[44] Peru, for its part, had a new military government in 1975, headed by General Morales Bermudes. The replacement of General Velasco had been made necessary because of health problems and, more importantly, because his economic strategy was in a shambles, with the country almost bankrupted. Velasco had therefore become highly unpopular in many circles of Peruvian society and the military leadership had judged it best to replace him. With Velasco also went the most reform-minded of his ministers, with the result that the new military leadership, although vowing in public to pursue Velasco's economic program, was in the process of modifying the economic strategy followed since 1969.[45] One of the consequences of this change was a modification of Peru's position in the framework of the Andean Group. Officially this position was still one of complete support of Andean integration mechanisms, but in the course of the discussion it became very clear that Peru would not oppose a downgrading of the most nationalist community policy instruments. This of course applied to Decision 24, although the Peruvian government, like that of Colombia, was prepared to compromise to save the integration scheme.

The other element of contention, in 1974–5, was the common external tariff. Here again Chile was asking for changes in the original agreement. Using the excuse that the deadline for adoption of the CET could not be met, the Chilean government started by proposing the complete elimination of tariff protection as a policy instrument of the integration scheme. Should the other member countries refuse to go along with this proposal, Chile's back-up position was to negotiate for an effective tariff protection of no more than 45 per cent.[46] This low level of tariff protection was of course consistent with Chile's new economic policy, which sought to make the local economy as open as possible to the external world. At the start of the discussions, Colombia had teamed up with Chile on this point because the Colombian government had itself started to open up the national economy at the beginning of the 1970s.[47] This new economic strategy had put Colombia at odds with most of the protectionist positions defended by others in the framework of the Carthagena Agreement, but here again Colombia was willing to compromise to save the integration scheme and consequently abandoned Chile in the course of the negotiations.

Venezuela and Peru, on the other hand, were the major proponents of a high tariff protection. This was consistent with the traditional situation in both countries and especially in Venezuela where the local industry had always benefited from very high tariff protection and where the government was always dedicated to a policy of industrialization by import substitution.[48] Bolivia and Ecuador, for their part, were in favor of a lower tariff protection than the one proposed by Peru and Venezuela, and Bolivia would have had no problem with the level proposed by Chile. The Bolivian government had traditionally espoused a policy of low tariffs and what the government wanted in the discussions on the CET was to be permitted to proceed at a slower pace because of the low level of industrialization of the country, while being permitted at the same time to exempt its mining sector from application of the CET. Chapter VIII of the Junta's CET proposal was in fact proposing exceptions for Bolivia which made it much less costly for the Bolivian government to adopt the proposed CET. This was a major reason in deciding Bolivia against siding with Chile on this subject.

Industrial programming was also an element of contention during the crisis of 1974–8. Arguments here were not put as strongly as was the case with the CET and Decision 24, but for those who could read between the lines a major debate was going on concerning industrial programming and, more specifically, sectoral programs. Formal opposition to industrial programming was never made openly in the course of the discussions but it became evident that this was also a point of contention for the new Chilean government. Chile's official position was that, since the deadline for adoption of the remaining sectoral programs could not be met, it was best simply to abandon the whole scheme of sectoral programs. This position was a cover for the very real opposition of Chile to the whole idea of industrial programming. One of the reasons for this opposition was that the Chilean government did not accept the high level of tariff protection included in the sectoral programs. Another was that Chile wanted to start production of items already assigned to other member countries in the framework of the metal-working and petrochemical programs.[49]

But the most important reason underlying Chile's opposition was the military government's refusal of the role assigned to the state in the functioning of industrial programming. As seen before, the original integration project had the state play an important role in determining where and what was to be produced in each sectoral program. Considering the impact of the Chicago School's economic ideas on Chile's new economic strategy and the very small role afforded to the state in that model, it was natural for Chile to oppose the type of industrial programming considered in the Andean Group. Here again Venezuela and Peru were the main opponents to Chile, supporting the original scheme of industrial programming. The Peruvian government was not prepared to openly reverse course on the positions adopted in Peru since 1969, while Venezuela, with its petroleum revenues, was the best equipped to take advantage of industrial programming.

Colombia and Ecuador were not very vocal concerning industrial programming. With her petroleum revenues, Ecuador was in a position similar to that of Venezuela in the sense that she had the means to benefit from sectoral programs, which the government also considered a useful mechanism to complement its policy of industrialization by import substitution. In addition to that, it did not seem as though Ecuador had experienced the problems that would affect Bolivia in relation to sectoral programs. Therefore, the government of Ecuador had no problem in siding with Venezuela on this aspect.

As the Colombia, it was a well-known fact that this country had not been a staunch supporter of industrial programming, mainly because the Colombian government did not like the role assigned to the state in industrial programming and was not in favor of the high tariff protection included in the sectoral programs. This position was supported by those Colombian business elite who were disappointed with the role played by the state development bank in promoting local industries.[50] Consequently Colombia did not support industrial programming and would have been quite happy with the elimination of this mechanism, but again she was not willing to side with Chile on this subject in order to keep the integration process afloat.

That left Bolivia, whose main reason for joining and remaining a member of the Andean Group was directly related to industrial programming. This was in effect a major community policy instrument from the point of view of Bolivia, but the Bolivian government had become somewhat disillusioned about existing sectoral programs. This was particularly the case with the metal working program in which other member countries had not discouraged production by local companies of items reserved for Bolivia and which the Bolivian government considered important in Bolivia's industrial development.[51] There was also the problem of the high tariff protection included in sectoral programs. This was particularly painful for the Bolivian mining industry, which had to buy on foreign markets items reserved for sectoral programs but not yet produced in the region. Finally, domestic politics was involved since the Banzer government had to rely more and more on Bolivia's commercial elite for support. These people were penalized by the integration scheme in various respects and were therefore less favorable to the Andean Group. Ultimately the Bolivian government nevertheless took a position in favor of industrial programming in a kind of trade-off with the Junta in which was promised the establishment of a special aid program for Bolivia in the near future.[52]

The crisis of 1974–8 consequently ended with the withdrawal of Chile from the integration process. This withdrawal, along with the preceding discussions, was not without effect on the future course of integration in the Andean region. New deadlines were established for the adoption of the common external tariff and the remaining sectoral programs, and Decision 24 was modified to ease the rules concerning foreign investment. But, more importantly, it was evident for all to see that the initial momentum had been broken.

During this period, the major determinants of member countries' behavior can be summarized as follows. The changing international economic environment was a major influence in modifying the attitudes of some of the member countries, notably Peru. The incompatibility between national strategies of economic development and the integration model also affected the behavior of Chile, Peru and Bolivia and was the main factor in Chile's decision to withdraw from the Andean Group. Finally the perception of costs and benefits was an important variable in the decisions taken at that time by Bolivia and Colombia.

The Second Crisis (1981–3)

The international economic environment of the early 1980s was particularly hostile to integration processes in the Third World and especially in Latin America. The second oil shock of 1979 and the world recession of 1980–82 had particularly devastating effects on the Latin American economies, whose governments had been borrowing heavily on international financial markets since the middle of the 1970s.[53] With the exception of Colombia, all the Andean countries were severely affected, the worst cases being Peru and Bolivia, which were for all intents and purposes in a state of complete bankruptcy. This situation was of course to constitute a major influence on the course of events in the Andean integration process at the time.

The Andean crisis of the early 1980, resulted officially from the impossibility of meeting the deadlines previously established for the adoption of the CET and the sectoral programs. More fundamentally it was brought about by the general non-compliance with community regulations by most of the member countries.[54] Some of these countries had also witnessed a change in their political regime and the border clashes between Peru and Ecuador in 1981 did not help the situation either.[55] The decade had started with a small success when the member countries had managed to agree in adopting two sectoral programs, fertilizers and metallurgy, which then brought the total of sectoral programs to eight.[56] But very soon afterwards, the junta was sounding the alarm by underlying clearly the problem of non-compliance, which had become a major burden for the integration process as a whole.[57] The ensuing discussions only served to show how the Andean countries' positions had changed since the middle of the 1970s and to what extent faith in the integration process had diminished.

Bolivia was not part of the sectoral program adopted in 1980 and the country was almost expelled from the Andean Group following the military coup of General Garcia Meza. The return to civilian rule did not alter very much Bolivia's overall dissatisfaction with the integration process, a dissatisfaction which had been growing constantly since 1972 and which was based on major criticisms made by the Bolivian government with respect to the functioning of the integration process. Although trade with other Andean countries had never been a major part of Bolivia's external trade, the Bolivian government accused its Andean partners of being responsible for Bolivia's limited trade benefits in the framework of the integration process by establishing unfair trade barriers. Data show that Bolivian exports to the Andean Group had in effect fallen constantly since the mid-1970s,[58] but Bolivia was not the only member country in this position and her trade performance had probably more to do with Chile's withdrawal from the Pact than with unfair trade barriers.

The other complaints concerning unfair practices in the case of sectoral programs and the malfunctioning of the special aid programme for Bolivia were much more serious and were confirmed by the junta's evaluation of the integration process.[59] All this strongly contributed to forging an image in Bolivian political circles that the integration process was not bringing to Bolivia the benefits foreseen when the country signed the Carthagena Agreement. If perceptions of limited benefits was a major factor in Bolivia's attitude towards the integration process in the early 1980s, another important determinant was related to economic strategy. Although Bolivia's economic strategy was not clearly defined at the start of the 1980s, some measures taken at the time announced the important shift in policy that was to be made public by the Movimiento Nacionalista Revolucionario (MNR) government in August of 1985.[60] The move towards a market-oriented economic strategy implied that there was no longer any place in Bolivia's economic philosophy for control of foreign investment, high protection tariffs and state intervention in the economy. This involved a complete shift in Bolivia's attitude towards industrial programming, the CET and the community regulations concerning foreign investment.

Ecuador experienced much the same problems as Bolivia with sectoral programs but was less critical towards that community policy instrument and had sided with Venezuela in supporting the developmental strategy of the integration process until the early 1980s. Things then started to change and the change became very apparent with the election of Leon Febres Cordero as president of Ecuador in 1984. Ecuador then openly led the battle for the dismantling of Decision 24 and adopted national economic measures similar to the ones in Bolivia, having the effect, at the community level, of shifting the Ecuadorian position against industrial programming and state intervention in this field, and against high tariff protection in the framework of the CET.[61] Things had also changed drastically in Peru when the military left power in 1980, leaving a legacy of economic disaster. Civilian rule was then restored and elections brought back to power the same Fernando Belaunde who had been forced to leave the country in the middle of an October night in 1968. Immediately upon taking office, the new president announced an important reorientation of economic policy towards a market-oriented strategy accompanied by an IMF stabilization program.[62] This implied drastic economic changes for the Peruvian economy and was directly related to Peru's demands for modifications in the community foreign investment code and in industrial programming.[63] Furthermore Peru's drastic lowering of tariffs on industrial products made it impossible to make progress in the adoption of a CET.

Adding to all this, Colombia, as we have seen, had never been very favorable to industrial programming or to the Andean code on foreign investment. The Colombian government had been the main proponent of a commercialist strategy in 1966 and Colombia had been faithful to that position all along while accepting to compromise on other aspects of integration policy in the hope of reaping a major part of eventual commercial benefits arising from the integration process. After some 15 years of integration activity, it was clear that Colombia had been and still was the major partner in intraregional trade[64] but it was also evident that her position in this respect had not changed much since 1970.[65] Furthermore it was not certain at all that Colombia's trade advantages were a direct result of the integration process. The outcome might not have been different in the absence of the integration scheme.[66] But Andean integration had always been a major issue of a Colombian foreign policy, which had otherwise been very low-profile for many years. The emerging process of coordination of Andean foreign policies and its possible impact in Latin America was considered an interesting development by the Colombian government,[67] which helps therefore to understand why Colombia was not prepared to abandon completely the integration scheme. But the Colombian government felt that the time was now ripe to press for modifications to the original integration arrangements along the lines of the more commercialist strategy that Colombia had always favored. With the passage of time, Colombia became more insistent on this aspect.[68]

That left Venezuela as the only member country supportive of the original developmental strategy. But that support was also faltering because Venezuela, herself now caught in the debt stranglehold, had to consider economic policy changes.[69] Pressed by its local industrial community, the Venezuelan government continued to push for high community tariff protection[70] but did not oppose modifications to industrial programming and supported a watering down of the Andean code on foreign investment.[71] The return to power of Carlos Andres Perez at the end of the decade completed the process of economic reorientation which was begun under the Lusinshi government in Venezuela in the early 1980s. The economic package made public then was a perfect illustration that the former main proponent of a developmental strategy in the Andean region from 1974 to 1978 had now become a staunch supporter of a market-oriented strategy.

The Andean crisis of 1981–3 was therefore a result of the combination of external and internal factors.[72] The world economic recession, combined with Latin America's external debt crisis in the early 1980s, had a major effect on Andean countries whose economies were already in a shambles at the end of the previous decade. This situation created a favorable context for the development of a protectionist attitude which was in a major way responsible for the non-compliance behavior of the member countries of the integration scheme. Non-compliance became in turn a major component of a politicization process in which every aspect of the integration process became a question of national interest for each member country which became less and less willing to compromise on matters related to the functioning of the integration scheme.

This blocking of the situation came about at the same time that member governments, severely affected by adverse economic conditions, started to modify radically their economic strategy. Bolivia, Peru and Ecuador were then in the process of very substantial economic reorientations whose effect would be to make their economic strategy less and less compatible with the community strategy, the major points of contention being industrial programming, community tariff protection and regulations concerning foreign investments. With similar changes appearing progressively in Venezuela, it became evident that the Andean Group could not continue on the course established in the 1970s.

CONCLUDING REMARKS ON THE ANDEAN INTEGRATION EXPERIMENT AND BRIEF ASSESSMENT OF RECENT DEVELOPMENTS

The crisis lingered on for some years until the adoption of the Quito Protocol in May 1987. The adoption of the protocol, which nearly ended in diplomatic disaster, was a clear testimony to a severe downgrading of the original Carthagena Agreement. The protocol changes completely the fundamental nature of the Andean Group by abolishing the Andean code on foreign investment. It scraps the sectoral programs and quietly forgets the common external tariff. All in all, the Quito Protocol extends the logic of regional integration to its limits by abandoning the multilateral foundations of the Andean scheme and replacing them with bilateralism as a valid instrument for integration.[73]

Two years later the member countries had to recognize that they could not even comply with the less demanding measures contained in the Quito Protocol. The Carthagena Manifesto, issued on 26 May 1989, was basically a call to member countries to respect the earlier integration commitment.[74] But it was evident that the integrationist flame was no longer burning brightly, with only Venezuela and Ecuador being really interested in holding on to the Quito Protocol. Colombia, for her part, seemed more interested in free trade on a Latin American scale than in sub-regional integration. The Macchu Picchu summit of 23 May of 1990 managed to keep the integration scheme afloat.[75] On this occasion the summiteers agreed to coordinate their economic policies and foreign debt negotiations while engaging in the establishment of a joint commercial and industrial policy. They also decided to cooperate on energy policy matters and engage in the creation of a directly elected Andean parliament.[76] Finally the joint declaration proposed the creation of a European-style common market.

The last step was taken in December 1991 with the signing of the Act of Barahona.[77] In signing this act, the presidents of the Andean countries decided on the following: to advance the effective date of the common external tariff to 1 January 1992; to cease all exemptions in January 1992, except for Ecuador which is allowed a delay of one year; to remove all forms of export bounties in the course of 1992; to allow Peru and Ecuador six months for implementation of the free trade zone; and, finally, to start negotiations with Mexico, the Mercosur, Chile and the US with the object of establishing a Latin American common market and eventually a hemispheric one. How do these latest developments fit in the evolving experiment in regional integration in the Andean countries? What are the chances for success and what do they imply for the future?

Most analysts agree that the Andean Pact has not been very successful in meeting its initial objectives. Some progress was achieved in the early years in terms of reduction of intraregional trade barriers. The adoption of Decision 24 and of the first sectoral programs can also be considered a success in terms of regional negotiations, although the implementation of these decisions was not that easy. Institution building at the community level can also be considered a success of the integration scheme, but implementation of community decisions has not been, generally speaking, very successful and the need for member countries to respect regional decisions was a constant theme in the Andean Pact during most of the 1980s. Furthermore, there has been very little progress in the growth of intraregional trade and complete failure in the efforts to establish a common external tariff and to harmonize commercial and economic policies. Finally the Andean Pact has not been successful in meeting its most important initial objectives of balanced economic growth between member countries and of a more equal position in negotiations with the outside world.

What are the reasons for this bleak outcome? Interviews conducted by the present author at the end of the 1970s with high-ranking officials associated with the Andean Pact since the beginning revealed that the climate of community decision making had been very good up to the start of 1974, when things began to deteriorate. Three events happening in 1973 were responsible for this deterioration: the first was Venezuela's entry into the Andean Pact, which was a positive move in terms of boosting the membership and adding to the economic power of the integration scheme but also caused some problems in the decision-making process by making it necessary to renegotiate sectoral programs already approved. The initial impetus of the integration movement was therefore stopped and the renegotiation of sectoral programs assignments became an occasion for countries like Bolivia to express their dissatisfaction with the benefits arising from the integration process.

More important than this were the coup d'état in Chile in September 1973 and the significant rise in petroleum prices in the context of the Yom Kippur War. The first event had dramatic consequences for the Andean Pact since, six months after taking power, the military establishment of Chile adopted a new economic policy which was extremely liberal in orientation and completely opposed to the more protectionist policies pursued in the framework of the integration process. As is well known by now, this opposition led directly to the exit of Chile from the Andean Pact. This being said, the event that had the most profound effect on the integration scheme was certainly the dramatic rise in petroleum prices. This rise was catastrophic for Third World non-petroleum producers such as Bolivia, Peru and Colombia. The governments of these countries started to experience heavy balance-of-payment deficits which gave rise to a mood of protectionism in the framework of the regional negotiations. This created a particularly difficult situation in the context of give and take necessary for the progress of an integration scheme. The rise in petroleum prices also had the effect of opposing Venezuela and Ecuador, on one side, to Colombia, Peru and Bolivia on the other. The former, much richer than before, wanted to use their new revenues to foster industrialization along the lines of the existing integration model, while the latter, forced to borrow on world markets, wanted to adopt a more liberal strategy of regional development.

What we have here, consequently, is a clear example of the way external factors brought about dramatic changes in the economies of the region. These changes, in turn, caused the local governments to change their economic policies, more protectionist in some cases and more liberal in others, which created a stalemate which the integration process never managed to overcome. The latest developments leading to the Act of Barahona are analyzed by some as an important shift in strategy of the Andean integration process.[78] It is seen as a move from a protectionist to a more liberal strategy which should align the Andean Pact with other integration schemes in the Americas and eventually prepare the way for a Latin American or even hemispheric common market or free trade zone.

In order for this to happen, at least two basic conditions must be met. The first is that the Andean countries themselves succeed in establishing a free trade zone and eventually a customs union. The latest indications are that this is not going to happen in the near future, since some of the January 1992 deadlines have still not been met, while it is not sure at all that Peru and Ecuador will be able to comply after the six months delay permitted them. Furthermore nobody knows where the Peruvian government is going, especially after the dismantling of parliamentary institutions. This led to the breaking of diplomatic relations with Peru by the Venezuelan government, which of course complicated further regional negotiations.

The second condition implies a perception by Andean countries that more benefits will come from an association in the Andean Pact than from other types of association. And again this is far from certain. With the developments unfolding in the Mercosur, it is not at all impossible that in the near future Bolivia may find more attractions there than in the Andean Pact. As for Colombia and Venezuela, potential gains may be greater from closer links with Mexico, in the already existing framework of the Group of Three, and the Caribbean countries than from the existing Carthagena Agreement, in which case the Andean Pact would be doomed, with Peru and Ecuador the biggest losers.

Strong centrifugal forces are therefore at work in the Andean region and they do not bode well for the future of the Andean Pact. Only time will tell if the new strategy contained in the Act of Barahona has a chance of success, but right now the odds are clearly against since the integration scheme does not seem to be able to overcome the combination of adverse internal and external factors.

Notes and References

1. Guillermo Ondarts, 'La nueva integracion', *Integration Latinoamericana*, vol. 175 (Jan.–Feb. 1992), pp. 3–12.
2. Stuart S. Nagel, 'Evaluating Public Policy Evaluation', (Canadian Political Science Association) *Bulletin*, XXI, 2 (Aug. 1992) p. 106. See also on public policy evaluation Stuart S. Nagel, *The Policy-Studies Handbook* (Lexington, Mass.: D.C. Heath, 1980) and *Policy Studies: Integration and Evaluation* (New York: Praeger, 1988).
3. For an analysis of LAFTA's problems see M. Kaplan, 'La Crisis de la Asociacion Latinoamericana de Libre Comercio', *Foro Internacional*, vol. IX (July–Sep. 1968), pp. 20–42; G. Magarinos, 'La ALALC, la Experiencia de Una Evolucion de Once Anos', *ALALC Sintesis Mensual*, Suplemento, no. 7, (Aug. 1972), pp. 1–24; H. Sautter, 'Lafta's Successes and Failures', *Inter-Economics*, vol. V (May 1972), pp. 149–52; J.W. Sloan, 'Lafta in the 1960's: Obstacles to Progress', *International Development Review*, vol. XIV (1972), pp. 16–25; M. Teubal, 'El Fracaso de la Integracion Economica Latinoamericana', *Desarollo Economico*, vol. VIII (April–June 1968), pp. 61–92; M.S. Wionczek, 'The Rise and Decline in Latin American Integration', *Journal of Common Market Studies*, vol. IX (September 1970), pp. 49–67.
4. These documents were the Declaration of Bogota and the Bases for a Programme of Immediate Action. The major documents concerning the Andean Group prior to 1974 are included in F. Vinces Zevallos and A. Kuljevan Pagador, *Estructura Juridica del Acuerdo de Cartagena*, vol. I (Lima: Officina Nacional de Integracion, 1974).
5. See the original document in F. Vinces Zevallos and A. Kuljevan Pagador, op. cit., pp. 91–125.
6. D.E. Hojman, 'The Andean Pact: Failure of a Model of Economic Integration?', *Journal of Common Market Studies*, vol. XX (December 1981), p. 139.
7. For a detailed presentation of the institutional structure of the Andean Group, see ONIT, Acuerdo de Cartagena (Codificado con el Protocolo de Lima) (Lima: Ministerio de Integracion, 1976); D. Sidjanski, *Problèmes actuels d'intégration économique* (New York: United Nations, 1973) Doc. F.73.II.10; X. Falegeau, 'Naissance et orientation du "Groupe Andin"', *Revue de la Défense nationale*, vol. 26 (Dec. 1970), pp. 1841–45; F. Villagran, 'Sistematizacion de la Estructura Juridica del Acuerdo de Cartagena', *Derecho de la Integracion*, vol. VI (March 1973), p. 23 ff; K.C. Kearns, 'The Andean Common Market: A New Thrust at Economic Integration in Latin America', *The Journal of Inter-American Studies and World Affairs*, vol. XIV (May 1972) pp. 225–49; M. Caraud, *L'intégration des pays andins* (Paris: Economica, 1981), G. Mace, *Intégration régionale et pluralisme idéologique au sein du groupe andin* (Québec/Bruxelles: CQRI/Bruylart, 1981) Part one.
8. The establishment of the tribunal did not, however, settle all problems related to the application by member countries of community Decisions. Two years after its creation, the tribunal still had difficulties in this respect. See 'Presentan un proyecto modificatorio del Tratado del Tribunal

Andino', *Integracion Latinoamericana*, no. 113 (June 1986), p. 52.

9. R. Vargas-Hidalgo, 'The Crisis of the Andean Pact: Lessons for Integration Among Developing Countries', *Journal of Common Market Studies*, vol. XVII (March 1979), p. 217.

10. Mention should be made of the Council of Foreign Affairs Ministers, which became an important instrument for foreign policy coordination from the middle of the 1970s.

11. For a good overview of the Andean Development Bank, see F. Vendrell, *La Société Andine de Développement* (Geneva: Institut Universitaire des Hautes Études Internationales, 1974).

12. A. Linares, 'El Financiamiento de la CAF en los Planes de Desarollo de la Subregion Andina', *Boletin de la Integracion* vol. VII (Aug. 1972), pp. 455–66.

13. The idea of levels of economic integration in the third world was first introduced by Lynn Mytelka and Andrew Axline. See L.K. Mytelka, 'The Salience of Gains in Third-World Integrative Systems', *World Politics*, vol. XXV (January 1973), pp. 236–51; L.K. Mytelka, 'Direct Foreign Investment. Technology Transfer and Andean Integration', paper prepared for presentation at the IPSA Meeting in Edinburgh, August 1976; W.A. Axline, 'Underdevelopment, Dependence and Integration, the Politics of Regionalism in the Third World', *International Organization*, vol. XXXI (Winter 1977), pp. 83–105.

14. Bolivia and Ecuador could go at a slower pace as part of the preferential treatment for less developed countries.

15. Successful in terms of its application by the member countries and partly successful in terms of access to the regional market, which still favors mostly Colombia and, to a lesser extent, Venezuela. See Hojman, op. cit., pp. 140–7.

16. For a more detailed presentation of the Andean Group's external common tariff, see A. Hazlewood, 'A Common External Tariff for the Andean Group', *Bolsa Review*, vol. 7 (1973), pp. 274–80; R. French-Davis 'La Planificacion en el Pacto Andino y el Arancel Externo Comun', *Revista de la Integracion*, vol. VII (Sep. 1977), pp. 87–103.

17. The text of the Quito Protocol appears in *Integracion Latinoamericana*, no. 134 (May 1988), pp. 62–72.

18. Preferential treatment measures are presented in E. Ocampo, *El Pacto Andino o Acuerdo de Cartagena* (Lima: Editorial Universo SA, 1974).

19. 'Grupo Andino: Apoyo subregional a Bolivia', *Integracion Latinoamericana*, vol. XX, no. 14 (June 1977), p. 46.

20. 'Agricultural Policy in the Countries Signatory to the Andean Subregional Integration Agreement', *Economic Bulletin of Latin America*, vol. 16 (July–December 1971), pp. 91–119.

21. For a more detailed presentation, see 'JUNAC: La Racionalizacion Industrial en el Grupo Andino', *Comercio Exterior*, vol. II (May 1977), pp. 54–9.

22. On this subject, see D.M. Schydlovski, 'Allocating Integration Industries in the Andean Group', *Journal of Common Market Studies*, vol. 9 (June 1971), pp. 299–307; J. Silva Ruete, *La Programacion Industrial en el Grupo Andino* (Lima: Junta del Acuerdo de Cartagena, 1973); J.L.

Galves and A. Llosa, *Dinamica de la Integracion Andina* (Lima: Ediciones Banco Popular del Peru, 1974); Mace, op. cit., pp. 177–201; Hojman, op. cit., pp. 156–9.

23. G. Salgado, 'The Andean Pact: Problems and Perspectives', in A. Gauhar (ed), *Regional Integration: The Latin American Experience* (Boulder: Westview Press, 1985), pp. 178–90.

24. I. Cohen-Orantes, *Regional Integration in Central America* (Lexington, Mass.: D.C. Heath, 1972).

25. The text of the code appears in Vinces Zevallos and Kuljevan Pagador, op. cit., pp. 262–81. The reader can find a more detailed presentation of Decision 24 in F. Armstrong, 'Political Components and Practical Effects of the Andean Foreign Investment Code', *Stanford Law Review*, vol. XXVII (1975), pp. 1597–1628; G. Fernandez-Saavedra 'El Regimen Comun de Inversiones Extranjeras', *Derecho de la Integracion*, vol. VI (Nov. 1973), pp. 261–8; P. Schliesser, 'Restrictions on Foreign Investment in the Andean Common Market', *The International Lawyer*, vol. V (1971), pp. 586–98; C. Vaitsos, 'Foreign Investment Policies and Economic Development in Latin America', *Journal of World Trade Law* (Nov.– Dec. 1973), pp. 619–65; Mace, op. cit., pp. 203–28; L.K. Mytelka, *Regional Development in a Global Economy. The Multinational Corporation, Technology, and Andean Integration* (New Haven: Yale University Press, 1979).

26. For example, the rules did not apply to multinational corporations established in the region but exporting more than 80 per cent of their production outside the Andean market.

27. S. Woodby and M.L. Cottam, *The Changing Agenda, World Politics Since 1945* (Boulder: Westview Press, 1988), chaps 2–5.

28. 'Peru: Decree Law 18350 on the Law of Industries', *International Legal Materials*, vol. IX, no. 6 (November 1970), pp. 1225ff. For a more general analysis of state support in favor of integration during this period, see also Instituto de Ciencia Politica, *Variables Politicas de la Integracion Andina* (Santiago: Ediciones Nueva Universidad, 1974); B. Ernesto Tironi, *Estrategias de Desarolle e Integracion: Divergencia en el Caso Andino* (Santiago: CIEPLAN, 1977); Mace, op. cit., pp. 79–148; J.-F. Petras and M.H. Morley, 'Rise and Fall of Regional Economic Nationalism in the Andean Countries, 1969–1979', *Social and Economic Studies*, vol. 27 (June 1978), pp. 153–70; M. Urrutia, 'Colombia and the Andean Group: Economic and political determinants of regional integration policy', *Quarterly Review of Economics and Business*, vol. 21 (summer 1981), pp. 182–203; E.G. Ferris, 'National Political Support for Regional Integration: The Andean Pact', *International Organization*, vol. 33 (winter 1979), pp. 83–104; E.G. Ferris, 'National Support for the Andean Pact', *Journal of Developing Areas*, vol. 16 (January 1982), pp. 249–69; W.P. Avery, 'The Politics of Crisis and Cooperation in the Andean Group', *Journal of Developing Areas*, vol. 17 (January 1983), pp. 155–83.

29. On this subject see, among others, J.S. Jaquette, 'Revolution by Fiat: The Context of Policy-Making in Peru', *The Western Political Quarterly*, vol. 25, no. 4 (1972), pp. 667–85; M.O. Dickerson, 'Peru Institutes Social Property as Part of its "Revolutionary Transformation"', *Inter-American Economic Affairs*, vol. XXIX, no. 3 (winter 1975), pp. 23–33.

30. On the Velasco experiment, see Mace, op. cit., pp. 102–17; A. Lowenthal (ed.), *The Peruvian Experiment: Continuity and Change under Military Rule* (Princeton: Princeton University Press, 1975); A. Quijano, *Nationalism and Capitalism in Peru, A Study in Neo-Imperialism* (New York: Monthly Review Press, 1971).

31. On the economic strategy of the Popular Unity government, see Mace, op. cit., pp. 89–102; J. Faundez, 'The Chilean Road to Socialism: Problems of Interpretation', *The Political Quarterly*, vol. XLIV, no. 3 (1975), pp. 310–25; J. Garcia, *Allende et l'expérience chilienne* (Paris: Presses de la Fondation Nationale des Sciences Politiques, 1976); I. Roxborough, P. O'brien and J. Roddick, *Chile, The State and Revolution* (New York: Holmes and Meier, 1977).

32. Somavia's close personal relationship with Allende probably had very much to do with this.

33. C.M. Conaghan, *Restructuring Domination, Industrialists and the State in Ecuador* (Pittsburgh: University of Pittsburgh Press, 1988), chaps 4 and 5.

34. G.M. Ingram, *Expropriation of U.S. Property in South America. Nationalization of Oil and Copper Companies in Peru, Bolivia and Chile* (New York: Praeger, 1974).

35. M. Urrutia, 'Colombia and the Andean Group: Economic and Political Determinants of Regional Integration Policy', *Quarterly Review of Economics and Business*, vol. 21, no. 2 (summer 1981), p. 193.

36. Avery, op. cit., p. 163.

37. Escuela de Negocios de Valparaiso, *La Economia de Chile Durante el Periodo de Gobierno de la Unidad Popular* (Valparaiso: Fundacion Adolfo Ibanez, 1974), pp. 3–57.

38. Oficina de Planificacion Nacional, *Analisis Economico de los Ocho Primeros Meses de Gobierno (Octubre de 1973–Mayo de 1974)* (Santiago: ODEPLAN, 1974), p. 5.

39. See the text in 'Chile: Decree Law Containing the Foreign Investment Statute', *International Legal Materials*, vol. XIII, no. 5 (September 1974), pp. 1176–88.

40. T.H. Moran, *Multinational Corporations and the Politics of Dependence. Copper in Chile* (Princeton: Princeton University Press, 1974).

41. Mytelka, 'Direct Foreign Investment', pp. 30–31; Mace, op. cit., pp. 220–22.

42. R. Grosse, 'Foreign Investment Regulation in the Andean Pact: The First Ten Years', *Inter-American Economic Affairs*, vol. XXXIII (spring 1980), pp. 90–91. See also Ferris, op. cit., p. 98.

43. V. Sukup, 'Le Venezuela et le Pacte Andin: Problèmes et perspectives', *Cahier des Amériques latines*, nos 21–2 (1980), p. 174.

44. Urrutia, op. cit., p. 195.

45. E.V.K. Fitzgerald, 'The Political Economy of Peru, 1968–1975', *Development and Change*, no. 7 (1976), pp. 7–33; G. Philip, 'The Soldier as Radical: The Peruvian Military Government 1968–1975', *Journal of Latin American Studies*, vol. VIII, no. 1 (1976), pp. 65–79. See also Mace, op. cit., Part II.

46. For a more complete discussion of this element, see Mace, op. cit., chap. 4.

47. Urrutia, op. cit., p. 189.

48. Sukup, op. cit., pp. 160–1.
49. For a more complete discussion of the debate on industrial programming, see Mace, op. cit., chap. 5.
50. Urrutia, op. cit., p. 189.
51. One major example was oil drills.
52. Mace, op. cit., pp. 195–7.
53. See, for example, M.S. Wionczek (ed.), *Politics and Economics of External Debt Crisis: The Latin American Experience* (Boulder: Westview Press, 1985).
54. R. Vargas-Hidalgo, 'The Crisis of the Andean Pact: Lessons for Integration Among Developing Countries', *Journal of Common Market Studies*, vol. XVII, no. 3 (March 1979), pp. 219–22.
55. On this conflict, see G. Mace, 'L'Amérique latine et les Caraïbes', in A. Legault and J. Sigler (eds) *Les conflits internationaux, les régions et le Canada – 1981, rapport annuel sur les études stratégiques et militaires* (Quebec: Centre québécois de relations internationales, 1983), pp. 196–9.
56. *Integracion Latinoamericana*, no. 56 (April 1981), pp. 45–6.
57. *Integracion Latinoamericana*, no. 62 (October 1981), p. 63; and 'Looking on the bright side', *Latin American Weekly Report*, 6 November 1981, p. 6.
58. Avery, op. cit., pp. 168–70. See also D. Kisic, 'Evolucion del comercio de las paises del Grupo Andino en el decenio de 1980', *Integracion Latinoamericana*, no. 135 (June 1988), pp. 15–27.
59. J. Palomino Roedel, 'El tratamiento especial en favor de Bolivia y Ecuador en el Acuerdo de Cartagena', *Integracion Latinoamericana*, no. 69 (June 1982), pp. 21–33; J. Vega Castro, 'Analisis de la evolucion y los perspectivas de la integracion andina', *Integracion Latinoamericana*, no. 87 (January–February 1984), pp. 20–21; A.L. Fuentes and G.E. Perry, 'Participacion de los paises de menor desarollo economico relativo en la integracion subregional andina', *Integracion Latinoamericana*, no. 110 (March 1986), pp. 24–5.
60. 'Victor Paz sheds populist mantle', *Latin America Weekly Report*, 30 August 1985, p. 10.
61. 'Need for reform agreed in Lima', *Latin America Weekly Report*, 4 January 1985, p. 4; 'Tariff system is overhauled', *Latin America Weekly Report*, 29 March 1985, p. 5; 'Dismantling Decision 24', *Latin America Weekly Report*, 21 June 1985, p. 9. The position of the Febres government on tariff protection was opposed by the industrialist business elite in Quito which was part of the traditional feud between industrialist-oriented Quito and commercialy-oriented Guayaquil. See Conaghan, op. cit., chap. 6.
62. 'Government sure of refinancing', *Latin America Weekly Report*, 20 May 1983, p. 2. See also Avery, op. cit., pp. 162–3.
63. Ferris, op. cit., p. 154.
64. Avery, op. cit., pp. 168–71, Vega, op. cit., pp. 24–5.
65. Hojman, op. cit., pp. 145–6.
66. L.J. Garay, *Efectos del programa de liberacion sub-regional en el comercio exterior de Colombia* (Bogota: FEDESARROLLO, 1979). Cited in Urrutia, op. cit., p. 183.
67. Ibid., p. 192.

68. 'Un ministro de Colombia urgio el replanteamiento del proceso andino de integracion', *Integracion Latinoamericana*, no. 113 (June 1986) p. 52. See also 'Colombia/Violating Decision 24', *Latin America Weekly Report*, 18 January 1985, p. 7.
69. See R. de Krivoy, 'Venezuela ante el proceso de integracion andina', *Integracion Latinoamericana*, no. 127 (September 1987), pp. 20–48.
70. *Latin America Weekly Report*, 1 January 1982, p. 11.
71. 'Trimming of Decision 24', *Latin America Weekly Report*, 22 February 1985, pp. 2–3.
72. R.P. Figueredo, 'El comercio internacional y las politicas para el establecimiento del mercado subregional andino', *Integracion Latinoamericana*, no. 98 (January–February 1985), pp. 14–31.
73. 'Andean Pact: Little substance left', *Latin America Weekly Report*, 28 May 1987, p. 6. See also *Integracion Latinoamericana*, no. 134 (May 1988), pp. 62–72.
74. 'Summit Produces New Manifesto', *Latin America Weekly Report*, 7 June 1990, p. 3.
75. 'New target is to emulate Europe', *Latin America Weekly Report*, 7 June 1990, p. 3.
76. The current one emanates from national legislatures.
77. For a summary, see *Integracion Latinoamericana*, no. 176 (March 1992), pp. 1–2.
78. Jorge Rodriguez Mancera, 'Reflexions sobre la integracion Andina en un contexto de apertura economica', *Integracion Latinoamericana*, vol. 176 (March 1992), pp. 3–12.

Part II

Social Policy

Part II

Social Policy

3 Social Policy and Political Dynamics in Latin America

Ernesto Aldo Isuani

SOCIAL POLICY IN LATIN AMERICA

Among the various problems that have characterized social policy in Latin America, there are some that are particularly important. Maybe the most dramatic feature of Latin American social policy is the limited sector of the population that has access to social services or to the income transfer in this respect. Undoubtedly the scope of public action in areas such as health, education or housing varies according to the country but, even in those with a wider scope, a great part of the population does not benefit from the different services.

When using one of the main institutions of social policy, that is, social security, as an indicator of the level of coverage, it is possible to get an idea of the magnitude of the inclusion/exclusion phenomenon in the region. Towards the year 1980, countries such as Mexico, Venezuela, Colombia, Guatemala, Peru or Bolivia were unable to protect more than a third of the workforce. Panama, Costa Rica, Brazil, Chile and Argentina had been unable to extend coverage beyond two-thirds of the labor force. Only Uruguay and Cuba had gone further (Isuani, 1985). Whilst social security is closely related to the formal labor market and the principle of contributions, other areas of social policy were structured on the basis of universal and free services. This is basically the case of the public-health and education systems, but, despite universal principles, large sections of the population do not benefit from the services. Although the right to health care does not admit, from the legal point of view, any limitation whatsoever on access, in several public-health-care systems, resources allotted and the existent infrastructure tend to leave more or less significant gaps in such care. Thus, in many cases, people in certain geographical areas lack access to public-health infrastructure or the paucity of resources hinders the satisfaction of these care needs. It is not easy to

55

determine this 'lack of access' except through surveys concerning utilization of services, which are not used in the region. However a study on Mexico showed that 21 per cent of the population had no access to public health-care services (McGreevey, 1990).

It is possible to get an idea of the difficulties faced, as regards the expansion of essential requisites for health preservation, by taking a look at what happens with the provision of public-health and sanitation services. For example, in the mid-1980s, less than 60 per cent of the population in Bolivia, Honduras, Guatemala, El Salvador and Peru had access to safe water and sanitation services. Only Chile, Costa Rica and Panama had sanitation services that reached over 80 per cent of the population (UNDP, 1990).

Basic education is the field of social policy where the universal trend is more clearly traced. Only in El Salvador and Guatemala was the gross enrollment rate below 90 per cent. However the universal nature of basic education *vis-à-vis* other areas of social policy is affected if the net enrollment rate or illiteracy rate are taken into account. Considering the latter as an indirect measure of the real capacity to universalize basic education, it must be pointed out that only Argentina, Costa Rica, Cuba and Uruguay had literacy rates over 90 per cent. In the Dominican Republic, Brazil, Colombia, Bolivia and El Salvador, the percentage of illiterates surpassed 20 per cent and in Honduras and Guatemala it was over 40 per cent. The gross enrollment rate in secondary levels of education also shows the limitations of the Latin American educational systems: only in Argentina, Cuba, Chile and Uruguay was this rate over 65 per cent (CEPAL, 1989).

Exclusion shows sharp differences according to social or geographical levels. For example, whilst in Brazil over 90 per cent of the employed population with the lowest salary level was excluded from the social-security system, the percentage came down to 14 per cent among those that earned the highest salaries. The same phenomenon appeared in the Dominican Republic, where coverage increased the higher the ranking on the income scale (Isuani, 1985; 1989). In several countries, among them Argentina, Bolivia, Chile, Colombia, Costa Rica, Ecuador, Mexico, Panama, Peru and Uruguay, the states or provinces with a greater economic and social development usually have a greater coverage rate (Mesa Lago, 1990).

So far the exclusion phenomenon existent in Latin American social policy has been stressed, but disparities that affect the beneficiaries thereof are very marked and clearly appear, for instance, through different possibilities of access to benefits according to the type of services.

An example is the difference that exists between the medical services provided by social security and by the public sector. In general, public-health services have fewer resources than the social-security system in relation to the potential 'clients' they must serve. For example, in Bolivia public expenditure on health was three times less than that spent by the social security, despite the fact that the coverage of the latter was not more than 20 per cent of the economically active population. In Colombia, the spending of both types of institution are similar but social security only reaches 20 per cent of the population. This situation also occurs in the Dominican Republic, Ecuador, Panama and Peru (Mesa Lago, 1990).

The position in the productive structure is also a fact that greatly discriminates the amount and quality of benefits received. In Argentina expenditure per capita on medical care of the *obras sociales* (trade union social security schemes) shows marked differences: the analysis of a small sample of these social-health schemes indicates that some of them spent up to nine times more on each of the insured than others did (Isuani and Mercer, 1988). The same differences were detected in Venezuela among the different social-security institutions existent in the public decentralized sector (Chona, 1990).

The income level of the population and the geographical region are other elements that mark differences in social policy. In some cases social policy has played a progressive role since spending on public health and basic education tends to favor lower-income sectors to a greater extent. For example, it was noted that in Argentina, Chile, Costa Rica, the Dominican Republic and Uruguay, the poorest 40 per cent of the families increased their share in income when access to public-sector health care was taken into consideration (Mesa Lago, 1990). Anyhow, in no way was it an increase that could be considered significant. It must be noted that frequently so-called 'progressive-ness' is due to the fact that services are of low quality or of extreme austerity; the poor have access thereto because the non-poor have no interest in using the said services. Nobody would dare question the fact that charity given by the rich to the poor is a progressive act, but we also know that charity incorporates certain meanings that disqualify it from being termed progressive.

Other types of expenditure, among them social-security spending, have a clearly regressive effect from the point of view of redistribution. Appropriation of benefits also differs according to the environment: there are different levels of benefits in view of greater industrialization, urbanization or other development or modernization indicators.

Thus the amount and quality of financial, physical and human resources of the educational and health sectors are usually greater in the most developed regions.

So far reference has been made to the main problems concerning social policy equity; a few comments will now be made on problems related to efficiency or rationality. Overlapping of actions and investments, which shows a deficient allotment of resources, is a feature of social policy in Latin America despite all sorts of restrictions that have affected the area and may easily be detected in health care, with the existence of the public sector, on the one hand, and social security, on the other. These institutions provide services in a practically autonomous manner. This leads to investments in technology, infrastructure development and utilization of human resources which may have a sectoral rationality but that bring about a global inefficiency due to the ill-use of expensive medical resources.

Administrative costs are frequently very high. In Nicaragua, Honduras, the Dominican Republic, Venezuela and Mexico, administrative expenditure in the field of social security represents over 20 per cent of the total expenditure (McGreevey, 1990). It is also important to point out that many public social services are extremely bureaucratic and centralized and could sensibly reduce operational costs if alternative supply models and systems were used. Moreover it is not by chance that there is low expenditure implementation and a lack of modern and reliable information, evaluation or follow-up systems to enable an improvement in the effectiveness and efficiency of actions. Finally the low qualifications of those in the public sector, both at central and local level, is one of the greatest obstacles to a better and greater impact of social policies.

With respect to the determinants that explain the above problems, the following may be stated. The lack of universality in social policy is due to several factors. One is the weak process of accumulation and production that hindered the creation of a material basis for development on a wide scale of the social policy, as happened in the central countries, especially in the second postwar period. Another particularly important element in explaining the difficulties in expanding social security is the high rate of underemployment in the region that affected 42 per cent of the economically active population in 1980 (PREALC, 1981); in other words, social security has shown a lack of capacity to expand beyond the boundaries of the formal labor market, leaving aside important segments of the low-income population.

Appropriation of public resources by the strongest social groups and the lack of will or capacity of the forces that govern the state in order to respond to the most essential needs of the population as a whole are the main elements that explain the exclusion of sections of the population and the stratification phenomenon. In other words, differential access to government resources by different organizations of civil society, together with the action or omission of the state machinery may also explain the enormous differences noted in the distribution of benefits.

The efficiency problems stated above are mainly related to the weakness of the state machinery in many countries of the region and the resulting incompetence to reverse or reduce institutional fragmentation of the systems for social service delivery. That is to say, the lack of integration, coordination and convergence among the different agencies of the public sector, and between the latter and the private sector, may explain irrational phenomena that severely affect social policy. The insufficient professionalization of the civil service, obsolete norms and procedures, 'clientelistic' policies and cultural phenomena that degrade all that is 'public' are also elements that help to explain this type of problem. It must be noted that both the efficiency and the equity problems mentioned above show a social and political fabric that is incapable of structuring the supply of social services on universal grounds. A brief historical review may serve to clarify this concept.

In Latin America, as had happened before in Europe, social policy was associated, at a first stage, with state actions focused on those unable to earn an income through their work (the elderly, disabled, orphans and so on). At that time there prevailed the idea of charity for the poor and the concept of self-reliance (Bendix, 197) with respect to workers. At a second stage, the idea of a social policy expanded in order to include state actions aimed at protecting the salaried labor force. As also happened in the European countries, after the implementation of social security at the end of the last century (Rimlinger, 1971), in many Latin American countries salaried workers became the main objective of the state's social policy. On the one hand, trade unions were accepted and, on the other, the right to vote was extended and popular movements grew rapidly. These events paved the way for the development of labor regulations to protect workers (women and children in the labor force, working hours, hours of rest) and for the creation of social-security institutions (insurance against employment-related accidents, pensions, health and so on). In some cases this was the result of the pressure of organized workers and in other instances of state measures aimed at preventing and eliminating the risks of social protest or at attracting political support.

After the Second World War, and particularly with the publication of the Beveridge Report, there was a change in the concept of social policy which influenced a great part of Europe. Benefits were considered a right of the individual in his capacity of citizen. Undoubtedly, the development of national solidarity practices, public regulation of consumption and a more equitable distribution of the burdens imposed by the war enabled the flourishing of more universalist ideas and more equitable service schemes (Flora and Heidenheimer, 1982). These universalist ideas also arose in Latin America, mainly in the fields of public health and education, but in essence were not implemented except in the Southern Cone countries. Although in these countries it is not possible to talk of universality, coverage was wide.

Consequently Latin America generally speaking, maintained a double political profile: the social-security system for workers in the formal labor market and social assistance for the poorest sectors of society. However the latter, like its predecessor in the nineteenth century, delivers some type of assistance to a relatively small section of the poor. Resources allotted to this component are scarce *vis-à-vis* the wide segments of population to be covered. For example, in Argentina, public expenditure specifically allotted to social assistance programs represents only 5 per cent of public social expenditure (Isuani and Tenti, 1989).

THE ECONOMIC CRISIS OF THE 1980s

Although, before the 1980s, Latin America presented the above picture in the field of social policy and marked inequalities in income and wealth distribution, the situation deteriorated markedly during the 1980s, giving rise to one of the region's most critical periods. Growth rates of GDP per capita, which had been over 3 per cent in the 1970–74 and 1975–9 quinquennia, fell to 1 per cent in 1980–81 and dropped to 0.8 per cent in the 1982–8 period. At that point, regional inflation rates, which had averaged for every quinquennium between 1950 and 1980 a percentage not above 50 per cent per annum, rose to 240 per cent. Gross fixed investment in GDP, which was around 22.7 per cent in 1980, dropped gradually, to reach 16.4 per cent in 1989 (Eclac, 1990). Unemployment, with its negative consequences on workers' income, rose between 1970 and 1985 in all countries except Brazil and Mexico. The figure doubled in Uruguay, Peru and Ecuador and tripled in Bolivia and Chile (PREALC, 1987).

The external debt of the region meant an annual transfer to creditors of resources equivalent to 5 per cent GDP. At the same time the income of the labor force dropped significantly and regression in the functional distribution of income was emphasized. On the other hand, the drop in investments coexisted with a fall in consumption of wage-earners but, at the same time, there was an increase in consumption of the sectors that were better off (PREALC, 1988). A greater regression in income distribution, greater unemployment and inflation rates and a drop in investments, production and salaries explain the growth of poverty and the clear indication of a dual social structure; that is, a strong reduction in middle class strata. During 1960–80, poverty had gradually decreased in relative terms, the percentage of poor having dropped from 51 per cent to 33 per cent, although it remained quite constant in absolute terms. But towards 1985 the situation had deteriorated considerably. The percentage of poor rose to 39 per cent and, in absolute terms, the number of people in poverty increased from 119 million in 1980 to 158 million in 1985 (PREALC, 1988).

Within the context of an extremely severe crisis during this decade and of the adjustment policies implemented that, as a whole, helped to produce the results described above, it could not be expected that Latin American social policies would overcome the problems of social policy. Indeed they seemed to get worse. Efficiency problems were aggravated by the fiscal crisis and its impact on the deterioration of public institutions, which resulted in low salaries a drop in civil servants, morale, an exodus of the most qualified personnel, lower spending on infrastructure investment and maintenance, and so on. On the other hand, although this is a subject that must be looked into, there are signs that indicate stagnation in social-security coverage. In Venezuela, coverage showed a downward trend in the last few years (IVSS, 1990) and in Chile, although it grew slowly, at the end of the 1980s it had not recovered the level reached in the mid-1970s (Arellano, 1989).

RESPONSE TO THE CRISIS

The persistence of the crisis and its social and political effects on the one hand, and the chronic problems of social policy on the other, have led to a deep questioning of the latter and to the emergence of new ideas aimed at changing prevailing models. Among these ideas there are three on which great hope has been placed with a view to attaining greater equity and efficiency levels: selective assistance, privatization and decentralization. The first of these arises from evidence that the state's social expenditure, except for a small proportion, does not reach the poorest sectors. Consequently it is necessary to redirect spending so as to concentrate it on the poorest segments of the population. Maybe the best example of attempts at selective assistance in the field of social programs is the recent abundance of emergency, development or social investment funds. One of the countries that first established these funds was Bolivia, immediately followed by Honduras, Chile, Panama, Venezuela and others (World Bank, 1990). These funds have developed several types of action such as nutritional surveillance, food support, health and sanitation actions and income-generation programs. Although the idea of a fund is not new, since the existence of public entities with resources used for benefiting low-income groups is a long-standing institution, the new generation of funds appeared so as to enable a more efficient management of available resources. In this way the funds financed both public and non-governmental programs aimed at sectors of the population living in poverty and entailed a rejection of conventional institutions and modalities for social service delivery. It is perhaps for this reason that they were not assigned to the so-called 'social' ministries but instead were granted great political and financial autonomy with respect to the rest of the bureaucratic structure, and some worked directly under the highest political authority. Furthermore there was such little trust in the state machinery and its procedures that in some cases private commercial firms were requested to implement the activities (Bustelo and Isuani, 1991).

Privatization has been presented as a response to alleviate the fiscal crisis, to avoid irrational use of resources brought about by public services delivered free of charge and to increase progressive public expenditure so as to avoid the better-off sectors receiving disproportionate (greater) benefits in view of their contributions towards the financing thereof. Despite the number of privatizing proposals in most countries, privatization progress in the field of social policy has been weak. Perhaps the most significant symbol has been the reform of the pension system in Chile under the military government, which meant a radical change in the prevailing logic of the Latin American social-security systems, leaving aside a 'pay as you go' scheme and adopting a full capitalization scheme administered by private entities (administrators of pension funds). In the same way, long ago Argentina implemented a privatization process in medical care delivered by the social-security system; instead of delivering services, the social health schemes started financing health services hired from the private sector.

Decentralization is considered in the same way as privatization, as a tool to enable an increase in the efficiency and effectiveness of expenditure, in this case by bringing together problems and management. The starting-point is thus a questioning of the size, red tape and inefficiency of the service-delivery systems administered by the national governments, which tended to consolidate themselves in the field of education or health in several countries after the Second World War. At the end of the 1970s, public health and basic education systems in Argentina were decentralized, with hospitals and primary schools transferred to provincial governments. A process of decentralization has also taken place in Brazil (Draibe, 1989). For instance, health services of the once upon a time powerful Instituto Nacional de Atención Médica de la Previdencia Social (INAMPS) were decentralized, prior to cession of its infrastructure to the Ministry of Health. In Venezuela, a law has been enacted for decentralizing health services, although the modality and magnitude of the process is still subject to discussion.

STRATEGY EVALUATION

Undoubtedly, directed assistance is a puzzling concept, and its main challenge is the distribution struggle and the political conflict. It is impossible to believe that it is only necessary to have solid technical proposals in order to obtain expected results. Crisis brings about an increase in the distribution struggle (Hirschman, 1985): public resources are not waived; there is a battle concerning their allotment. For example, in Argentina certain wage-earners with inferior organizational capacity and few economic resources no longer have access to medical care within the social-security system because of a suspension of services by private deliverers. Consequently these workers resort to public-health institutions which cannot cope with all the requests for medical care and end up by excluding low-income sectors that before had access to the public hospital. Moreover,even when an evaluation has not yet been made of the existent social funds in Latin America, the information available seems to indicate that so far resources have not been focused on actions and programs that really benefit the poorest social sectors. To date, it is the better organized sectors that have been able to appropriate the available resources of these funds.

There are two basic reasons that hinder a significant redirecting towards the poor of the spending that benefits the middle- and high-income sectors. In the first place, the needy lack the necessary organization successfully to exert pressure in the distribution struggle; in the second place, those in charge of conducting the adjustment strategies in the countries of the region, in general, do not seem to have been representatives of the poor sectors, ready to reverse power relations in their favour. If redirecting social expenditure towards the poor is difficult for the above stated-reasons, it is by no means easier to use a strategy of parallel organizations such as the social funds. Despite the greater autonomy and technical capacities of the funds, they count on only a small (generally very small) proportion of resources allotted to social policy. Consequently reform of traditional sectors of social policy must be carried out to avoid a situation where assistance benefits only a small number of the needy. This is undoubtedly another important risk in selective assistance, since it is most probable that it will turn into a sort of neo-charity, now in the charge of competent technicians instead of charity ladies, as in the last century.

As regards the greater efficiency which would be granted by privatization, things are not as simple as they seem. There are cases of privatized systems that end up by introducing more irrational levels than those they intended to solve. Social-security health policies and the housing policy in Argentina are clear examples. The Argentine social-security system operates almost exclusively through the hiring of health services from the private sector which have produced such levels of over-delivery that overall inefficiency is alarming (Perez Irigoyen and Isuani, 1989). The same happens with the housing policies based on the subcontracting of private building companies that declare very high costs in relation to the product they offer (Lumi, 1989).

Privatization may entail greater efficiency within the framework of a state with real regulating capacity and/or with high levels of participation and control by the users. The current Latin American context does not tend to favor the existence of a state with regulating capacity but instead seems to reduce the little that is left. Anyhow a privatization process that relies mainly on the profit-earning sector is not the most adequate for enabling users' participation and control. With respect to equity, the idea that privatization releases resources in order to assign them to those who need them most is problematic. In general, only the high- income sectors can pay for the social services they use out of their own pockets. In the case of the middle-income wage earners, the elimination or reduction of state services as a result of privatization processes does not mean, as stated above and especially in a situation crisis, that these sectors will waive the remaining public resources in favor of the poorest; thus privatization rarely makes it possible to release an important amount of resources for the poor.

As mentioned above, it does not seem clear that the privatization of social policy will progress at a great pace since it comes up against the resistance of the trade unions that consider privatization a menace to sources of employment and, within the context of democratic institutions, it is not easy to ignore or overcome such resistance. Users may also hinder privatization; in general, the benefits of the welfare state have been incorporated into wide sectors of the population as a right that cannot be waived; the crisis of these institutions generates claims for their functions to be fulfilled and not for them to be dismantled or replaced by private initiatives. This may explain the enormous difficulties encountered when trying to modify or reform the pension system that is practically bankrupt in several countries of the region and the fact that to date privatization has been carried out in an authoritarian context, as was the case of Chile.

Finally it is not easy to reduce social public expenditure. Although limited by the lack of a common methodology to consolidate social expenditure in the region, a recent study (Grosh, 1990) does not show public expenditure as an 'adjustment variable' of the crisis of the 1980s. Its main conclusions are the following: in the 1980–85 period in nine countries where the study was carried out, GDP per capita dropped 7 per cent and the share of public expenditure in the GDP 2 per cent. However the share of social expenditure in global public expenditure increased 4 per cent. Within social expenditure, health spending fell slightly; education expenditure maintained the same level and social security spending increased. This coincides with the experience of the OECD countries in which social expenditure increased constantly between 1960 and 1981, having reached a peak in 1974 and 1975, particularly critical years. In these countries it may be noted that the growth rate of social expenditure decreased between 1974 and 1981 but the growth rate of total public expenditure in this same period was even less (OECD, 1985). That is to say, social public expenditure seems to have remained constant or suffered less reduction than public expenditure as a whole, to such an extent that it is asserted that the welfare state in these countries is being consolidated and not dismantled (Alber, 1988).

The information provided shows the difficulties encountered in reducing the size of the welfare state, thus promoting privatization. In Latin America it may be noted that the role of the state as an entrepreneur has been severely questioned. From the ideological point of view, it is easier to assert that the state must put aside its actions in the field of the economy than to question state responsibility in the field of social policy; in this respect, even non-democratic regimes may pay a high price as regards legitimation. In other words, the institutions of the welfare state still seem necessary to solve the legitimacy problems that the crisis is generating in the labor market and income distribution. Only a great deterioration of public services is likely to create more favorable conditions for privatization (Isuani, 1991). On the other hand, the upward trend of the more regressive social expenditure such as social security, at the expense of the most progressive such as health and education, may be considered an indicator of the success of wage-earning sectors with greater organization, power and income in the battle for public resources.

Decentralization will probably help to improve efficiency levels of the public sector by enabling greater contact between suppliers and users, a better identification of needs or a greater degree of innovation in the response to problems, but this is not something automatic. In Argentina, decentralization processes in the fields of education and health gave rise in the provinces to systems as centralized and bureaucratic as the one that existed at the national level. As regards equity, decentralization can only contribute to improving the weakest sectors of society when there is a central state capable of moderating disparities that arise when each institution is left to stand on its own. Delivery by different regional entities in terms of capacity and resources highlights the problem of existent inequalities and, therefore, the great inequity of such a system of production of goods and services. A feasible scenario would probably be more for those with more resources power. When there is no central institution capable of conducting, coordinating and compensating, each social group that struggles to obtain resources brings about greater disparities.

In summary, a scenario that must be borne in mind with regard to the proposals we have analyzed and which seek to overcome the chronic problems of social policy and the consequences of the economic crisis is the following: the implementation on a large scale of privatization processes, although not feasible, as already mentioned above, would leave the poor without a chance of access to the necessary care; decentralization, without a central state capable of taking political decisions to correct disparities, would leave the weakest social sectors adrift;

and attempts at selective assistance would probably mean going back to old charity practices, which entails giving little to very few.

SOME FINAL CONSIDERATIONS

Undoubtedly it is not possible to defend a style riddled with inequity and irrationality that, generally speaking, has characterized social policy in the region and that we described at the beginning of this chapter. Centralized delivery by the state machinery has indeed tended to standardize services and, consequently, impoverish responses to a series of situations. Excessive red tape that has characterized public action has brought about rigid and slow responses; and inefficiency seems a serious problem when those in charge of the administration consider public resources as alien and not common resources. Finally – and this is of utmost importance – the exclusive responsibility of the state in social policies has dulled the capacities of the population and led it to a perverse subordination to the state.

But we have also warned of the risks of possible changes in social policy, referring to the ideas of directed assistance, privatization and decentralization. However these problems must not discourage the necessary search for changes in social policy if the aim is for it to contribute to reducing inequalities and minimizing deficiencies in resource allotment. As a starting-point, it is convenient to say that the fact of guaranteeing that no inhabitant is below the level of satisfaction of basic needs is a goal that cannot be waived, especially when existent marginality in the region is not due to an absolute lack of resources but to a regressive income distribution. Therefore, in societies like those in Latin America, the search for basic levels through social and economic policies must not run separate from a fiscal policy with a more progressive profile.

It may be convenient to define policies instead of focusing on segments of the population. Undoubtedly food policies may and must be directed at the population that needs food; there is no justification for giving food aid to those who do not need it; but the segment of the population that cannot meet health, education and housing needs on their income is just as important. In this case we cannot speak of 'directed assistance', since this requires minorities not majorities. Thus, whilst it is ensured that the most basic need, food, reaches those who really need it, it is necessary to work in fields such as basic education or health, on the existence systems, modifying health care structures and models, coordinating institutions and giving them priority in the distribution of resources, so that all those who cannot finance pay for these needs from their own resources may be benefited.

Certain mechanisms, such as the social funds, may play an important role since they have remarkable advantages, such as being able to break away from the rigidity imposed by all the red tape more easily than the traditional sectors of social policy. Therefore they are capable of promoting innovative experiences and creating a demonstrative effect that will make it possible to alter the dynamics of the traditional sectors of social policy. There is in fact a wide scope for developing creative social intervention technologies, at a low cost, that are capable of being widely reproduced.

This search for universal coverage of basic needs should not lead to identifying universality with statism. Universal access to basic commodities and services does not depend on whether the state has the exclusive right to production and distribution of the same. On the contrary, it is only the participation of the population, through numerous organizations of civil society and in the management and control of public action, that may act as an antidote to the red tape, wastage or indolence that has so many times characterized the state's action. Not only is it necessary to strengthen the responsibility of civil society in the direct delivery of services and to decentralize actions as a way to increase efficiency and effectiveness, it is also necessary to once again give the state a more powerful role with respect to its regulating capabilities in order to avoid the fragmentation brought about by the spontaneity of civil society and the inequality that stems from social dynamics acting without impediment. To promote social energies, correct inequalities, control quality of social services and goods, optimize the use of resources by civil society and especially to see to the protection of the weakest should be important aims when the role of the state in the present situation is rethought.

In summary, we deem it convenient, in the first place, to establish priority actions for achieving the objective of enabling access on a universal basis to the most basic human needs and not to direct actions at 'the poor'; in the second place, to ensure wide fields of action to solidarity organizations of civil society instead of promoting profit-earning organizations; and finally, to strengthen the state's leading and regulating capacity in order to control the quality of the services and to counter regional and social inequalities brought about by a decentralization process. These notions are subject to the criticism made above of the directed assistance, privatization and decentralization strategies. Finally social dynamics (and the distribution struggle entailed, especially in times of crisis) is an element that goes against the possibilities of meeting basic human needs on a universal basis and building up a state oriented towards the reduction of social disparities. On the other hand, the low organizational capacity of the poorest and a certain statist culture in civil society go against the possibility of enabling the participation of the former and hinder a more leading role of the latter.

No doubt greater equality and rationality in social policies are not possible without the presence of social and political forces with enough power to promote these values both in civil society and in the institutional machinery of the state. It is clear that the current context is not the best for the flourishing or development of this kind of social and political force. But we have ventured to set forth the above strategy, which is difficult but not impossible to achieve, because it proposes, in our opinion, a more desirable horizon than the prevalence of charity, inequity and anarchy that can result from certain forms of directed assistance, privatization and decentralization.

References

ALBER, J. (1988) 'Continuities and Changes in the Idea of the Welfare', *Politics and Society*, vol. 16, no. 4.

ARELLANO, J.P. (1989) 'La seguridad social en Chile en los años 90', *Estudios CIEPLAN*, no. 27 (Santiago de Chile).

BENDIX, R. (1964) *Nation-Building and Citizenship* (Berkeley: University of California Press).

BUSTELO, E.S. and E.A. ISUANI (1991) El Ajuste en su Laberinto: Sobre Fondos Sociales y Politica Social en América Latina, *Cuadernos de Trabajo CIEPP*, no. 5 (Buenos Aires).

CEPAL (1989) *Anuario Estadistico de América Latina y el Caribe* (Santiago de Chile).

CEPAL (1990) *Tranformación Productiva con Equidad* (Santiago de Chile).

CHONA, G. (1991) *Venezuela: Los Costos de Seguridad Social en el Sector Público Descentralizado* (Caracas: Ministerio de Hacienda de Venezuela).

DRAIBE, S. (1989) 'Una perspectiva del desarrollo social en Brasil', *Revista de le CEPAL*, no. 39 (Santiago de Chile).

FLORA, P. and A. HEIDENHEIMER (1982) *The Development of Welfare States in Europe and America* (London: Transaction Books).

GROSH, M. (1990) *Social Spending in Latin America: the story of the 1980s*, World Bank Discussion Paper no. 106 (Washington, DC: World Bank).

HIRSCHMAN, A. (1985) 'Reflections on the Latin American Experience', in

L. Lindberg and C. Maier (eds), *The Politics of Inflation and Economic Stagnation* (Washington, DC: The Brookings Institution).

ISUANI, E.A. (1985) 'Universalización de la Seguridad Social en America Latina', *Desarrollo Economico*, vol. 25, no. 97 (Buenos Aires).

ISUANI, E.A. (1989) *Seguro Social en República Dominicana* (Washington, DC: Banco Mundial).

ISUANI, E.A. (1991) 'Bismarck o Keynes: Quien es el culpable?: notas sobre la crisis de acumulación', in E.A. Isuani, R. Lo Vuolo and E. Tenti, *El Estado Benefactor: un paradigma en crisis* (Buenos Aires: Ed. CIEPP/Miño y Dávila).

ISUANI, E.A. and H. MERCER (1988) 'La fragmentación institucional del sector salud en la Argentina: pluralismo o irracionalidad?' Centro Editor de América Latina, *Biblioteca Politica Argentina*, no. 241 (Buenos Aires).

ISUANI E.A. and E. TENTI (1989) 'Una Interpretación Global', in E.A. Isuani *et al.*, *Estado Democrático y Politica Social* (Buenos Aires: Editorial Universitaria de Buenos Aires).

IVSS (1990) *Población protegida y recursos asistenciales del IVSS por entidad Federal* (Caracas).

LUMI S. (1989) 'Hacia una Politica Habitacional', in E.A. Isuani *et al.*, *Estado Democrático y Politica Social* (Buenos Aires: Editorial Universitaria de Buenos Aires).

McGREEVEY (1990) *Social Security in Latin America: Issues and options for the World Bank*, World Bank Discussion Paper no. 110 (Washington, DC: World Bank).

MESA-LAGO, C. (1990) *Economic and Financial Aspects of Social Security in Latin America and the Caribbean: Tendencies, Problems and Alternatives for the year 2000*. Banco Mundial, Internal Discussion Paper (Washington, DC: World Bank).

OECD (1985) *Social Expenditure 1960–1990* (Paris).

PEREZ IRIGOYEN, C. and E.A. ISUANI (1989) 'Politica de Salud en la Argentina', *Cauces*, vol. 1, no. 1 (Buenos Aires).

PNUD (1990) *Desarrollo Humano, Informe 1990* (Bogotá: Tercer Mundo Editores).

PREALC (1981) 'Dinámica del subempleo en América Latina, *Estudios e Informes de la CEPAL*, no. 10 (Santiago de Chile).

PREALC (1987) *Ajuste y Deuda Social: Un enfoque estructural* (Santiago de Chile).

PREALC (1988) *Deuda Social? Qué es, cuánto es y cómo se paga?* (Santiago de Chile).

RIMLINGER, G. (1971) *Welfare Policy and Industrialization* (New York: John Wiley and Sons).

WORLD BANK (1990) *Social Investment in Guatemala, El Salvador and Honduras* (Paris).

4 Dilemmas and Solutions in the Implementation of Social Policies in Latin America

Bernardo Kliksberg

POVERTY KILLS

By 1980, almost 38 percent of the Latin American population was affected by poverty as defined by the United Nations system. Almost four out of every 10 inhabitants in the region were below the poverty line at the beginning of the 1980s. At the last Regional Conference of Latin American countries on Poverty held in Quito (September 1990), by fine-tuning the handling of categories and measurement instruments, the Regional United Nations Project to Overcome Poverty estimated that 270 million Latin American Inhabitants lived in poverty, that is close to 62 per cent of the population.[1]

If we apply a measuring method similar to the one used in the 1980s, the figure is not, at any rate lower than 50 per cent. If we apply more stringent criteria, we approach the 62 per cent figure mentioned above. That is to say that the 1980–90 period witnessed an overwhelming increase of poverty in Latin America. Therefore the discussion of this subject in this region of the world means referring to a situation affecting one out of every two Latin Americans. It also means facing a problem which is not decreasing; nor is it an isolated case within the progress of the modern age: it is one that has grown considerably during the 1980s.

Also to analyze poverty is not the same thing as dealing with other aspects which are a legitimate cause of concern to social science. To speak of poverty means facing a process having daily impacts on the very concrete lives of people. Peter Townsend, studying living conditions in England of workers and almost marginal sectors of English society as compared to the middle class, reaches the conclusion that 'poverty kills'. The researcher demonstrates how life expectancy of sectors affected by economic difficulties is clearly shorter than for other sectors of the social structure, and the gap keeps growing. In Latin America, this situation occurs exactly as the author depicts it. In Latin America, poverty does indeed kill. So much so, that it has become the main cause of death in the region. Every year, one and a half million people die for reasons related to poverty, of which 700 000 are children, the most affected by the specific features of poverty in the continent. Witness to this fact is the upsurge of once conquered diseases, belonging to another century such as cholera. Cholera is not an isolated erratic phenomenon suddenly showing up in Latin America; it absolutely correlates in many aspects with core factors related to poverty in the continent, such as malnutrition, environmental conditions and the lack of water.

This is why the Director of the World Health Organization, Miroshi Nakajima, pointed out in Lima the responsibility carried by some policies entailing silent social impacts and the neglecting of basic essential conditions, favorable to the massive presence of cholera. Developing nations must face, with their scarce resources, the imposed drastic adjustment policies, thus neglecting, among other things, environmental sanitation measures. Health infrastructure is in a deplorable condition and the lack of water supply may turn the epidemic into an endemic situation in the near future.[2]

We would like to explore some aspects of the process aimed at implementing social policies in the struggle against poverty in the region, stressing its institutional and managerial aspects. First, we would like to focus on some myths in dealing with the problem and its solutions, which we feel stand in the way of a rational approach towards the search for truly effective action proposals. Second, we will attempt to establish the framework for some of the main institutional and organizational problems arising in the struggle against poverty and to suggest some criteria on experience and significant approaches of organizational solutions which are being tested in Latin America. Third, we will explore some thoughts on the overall situation. Needless to say, the struggle against poverty can in no way be solved exclusively at the implementation and management levels. It clearly has to do with the design of economic and social policies. However the organization and institution elements are of great importance, and meaningful initiatives can be carried out in this field, as facts have already proved.

CONFRONTING MYTHS

We will now review several generally accepted myths and one specifically related to the organizational and managerial aspects. We feel a discussion of these myths is essential before we can explore concrete problems and solutions, because they are present as a daily occurrence, in mass media as well as in the type of debate on the subject pursued, often in a very 'light- hearted' manner, in Latin America.

The Illusion of Development by Spillover

First, there is a myth in the region which has become the so-called 'spillover theory'. Very briefly described, it states that, if all efforts concentrate exclusively in the direction of economic development, measured according to common criteria, of a solely macroeconomic nature (gross product, per capita income, balances and so on), progress will be made, and will ultimately 'spill over' towards society at large. Thus it suggests a long period of waiting, filled with all kinds of sacrifice, culminating at the end through a 'spillover' of benefits.

In 1990, the United Nations Development Programme prepared a large-scale report on 'Human Development' in the World; it was based on research and on statistical data from over 130 countries, and it contradicts the 'spillover' theory in a very straightforward manner. It expresses very serious doubts as to the definition of development, how to measure it, and when it can be said that there is development by questioning the purely macroeconomic indicators. It also underscores that, even though there may be development as measured by traditional macroeconomic parameters (gross per capita product, increase in reserves and so on), not only could it be devoid of 'spillover' but, furthermore, there could be a worsening of the situation, which can be ever more regressive from the Human Development point of view: 'If there is unequal income distribution and a reduction of social expenditure, or if the latter is distributed in a non-equitable manner, human development will not be able to evolve in a satisfactory fashion despite a rapid growth of the Gross National Product.'[3]

This wide-ranging analysis suggests a different approach to the two main issues. It questions the fact that true progress means moving in the direction of purely macroeconomic indicators. It points out that the ultimate objective, obviously, is human development, people. Thus development implies increasing opportunities of all that is vital to human beings, from the most basic needs related to subsistence to those having to do with quality of life, such as freedom, participation, enjoyment of cultural and spiritual goods.

If the ultimate objective of societies is to progress towards human development, we would have to find a way to measure it, which would become the frame of reference to govern all other parameters as markers of this direction. The report offers an effective proposal to measure such human development. It starts of with three indicators: it builds a combined index including life expectancy as an essential measurement of health-related matters and various other aspects, making up one indicator; it also weighs schooling, as a progress indicator in the field of education, with obvious implications in the economic sector and the access to occupational structures; and it uses per capita gross product but with a variation: it is weighed in relation to income distribution. It is also updated in terms of purchasing power. The resulting integrated indicator is one of the first human development indicators ever produced in the world. Its application demonstrates that it is possible to have economic development, according to traditional categories, but severely lacking in matters of human development. Measurements of 130 countries were performed with the developed patterns and criteria, and the table of world progress according to human development was rebuilt.

What Latin American countries show the highest human development figures? Generally, any of these indicators are associated with the larger countries. However, in this instance, a small country produces very advanced figures. It has limited resources and three million inhabitants (1988): Costa Rica. Brazil, on the other hand, ranked eighth industrial power in the world, is far below Costa Rica from the human development point of view. The difference between life expectancy, the level of schooling and literacy makes for a large gap between these countries. This is obviously true elsewhere as well. For instance, a very modest Asian country, with serious economic difficulties and a very low per capita income, Sri Lanka, has human development indicators three times higher than Saudi Arabia, a country with enormous economic resources. This means that the problem is far more complex than is usually submitted.

Thus it can be seen that, in the presence of economic development, as measured by traditional patterns, the situation may be bad, and even regressing, despite the illusion of development. Naturally the degree of inequality in income distribution has great influence on the situation. According to official data, the situation in Brazil, for instance, already very unequal, continued to deteriorate during the 1980s. In

1980, 10 per cent of the population had access to 46.6 per cent of the gross product. In 1990, 53.2 per cent of the gross product was in the hands of the same 10 per cent. On the other hand, 50 per cent of the population had access to only 13.4 per cent of the gross product in 1980, and by 1990 this had become even less, only 10.4 per cent. Thus income distribution became even more unequal throughout the decade, a fact for which very high social costs have to be paid, as expressed by Peter Townsed. In the case of Brazil, this is illustrated by the dramatic increase in abandoned children. There are at present eight million children living on the streets in Brazil. Over recent years, they have been subject to horrible extermination operations: as denounced by various international organizations, 2100 have been murdered over the last five years and, in 1991, the average figure was of three children murdered every day in the main cities. According to accusations, the murderers are groups of bullies with police connections, hired by businessmen who feel these children make an unfavorable impression on sidewalks and are a hindrance to them. President Collor de Melo recently declared 'Our conscience bears the burden of extermination practices of children and youth in various of our main urban areas. . . . Brazilian society and world public opinion are indignant with the proven truth of denounced violence.'[4]

International experience demonstrates that 'the illusion of development by spill-over' must be proved false so that greater depth can be reached and also that development must be measured by means methodologies of larger scope than those traditionally used. 'Human development' explores the reasons leading some societies to far greater success than others even though endowed with lesser natural resources and lower levels of development according to traditional indicators. The reasons pointed out include the existence of active social policies to protect the most vulnerable people, permanently implemented with a high degree of organizational efficiency, as well as the existence of a structure for equitable income distribution, allowing for progress in economic development to flow towards large sectors of society instead of concentrating in reduced segments.

Another example to illustrate possible gaps between economic and human development is Chile. Chile reached significant indicators in terms of economic development during the dictatorship. At the same time the once invisible and now evident reality, which is nowadays the highest priority for the democratic government, lies in the fact that, while the number of people living below the poverty line at the time the military dictatorship took office represented approximately

20 per cent of the population, it had more than doubled to over 40 per cent by the time it surrendered power.

Consequently and a large proportion of the central government's main efforts are at present concentrated on a very difficult struggle to overcome the conditions of poverty prevailing at the time it came into office.

The Non-legitimate Nature of Social Expenditure

The second myth to be confronted by those who make a serious attempt to engage in social policy in Latin America, both at the social macropolitical level and in concrete field programs, is the myth of the non-legitimate nature of social expenditure. This constitutes a permanent, sometimes overt, often implicit, pressure, *implying that investing resources in social aspects would be making bad use, from the macroeconomic point of view, of resources which could be much better invested for other purposes.* This myth does not hold up when significant empirical evidence is analyzed. International experience shows that the opposite is true: an efficient social investment has one of the highest return rates known in economics. One instance, among many, is that, if we were able to invest the necessary resources to increase primary schooling among mothers in Latin America, the child mortality rate would be reduced in one single year by nine per thousand. This would occur because, as the World Health Organization points out, 'mothers are the main health producers'. Their knowledge during the pre- and post-natal periods has a great impact on the health of their children. With another year of primary schooling, infant mortality would be considerably reduced. Measured in human terms, the 'return rate' would be staggering. Even from the macroeconomic viewpoint, there would be tremendous savings in hospital infrastructure and in the cost of medical therapy.

Another illustration: it has been proved that a farmer with primary education has a 70 per cent higher productivity than one lacking it. Conclusions on social expenditure of this kind were arrived at by some of the rapidly industrializing Asian societies. Thus, in Korea, the rate of secondary school age youngsters completing secondary schooling is 92 per cent. This fact has implications for the quality of industrial manpower, as well as for competitive capability. Also the World Health Organization has verified that with only 2.5 to 4 US dollars per inhabitant per year, it is possible in any country to provide primary medical care to the entire population, with the ensuing social and economic impacts.

The 'useless' social investment therefore has return rates such as those mentioned, having also very important consequences both in the short and long term. In the face of this information, how can the myth concerning the non-legitimate nature of social expenditure be explained? What stands out clearly is the overwhelming lack of sensitivity and of historical flexibility of those sectors which systematically support and argue in favor of this myth, thus protecting narrow interests.

The Inborn Lack of Efficiency of Social Management

The third myth we would like to examine has to do with the assertion that social expenditure suffers from some kind of inborn lack of efficiency – that eveything done in the field of social programs in Latin America is bound to lead to corruption, to waste, to misuse of resources. This is why one of the first problems facing any manager of social programs in the region is the need to make a case against the sectors claiming that no resources should be allocated to the said programs because they will be wasted, as well as against those stating that things will inevitably turn out badly, one way or the other, even before the start of any operation whatsoever.

Again there is no empirical evidence to support these adamant attitudes. Where is the research sustaining statistical correlations between what happened in reality and what this myth describes? Given the fact that the management social programs are a complex matter, it is possible to make a long list of cases in the region showing that organizations aiming at certain goals in this field may achieve considerable results by means of modern managerial methods and the active participation of the assisted population. In all Latin American countries, there are social programs which have been implemented with excellent results, while others have not worked well.

Among the many examples illustrating the open possibilities of efficient management are the family consumer fairs in Venezuela; 'Villa Salvador' in Peru, winner of the 'Principe de Asturias' award, is considered by the United Nations system as a model of social development at the world level: the development of indigenous technology suited to specific conditions as undertaken in a number of countries such as Ecuador and Colombia, among others. All of these have operated with very limited financial resources, and mainly by optimizing social energies in relation to well-defined organizational projects and goals of interest to large portions of the community. There is no inborn flaw 'dooming' social programs to inefficiency.

A Merely Bureaucratic Approach to Social Management

The fourth myth lies in the usually implicit belief that *social problems can be solved at the bureaucratic level*: that, once adequate decisions are made, the bureaucratic apparatus can implement them. Thus, if the apparatus does not implement them and strays very far away from the goals, the blame will be put on 'inefficient bureaucrats', and not on errors in policy making, or flaws in the approach to the problem, or insufficient grasp of the complexity of implementation processes.

This myth is very relevant to the question of how to implement social programs from the managerial and organizational side of things. It is deeply rooted in an extremely formalistic concept on the way organizational processes actually operate within the economy and in society. In fact, social programs work in the midst of contexts and forces at play, which introduce all kinds of variations. Thus Harold Seidman, a very sharp analyst on the subject of public policies, points out that 'many of the social policies he has analyzed are actually expressed through regulations and decisions with a high degree of internal confusion and contradiction, making it difficult to enforce the law or the standards because of ambiguities, contradictions, lack of definition leading to conflicts and difficulties in practice'.

Actually, he points out, this is not surprising, as they result from transactions between the many groups of all kinds of interests normally involved in the environment of social policy making. These agreements lead to ill-defined policies which later, in practice, leave room to continue these transaction processes or direct confrontation. The play of interests around implementation has to be added to the 'original confusion' of the policy: for instance, the conflict of interests involved in a 'glass of milk program' in Venezuela, in Peru or any other country; all the pressures from local, regional and central lobbies, from outside the apparatus. The 'who gets what?' of social policies has to do with a very lively dynamic process involving conflicts, negotiations and a power struggle over resource allocations, occurring over a number of steps.

The myth of believing that once a policy is adopted its implementation will be more or less automatic has little to do with reality. Such myths practically pervade daily life. After going beyond them in our conceptual approach, we will undertake the analysis of key problems of policy implementation in the social field.

STRATEGIC PROBLEMS IN SOCIAL MANAGEMENT

We will review some problems which are very relevant to Latin American practice as well as some possible solutions as an alternative to traditional approaches.

Lack of Linkage between Economic and Social Policy

It will be difficult to achieve progress in this field unless there is linkage between economic and social policies. It is useless to evade the subject. The interrelation exists in practice, with multiple links both backwards and forwards. In the background of a social program there are economic situations having different effects on what is occurring now and what will happen in the future. In the foreground there are the possible effects that could be derived from the abovementioned example of the impact of secondary education on industrial manpower in Korea. Economic and social realities are connected to each other. The question is how to link them correctly. Thus questions should be asked, such as: What direction will the linkage have? Will it be aimed solely at orthodox quantitative economic development or at human development? The latter, of course, is not incompatible with the former – on the contrary. Economic development aimed at human development has many possibilities for enhancing mutual potential. In the Latin American situation, there is a lack of linkage, and the sector having the greatest power and influence, which is clearly the economic sector, leads and biases the interrelation, often leaving out social impacts and costs of economic decisions.

Also the public social sector suffers from 'institutional weakness'. The institutional problem of the social sector does not evolve mainly around the design of its organizational chart, or whether a body has to be relocated or function descriptions are to be modified. These aspects are only part of the overall problem, which should be solved following advanced technical principles. The essential difficulty has to do with the weak spots of the sector's profile within the overall power play of the public apparatus in the region. It is removed from places were basic decisions are made. Ministers of social affairs, with a few exceptions which are quite racent, do not participate at the level where policies are adopted on subjects such as the terms of external debt rescheduling, important definitions concerning investment flows and so on. Also, in Latin America, the public social sector in usually made up of organizational structures located at the lower end of a scale ranking the degree of development of the various organizational structures of the public sector in the region.

Health and education ministries, the basic operational ministries in the social sector, are usually to be found among the most backward sectors from the managerial point of view. Thus it is a technologically lagging sector, with no access to fundamental decision making and with a continuously challenged and haggled-over financial situation. Furthermore, when the time for cuts arrives, under the pressure of any given international financial institution, their already scanty budget is one of the first to be affected by the cuts. This explains why the United Nations' 'Human development' points out, among other practical conclusions, the need to suggest to international financial institutions that, together with the very harsh clauses often adopted in the economic field, they should include equally harsh clauses in the social aspect. Thus, for instance, no loans will be granted to any government not allotting a given percentage of its gross internal product to social expenditure.

The social sector is usually at a disadvantage in most fields. The linkage between economic and social policy takes place within this environment. To modify these conditions, changes leading to a 'social tuning' of the economic policy and to the strengthening of the social sector are required. From the instrumental point of view, some technical mechanisms essential for coordination must be set up. For instance, measuring homogeneous categories of the same problems: the social and economic sectors should use a standard measuring scale so that there is a common language in the analysis of the evolution of poverty, the worsening of conditions for middle classes, the increase of marginal populations – in other words, a standardized system to measure 'social accounts'.

It must also be said that linking economic and social policies cannot be achieved by the monthly meeting of any given ministerial cabinet. Although this is an important exercise, that should exist and be developed, day-to-day linking is also required. In the field of modern management there are possible mechanisms to achieve this: for instance, the setting up of a joint working group to monitor on a daily basis what impact public policies are having on both fields, as well as the reciprocal linkages. Thus there is a need to review, in depth, both the substance and the technical aspects of the linkages between the two sectors.

Strategies to Address Poverty

The second problem is related to changes in approach to basic organizational strategies in the struggle to overcome poverty. In the region there seem to be some indications of paradigm changes in this matter. Steps are being taken away from the bureaucratic, autocratic approach, in terms of which it was felt that the vertical process of imposing a social program from above, deciding at the top the supposed needs of the population, could operate adequately. This patronizing approach has revealed serious limitations in practice in the face of the very specificity of social programs, which call for interaction with population groups having their own ideas about their needs; there must be true respect for these ideas to reach efficiency levels, and people also want to become an active part of the program, not merely passive recipients.

All this calls for a review of the traditional organizational strategy. Likewise, in-depth changes will be required in the light of the increasingly widespread acceptance of the idea of sustainability. To illustrate, it has been shown that, if aid is provided to a community, for instance to build an excellent road connecting it to important places to which it had no access, unless there is sustainability this will be a short-lived solution. Unless local capability is developed for the permanent maintenance such a road requires, its use will become precarious.

Any social program which fails to develop self-sustaining ability once the cooperation and its officials have gone, and people have changed, will certainly be transient and will not have a real impact or effect profound changes. One of the essential limitations of the patronizing approach has to do with its inability to generate self-sustaining capacity. This is also true for the version of this approach sometimes called manipulative technocracy. This is not patronizing, but it is all about inducing the same attitude, in an elegant and more sophisticated manner.

As far as social programs are concerned, it would seem that we are about to witness a new paradigm where emphasis is given to a greater respect for the characteristics of the community and its involvement, at the highest possible levels, with the entire process, from planning, to implementing, monitoring and assessing policies.

The international technical debate on this matter is not limited at present to questioning the flaws of public bureaucracy. It also analyzes what happened when public bureaucracy delegated a great deal of its programs to external agencies; some of these, in turn, began to implement them in a patronizing fashion, and set up ever-growing bureaucratic apparatuses. It is necessary to find a way different from unilateral action by public or private bureaucracies. At the Copenhagen Round Table,[5] the need to combine actions of the public sector, of NGOs and assisted communities was stressed, and suggestions were made to train the community to improve its negotiation capacity vis-à-vis bureaucracies, both from outside and within the state. At the same time, it is necessary to train both kinds of bureaucracies to exercise participation in a consistent and serious manner. In Latin America, there is a need to take the step from talking about participation to practising it in a significant way. To this end, basic organizational strategies will have to be substantially reviewed.

García Huidobro's remark is very much to the point when he underlines the fact that, in social programs, 'both the policies and the core project aim at the participation of people, for them to become the subject, a community with the ability to generate its actions and goals', and therefore, in the said programs, 'the way in which things are done is as important as the things being done'.[6] Objectives must be reached, but through methodologies of participation creating conditions for sustainability.

Changing Linkages within the Social Sector

The third organizational problem we wish to bring up is related to the inner linkages of the public sector. At present, the low level of linkages among ministries and institutions of the social sector is one of the reasons weakening its position as compared to the economic public sector, which displays a growing degree of unification in Latin America.

The 'organizational scenery' is quite similar throughout the region: a large social public sector with many institutions, including five or six ministries, involved in permanent debates and competing in the struggle to obtain financial allocations, human resources and journalistic space. There is no coordination among them, unless this is made compulsory, in which case they seemingly oblige, only to continue their discussions as soon as they leave the meeting. Traditional approaches have not produced any significant solutions to this lack of linkage.

Traditionally the problem has been approached in a formal, bureaucratic way. The argument goes that the institutions in the social sector are not complying with legal mandates which, although sometimes confusing, attempt to create an organized linkage. Thus, it goes on, they should adjust to regulations, the organizational chart should be redesigned with greater precision, and standard manuals should be drafted. Are we sure that by doing all this we would really be addressing the underlying causes of the lack of linkage? It would seem, according to regional and comparative experience, that there is much more to it. For instance, it is quite likely that one of the reasons for the 'confrontation' being harsher in the social sector than in other public sectors is the influence of 'metapowers'. These papers suggest that part of the supposed power of the sector's organizations to use resources and define programs are taken from them by external lobbies.

Thus competition among organizations to gain the remaining reduced power is activated. A complete 'field case' of this 'stealing of power' process is recapitulated by Merilee Grindle, a Harvard researcher in Mexico.[7] It tells the manner in which the large CONASUPO program, which made low-cost food items available to the poor farmers throughout the country, was coopted and interfered with at its various stages by several sectors – *caudillos*, local politicians, businesspeople in the different areas, strong commercial pressure groups – thus diverting it from its original objectives. Given that situation, along what possible lines could innovative solutions be found? A network approach, with an egalitarian involvement by all players, seems promising.

Attempts at approaching organizational coordination are being made by setting up a network including the public sector, NGOs, the assisted communities which have an essential role to play, as well as support from the civilian society. The idea is for the network to function as a permanent arena for negotiations, where interinstitutional conflicts can be discussed and attention is focused on developing mutually beneficial programs. Naturally there will be conflict, but also significant matters in common to benefit the entire network. That is to say, some games will end in zero, but others will allow gains for all, and no losers: for instance, exerting pressure, as a block, to obtain external financing or a better ranking position for internal financial sources, producing quality information for the network as a whole, cooperating in the training of specialized human resources. By following this line, it is possible to set up networks aimed at finding the synergic potential to benefit the entire system, and this is a non-traditional approach to the problem of lack of linkage.

Towards Non-conventional Organizational Models

A process to change the paradigm concerning organizations in general is taking place at the international level. Both in the public and the private sectors, traditional formal bureaucratic models are regressing while significant moves are being made in non-conventional approaches: from organizational models based on projects which are dismantled after conclusion, to models attempting to optimize flexibility through the design of organizational relations stressing open, ambiguous structures and horizontal relations. The social sector is lagging in this field: ministries of health, of education and so on use outdated models very keen on hierarchy and vertical arrangements, and with great rigidity.

But we are close to the year 2000, a time for the collapse of the bureaucratic model. The most successful enterprises in the world are at present ever more decentralized, totally flexible, and some of them have even done away with the organizational chart in order to optimize the capability to adapt to an environment that keeps changing very rapidly. This is a time of transition 'from administration to management'. The inclusion of the social sector in the new era and the setting up of non-conventional organizational structures within it have become an important requirement. This is not a matter of economic investment, but of changes in organizational culture. The social sector should take advantage of the advanced managerial know-how, instead of remaining attached to the old model, which is not conducive to efficiency, to the ability to adapt, and to following essential guidelines for its task, such as full openness to community participation.

Decentralization, Municipalization and Participation

Decentralization of social programs opens up a number of significant possibilities. It is however essential not to turn it into a myth. It has both advantages and disadvantages, but if the latter are carefully dealt with through specific policies, the balance may be extremely positive. One of the greatest potential advantages of decentralization processes is their very operational capacity. Thus decentralization may be a channel to democratize society, to bring the state close to the community. Contact of this kind is absolutely essential where social programs are concerned. Programs should not be global, but seize the specific traits of every community – what is actually happening in it.

Also active participation requires significant room for decentralization. From the practical operational point of view, this is very difficult to achieve in huge macro organizations. What do statements such as 'the population took part in the formulation of national plans', as has been often claimed in Latin American countries, mean? What did it take part in? Did the people watch it on television? Did they send in their suggestions? That is all. True participation is far more possible in the framework of decentralized social programs. In such instances, programs are taken to a community unit and this provides an arena for joint work between the people in charge of the programs and the community, for a dynamic exchange of ideas in horizontal conditions.

The central strategy for decentralization in social programs in the region should lie in municipalization, as municipalities are the basic historical units in Latin America, with a good, largely unexplored potential. This entails the prior strengthening in much more global terms of the municipal regime, as well as its resources and capacity. However municipalization cannot be considered to be the ultimate goal of decentralization. It would be desirable to take further steps towards a joining of efforts between civil society and the municipality. A state reform is taking place in Sweden, a state which, according to all indicators, functions very efficiently, aimed at enhancing as much as possible the citizen's freedom of choice. A Law for the Conditional Delegation of Power has been adopted, among others, by means of which, in an already very decentralized state, additional resources will be provided to municipalities if they demonstrate that they use them in programs with a high degree of community participation: that is, not only resources for municipalities, but direct pressure so that decentralization may be combined with active community participation.

In the case of the Swedish model, as in other comparative research, there is evidence to show that, the more specific the situation for resource use, the greater the possibility for resources to be put to good use. And the closer the public organization to the assisted population, the lower the administrative cost. Also the greater the possibility of social control by the community over the working of the program, with the ensuing advantages.

Managing the Social Sector

What managerial style is appropriate for a social program? What kind of concrete problems are encountered in practice by a social program and, therefore, what is the profile of the kind of manager required, to be trained in the social field? These and other similar questions are of utmost importance, because human resources are the very decisive point at which the success of programs is ensured in practice. The leader of a social program has, in turn, a strategic role in the answers given. For instance, the manager will define the existence of participation, or the opposite; that is, whether 'participation' is argued for, but nothing done for it in fact. How can appropriate managerial skills be developed?

First, the manager must be trained for his task. Often in Latin America there is a belief that a massive health program should be conducted by a physician, and education programs by an educator. In practice this has not worked very well, notwithstanding individual personal qualifications. Managerial problems in a social program usually exceed by far the capability of professionals in other fields, but lacking the specific training for this kind of situation.

Second, the problem will not be solved by replacing physicians, educators and others with professional administrators. In Latin America, the latter have often been trained solely to manage formal, bureaucratic structures. They learn everything about organizational charts, standards manuals, job descriptions and filing memos. This does not qualify them to manage a social program, under the pressures of political lobbies, of the assisted population and with daily variations, and where part of the population may even disappear because part of the land they are settled on becomes uninhabitable.

Progress should be made towards a more sophisticated kind of management. Dennis Rondinelli remarks on development programs that 'no matter how comprehensive the project planning or the manner in which the technical analysis was performed, very seldom is it said that the problems encountered were unpredictable'.[8] They were not included in previous planning, nor were they within the most probable assumptions. They resulted from reality, because reality means that, all of a sudden, there are budget cuts in social expenditure, that the minister has been replaced, that a local group has set up a power coalition to hinder supplies being delivered in one way and trying to do it in another, and so on, as well as the many variable deriving from the dynamics of the community in this interaction. Some such as the foregoing, are negative and others can be positive, as for instance enhanced maturity of the community *vis-à-vis* the situation, and its readiness to move towards more advanced stages.

Management in the social field, according to Rondinelli, has no prior design and later action: both should melt into the day-to-day events. One must act and feed back, and management must be entirely adaptive. Human resources, requiring an ad hoc profile, must be trained for this purpose. One of the main features of such a manager must be an important change in basic mental structures. Latin American managers in almost all fields are trained to rely on the past, to project historical data in budgets, marketing, social programs. This style can be questioned as we live in times of accelerated change, in which what comes is quite different from what was. Therefore there is a need to work looking into the future through more sophisticated methods than merely projecting the past.

Also our managers are used to thinking in terms of a single scenario. An adaptive manager must have the ability to think in terms of multiple scenarios: what may occur is (a), (b), (c) or (d); what will I do in each instance? Training is necessary to replace the single scenario model with multi-scenario thinking. What is needed is a social manager with a very high degree of sensitivity towards the community: that is one who is tuned into it. The public service orientation underlines the fact that municipal bureaucracies in Europe have been offering all along services according to their training, their knowledge and the 'state of the art' in the field, whatever they find more modern. They stress the need to start from the opposite end, from what the community considers are its basic priorities, those the community 'feels for'.[9] These are some of the features of the desirable manager in the social field.

The proposed lines of work concerning the strategic problems of social management dealt with include economic and social policy, revamping the overall strategy to work in the field of poverty, linking the social sector internally on the grounds of networks, organizational structures related to advanced management, decentralization and adaptative management. These seem promising roads to improve the final effectiveness of social programs.

ACTION AS A PRESSING MATTER

'Adjustment with a Human Face', the well known UNICEF publication, demonstrates that orthodox adjustment policies have failed in over 80 countries, that no good results have been achieved in the economic field, and that they have been disastrous in the social area.[10] It warns about the seriousness of the situation and that 'the worst is yet to come'. UNICEF's Director General, James Grant, spoke about the 'millions of children suffering from the consequences of economic and financial policies which have barely taken into account the basic needs and future conditions for the wellbeing of children and other vulnerable groups', and pointed to the likelihood that the situation will continue deteriorating.

This was a premonition for Latin America. It was written a few years ago and, unfortunately, cholera seems to have come as a confirmation of that warning. In this field, it is necessary to keep an open mind, forget all about myths and dogmas, and to review what is happening in reality: to try to aim at 'human development'; not to forget the ultimate goal, and to evaluate whether what is being done serves that purpose; and, together with the unavoidable re-examination of economic and social policy, to thoroughly review what is being done on the implementation side.

In the light of the disarraying data on the explosive growth of poverty during the last decade in Latin America, the warning of Grant should be taken very seriously. Action is a pressing matter.

Notes

1. UNDP Regional Project to Overcome Poverty, *Development without Poverty* (Bogota: Editorial Presencia Ltda, 1990).
2. Statement by Hiroshi Nekajima, El Universal, 4 April 1991; Caracas.
3. United Nations Development Programme, *Human Development Report* (1990).
4. Reuter, El Universal, 5 April 1991.
5. International Institute of Administrative Sciences, Ministry of Finance, Denmark, Copenhagen Round Table, July 1991, Management of Social Services. See Bernardo Kliksberg (General Co-rapporteur of the Congress), 'Conclusions of the Copenhagen Round Table', *Revista de Investigación y Gerencia*, Caracas, 1991.
6. Juan Eduardo García Huidobro, 'Social solidarity and people's education programmes' in *Methodological aspects of social development policies*, ILPES/APSAL/ISUC, 1985.
7. Merilee S. Grindle, 'Political restrictions in the implementation of social programmes: the Latin American experience', in Bernardo Kliksberg (ed.), *Addressing Poverty: innovative strategies and organizational experience* (Buenos Aires: Grupo Editor Latinoamericano, 1989).
8. Denis A. Rondinelli, *Development Projects as Policy Experiments: an adaptative approach to development administration* (New York: Methuen Editorial, 1983).
9. John Stewart and Michael Clarke; 'The Public Service Orientation: Issues and Dilemmas', *Public Administration*, 1987, Royal Institute of Public Administration.
10. G. Cornia, R. Jolly and F. Stewart, 'Adjustment with a Human Face', *Siglo*, XXI (1987).

Part III

Technology and Environmental Policy

5 Administering Electronics: The Experience of India and Brazil

Jørgen D. Pedersen

INTRODUCTION

The revolutionary changes implied by the 'electronic revolution' pose major challenges to countries in the Third World. On the one hand, the spread of new production methods in all fields of industry puts increasing pressure on already established industrial strongholds of the more advanced developing countries. The rapid changes and high 'rate of obsolescence' that characterize the new industrial technologies further intensify this pressure. On the other hand, the new technoeconomic paradigm underlying the new economic dynamism has shifted the strategic center of industry towards, in particular, the electronic industries, but also towards other R&D-intensive industries such as those producing new materials and biotechnology.

While these economic changes pose problems for all countries, developing countries face particularly severe problems, for a number of reasons. The general lack of capital and of technological capabilities makes it extremely difficult for these countries to keep up in the technological race, and most developing countries will never attempt to get into the race precisely for that reason. For others, who until now have been able to advance industrially and who aspire to continue in the race, additional problems have emerged – in particular problems of state management of economic development. One problem concerns the management of the relations with those external actors – transnational corporations based in the most advanced developed countries – that increasingly monopolize the new core technologies. The other problem concerns the domestic introduction of the new technologies in societies so different from the ones in which the technologies emerged.

Both types of problem point towards the crucial role of the state in developing countries as the key manager of economic change. Can states that in part were successful in transforming their countries industrially under the 'old model' repeat this performance under new circumstances? Is the traditional structure and functioning of the state compatible with new demands of intensive management on the external front as well as on the domestic front? If not, what then are the required changes in the functioning and organization of the state for successful management of the new challenges? These are the questions which we address in this chapter. It begins with a consideration of some theoretical issues of a more general nature which are expanded and specified in order to relate them to the problems faced by developing countries. Then follows an analysis and comparison of two Third World states struggling to manage the new challenges within the electronics/computer sector – India and Brazil. On the basis of these two case studies an attempt is presented to specify some preliminary conclusions with regard to the role of public administration in the management of technological development.

SOME THEORETICAL CONSIDERATIONS

Three main theoretical sources of inspiration provide the framework for the discussion in this chapter. A main source of inspiration comes from what has been called the 'French Regulation School' and its theoretical work on the changes in the advanced capitalist economies from 'Fordism' to 'Post-Fordism'. A second, and closely related source is the recent debate on the implications of the new and emerging technologies grouped under the heading of 'flexible specialization'. Finally these theoretical strands are combined with and extended by Weberian theories on the role of public administration in capitalist development and considerations on the specific economic role played by the state in the economic development of countries in the Third World.

The French Regulation School has been concerned with the structural changes in the economies of the Western world during this century and the accompanying systems of social and economic regulation (Aglietta, 1979; Lipietz, 1987). Basically these theories argue that there exist various distinct modes of capitalist growth termed 'regimes of accumulation', each accompanied by a specific 'mode of regulation' that provides a certain degree of stability to the otherwise contradictory and inherently unstable national economic systems. The prime example is the transformation to 'Fordism': a regime of accumulation characterized by industrial mass-production and a mode of regulation comprising the central institutions of the Keynesian interventionist welfare state that ensure a mass-consumption market. This Fordist mode of development has from the 1970s onwards been in crisis, the way out of which is seen in the transformation to a not yet fully defined 'Post-Fordist' regime of accumulation (For an overview, see Jessop, 1990b). While acknowledging the unique role played by the state in social and economic regulation, most work done by the regulation theorists has concentrated on economic issues, neglecting the closer analysis of the state (Jessop, 1990a, 315ff; Jessop, 1990b, pp. 196–200). There is, however, nothing inherent in the regulation approach that excludes considerations on the state, on the importance of different forms of the state for the mode of regulation and eventually for the regime of accumulation.[1] It would therefore seem fruitful to extend the analysis of the connections between the economic structures and the regulatory mechanisms further to include also an investigation of the administrative and political institutions involved in these regulatory practices.[2] Before this is considered further, another supplement to the regulationist approach should be considered.

This theoretical addition mainly concerns the specification of the ongoing changes in the economic sphere. According to some theorists the development and diffusion of new production technologies based on the use of microelectronics can be interpreted as marking a significant transformation away from the old 'technoeconomic paradigm' (Perez, 1985) of mass-production based on electromechanical techniques towards a new paradigm of what has been termed 'flexible specialization' (Piore and Sabel, 1984) or 'systemofacture' (Kaplinsky, 1989). These theories are clearly inspired by and conveniently fit into the concern of the regulationist school theories with the development of a new 'Post-Fordist' regime of accumulation (Kaplinsky, 1989; Perez, 1985; for a polemic/critical review, see Hirst and Zeitlin, 1991). In some of these theories a claim comparable to that of the regulation theorists on the important implications of the economic and technological changes for the 'socioinstitutional' framework including the regulation of markets, the separation between public and private responsibilities and their interrelations, the structure of the educational system and broad features of international economic relations has also been made (Perez, 1985, pp. 445–6). The electronics industry (especially when combined with the telecommunication infrastructure – the 'informatics industry') has in this perspective been regarded as the future economic core sector of this new era. Flexibility, information intensity, creativity, decentralization and the absence of hierarchy are some of the most important organizational consequences accompanying this change in production structure that are visualized in these theories (Perez, 1985).

While the theories outlined above have their main focus on the changes in the nature of the production processes and only pay limited attention to the broader social consequences, it is suggested that it would be useful to extend the argument to include also the political and administrative arrangements that reflect upon and are affected by the economic changes. A starting-point for such considerations can be taken in the classical works of Max Weber on the proper administrative form for capitalist societies and its extension in more recent theories. For Max Weber the optimal form of administration in a capitalist society was 'bureaucracy' – a legal–rational 'administrative machine' that, organized in a hierarchical structure, worked in a calculable, predictable, impartial and dispassionate manner, staffed by technically competent and carefully selected personnel (Weber, 1978, pp. 956–1005). Furthermore for the optimal working of this kind of administration the existence of some external controls was considered essential in order to avoid undirected bureaucratic actions. These controls could, according to Weber, best be provided by an effectively working parliament consisting of 'able politicians' and the existence of such controls would be particularly important should the bureaucracy engage in the direct management of economic enterprises (Weber, 1978, p. 1456). The parliamentary committees in which the working of the administration could come under close scrutiny would thus be a crucial feature of a democratically organized state and, together with the budgetary prerogatives, they would constitute the most important means of parliamentary control over the executive (Weber, 1978, pp. 1381–469). It is interesting to note that, contrary to much recent theorizing on the prerequisites for the strong developmental states (see IDS Bulletin, 1984), Weber does not visualize an 'insulated' or 'autonomous' state as being the optimal regulatory structure for a capitalist economy. On the contrary, he repeatedly stresses the negative features of an insulated bureaucracy, free and unhindered by outside forces.

In a periodization of capitalist development in specific phases in the style of the French regulationists, it is possible to regard Weber's ideal model of bureaucracy as reflecting the structure of an early capitalist epoch characterized by a non-interventionist state and a free (competitive) market economy. Following Göran Therborn, it can then be argued that in addition to the legal–rational mode of administrative functioning there has at a later stage emerged within the state what he terms a 'managerial–technocratic' mode of functioning required by the expansion of public interventions in an increasingly complex and thoroughly regulated (Fordist) economy (Therborn, 1978, pp. 49–63, 87–97). (The archetypical example of this would probably be the socio-economic planners). From this perspective it becomes important to inquire whether a full transition to a new phase of Post-Fordism, or flexible specialization, in the wake of the microelectronic innovations will in the same manner require changes in the administrative and political arrangements needed for the regulation of this transition and for the stabilization of its working.

The considerations on the political and administrative requirements of the new technoeconomic paradigm furthermore become of special importance in the case of developing countries where the role of the state is of substantial importance in the overall regulation of the economy. As an initiator, protector and regulator of economic change, the state in developing countries will not only act as an 'outsider' intervening in the economic processes, but will usually also be a key participant in these changes. This crucial role that is forced upon the state because the new 'technoeconomic paradigm' in these countries has not only to be regulated, but also to be introduced, makes it plausible to argue that the political and administrative structures will be of extreme importance for a successful regulation.

To sum up: the new opportunities for a renewed economic growth promised by the microelectronic innovations and the vision of a new emerging 'technoeconomic' paradigm pose the question whether the existing socioinstitutional arrangements have to be transformed in order for these potentials to be fully realized and a new stable 'mode of development' established. According to the theories outlined above, this is precisely what should be expected, but until now very little empirical research has been done in this area. This may be due to the fact that most discussions on the subject of the implications of the econ_omic_ changes have been concerned with the consequences in the advanced capitalist countries, but it would appear fruitful from both a theoretical and an empirical perspective to inquire more closely into the political and administrative repercussions in those developing countries that have tried to take advantage of the opportunities offered by the microelectronic revolution.

MANAGING 'THE ELECTRONICS REVOLUTION':
THE EXPERIENCE OF INDIA AND BRAZIL

The microelectronic revolution has placed developing countries in a fundamental dilemma. On the one hand, developing countries as with any other branch of industry, face the problem of overcoming dependency: that is, the problem of creating a domestically controlled electronics-producing industry and obtaining the ability to master and subsequently develop appropriate related technologies. On the other hand, and to some extent in contradiction with the first objective, developing countries face the problem of optimal utilization of the new technologies in all productive spheres. Choosing to tackle the problem of dependency will often involve a delay in the introduction of the new technologies, while deciding to import and disseminate new technologies may preclude the emergence of an indigenous, self-reliant electronics industry. This fundamental dilemma can furthermore be expected to surface in the domestic struggle of diverse economic interests over the course of actual policies regulating the industry. The issue then becomes one of performing a balancing act between the pursuance of self-reliance, on the one hand, and the unrestricted import and dissemination of new technologies and new electronic products, on the other.

Achievements

India and Brazil have since the early 1970s made remarkable progress in electronics. At that time both countries took their first steps towards the creation of an indigenous computer industry, and by the end of the 1980s both countries were in possession of a thriving national computer industry producing various types of hardware and, in addition, both had growing software industries. In the late 1980s there were around 40 companies in India producing some 60 000 personal computers annually (Bowonder and Mani, 1991, p. M7). In 1989, Brazil had more than 300 national companies operating in the computer and peripherals market – and probably more than 50 in computers alone (Schwartzman, 1988, p. 71) – generating sales of over US$ 3.6 billion, up from US$ 1.5 billion three years earlier (*IHT*, 10 July 1990; Schmitz and Hewitt, 1989, p. 3). While the Brazilian market for electronics in general and computers in particular has been much larger than the Indian market, the rate of growth of the Indian market and of the production of the Indian computer industry has during the 1980s been somewhat higher.[3] In addition, Brazil has obtained a significant though of late somewhat stagnating export of computers, while India still only has a marginal though rapidly increasing export (*Report*, 1990, p. 319; Evans and Tigre, 1989a, p. 14).[4] In software India seems to be ahead of Brazil at least with regard to exports. The Indian export of software has expanded dramatically in the late 1980s, while Brazil so far has not made any significant impact in the export markets.

While these achievements in broad terms seem quite impressive, a closer inspection reveals some more disturbing features, especially with regard to the continuing dependence on foreign suppliers of technology, the inability to produce more advanced computers, the dependence on import of components and key raw materials and the dependence on the marketing channels of foreign companies when exporting. Despite successful efforts in developing a domestic software industry, there still exists a considerable dependence in this area as well, especially with regard to standard application software. A recent threat to the Indian industry comes from the growing practice of foreign companies to recruit software engineers from India, thus depriving the country of much of its best manpower (Lakha, 1990). And in Brazil the precarious financial situation makes it difficult to expand public computer education and increase funds for research and development.

Despite the persistence of various forms of dependency, it must be acknowledged that both countries have achieved a degree of self-reliance and a level of capability within the electronics/computer sector that only very few other developing countries can match.[5] These achievements may not protect the national electronics industry from sliding backwards into higher degrees of dependency in the future, but they have provided both countries with a much better bargaining position and a capacity to choose between a range of alternatives in negotiations with technology suppliers (Schmitz and Hewitt, 1989, p. 21). An example of this is the remarkable willingness of large international computer companies to enter into collaboration agreements with local firms in both countries from the mid-1980s onwards (Schmitz and Hewitt, 1989, p. 22; *India Today*, 31 March 1988; Bowonder and Mani, 1991, p. M10).

Explanations

Explanations of these in many ways impressive achievements in a crucial high-tech industry have generally focused on two sets of important factors: (1) the institutional arrangements within which key groups of social actors have promoted their vision of an appropriate public policy for encouraging the industry; and (2) the particular external circumstances conducive to the successful implementation of the strategy – internationally as well as in the domestic arena. As for the first set of explanatory factors, it has been pointed out that in both countries a dedicated and highly motivated group of technically competent persons with a strong nationalistic orientation succeeded in penetrating the state apparatus, creating new strong institutions and through these initiating a process of support for the establishment of a domestic computer industry. Through an intricate process of 'bureaucratic politics' contesting strategies were fought over, modulated and subsequently implemented leading to the creation of a vigorous domestic industry.

With regard to the second set of factors, it has been pointed out that international opportunities presented themselves through the rapid technological developments in the field and the presence (initially) of a large number of companies willing to share their technological know-how for an acceptable price with emerging companies in developing countries (Grieco, 1984, ch. 3). Domestically it has been pointed out that the strength, capabilities and orientation of local companies *vis-à-vis* foreign companies within the sector influenced the strategies and instruments used by the two states and shaped the final outcome.

Strategies, Instruments, Phasing

A closer look at the strategies, the instruments and the phasing of policies reveals some interesting parallels as well as important differences between the two countries. In India, the idea of establishing a domestic computer industry emerged in the 1960s following the war with China, but it was only in the early 1970s that serious actions were initiated. A separate Department of Electronics was set up in December 1970 under the supervision of a high-level Electronics Commission established shortly after (in February 1971) both with direct reference to the prime minister.[6] The Department and the Commission were largely staffed by nationalistic, technically educated officials from the research community (the 'network') centered around the influential Atomic Energy Commission. These specialized scientists eager to develop an indigenous capability in electronics thus emerged as winners in the dispute with the military establishment located in the Ministry of Defense which was more inclined to establish international links in order to get access to the most advanced technologies and besides favored the expansion of their own state-run electronics company. In the staffing procedures the Department, because of the perceived technical nature of its tasks, was to some extent exempted from normal regulations, a fact that must have caused some annoyance within the established bureaucracy (Grieco, 1984, p. 119).

The strategy mapped out by the new institutions was largely one of challenging the then dominant position of foreign producers of computers (IBM and ICL) by promoting a 'national champion' in the form of the state-owned Electronics Corporation of India Limited (ECIL). During the 1970s ECIL succeeded in manufacturing its own computers thanks to access to foreign technology and, assisted by import restrictions in combination with restrictions on the activities of, primarily, IBM, the company also managed to sell some of them. In addition, a separate state-owned Computer Maintenance Corporation (CMC) was established to service the plethora of different (imported or locally produced) non-ECIL computers, primarily IBMs. When IBM in 1978 withdrew from the Indian market in protest against the enforcement of the general rules on foreign ownership of companies, it seemed that the strategy had succeeded in the sense that ECIL (with CMC) now had a good chance of securing complete dominance over the Indian market.

The forces that prevented this from materializing came from sections of local private capital eager to enter the computer industry, as well as from customers (private and public) dissatisfied with ECIL's services and products. As a result of these pressures policies were changed, allowing selected private companies to enter the market for microcomputers. At the same time the administration of the electronics/computer policy was reevaluated by an official commission, the 'network' was broken up and the bureaucracy obtained a much firmer grip on the affairs of the Department of Electronics through the establishment of an interdepartmental committee to coordinate policies and through the replacement of former key officials in the Department.[7] Following upon this reorganization, the computer policy in the first half of the 1980s underwent a significant liberalization (BICP, 1988, pp. 21ff). Licencing conditions were relaxed, as were import restrictions, and as a result the private companies that had entered the industry in the late 1970s were joined by several newcomers. All new entrants based their products on imported technology obtained through extensive collaboration agreements with different foreign companies (not including IBM), imported components and only modest attempts at local technological development (BICP, 1988; Bowonder and Mani, 1991). By the end of the 1980s the computer market was bifurcated, with the market for smaller computer crowded with a substantial number of local private companies assembling computers from imported components technically assisted by foreign collaboration agreements. The much smaller market for larger mainframe computers was shared by the state-owned ECIL plus a private company affiliated to the (then) British company, ICL.

In software gains were considerable. Based on the huge pool of educated, cheap and English-speaking manpower available in India, a number of software producers emerged, assisted by an increasingly liberal policy that from 1986 allowed free import of necessary hardware to exporters and liberal access for foreign investors. In partial contrast to the hardware industry, the software industry became dominated by companies belonging to large industrial houses (in particular Tata) and the industry has been strongly export-oriented, establishing close links with US companies and with the US market (Lakha, 1990). While large private companies dominate the export of software tailored to customer requirements, larger independent consultancy tasks in the nature of system construction have lately been taken up quite successfully by the state-owned companies, primarily by CMC, but also by ECIL (Evans, 1990). Finally, in the field of more advanced computer research, India has maintained its aspiration to stay in the absolute front line with state-funded research projects in supercomputers and other fields of advanced technology (DoE, 1989).

From the initial strategy of promoting a 'national champion' in hardware (and some software applications), the new strategy that has emerged as a result of incremental policy changes during the 1980s appears to be one of adapting to conditions on the world market by de facto giving up ambitions to develop a wholly indigenous industry capable of operating internationally in the highly competitive sector of small computers and in standard software, relying instead on extensive foreign collaborations in order to satisfy domestic demands. In contrast, efforts have been concentrated in more advanced software applications, to some extent in larger computer systems and in basic research – all areas where competition is based to a lesser degree on manufacturing capabilities and more on technological expertise and human intellectual skills. The export strategy has centered on software exports through collaboration with international companies; witness the collaboration of the largest software exporter, Tata, with the American company Unisys (Lakha, 1990). The activities of the state became confined to the production of research intensive products, pursuance of costly basic research and the provision of skilled personnel through the educational system. As a new ingredient in the overall computer policy, the Indian state, through the marketing of a range of low-cost personal computers by the state-owned Electronics Trade & Technology Development Corporation, has recently attempted to stimulate demand while at the same time ensuring a certain level of competition in the market for personal computers (*India Today*, 31 December 1989; Bowonder and Mani, 1991, p. M10).

More generally the strategy worked out by the Indian state can be interpreted as a particular solution to the fundamental dilemma of developing countries outlined above: in order to ensure the spread of computer technologies, the markets for smaller computers have been entrusted to private companies, complemented recently by selective state interventions aimed at ensuring a competition environment and low prices. This has effectively meant the abandonment of the goal of total self-reliance. Some measure of self-reliance is, however, still being pursued through state activities in the less competitive and technologically more advanced sectors mentioned above and through various fiscal arrangements aimed at promoting local supply of peripherals and components.

Comparing this development with the evolution of the electronics/computer industry in Brazil, one is struck by the apparent similarities in policies and instruments, as well as in the timing of the strategies. Important differences remains, however. As in India, the first serious initiatives to develop an indigenous computer industry were undertaken in the early 1970s. At that time Brazil was in the middle of an economic boom, making the country an extremely attractive market for foreign companies. The computer requirements of the country were largely served by imports and by local production of subsidiaries of foreign companies, primarily IBM.[8] A fusion of a group of 'frustrated nationalist technicians' (Evans, 1986) all experienced in electronics with some 'developmental nationalist' segments of the state apparatus, especially the National Economic Development Bank (BNDE), provided the nucleus of what was later called the 'ideological guerrillas' (Adler, 1986, 1987) – a group of highly committed individuals who, because of crucial support from within the military establishment (the navy in particular) in the early 1970s, were able to create and staff new public institutions with the ambition of providing Brazil with an independent local computer industry. In 1972 a special commission for coordinating efforts in data processing (CAPRE) was created under the Planning Ministry, and two years later a state-owned company – COBRA – was set up to undertake the development and manufacturing of smaller computers.[9] In 1975 CAPRE was given the authority to regulate all imports of computers and computer-related items, which de facto meant complete control over the development of the local computer industry. In 1976 a dual computer policy was devised: in the market for large computers considerations of efficiency and optimal utilization of resources were to prevail, which in reality meant leaving this segment to the multinational corporations (IBM and others). In the market for smaller computers and peripherals, presumably with technologies easier to master, a policy of fostering national productive capabilities was given high priority. At the same time, CAPRE was authorized to control all purchases (as well as rentals and so on) of data-processing hardware and software by public authorities. In 1977 CAPRE decided after a round of bidding to reserve the market for smaller computers to COBRA plus three (later four) local private companies, all with foreign technological tie-ups, but none under foreign control. This 'market reserve' policy aimed at creating a local, predominantly privately owned, computer industry thus replaced the earlier policy of creating a single state-owned 'national champion' (COBRA).

Shortly after this apparent victory for the 'ideological guerrillas' their main institutional base of operation, CAPRE, was abolished following a critical report ordered by the National Intelligence Service (the 'Brazilian CIA', SNI) on its activities. It was replaced by a new Special Secretariat of Informatics (SEI) attached to the National Security Council and staffed with almost entirely new personnel – the former employees in many cases establishing their own private computer companies. Somewhat unexpectedly, SEI continued the policies pursued by CAPRE, and even broadened the policy by including in the market reserve policy some new sub-sectors and strengthened it by promoting a law on informatics in 1984. While IBM in 1980 managed to penetrate a section of the reserved market by obtaining permission for local production of a medium-sized computer that effectively competed with the minicomputers reserved for the national producers, restrictions on the activities of the company prevented extensive damage to local companies (Adler, 1986, p. 697). In October 1984 the Brazilian Congress voted through the National Informatics Law that for a period of eight years restricted the access of foreign companies to the manufacturing of small computers, extended the market reserve policy further to include the requirements of the telecommunications sector, some more peripherals and components, and provided various support mechanisms for strictly nationally controlled companies. In addition the law established a new institution, the National Council for Informatics and Automatization (CONIN) to supervise the activities of SEI, thus freeing the organization from the grip of the National Security Council. The military grip was further loosened after a civilian government took office in 1985 and created a separate Ministry of Science and Technology to coordinate the activities of CONIN. Finally, in 1988, the administrative structure was changed once more, making CONIN directly responsible to the president, while SEI came under the authority of the Ministry of Industry and Trade (the Ministry of Science and Technology being abolished) (Meyer-Stamer, 1989, p. 33).

The similarities between the strategies and instruments chosen by the Indian and Brazilian state are many. Both countries tried initially to promote a 'national champion' in the form of a state-owned company protected by import regulations; both had to bow to pressures from local private companies wishing as manufacturers to enter the profitable (lower-end) segment of the computer market or as customers wishing to obtain access to imported up-to-date technologies. In both countries dedicated groups 'pioneering' the activities had to give way to more established/traditional groups within the state apparatus, but notably without significant reversal in the overall strategy in Brazil. Likewise the state in both countries came to be responsible for most research efforts, either through the state-owned computer companies that in both countries were significantly more research-oriented than the private companies, or in public research centers and universities. And finally the public sector in both countries provided a large and relatively secure market for the local producers, mostly so in Brazil.

Differences in strategy and outcomes are as many as the similarities, however, reflecting the different social and economic circumstances prevailing in the two countries. India's strategy has all along been more ambitious in the technological field, while Brazil has emphasized commercial considerations much more. This in part reflected the relative position of international companies versus private and state-owned national companies in the two countries. The strong presence of IBM and other foreign companies in the large and dynamic Brazilian market made it virtually impossible for the Brazilian state to challenge their leadership in the manufacturing of large computers without running the risk of incurring very high costs. The Indian state in an environment of slow growth and a restrictive environment for foreign companies in general found it much easier to challenge IBM, even if the eventual exit of the company from the country was probably not intended. Combine this with a strong Indian tradition for self-reliance and serious engagement in science and technology and the chosen strategy is almost preordained. While India ended up leaving the market for small computers to private companies doing little more than assembling imported components, Brazil through the market reserve strategy continued its bid for private national dominance, including technological mastery within this sector. The Brazilian strategy proved initially to be a commercial success, probably helped by the entry of the large private financial conglomerates that by combining the roles of producer and of large customer greatly facilitated the process of marketing. In the longer run it seemed difficult, however, for the Brazilian producers to keep up with the rapid international development in the sector that meant a continuous stream of new technologies and a constant lowering of prices on the international markets. By the end of the 1980s opposition to the market reserve policy had grown considerably – not only international opposition (from the US in particular), but also domestic opposition from customers increasingly dissatisfied with being compelled to use expensive and old-fashioned equipment (Meyer-Stamer, 1989, pp. 24ff). It remains to be seen whether the Brazilian companies can withstand international competition when (and if) the market reserve policy is terminated, by 1992.[10] As for India, it still has to be seen whether local private companies will be able to indigenize and commercialize the technologies involved in the manufacturing of small computers.

Both countries still have to reap the full benefits of a dissemination of the new technologies throughout the economy, but in this respect Brazil seems to be better off. The presence of IBM in particular has secured for Brazilian customers a continued access to large up-to-date computers, while India's break with IBM, despite the possible attraction to other companies of not having to compete with the 'Big Blue' in the Indian market, has somewhat cut the country off from the mainstream of developments in computer technologies.[11]

THE ROLE OF POLITICAL AND ADMINISTRATIVE STRUCTURES

Returning to the theoretical questions raised in the second section, it can be asked whether the evolution of policies and their eventual outcomes were influenced by the political and administrative structures of the two countries, and whether lessons can be learned as to the proper management of high-technology industries from the two cases. More precisely, it can be asked whether a new paradigm for political and administrative regulation can be extracted from the history of computer policies in India and Brazil. Obviously a full answer to these questions cannot be given here – much more research will be needed for that – but it will be argued below that at least a tentative outline can be provided on the basis of the cases presented.

Starting with the importance of *the political regimes* under which the two countries pursued their strategies for developing the computer industry, the key question, according to Weber, concerns the role of parliament in influencing, controlling and correcting the actions of the administration. The differences between the two countries in this respect have caused differences in the weight and influence of various institutional interests, most importantly those of the military, in the shaping of the computer policy. It has also influenced the way in which important social forces have channelled their demands into the state apparatus and; finally differences over time in the type of regime may have exerted some influence on the policies.

For a start, it can be noted that Brazil's bureaucratic–authoritarian regime until the New Republic of 1985 – and possibly even after that – effectively excluded any significant interference in the affairs of the state through parliamentary channels. Always dominant, the political system established after the military coup in 1964 nevertheless provided the executive with an exceptional autonomy in economic policy making by cutting off the Congress from all decisions on and control over the implementation of economic policies (Packenham, 1971; Skidmore, 1973).[12] Furthermore the political structure not only gave the military a dominant role in politics, it probably also shaped their interests. While the Indian military establishment failed to ensure a decisive influence on the formulation and implementation of computer policies,[13] the Brazilian military was instrumental in initiating the process of development in the computer sector, and from 1979 onwards it even for a while strengthened its control over events in the sector. Contrary to the Indian military, the Brazilian military pursued a strongly nationalist policy – ideologically expressed in the doctrine of 'National Security and Development' (Alves, 1988, pp. 13ff) – which was probably reinforced by the fact that the responsibility for overall economic development resided firmly with the military institution, not like the situation in India with the civilian authorities. The Brazilian military, unlike their Indian counterparts, therefore found it more difficult to make economic demands on the public finances without considering the overall resource constraints of the national economy.[14]

The only instance when the Brazilian Congress was called on to take part in the deliberations over the computer policy was in 1984 when the Informatics Law replaced the previous practice of policy making by presidential decrees. The decision of the military government to involve the Congress, however, seems to have been motivated by a desire to protect the nationalistic policies from attacks from an anticipated future democratic government more than it was a case of truly parliamentary influence on the policy of the administration (Meyer-Stamer, 1989, p. 11). The 'insulation' of the administration from the parliament has not, however, been accompanied by the same degree of insulation from the interests of powerful social classes. Domestic and international business interests have in general succeeded in influencing the formulation and implementation of economic policies through a large number of formal and informal corporatist channels (Boschi, 1979). In computers, it appears that these interests, especially those of the domestic producers created as a result of the policies, first began to exercise some influence through their representation in the advisory Informatics Council after a reconstruction of SEI in 1981 (Adler, 1986, p. 697), but even then the close links with the military ensured the administration a relatively large degree of autonomy. The links between the SEI and the private industry have accordingly been characterized as being more like patron–client relations than those of private masters and public servants (Meyer-Stamer, 1989, pp. 34–5).

In contrast to the situation in Brazil, the Indian parliament has always had a number of instruments for controlling the government and administration at its disposal (Bhambri, 1971, pp. 78–112; Dwivedi and Jain, 1985, pp. 137–98). Basically it is the minister as political head of the administration who is accountable to the parliament, not only through questions and debates, but more importantly through a number of permanent committees and through the general audit of public expenditure. While one may doubt the efficacy of these instruments of control on the overall activities of the administration, it seems that the parliamentary controls have been exercised to a significant degree with regard to the electronics and computer policy. Indian politicians have demonstrated a continuous interest in the developments of the electronics policy through a stream of questions in parliament.[15] It is doubtful whether Indian politicians would be considered as 'able parliamentarians' in Weber's understanding of the concept, and it has been convincingly argued that the Indian parliament has only had little impact on the actual formulation of the electronics policies. There are stronger indications, though, that the parliament through the Estimates Committee, the Public Accounts Committee and the Committee on Public Undertakings has quite closely monitored the policy actions of the administration and the functioning of the state-owned electronics companies and many of the corrective actions proposed in the reports of these committees have in fact been implemented (Jain, 1985). The capacity for self-correction this has provided to the Indian state may have contributed to the gradual changes in policies during the 1980s.

The democratic regime in India has moreover meant that in addition to corporatist channels of influence the parliament and also the press have been used as channels of influence for domestic industrialists seeking to effect changes in policies.[16] Another aspect of the Indian condition that may be seen as at least a partial reflection of the democratic regime has been the existence of pockets of strong labor unions. In contrast to the situation in Brazil, labor unions in the Indian banking sector have been quite powerful and, out of fear of job losses, strongly opposed the computerization of banking services, thus delaying the emergence of what could have been a major market for computers and computer-related products.

A final observation on the importance of the democratic regime in India for the shaping of the computer policy refers back to the period of the Emergency of 1975-7, where essential features of Indian democracy were suspended. It was precisely during this short period that a number of crucial 'nationalistic' decisions were taken with regard to the computer policy.[17] The decision to promote ECIL as a national champion, the crucial democratic stages in the negotiations with IBM that made the company decide to leave India altogether, and the setting up of CMC all took place during the Emergency, that is in a period where the administration was more 'insulated' from interests in civil society and more free from interference from parliament (and the press) than ever before. It is interesting to note that this brief spell of 'strong rule' in India resembled the Brazilian regime in the strategy pursued and the methods involved in the computer industry. It was only after the restoration of democratic order that important policy changes were brought about, amongst other things through pressures from interested groups through the democratic channels – parliament and the press. That it was not just a change of government but a change of regime that was significant in this case is indicated by the fact that when Mrs Gandhi and the Congress Party, who had imposed the Emergency, were returned to power in the elections of 1980 the computer policy was not reversed. On the contrary, the changes in strategy initiated under the previous government were continued and accelerated by letting more independent private Indian companies enter the industry and by gradually liberalizing imports.[18]

It may be concluded, then, that the democratic regime in India provided a broader range of channels of access for interests in civil society to influence government policies in the computer sector than seems to have been the case in authoritarian Brazil. Whether this has been beneficial for the overall development of the industry, or for the dissemination of microelectronic/computer technologies more generally, will be discussed in the conclusion to this chapter. Before that, the importance of the different administrative structures in the two countries should be considered.

The general *administrative structures* in the two countries have differed considerably, and these differences have also affected the administrative arrangements related to the electronics/computer policies and influenced the outcomes of the policies. India has been famous for the administrative system inherited from the British, a system built around the unique elite civil service, the Indian Administrative Service (IAS). The IAS has effectively monopolized the top layers of the Indian administration, thereby giving it a strong resemblance to Weber's ideal-type legal–rational bureaucracy, but in some areas the IAS has had to give way to more specialized services – a sort of Indian parallel to the Brazilian technocrats. The overall bureaucratic 'steel frame' has, furthermore, largely been preserved despite the changes and expansion in the size and range of activities of the Indian state. Even the proliferating state-owned corporations operating in a large number of industries have to a large extent been managed by IAS men.[19] 'Bureaucracy' in the Weberian sense has thus very much been a characteristic of the Indian state, giving it a substantial measure of cohesion, but the dominance of the bureaucratic tradition over the technomanagerial mode of functioning has also made the Indian state less flexible and less oriented than the Brazilian towards entrepreneurial activities. In addition it can be argued that the organization of many Indian technocrats in a 'service tradition', that is organized in a parallel fashion to the IAS, has made them more 'bureaucratically' oriented than their Brazilian counterparts.

Brazil has never had the same bureaucratic tradition as India. The few attempts to create an elite civil service have all failed (Graham, 1968) and, despite US support for various administrative reform measures, the Brazilian administration cannot be said to be fully 'bureaucratized'. The only important institution organized along bureaucratic principles has apparently been the military, which, however, by virtue of being in power lost some of its 'professionalism' and never succeeded in installing bureaucratic features within the civilian administration.[20] Instead the Brazilian administration has preserved strong patrimonial features with appointments based on patronage/clientist relations rather than on individual merit.[21] This lack of a unified bureaucracy has resulted in a segmented or 'feudalized' state, with many of the new 'developmentalist' institutions acquiring an exceptionally independent position, most visible in the case of the large state-owned corporations like the oil company, Petrobrás, but also institutions like the National Development Bank, BNDE (Assis, 1984). In the wake of the military coup of 1964 there were extensive purges in the public administration (Alves, 1988, pp. 41ff). This probably to some extent weakened the traditional 'patronage system' to the benefit of the 'tecnicos' – the technically educated experts whom the military regime promoted as the managers of its drive for modernization and whose influence increased as a result of the establishment and growth of new institutions under the military rule (Mendes, 1980).

With specific reference to the administrative arrangements pertaining to the electronics/computer policy it has been claimed that 'policymakers must combine ... comprehensiveness with selectivity and flexibility, in the same way as the electronics industry' (Erber, 1985, p. 306). Expanding this line of thought somewhat, the claim is that the politico-administrative set-up ideally has to possess the following attributes:[22]

(1) *flexibility*, the ability to *adapt* to changing external circumstances, technological as well as social and political;
(2) *selectivity*, the ability to *choose* appropriate strategies, including the choice between different technologies, between industrial subsectors and between public, private national or private foreign ownership;
(3) *comprehensiveness*, the ability to *coordinate* activities in different sectors: this is especially important in electronics, because developments in this sector affect (and are affected by) the performance of a broad spectrum of social and economic activities.

It can be argued that these different attributes will be important for the proper management of the electronics/computer industry in general. They must, however, be complemented by one more ability, particularly important in developing countries where state-owned companies form an integral part of government interventions in the economy:

(4) *entrepreneurship*, the ability to *commercialize* – to operate efficiently in a market-like economic environment.

If we use these preliminary characteristics to discuss the administration of the computer policies in India and Brazil, it can be argued that variations between countries and over time in the possession of these abilities have affected the policies pursued and the outcomes achieved.

The evolution of computer policies in India and Brazil illustrates one additional point, namely the importance of the administrative structures being *permeable* to new emerging actors – in Brazil the 'ideological guerrillas', in India the 'network' around the Atomic Energy Commission. In both cases the introduction of an institutionalized electronics/computer policy catapulted new actors into policy making – the scientists. In Brazil the scientists worked in close alliance with nationalist economists (in the BNDE and the Ministry of Planning), while in India the scientists reigned almost supreme in the Department of Electronics. This permeability to new forces was only a temporary phenomenon, however. As the electronics sector grew in importance the traditional administrative structures reasserted themselves. In Brazil this happened through the military establishment strengthening its controls, in India through the creation of bureaucratic structures (interministerial coordination committees and so on) that ensured some sort of coordination within the larger administrative framework of the Indian state. ECIL, the state-owned electronics company, was kept for a longer time in the hands of the scientists because of its strong research orientation and privileged administrative position, being placed under the Department of Atomic Energy. Eventually even this company had to adopt a more commercial orientation to its activities.[23] The relatively successful performance of ECIL and CMC in the late 1980s is evidence of both flexibility and selectivity. Their success probably reflects a choice of activities (away from production of small computers, more emphasis on larger system-constructing operations involving software design and application, continued research and development) that demonstrate an ability to adapt to the prevailing economic and social environment, primarily a change to activities complementing the capabilities and interests of the local private Indian companies, but also an adjustment to the technological changes and competitive situation prevailing in the international markets. Furthermore, and in contrast to many other state-owned enterprises, it seems that a stronger entrepreneurial attitude has been installed in the working of both companies. This has been accompanied by organizational changes. There is evidence of changes in both ECIL and CMC, and even in the Department of Electronics, making these organizations more flexible and their structure less hierarchical, and more examples of similar changes in some newly established organizations within the broader 'informatics' sector can be found (Evans, 1990).[24]

Despite the efforts in coordinating the electronics/computer policy with other policy areas through bureaucratic structures since the early 1980s, it is officially recognized that technological developments like the integration of microelectronics with telecommunications require further administrative adjustments and that they have to be accompanied by changes in other policy areas. The proposals advanced – a creation of a (super-) Ministry of Informatics – however demonstrate the prevalence in India of a traditional bureaucratic orientation when it comes to suggestions for new administrative arrangements (BICP, 1988).[25]

Compared with India, the lack of a strong bureaucratic tradition in Brazil seems to have facilitated the creation of new, relatively autonomous, institutions and the fusion of technological prowess with an entrepreneurial spirit providing for a high degree of flexibility (Erber, 1985, p. 307). The key institutional structure managing the electronics policy – CAPRE, later SEI – has been working quite efficiently and the organization is reputed to be one of the few Brazilian public institutions free of extensive corruption (Meyer-Stamer, 1989, p. 33; Schmitz and Hewitt, 1989, p. 19). The basic problem in Brazil seems, accordingly to informed sources, to have been the lack of coherence and comprehensiveness in the policies pursued. The computer policy has not been coordinated within the framework of a general industrial policy, and only partially with an educational policy that could secure a steady supply of well-educated manpower (Erber, 1985, p. 307; Evans and Tigre, 1989b, p. 1756; Meyer-Stamer, 1989, pp. 30, 91). This lack of comprehensiveness can be interpreted as a result of the segmented and non-bureaucratic nature of the Brazilian administration, and it has apparently not been possible for the military to compensate fully for this situation. Furthermore the segmented character of the Brazilian state may have made interinstitutional conflicts more frequent. SEI has thus been engaged in a number of conflicts with other public institutions on specific policy issues (Meyer-Stamer, 1988, pp. 42–5). The lack of bureaucratic resistance and the backing of the military probably constituted the key factors allowing for the emergence of the scientists and the economic nationalists as a strong unified group capable of exploiting a situation of enhanced autonomy for the state institutions. On the other hand, it can be argued that the resulting strategy of national self-reliance lacked some of the correcting mechanisms that bureaucratic structures linked to interests in civil society through corporatist or through parliamentary channels might have provided. While the private companies have thrived in Brazil, the state-owned COBRA seems of late to have had difficulties in defining its proper role. Since 1988 the company has been earmarked for privatization, and its possible role in promoting the more costly and less market-oriented research in both hardware and software seems not to have been exploited (Evans, 1990, p. 25). The recent abandonment of the company's project of introducing a standard software program equivalent to the Unix program may signal the end of its striving for technological excellence, and leave the company with no apparent reason for continuing as a state-owned corporation (*Gazeta Mercantil*, 22 April 1991).

It conclusion, it seems that in India the strong bureaucratic tradition made policy coordination and interest mediation easier, but the lack of technomanagerial attitudes made it difficult for the state to fulfil the objectives of producing and disseminating computer technologies. Some measure of flexibility, however, was demonstrated through selective administrative intervention in sectors that were more research-oriented, less commercially oriented, and better adapted to the Indian resource endowments.

In Brazil the state administration, by virtue of its segmented character, did provide for substantial flexibility and a commercial orientation due to the promotion of the techno-managerial ('tecnicos') mode of functioning under the military regime. The comprehensiveness and coherence that a unified bureaucratic structure might have provided was to some extent achieved through the intervention of the military (through the SNI) in the management of the computer policy, though this was not sufficient to change the basic character of the civilian administration. The gradual change to civilian rule in the 1980s has further eroded this particular form of policy-coordinating mechanism without yet replacing it with another.

CONCLUSION

The development of the computer industry in India and Brazil has taken place within certain structural constraints related to the character of the industry, the international context and the domestic socio-economic situation. In combination with the different political and administrative arrangements, this has decisively shaped the policies and their outcomes in the industry. The general conclusion regarding the determinants of developments in the computer industry may be summarized as follows, with special emphasis on the role of political and administrative structures:

(1) Structural constraints of a socioeconomic and technoeconomic nature have shaped the computer policy and its outcome in both countries. Differences in the degree of economic dependence, that is in the interrelationship and relative positions of economic and political power between local and foreign companies, have, in combination with the fundamental dilemma with regard to the electronics industry in general, made for different limitations in the available policy options. Similar strategies may at times have been pursued, but outcomes have differed. India succeeded in obtaining some degree of self-reliance in the capacity to produce larger computers and in the provision of larger software-based systems engineering, primarily because of the retreat of IBM, but at the cost of a lagging behind in the dissemination of such computers and computer-based systems. Brazil's policy of leaving this sector to the multinationals ensured a much wider availability of computer services. The change in the Indian policy towards wholesale imports of technologies for the manufacturing of smaller computers led to a rapid proliferation in the use of these machines. The Brazilian policy of self-reliance, while ensuring a similar outcome, also implied a continuous lagging behind in technology and a constant threat to the established positions of local companies. Despite structural constraints, both countries experienced some very real advances in the capacity to produce various types of computers and in the spreading of the use of computers and electronics in general in different spheres of the economy.

(2) The experience of both countries demonstrates their ability to cope with rapidly changing technologies. This ability has been conditioned by the prevailing political and administrative structures in the two countries, and some of the administrative structures have been transformed in the process of regulating the electronics/computer industry. The authoritarian political system in Brazil, coupled with a segmented administrative set-up, made an initially flexible response to new opportunities and ambitions of new political actors possible, while ensuring through the considerable autonomy of the state apparatus a powerful and persistent support for the chosen policy. A subsequent adaptation to changing circumstances in the form of new social and economic interests and new technological developments seems, however, to have been hampered by the authoritarian structure, and the lack of a coherent bureaucratic framework has restricted the coordination of overall policies. The Indian democratic system, on the other hand, has ensured a degree of adaptation of policies to changing economic interests in society, while the bureaucratic administrative structures

have facilitated more coordinated efforts in the pursuance of policies. The administrative structures of the state, including those of the state-owned enterprises within the sector, underwent significant changes that eventually led to a new balance between the bureaucrats keen on regulating and coordinating policies, the economic planners/managers keen on achieving commercial successes and ambitious scientists keen on achieving as high a degree of technological self-reliance as possible. In Brazil some changes in policies and administrative structures implying an adaption to the strengths of the various interests present in the Brazilian society were discernible parallel to the gradual democratization, but as yet conclusive changes have not been effected.

(3) On the basis of the experiences of the two countries it would be tempting to seek a generalized model of the 'best policy' for developing countries in their management of the electronics/computer industry. For a number of reasons, however, this would be premature. The two countries are far from typical developing countries; the international circumstances under which they pursued their initial policies are not likely to be repeated; and the domestic socioeconomic configurations through which the policies take effect are likely to vary to a degree that eludes easy generalization. The only conclusion of a general nature that can be reached on policy matters is probably that the 'best policy' in this as in other policy areas is one that is adapted to the given socioeconomic and technological circumstances, while at the same time exploiting to the maximum the possibilities for desirable changes inherent in the situation.

While this conclusion opens up a whole spectrum of different 'best policies', it can nevertheless be claimed that some general principles for a possible 'best model' of the political and administrative structures through which the development of the electronics/computer industry is regulated can be identified. The evidence presented here is far from sufficient for claiming that a new 'Post-Fordist' model of politics and administration has emerged, but still it is possible to sketch a tentative 'ideal-type' model for successful public administration of electronics/computer policies (see Figure 5.1).

The administrative organization should, according to the model, be flexible and selective in its approach, and it should be able to coordinate policies. At the same time the policies should be continuously adapted to (a) the prevailing political and social environment, as expressed through the political system proper or through interest representation via the bureaucratic structures ('corporatism'), and (b) the

Technoeconomic environment

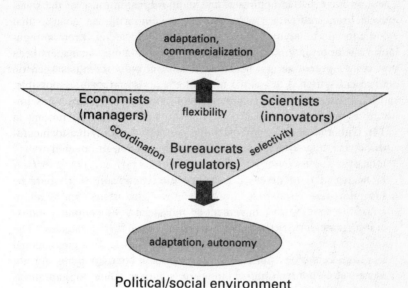

Figure 5.1 A tentative model of a new administrative paradigm

technological and economic environment, as expressed through changes in the structures and dynamics of the market. The ability to accomplish these tasks will, as illustrated in the model, require a personnel structure that combines and balances different types of 'administrators': the bureaucrats (regulators), the economists (managers) and the scientists (innovators). It may also imply changes in the organizational set-up conducive to the exercise of the tasks outlined above: a more decentralized but still coordinated structure; an openness towards outside interference while retaining a considerable degree of autonomy and so on.

From the experience of India and Brazil it can be hypothesized that, before this model is brought into proper function, a certain level of development of the industry has to be achieved: the computer industry has to be installed first, so to speak. In both countries this was achieved through a phase of authoritarian rule that provided an enhanced degree of autonomy for the state. While this may not be the only way to reach a viable initial level of development for the industry, the experience of India in particular, but of late also of Brazil, may lead to an expectation that a democratic regime – all things equal – should have better opportunities for managing the complexities of the electronics/computer industry than an authoritarian system, provided appropriate administrative changes are effected. Democracy may thus be a necessary, but not sufficient, condition for the full utilization of the potentials promised by the 'electronics revolution'. That the present writer is not alone in ending with this hopeful conclusion can be illustrated by the following quotations:

> The elaboration and implementation of such a policy [of managing the conflicting interests associated with developing an electronics industry, JDP] cannot be left to the bureaucrats and entrepreneurs alone, since it involves so many different interests. In this sense, too, electronics presents one of the most important challenges to Brazil: to develop and implement an industrial policy within a democratic framework (Erber, 1985, p. 307).

> Because technology policy/selection can be a complex issue, a more democratic approach to technology selection is bound to help in the long run (BICP, 1988, p. 83).

Notes

1. As argued by Jessop: 'we should not ignore the role of the bureaucrats and other non-party intellectuals in developing the norms, modes of calculation and procedures which sustain a given mode of regulation' (Jessop, 1990, p. 319).
2. It has been argued that a successful transition towards Post-Fordism will require popular participation through democratic structures at all levels of society (Mathews, 1989).
3. Average annual growth rates of the value of computer production of 44 per cent during 1983–9 (reduced to around 34 per cent if converted into US$) in India compares with 26 per cent average annual growth during 1981–8 in sales figures (in US$) of national producers in Brazil (Bowonder and Mani, 1991, p. M11; Meyer-Stamer, 1989, p. 12).
4. To the extent that the Indian export of computers is directed towards Eastern Bloc countries, the optimism for future expansion may be overstated. I have no firm information on the direction of export, however.
5. The only other developing countries with similar levels of capabilities would probably be Taiwan and South Korea.
6. The description of Indian electronics/computer policies is based on Grieco, 1982, 1984; Agarwal, 1985; BICP, 1988; Mahalingam, 1989; Evans, 1990.
7. ECIL, however, continued to be under the authority of the Department of Atomic Energy.

8. For general descriptions, see Tigre, 1983; UN/CTC, 1983; Erber, 1985; Evans, 1986; Adler, 1986, 1987; Ramamurti, 1987; Meyer-Stamer, 1988, 1989.

9. Initially the company was a joint venture between the Brazilian state (or rather various state-owned institutions), a private Brazilian company and a foreign company. In reality, and later also formally, COBRA was entirely controlled through the state-owned national development bank, BNDE.

10. Optimists point to the abilities of Brazilian companies in 'creative imitation', while pessimists point to the exceptional circumstances that led to the initial success and to the increasing costs of research in the development of new models (Schmitz and Hewitt, 1989; Schwartzman, 1988).

11. According to some, IBM should not so much be regarded as a major competitor in the computer market, but more as an 'environment' that everybody in the industry has to adapt to (Meyer-Stamer, 1989, p. 49).

12. 'the Congress is expendable. It functions when the interests of the state requires the "normal" functioning of the federal, democratic state. When it does not, the Congress is closed, and the state, of course, continues to function' (Roett, 1978, p. 55).

13. It should be recalled that the Indian military through its own production facilities, in particular *Bharat Electronics Ltd* (BEL), had its vital interests served and that it all along managed to obtain abundant economic resources for defense-related research, including research and services conducted by otherwise civilian public enterprises and institutions.

14. This argument seems to be supported by evidence of declining military budgets under the military regime, followed by increases under the civilian regime from 1985 (Stepan, 1988, pp. 72–80).

15. Grieco (1984) is to a large extent based on transcripts of the debates in parliament and the reports from various parliamentary committees; cf. his references cited on pp. 210–11. Jain (1985), pp. 271–3 also contains references to a large number of parliamentary debates, and an annual report of the Department of Electronics mentions that in the year 1988 alone more than 300 questions pertaining to electronics were asked in Parliament (DoE, 1989, p. 53).

16. For examples of press campaigns in the late 1970s, see Grieco (1984) pp. 131ff. Jain (1985) p. 256, argues that domestic producers tried to protect their interests through influencing members of parliament. In the 1980s domestic producers have on several occasions with some success influenced the policy making in the administration, mostly with an eye to avoiding competition from imports.

17. This information is collected from Grieco (1982) pp. 625–8; Grieco (1984) pp. 30–1, 73–81 and *passim*. Grieco does not mention the Emergency, but he does distinguish between a period of 'strong state' (1973–7) and a period of when the state is weak and open to external forces (1978–80). Knowing the situation prevailing during the Emergency, it is ironic to note that Grieco ascribes the tough stand towards IBM at the time to 'domestic political limitations' (p. 50) – at no time during Indian independence had 'political limitations' been of so little importance!

18. In an official report it has been noted that the liberalizations in the 1980s were a direct consequence of reappraisals of policies undertaken in the late 1970s by various official commissions, (BICP, 1988, p. 17).

19. General descriptions of the Indian administration and the IAS can be found in Potter (1986) and Misra (1986).
20. The creation of the National Information Service, SNI, can be seen as an unsuccessful attempt to create a bureaucratic framework for the civilian administration (Stepan, 1988, pp. 13–20).
21. For general descriptions of the Brazilian 'bureaucracy', see Daland (1967), especially pp. 210ff; Roett (1978) pp. 126–30 and *passim*; Daland (1981); Geddes (1990).
22. See also Evans and Tigre (1989a) p. 1761; 'support for the policies must have both breadth and coherence within the state apparatus . . . this implies a diversified but coordinated organizational base'.
23. Witness the following extract from a report by the comptroller and auditor general, quoting a statement by the Company: 'The Company stated (September 1980) that historically they had given secondary considerations to business aspects and the growth was primarily based on the vision of R&D personalities who get out to conquer unchartered markets, not fully mindful of the business risks involved. The Company feel that it is essential now to de-link projects from personalities and try to institutionalize the organization' and that "a systematic integration and rationalization of activities so as to form efficient systems to satisfactorily cater to the market needs is unavoidable"' (*Report*, 1983, p. 104).
24. The Centre for the Development of Telematics (C-DOT), established in 1984, is often seen as a model for future organizational structures in high-tech industries. The Centre combines a high degree of autonomy with flexibility, a 'flat' structure and a highly motivated, highly educated staff. In part because of its high-profile director, Sam Pitroda, it has been involved in a number of political controversies in recent years.
25. The BICP report suggests the creation of a Ministry of Informatics to coordinate electronics policies with developments in telecommunications (BICP, 1988, pp. 62–3). It can be doubted whether such a traditional (bureaucratic) solution alone will be able to satisfy the report's own demands on policy making: 'the Government's role will have to be self-correcting, flexible, and able to promote and accommodate creative forces' (p. 60). As the BICP belongs to the Ministry of Industry, this suggestion may also be interpreted as forming a part of a struggle within the bureaucracy over the future control of the industry.

References

ADLER, EMANUEL (1986) 'Ideological "guerrillas" and the quest for technological autonomy: Brazil's domestic computer industry', *International Organization*, vol. 40, no. 3 (summer), pp. 673–705.

ADLER, EMANUEL (1987) *The Power of Ideology. The Quest for Technological Autonomy in Argentina and Brazil* (Berkeley: University of California Press).

AGARWAL, SURAJ MAL (1985) 'Electronics in India: Past Strategies and Future Possibilities', *World Development*, vol. 13, no. 3 (March), pp. 273–92.

AGLIETTA, MICHEL (1979) *A Theory of Capitalist Regulation. The US Experience* (London: New Left Books).

ALVES, MARIA HELENA MOREIRA (1988) *State and Opposition in Military Brazil* (Austin: University of Texas Press).

ASSIS, J. CARLOS DE (1984) *Os Mandarins da República* (Rio de Janeiro: Paz e Terra).

BHAMBRI, C.P. (1971) *Bureaucracy and Politics in India* (Delhi: Vikas Publications).

BOSCHI, RENATO RAUL (1979) *Elites Industriais e Democracia* (Rio de Janeiro: Edicoes Graal).

BOWONDER, B. and SUNIL MANI (1991) 'Government Policy and Industrial Development: Case of Indian Computer Manufacturing Industry', *Economic and Political Weekly*, 23 February, pp. M7–M11.

BUREAU OF INDUSTRIAL COSTS AND PRICES (BICP) (1988) *Report on Electronics* (New Delhi: Government of India).

DALAND, ROBERT T. (1967) *Brazilian Planning. Development Politics and Administration* (Chapel Hill: University of North Carolina Press).

DALAND, ROBERT T. (1981) *Exploring Brazilian Bureaucracy: Performance and Pathology* (Washington: University Press of America).

DEPARTMENT OF ELECTRONICS (DoE) (1989) *Annual Report 1988–89* (New Delhi: Government of India).

DWIVEDI, O.P. and R.B. JAIN (1985) *India's Administrative State* (New Delhi: Gitanjali).

ERBER, FABIO STEFANO (1985) 'The Development of the "Electronics Complex" and Government Policies in Brazil', *World Development*, vol. 13, no. 3 (March), pp. 293–309.

EVANS, PETER B. (1986) 'State, Capital, and the Transformation of Depedence: The Brazilian Computer Case', *World Development*, vol. 14, no. 7 (July), pp. 791–808.

EVANS, PETER B. (1990) 'Indian Informatics in the Eighties: The Changing Character of State Involvement' (manuscript) University of California.

EVANS, PETER B. and PAULO BASTOS TIGRE (1989a) 'Paths to Participation in "Hi-Tech" Industry: A Comparative Analysis of Computers in Brazil and Korea', *Asian Perspectives*, vol. 13, no. 1 (spring–summer), pp. 5–35.

EVANS, PETER B. and PAULO BASTOS TIGRE (1989b) 'Going Beyond Clones in Brazil and Korea: A Comparative Analysis of NIC Strategies in the Computer Industry', *World Development*, vol. 17, no. 11 (November), pp. 1751–68.

GAZETA MERCANTIL (22 April 1991) 'Cobra Strategy Switch Brings 1990 Profit of US$ 1.15M' (obtained through Reuter's 'Textline' database).

GEDDES, BARBARA (1990) 'Building "State" Autonomy in Brazil, 1930–1964', *Comparative Politics*, vol. 22, no. 2 (January), pp. 217–35.

GRAHAM, LAWRENCE A. (1968) *Civil Service Reform in Brazil* (Austin and London: University of Texas Press).

GRIECO, JOSEPH M. (1982) 'Between dependency and autonomy: India's experience with the international computer industry', *International Organization*, vol. 36, no. 3 (summer), pp. 609–32.

GRIECO, JOSEPH M. (1984) *Between Dependency and Autonomy: India's*

Experience with the International Computer Industry (Berkeley: University of California Press).

HIRST, PAUL and JONATHAN ZEITLIN (1991) 'Flexible specialization versus post-Fordism: theory, evidence and policy implications', *Economy and Society*, vol. 20, no. 1 (February), pp. 1–56.

IDS BULLETIN (1984) 'Developmental States in East Asia: capitalist and socialist', vol. 15, no. 2 (April).

INDIA TODAY (31 March 1988) 'Computers: Thinking Big', p. 77.

INDIA TODAY (31 December 1989) 'Computers: Price Friendly. Cheaper PCs Storm the Market', p. 63.

INTERNATIONAL HERALD TRIBUNE (IHT) (10 July 1990) 'Brazil Takes Aim at Computer Police'.

JAIN, R.B. (1985) 'Electronics Policy and Indian Parliament', *Indian Journal of Public Administration*, vol. XXXI, no. 2 (April–June), pp. 239–74.

JESSOP, BOB (1990a) *State Theory: Putting the Capitalist State in its Place* (Cambridge, Mass.: Polity Press).

JESSOP, BOB (1990b) 'Regulation theories in retrospect and prospect', *Economy and Society*, vol. 19, no. 2 (May), pp. 153–216.

KAPLINSKY, RAPHAEL (1989) '"Technological Revolution" and the International Division of Labour in Manufacturing: A Place for the Third World?', *European Journal of Development Research*, vol. 1, no. 1 (June), pp. 5–37.

LAKHA, SALIM (1990) 'Growth of Computer Software Industry in India', *Economic and Political Weekly*, 6 January, pp. 49–56.

LIPIETZ, ALAIN (1987) *Mirages and Miracles: The Crisis of Global Fordism* (London: Verso).

MAHALINGAM, SUDHA (1989) 'Computer Industry in India: Strategies for Late-Comer Entry', *Economic and Political Weekly*, 21 October, pp. 2375–84.

MATHEWS, JOHN (1989) *Age of Democracy: The Politics of Post-Fordism* (Melbourne: Oxford University Press).

MENDES, CANDIDO (1980) 'The Post-1964 Brazilian Regime: Outward Redemocratization and Inner Institutionalization', *Government and Opposition*, vol. 15, no. 1 (Winter), pp. 49–74.

MEYER-STAMER, JÖRG (1988) *Informatik in Brasilien* (Hamburg: Institut für Iberoamerika-Kunde).

MEYER-STAMER, JÖRG (1989) 'Technologipolitischen Optionen für die brasilianische Informatikpolitik' (manuscript) (Berlin: Deutsches Institut für Entwicklungspolitik.

MISRA, B.B. (1986) *Government Bureaucracy in India 1947–1976* (Delhi: Oxford University Press).

PACKENHAM, ROBERT (1971) 'The Functions of the Brazilian National Congress', in Weston H. Agor (ed.), *Latin American Legislatures: Their Role and Influence* (New York: Praeger), pp. 259–92.

PEREZ, CARLOTA (1985) 'Microelectronics, Long Waves and World Structural Change: New Perspectives for Developing Countries', *World Development*, vol. 13, no. 3, pp. 441–63.

PIORE, MICHAEL J. and CHARLES F. SABEL (1984) *The Second Industrial Divide: Possibilities for Prosperity* (New York: Basic Books).

POTTER, DAVID C. (1986) *India's Political Administrators 1919–1983* (Oxford: Clarendon Press).

RAMAMURTI, RAVI (1987) *State Owned Enterprises in High Technology Industries* (New York: Praeger).

REPORT (1983) Report of the Comptroller and Auditor General of India Union Government (Commercial), 1982, Part V: Electronics Corporation of India Limited, New Delhi.

REPORT (1990) 'Report of the Study Team on Electronic Components for Eighth Five Year Plan for Electronics Industry', *Electronics – Information and Planning*, May–June, pp. 307–31.

ROETT, RIORDAN (1978) (2nd edn) *Brazil: Politics in a Patrimonial Society* (New York: Praeger).

SCHMITZ, HUBERT and TOM HEWITT (1989) 'Learning to Raise Infants – A Case Study in Industrial Policy' (manuscript), University of Sussex, Institute of Development Study.

SCHWARTZMAN, SIMON (1988) 'High Technology Versus Self-reliance: Brazil Enters the Computer Age', in Julian M. Chacel, Pamela S. Falk and David V. Fleischer (eds), *Brazil's Economic and Political Future* (Boulder, Col. and London: Westview Press), pp. 67–82.

SKIDMORE, THOMAS (1973) 'Politics and Economic Policy Making in Authoritarian Brazil, 1937–71', in Alfred Stepan (ed.), *Authoritarian Brazil: Origins, Policies, and Future* (New Haven and London: Yale University Press), pp. 3–46.

STEPAN, ALFRED (1988) *Rethinking Military Politics* (Princeton: Princeton University Press).

THERBORN, GÖRAN (1978) *What Does the Ruling Class Do When it Rules?* (London: New Left Books).

TIGRE, PAULO BASTOS (1983) *Technology and Competition in the Brazilian Computer Industry* (London: Frances Pinter).

UN/CTC (1983) *Transborder Data Flows and Brazil* (New York).

WEBER, MAX (1978) *Economy and Society*, ed. by Guenther Roth and Claus Wittich (Berkeley: University of California Press).

6 Bureaucrats as Technology Policy Partners

Elisa P. Reis

INTRODUCTION

There seems to be such a large gap between the bureaucracies of developed and underdeveloped societies that one is often led to think we would need a totally different body of assumptions, concepts and theories to deal with such different contexts. However an attempt is made to defend the opposite perspective here: that is to say, the need for a unified bodied of knowledge that would account for the similarities and differences between public bureaucracies worldwide. It seems to me that the apparent mismatch between the key political and economic concerns of less developed societies as regards bureaucracy, on the one hand, and the theoretical concerns of mainstream literature on bureaucratic issues, on the other, actually reflects a lack of comparative research.

An effort to elaborate a theoretical perspective on bureaucracies specific to the Third World, like any other attempt to build a 'parallel' theory to account for less developed countries, would be inappropriate and would run the risk of being irrelevant and tautological. While theories about the Third World may perform important sociological and psychological roles, they cannot play an adequate explanatory role if they are not part of, or interactive with, a general theory. This does not negate the fact that a productive theoretical perspective must undeniably account for many specificities of Third World contexts. Yet, while it may indeed be true that less developed countries (LDCs) share important features that distinguish them from developed societies, unless we have a common frame of reference, a single analytical model, we will miss a critical opportunity to use systematic comparison to throw light on the problems peculiar to bureaucracies in the Third World.

This chapter comments on three different approaches to dealing with patterns of interaction between politics and administration that were developed with mature democracies in mind, and examines to what extent each of them may be useful in assessing problems in the inter-

122

play between politics and bureaucracy in less developed societies. Next attention is drawn to science and technology policies in Brazil's recent history. The purpose here is only to illustrate the implications that policy-making styles have in democratization, contrary to the usual tendency to explore what implications regime type has as far as patterns of interaction between bureaucracy and democracy are concerned.

BUREAUCRATS AND POLITICIANS IN THEORETICAL PERSPECTIVES

What is the purpose of resorting once again to a dichotomous perception of bureaucratic and political roles? Despite the recurrent criticism of such dualistic schemes, they still constitute a basic reference for important theoretical developments related to mature democracies. Thus, while all call attention to the growing role of convergence and interdependence between bureaucracy and politics, not only does everyone continue to reason in terms of a dual point of departure (be it in logical or historical terms) but everyone also tends to stress the fact that persistent role differences remain relevant.

For the Third World, while there is a relative dearth of comparative studies on bureaucrats and politicians, the differences between these two typical actors are implicitly or explicitly deemed relevant, particularly when one or more of the following issues is in question: (a) the nature of the political regime; (b) the effectiveness of particular adopted policies; and (c) the role of the state in the productive sector. Thus under (a) we have a series of studies discussing either the characteristics of modernizing dictatorships or prospects for the consolidation of democracy. Under (b) what is most frequently subject to discussion is the proper mix of politics and administration. Finally under (c) we find a series of studies focusing upon ways to draw the line between the public and private spheres, between authority and market concerns, between interest representation and technical expertise, and so on.

Taking into account this persistent reference to the duality 'bureaucracy versus politics', we will examine three theoretical approaches that offer different possibilities for exploring the relevant convergences and divergences of roles. The first analytical frame to be considered is that of Aberbach *et al.* (1981). Informed by Weberian ideal types, the authors of this study depart from the bureaucrats v. politicians dichotomy, going on to elaborate a more complex typology. While this dichotomous model draws a sharp contrast between decision making and implementation, the three additional models of interaction that the authors propose suggest a progressive blurring of the frontiers between political and bureaucratic roles.

The second model, unlike the first, accounts for bureaucratic participation in decision making, but it remains tied to a dichotomous view to the extent that it sharply contrasts the behavior of the bureaucrat – grounded in 'knowledge of the facts' – with that of the politician, which is based upon 'interests'. The third analytical model sees interests informing the performance of both typical actors but differentiates between the nature and scope of the interests represented by each: bureaucrats stand for specific and well-organized interests, unlike politicians, who can stand for broad and diffuse clienteles.

Finally Aberbach and his colleagues suggest a fourth model – the 'pure hybrid' – which conflates bureaucratic and political characteristics. This last type, while pointing to a clear trend towards converging roles in the contemporary world, still permits the preservation of notable differences between the behavior of bureaucrats and politicians. And the analysis the authors offer for particular Western democracies strongly suggests that role specificities remain significant and relevant.

While this first theoretical perspective mainly seeks a descriptive approach to bureaucrats' behavior vis-à-vis politicians', the fact that it allows for systematic comparisons within or between nations opens up the possibility of building more exploratory hypotheses relating the performance of the two typical actors to particular characteristics of the surrounding context (Aberbach *et al.*, 1990). Moreover the somehow impressionistic generalizations the authors suggest concerning the predominance of one or another of the proposed typologies also deserve further elaboration if they are to fulfill more explanatory purposes. That is to say, their suggestions – (a) that the first two typologies are more suitable to lower bureaucratic echelons, while the last two are more suitable to the higher bureaucratic spheres, and (b) that there seems to be a progressive trend toward making each of the descriptive typologies predominant in a historical succession – lead us to stimulating new research questions. One could inquire, for example, to what extent the blurring of the frontiers between politics and administration, which increases as we move up the bureaucratic ledder, creates the need for greater coordination once differentiation reaches some critical level.

As to the historical 'progression' towards less contrasting roles along the administration versus politics axis, one wonders if this expresses a tendency away from the sombre picture of the soulless bureaucratic world Weber feared. It could be that what Aberbach and his colleagues suggest as a historical trend among Western European democracies may in point of fact express a key feature of democracy itself. Whether the growing affirmation of a pure hybrid type is more typical of mature democracies, or not, is something to be investigated through systematic comparative research. In any case, whatever the findings, they would contribute to a deeper understanding of the relationships between democracy and bureaucracy.

From the above it is legitimate to conclude that the typological approach in question opens up promising perspectives for systematic comparison of bureaucracies in LDCs. This analytical framework can be successfully used to compare Third World bureaucracies with each other or with the mature Western democracies for which it was designed to account. What is the actual role played by bureaucrats in Third World societies when it comes to specific policy-making activities? Does regime variation account for systematic variations in role definition? And what about the specificities of particular policy areas? These are some of the substantive questions that the approach offered by Aberbach and his colleagues could help us to pursue while researching bureaucracies in the Third World.

A second suggestive analytical approach to the pair 'bureaucrat–politician' is provided by B. Guy Peters (1987). While strongly rejecting the 'long-dead dichotomy between politics and administration', the author explores five patterns of interaction between career civil servants and political executives. Although these five models are intended specifically to capture the interplay of politics and administration in the policy-making process, they could easily be taken as broader political models, and to that extent permit explorations of the variable relationships between bureaucracy and democracy. A brief description of each of the five follows.

As in the previously discussed approach, Peters starts with the simple dichotomy depicted in Weber's ideal types, calling attention to the usefulness of taking the 'formal model' as an instrumental device against which to measure actual bureaucratic behavior. The model can also serve, Peters recognizes, as a normative standard against which to compare real patterns of interaction and of policy-making styles, or else as a functional fiction to which political systems resort. Despite its extreme artificiality, the formal–legal model can thus serve helpful descriptive and comparative purposes, he concludes.

Next comes the 'village life' model, which borrows its name from Heclo and Wildavsky (1974). The main element of this model is the assumption of a common socialization pattern experienced by bureaucrats and executive politicians, who share elite concerns, chief among them the maintenance of the government and the non-disturbance of the executive branch. As Peters indicates, there are in fact important areas of overlap in the motivational and behavioral patterns of bureaucrats and politicians. Reliance on the village life model can thus enhance our understanding of the politics of policy-making. Yet one deduces from Peter's discussion that this model is perhaps more useful in comparing variable degrees of elite coalescence across nations, and less adequate in describing any single system that always displays some area of non-convergence as far as career and occupational patterns are concerned.

The 'functional model' is the third analytical possibility the author discusses. Here, as in the previous model, the decisive aspect is the patterns common to bureaucrats and politicians, but these derive from functional specialization within the elite and not from the elite condition itself. A common policy area would link the civil servant and the executive politician, providing the ground for common motives and interests. As Peters observes, the functional model 'would bear some resemblance to numerous descriptions of corporatism or neocorporatism in a number of European countries, and to the literature on "iron triangles", "cozy little triangles", or "issue networks" in American politics' (Peters, 1987, pp. 260–1). The functional model shares with these approaches an emphasis on vertical integration across policy areas instead of horizontal integration, as presupposed in the village model. Actually the models can be superimposed, and the author even speculates that it may be that a significant degree of horizontal elite coalescence provides the most fertile ground for intra-village competition along functional lines.

It is precisely the possibility of coexisting models that suggests a hypothesis worth testing in the Third World context: to what extent may the 'corporatism', 'state corporatism', 'bureaucratic rings' and similar phenomena frequently observed by the specialists on LDCs be linked to the degree of elite coalescence? That is to say, are the narrow limits of the political community in the Third World, the persisting obstacles to citizenship extension there, and the tendency to portray as 'essentially administrative' what also constitute political allocations – thus favoring interest mobilization along functional areas – all closely related phenomena? Converted into research questions, such speculations might prove a powerful device in making theoretical perspectives on bureaucracy relevant to some of the most recurrent concerns of political science in the Third World, namely, the obstacles confronting democratic consolidation.

The fourth model in Peters' conception is the 'adversarial' one, which depicts an inverse situation to the village model. Here politicians and bureaucrats compete for power instead of forming alliances, while not necessarily conforming to the sharp differentiation found in the formal–legal model. The illustrations offered for mature democracies point to several possible sources of conflict and competition, placing civil servants on one side and executive politicians on the other. It does not take to much imagination to come up with similar situations in the Third World. Thus, for example, the very preference for bureaucratic innovation over bureaucratic reform that has often been observed by the specialists could possibly be conceived as a way of overcoming bureaucratic resistance to political changes and of avoiding the configuration of an adversarial model (Reis, 1990; Geddes and Nunes, 1987).

The last analytical possibility Peters explores is the 'administrative state model', which is the opposite of the formal model. Instead of displaying clear-cut lines that preserve the balance between politicians' and bureaucrats' respective areas of competence, this model perceives actual policy making as increasingly dominated by civil servants. As the author indicates, this model does not presuppose any conscious domination project on the part of bureaucracy, nor does it necessarily involve a normative posture against bureaucracy. In Peters' perspective, the tendency to see governmental decision making as dominated by bureaucracy derives from the objective complexity of technical concerns, and from the overload of tasks inflicted upon the modern state. Under such circumstances, the administrative staff is better equipped to face the job than is the executive politician. In short, like the pure hybrid model of the previous theoretical perspective, the administrative state model constitutes, logically, a situation opposite to the formal division between administrative and political competence that characterizes the analytical possibility from which both perspectives depart. Moreover, as in the pure hybrid situation, the administrative state model expresses a historical trend.

Further elaborations on the major characteristics of the five models allow Peters to draw a broad frame of reference that can be of great value in comparative analysis. As he explicitly states, his theoretical construct is more a research agenda than a formal statement of findings. In any case, it seems that the possible uses of the approach, as he briefly illustrates, makes its relevance for Third World societies striving to consolidate democracy rather obvious. And the fact that comparative empirical research on bureaucracy in less developed societies has been delayed for so long should not be attributed to the lack of promising theoretical frameworks.

While it is true that both of the theoretical approaches discussed thus far are mainly concerned with the bureaucratic actor, their respective focuses are centered upon the patterns of interaction between administration and politics, and thus both explore the pair 'bureaucrats–politicians'. We now move to a third analytical perspective, one which centers on bureaucracy and which explores the variable signals that inform bureaucratic behavior. This is Richard Rose's discussion of votes, markets, law and self-expertise as four informational components that bureaucrats may take into account (Rose, 1987). The predominance of one or another of these signals, Rose says, is an empirical question and a normative concern. In any case, his point of departure is the following assumption:

> A multiplicity of signals implies variety among civil servants. Ideal-type categories of officials may be differentiated according to the priority given to a particular type of signal, law-bound bureaucrats; servants of elected policy makers; professionals possessing expertise in a substantive programme; and employees of public enterprises that sell their output in the market (Rose, 1987, p. 211).

The predominance of law signals suggests a situation resembling the two first models discussed by Aberbach *et al.*, or even the one expressed in Peters' formal–legal model: bureaucrats act according to legal prescriptions and, when these do not provide enough guidance, they have to seek directions from representative politicians. As an ideal type, the law signal more adequately describes lower bureaucratic echelons.

The expertise signals are mostly relevant when we are dealing with substantive policy areas. They express the triumph of specialization acquired either through formal training or on the job. The monopoly of knowledge, as Rose indicates, tends to 'protect' experts against the interference of politicians. Naturally market signals are essentially relevant within public enterprises. A state firm, despite its peculiarities, has to be concerned with efficiency and productivity criteria, which makes the use of market information decisive. The bureaucratic actor here is highly influenced by motives that transcend the public sector.

In fact, the author observes, the public enterprise employee tends to identify with his production sector rather than with the public sector per se.

Finally signals from the electorate seem to be the ones least popular among bureaucrats. These signals are not clear and precise enough to orient policy making. Naturally to some extent the vote signal is channeled into the policy process through politicians. However the translation of voting preferences into policy decisions is a very imperfect process. Rose's conclusion is that, when an elected official wants 'to send a directive to those delivering the services for which he is nominally answerable, it must often be an "indirect" directive' (Rose, 1987, p. 216).

After characterizing each of the typical signals, Rose's concern is to identify which situation makes which of these directives more adequate than the others. As he convincingly argues, this constitutes the crucial political problem of public policy. His strategy is to identify 'the attributes of public programmes that cause signals to vary': he distinguishes between 'collective' and 'private' program outputs, and between market and non-market means of provision. From that we arrive at a fourfold typology of public program outputs: (a) pure collective goods (collective type and non-market provision); (b) deviant collective goods (collective and marketed); (c) merit goods (private and non-market); and (d) public enterprise goods (private and marketed). Each of these four alternative modes of providing signs ideally corresponds to a particular hierarchy of signals: pure collective goods are better served by directives coming from expertise and votes; deviant collective goods, such as debt interest payments, are better accounted for by law and market signals; the combination of law and expertise directives is more adequate in the case of merit goods, such as education and health; finally, the goods produced by public enterprise require priority to be placed on market and vote signals.

Rose concludes that multiple signals offer great advantages in guiding bureaucratic behavior. In his words,

> From the perspective of ordinary citizens, multiple signs can be regarded as a surety of better public policies. . . . A plurality of signals offers the potential to produce a more appropriate mix of public goods and services than placing total reliance upon only one signal, whether from laws, expertise, markets, or elected officials (Rose, 1987, p. 228).

Not that he assumes an automatic equilibrium between these signals, but he does seem to suppose that at both the positive and the normative level a democratic order poses the need for some sort of balance in the directives that guide public action. We can thus conclude that research on the actual empirical combinations of signals to bureaucracy can prove a very useful instrument in understanding concrete political regimes. Investigation along these lines could also meaningfully tie together the study of public policies and research on the prospects for democratization among latecomers.

POLICY MAKING IN POST-DICTATORIAL BRAZIL: REFLECTIONS ON SCIENCE AND TECHNOLOGY

After living through two decades of bureaucratic authoritarianism, and despite many divergences and controversies, Brazilian society displayed a remarkable consensus as regards the evaluation of bureaucracy. Bureaucratic procedures had come to be perceived as unequivocally 'bad'. To public opinion, the combination of technical expertise plus bureaucratic insulation had constituted the backbone of the dictatorship.

Certainly, the prestige of Brazilian politicians is not any higher at all today. But immediately after the retreat of the military from power, before the new rules of the political game had been established, many dreamed of a kind of 'purged' politics, in which the former technocratic caste entrenched in the state bureaucracy, and its political allies from the 'old regime', would be replaced by 'better' representatives. Today, six years after the return to civilian government, the complicated task of balancing politics and bureaucracy still seems a crucial challenge for the government. Even if not couched strictly in these terms, what we witness in media coverage are constant references to disputes between a 'bureaucratic' and a 'political' way of settling problems and arriving at policy decisions. Changes in cabinet offices often bring to the fore recurrent disputes and changing alliances involving bureaucrats and politicians. Ministers and top bureaucrats are classified according to how open they are to negotiations with Congress, civilian associations or specific private interests vis-à-vis their concern with expertise.

If the 'technocratic' style of governing, because of its association with past practices, is easily identified with 'non-democratic' politics, open reliance on interest negotiation tends also to be perceived by public opinion as 'immoral', 'corrupt', 'privatist'.[1] While it is true that either 'technical' or 'power bargaining' styles can indeed foster non-democratic practices, the point to make clear is that the Brazilian political system has had difficulty in striking a balance between bureaucracy and politics, between technical expertise and interest representation; also the struggle to consolidate democracy has been to a large extent an effort to legitimate power competition among and between these partners.

As a policy area, science and technology serves well to illustrate the difficulties encountered in balancing politics and bureaucracy, while at the same time it evidences how these two dimensions can only be separated artificially. Regardless of the political regime, science and technology policies tend to be clearly biased toward technocratic criteria, given the centrality of specialized knowledge that they require. Following Rose (1987), one can say that expertise is the decisive sign informing bureaucratic behavior in this policy area. Yet the exclusion of the large majority of the population from the political arena, which characterized the military regime in Brazil, contributed to making the 'experts' de facto allies of a highly elitist agreement.

It is true that technical decisions in the area, while contributing, for example, to the expansion of educational opportunities or to industrial development, ended up benefiting many of those outside the political arena. However it is important to keep in mind that the politics of science and technology – the proper space where policy alternatives are confronted and ranked – remained concealed from the public because effective political disputes took place within the bureaucratic arena, even though selected non-bureaucratic actors were also partners. In this sense the concrete patterns of interaction between the politics and the administration of an 'expertise domain' like science and technology reveal the distinctive characteristics of bureaucratic and political roles, on the one hand, and illustrate how central these patterns are in defining the nature of a political order, on the other. These two aspects orient the following discussion of Brazil's recent past and contemporary efforts to consolidate democracy.

Scientific and technological policies have been an important part of Brazil's growth model, based on the active state involvement in the economy that has characterized the nation since the 1930s.[2] However, while significant advances may have been made before 1964, the bureaucratic–authoritarian pattern adopted after the military coup was especially generous with scientific and technological development, and public investments to this end became part and parcel of the military's national growth strategy. Thus the first Basic Plan for Scientific and

Technological Development was adopted in 1973, funded by the National Fund for Scientific and Technological Development (FNDCT), established by federal legislation in 1969. As was explicit in the language of the planners, the objectives of science and technology policies ought to be derived from national development strategy (Guimaraes *et al.*, 1985).

Within this perspective the state assumed the responsibility of providing for expansion of the nation's technological base. Successful economic performance itself further stimulated investments in science and technology, as the so-called 'economic miracle' of the late 1960s and early 1970s sparked widespread optimism among policy makers and fueled the dream of a powerful domestic economy, increasingly free from technological dependence. State agencies were reformed or newly established to carry out a bold investment program in science and technology. The National Development Bank (BNDE) and the newly created federal agency for the promotion of economic–technological projects, FINEP, became the leading actors in the interface between technology and industry (Martins, 1985). In close connection with the former, the National Research Council, converted into the National Council for Scientific and Technological Development (CNPq), played a key role in monitoring scientific and technological concerns (Schwartzman, 1979 and 1980; Forjaz, 1989). Investments in science and technology expanded from 0.24 per cent to 0.65 per cent of GDP between 1971 and 1979 (Adler, 1988, p. 378).

As the voting process underwent a severe devaluation, relevant political decisions were made under the guise of 'exclusively technical' considerations. At the time, many analysts observed, bureaucracy became the strategic locus for articulating interests, while Congress played more of a symbolic role. This was the heyday of the new technocratic elite brought to power by the dictatorial regime.[3] So biased was the policy-making process that some went as far as to suggest that a 'state bourgeoisie' had emerged from within the ranks of the many state enterprises and from the top echelons of so-called 'direct administration agencies' (Martins, 1977). Others agreed with Cardoso's suggestion that state bureaucracies constituted the privileged locus for interest articulation, invoking the image of bureaucratic rings to convey the idea of the public and private alliance of interests that took place within the executive (Cardoso, 1975).

While it is true that even the more inclusionary regimes rank the vote sign low in policy making, there are significant differences between democracies and dictatorships with regard to who affects policy decisions. Certainly the political systems degree of inclusiveness provides greater or lesser opportunities for votes to influence policy. However, following Peters (1981), it could said that Brazilian bureaucracy became highly politicized under the military because, once free of political counterweights, bureaucrats tend to become fragmented around dividing interests. The trouble with this sort of politics is that it is highly discriminatory. Very few had a chance to voice their opinion, for example, when the decisive steps toward the development of a Brazilian nuclear energy program were taken. Those who objected to the policies adopted (and which afterwards proved disastrous) had very little chance to express their disagreement. Closed to public scrutiny on the grounds that expertise was necessary, nuclear policies were implemented by the technocratic establishment, in close alliance with foreign capital (Adler, 1987; Pinguelli Rosa, 1985).

The process was similar when it came to decisions on investments in microelectronics. A small group of experts working for the government, together with a select few private actors (mostly bankers and retired army officers), took charge of what became Brazil's 'politics for informatics'. This provides us with quite a clear illustration of the knots that bind policies and politics together. In the name of national interest, and with the concurrence of interested private investors, experts devised and implemented a policy that granted state protection against foreign competitors and at the same time fostered monopoly conditions domestically (Adler, 1987; Evans, 1966; Tigre, 1983). Unlike nuclear energy policies, Brazil's policies for technological and industrial development in microelectronics are usually considered a success story: they illustrate a situation in which a state bureaucracy, oriented by nationalistic goals, followed expertise and law signs and ended up generating adequate (if artificial) market signs. Setting legal barriers to foreign competitors, Brazil managed to establish a domestic microcomputer industry.

The case of microcomputer policy, converted into a 'national' cause, provides a dramatized illustration of the broader policy orientation typical of the period. The complete exclusion of the vote sign from the policy-making scene was taken as a 'technical' requirement needed to 'keep politics out of it'. In turn the reestablishment of politics and votes as valued goods, which marked the demise of the military regime, brought into question not only the ethical premises of an experts monopoly in policy making but also the market efficiency of such a monopoly.

At this point the policy-making style typical of bureaucratic authoritarianism had lost its ideological power to rationalize and simultaneously conceal politics. Under the military regime, the apparent predominance of bureaucracy over politics contributed de facto to reducing bureaucratic accountability but did not make policies politically neutral. Thus, for example, the scientific and technological choices of the period had definite consequences for those directly interested, as well as for society at large. The demise of the authoritarian regime brought to the forefront a questioning of the terms of the interaction between politics and administration and of its particular consequences for policy making.

The return to civilian government and the attempt to consolidate a democratic order posed new challenges to the interplay between politics and bureaucracy. The period right after the military stepped down was marked by a dramatic shift towards collegiality in policy making. Soon after the inauguration of the civilian government in early 1985, ad hoc committees were formed to revise major policy areas. As a natural reaction to 20 years of authoritarian decision making, and as a way of strengthening the new government's legitimacy, representatives from the various interests affected by specific policies were invited to get together and propose changes in education, health, social security, scientific research and so on.

The reform plans and policy changes recommended by such general assembly-like corps were, with a few exceptions, largely ineffective, partly because they were technically and/or politically unviable, partly because the intensification of the economic crisis besetting the country tied the government's hands. In any case, the attitudes and opinions that bureaucrats, politicians and 'clients' voiced about the proposed changes, as well as about the ultimate inefficacy of these changes, reveal to us important aspects of the actual patterns of interaction and the normative conceptions these typical actors hold regarding what the roles of bureaucrats and politicians should be in the policy process.

Mutual accusations were the rule within each policy area: politicians blamed the bureaucrats and technocrats, who in turn blamed politicians and their particular constituencies; the bureaucrats and technocrats pointed their fingers at the lack of political will among politicians, who in turn blamed the formality and rigidity of the bureaucrats. In the end, whatever was accomplished, observation suggests, it was the bureaucrats – who last longer in government and know the technical details – who played the leading role in negotiations with politicians to obtain congressional approval of policies, particularly ones related to welfare measures.

The scenario is in some sense different with respect to science and technology because the immediate 'beneficiaries' have much more bargaining power than the mass of those who are the targets of social policies first; the big economic interests at stake on the technology front render the market much more relevant to decision makers than in other areas of state action. Second, the power project of the state itself cannot neglect scientific and technological investments which, particularly for the military actor, are the guarantee of a minimal degree of autonomy and sovereignty. Third, international capital constitutes a powerful actor in the process, selling technology or establishing joint ventures with public and private domestic capital. Fourth, the academic–scientific community constitutes a very visible and articulated pressure group, if not a powerful one.

In any case, science and technology has become a much more disputed arena in post-authoritarian Brazil. Thus intrabureaucratic competition has increased, stimulated negatively by the severe economic crisis of the present and positively by expanded opportunities for political competition. New alliances have been made along the bureaucracy v. politics axis, as competing bureaucratic agencies seek to increase power or to consolidate positions, with the concurrence of external allies.

The chances for corruption may indeed be greater now that the voting process has been revalued. The shrinkage of economic resources seems to act to keep patron–client mechanisms relevant, and corruption salient, in policy decisions.[4] Moreover the fiscal crisis of the state increases the opportunity for private interests to have privileged access to government officials. Even the option of state shrinkage, thus far only a project, can make room for patrimonial dispensation of favors to private interests. That is to say, the particular rules presiding over the privatization of state bureaucracies can bring positive or negative signs as far as democratic consolidation is concerned.

Talks about privatization have generated the expectation that science and technology will become much more the responsibility of private capital, and that the patrimonial-like characteristics which the state has traditionally imprinted on its policies will thus disappear. With the vanishing of state protectionism, it is argued, science and technology will depend much more upon market criteria, owing to their close connections to industrial policy. Be that as it may, given the combined effects of the severe economic crisis, the collapse of the former technocratic growth model and the lack of any legitimate alternative political model for policy making, the prospects do not look too bright for the advancement of science and technology policies, nor for the consolidation of democracy in Brazil. Could our theoretical understanding of the relationships between bureaucracy and politics offer better prospects? We conclude with what is perhaps a surprisingly optimistic comment.

The three theoretical approaches discussed in the first part of this chapter offered alternative ways of looking at the interaction between politicians and bureaucrats in the policy process. While mainly providing conceptual devices for describing variable patterns, the approaches in question can also signal which patterns seem more adequate to particular policy areas as far as maximizing efficiency, on the one hand, and democracy, on the other, is concerned. A reliance on the comparative analysis offered by any of the theoretical alternatives in question is potentially a powerful instrument in helping us to strike a balance between bureaucratic and political criteria, or between technical efficiency and participatory goals. It would be interesting, for example, to refer to the models discussed by Aberbach *et al.* (1981) in comparing Brazilian policy process in science and technology and the Western democracies that the authors address. Tentatively one would say that comparative research making use of this theoretical perspective should concentrate on the exploration of models three and four, which assign bureaucracy a key role in dealing with interest articulation, in addition to stressing specialized knowledge.

While it is true that science and technology policy will remain mainly the territory of the specialists, one wonders to what extent the formal acceptance of an expanded role for political representatives in the policy process could increase bureaucratic accountability. It may be that in making explicit the diverging interests represented by bureaucrats and by politicians in this area, we help to legitimate disputes and to overcome the need for an authoritarian consensus. Comparative research along the lines suggested by Aberbach *et al.* (1981) could aid, for example, in exploring the chances for maximizing bureaucratic accountability.

The framework provided by Peters (1987) offers a very insightful perspective for exploring when and how patterns of interaction between politicians and bureaucrats contribute to furthering democratic procedures or to making policy decisions more discriminatory. While not intended to fulfil these particular purposes, Peters' research agenda can certainly add to knowledge along these lines. On could ask, for example, what have been the effective changes in Brazil with regard to the model underlying the interaction between bureaucrats and politicians in science and technology, and to what extent these changes contribute or not to enhancing democracy.

Finally Rose's discussion of the signals informing bureaucratic behavior remains highly relevant to our discussion. The constant references above to expertise, law, market and vote as possible criteria for decision making while addressing the Brazilian case is a clear indication of this. As the author has argued, a diversity of signs constitutes a positive reality and a normative ideal. Moreover different types of policy make particular signs more adequate. In any case, comparative research can once again help us to assess different mixes and their respective political and administrative consequences.

As Brazil seeks to consolidate democratic patterns of governance, science and technology policies – particularly because of their relevance to industrial policy – will play a critical role. How much room will be made for interest diversity? Will the state actually retreat from the market arena? If so, will this movement entail a radical change in the role assigned to particular policy makers? These and many other questions critical to democracy will put current patterns of interaction between bureaucrats and politicians to the test. Theoretical models can help us understand these changes and assess their implications. At the same time, comparative empirical research can provide a good opportunity for testing and revising bureaucratic theories.

Notes

1. Brazilian politics has traditionally had a very hard time legitimating interest pluralism. In offering explanations for this, reference is currently made to cultural factors, patrimonial legacies from the colonial past, particular characteristics of the state-building process and patterns of economic growth. The fact of it is that organic, holistic representations of the general interest have persistently made it suspect to defend special interests.
2. The central role of the state in Brazilian industrial development has been widely observed in the literature. Some even use the term 'state capitalism' to characterize Brazil's growth pattern after 1930. See, for example, Leff (1968); Martins (1966); Skidmore (1967).
3. For evidence on the recent recruitment of bureaucrats and technocrats for top positions in governmental agencies, see Martins (1985, pp. 196ff).
4. As Judith Chubb shows for Italy, economic crisis and shrinking patronage resources can act to expand the chances for power mediation and can grant brokers a further capacity to dispense privileges (Chubb, 1982). The economic crisis Brazil has been experiencing since the early 1980s has severely affected public investments in science and technology. Data for recent years reveal a dramatic shortage of funds: resources allocated for the National Fund for the Development of Science and Technology (FNDCT) in 1991 are about 20 per cent of what they were in 1986.

References

ABERBACH, JOEL, ROBERT PUTNAM and BERT ROCKMAN (1981) *Bureaucrats and Politicians in Western Democracies* (Cambridge, Mass.: Harvard University Press).

ABERBACH, JOEL, HANS-ULRICH DERLIEN, RENATE MAYNTZ and BERT ROCKMAN (1990) 'American and German Federal Executives – Technocratic and Political Attitudes', *International Social Science Journal*, vol. 123 (February), pp. 3–18.

ADLER, EMANUEL (1987) *The Power of Ideology: The Quest for Technological Autonomy in Argentina and Brazil* (Berkeley: University of California Press).

ADLER, EMANUEL (1988) 'O Papel das Elites Politicas e Intelectuais e das Instituicoes no Desenvolvimento da Informatica e da Energia Nuclear na Argentina e no Brasil', *DADOS*, vol. 31, no. 3, pp. 373–403.

CARDOSO, FERNANDO HENRIQUE (1975) *Autoritarismo e Democratizacao* (Rio de Janeiro: Paz e Terra).

CHUBB, JUDITH (1982) *Patronage, Power and Poverty in Southern Italy* (Cambridge University Press).

EVANS, PETER (1966) 'State, Capital, and the Transformation of Dependence: The Brazilian Computer Case', *World Development*, vol. 14, no. 7.

FORJAZ, MARIA CECILIA ESPINA (1989) 'Cientistas e Militares no Desenvolvimento do CNPq. (1950–1985)', *Boletim Informativo e Bibliografico de Ciencias Sociais – BIB*, vol. 28, pp. 71–99.

GEDDES, BARBARA and EDSON NUNES (1987) 'Clientelism and Political Insulation: Towards a Political Sociology of Contemporary Brazil', in John Wirth, Edson Nunes and Thomas Bogenschild (eds), *The State and Society in Brazil: Continuity and Change*, (Boulder: Westview Press), pp. 147–78.

GUIMARAES, EDUARDO AUGUSTO, JOSE TAVARES and FABIO ERBER (1985) *A Politica Cientifica e Tecnologica no Brasil* (Rio de Janeiro: Zahar).

HECLO, HUGH and AARON WILDAVSKY (1974) *The Private Government of Public Money* (Berkeley: University of California Press).

LEFF, NATHANIEL (1968) *Economic Policy Making and Development in Brazil, 1947–1964* (New York: Wiley).

MARTINS, CARLOS ESTEVAM (1977) *Capitalismo de Estado e Modelo Politico no Brasil* (Rio de Janeiro: Graal).

MARTINS, LUCIANO (1966) *Pouvoir et Developpement Economique: Formation et Evolution des Structures Politiques au Brésil* (Paris: Anthropos).

MARTINS, LUCIANO (1985) *Estado, Capitalismo e Burocracia no Brasil Pos 64* (Rio de Janeiro: Paz e Terra).

PETERS, B. GUY (1981) 'The Problem of Bureaucratic Government', *The Journal of Politics*, vol, 43, no. 1. pp. 55–82.

PETERS, B. GUY (1987) 'Politicians and Bureaucrats in the Politics of Policy Making', in Jan-Erik Lane (ed.), *Bureaucracy and Public Choice* (Beverly Hills: Sage), pp. 255–82.

PINGUELLI ROSA, LUIZ (1985) *A Politica Nuclear e o Caminho das Armas Atomicas* (Rio de Janeiro: Zahar).

REIS, ELISA P. (1990) 'Brazil: The Politics of the State Administration', mimeo.

ROSE, RICHARD (1987) 'Giving Directions to Permanent Officials: Signals from the Electorates, the Market and from Self-Expertise', in Jan-Erik Lane (ed.), *Bureaucracy and Public Choice* (Beverly Hills: Sage), pp. 210–30.

SCHWARTZMAN, SIMON (1979) *Formacao da Comunidade Cientifica no Brasil* (Sao Paulo: Nacional).

SCHWARTZMAN, SIMON (1980) 'Por Uma Politica Cientifica', in *Ciencia, Universidade e Ideologia* (Rio De Janeiro: Zahar), pp. 50–69.

SKIDMORE, THOMAS (1967) *Politics in Brazil, 1930–1964, An Experiment in Democracy* (New York: Oxford University Press).

TIGRE, PAULO BASTOS (1983) *Technology and Competition in the Brazilian Computer Industry* (New York: St Martin's Press).

7 Ecotourism: Toward a Policy of Economic Development and Environmental Balance in Latin America

Michele Zebich-Knos

It is simply not enough to raise the funds, put a fence around the forest, and call it preserved. The economic and social pressures will inevitably unpreserve it.

(Daniel Janzen)

INTRODUCTION

Tourism is big business. In 1989, an estimated $55 billion in tourist travel receipts was calculated for North and South America alone by the World Tourism Organization. Central American tourist receipts amounted to approximately $4.6 billion for the same year (World Tourism Organization, 1989). By 1990, tourism infused approximately $275 million into the Costa Rican economy and, for the first time, outranked coffee – $245 million in 1990 – as Costa Rica's second largest foreign currency earner. Bananas still ranked first, bringing in $315 million in revenue to Costa Rica, but tourism's position was very 'respectable' (*Europa World Yearbook*, 1992).

At the same time, a growing awareness of environmental preservation and sustainable development has encouraged a marriage between tourism's economic benefits and preservation of nature's finite resources. This marriage has spawned the growth of a sub-set within the tourist trade known as 'ecotourism', one of two terms much favored by those concerned with the travel industry and with economic development. The marketing of this relationship is expanding worldwide, particularly in Latin America. It is the intent of this chapter to examine the

140

environmental dilemmas and policy needs resulting from increased ecotourism in Latin America. Examples will be drawn from various ecotourist-related endeavors, primarily in Costa Rica and Ecuador.

Sustainable Development

The second frequently used term, 'sustainable development', became popular following its use by the World Commission on Environment and Development (Brundtland Commission) in its 1987 report entitled *Our Common Future*. As defined by the commission, sustainable development pertains to 'meeting the needs of the present generation without compromising the needs of the present generation without compromising the needs of future generations' (World Commission on Environment and Development, 1987). The World Bank extends this definition further to include meeting the needs of the world's poor. The World Bank does not distinguish between the 'goals of development policy and appropriate environmental protection'(World Bank, 1992). The bank explains that such a relationship between development and environment must be based on careful economic analysis and cost/benefit analysis. Conservationists often take issue with the attaching of purely economic indicators to the environment, but the term is used nevertheless by economists and conservationists alike to convey their concern about the depletion of natural resources and extinction of many flora and fauna under the guise of economic progress. Sustained development thus becomes an earth-sensitive term adopted by many because it conveys the feeling of 'doing what is right and just for the planet'.

Ecotourist proponents consequently tout this form of tourism as contributing to the 'right kind' of development – sustainable development. The ecotourist sector thus rides on the environmental bandwagon to successfully market tourism to areas that possess no Mona Lisa, Tower of Pisa, Acropolis or the Great Pyramids, yet are rich in natural history. The approach seems to be working in Latin America; for example, in Ecuador's Galapagos Islands, tourism grew between 1974 and 1987 by more than 335 per cent, from 7500 visitors to 32 595 (Boo, 1990).

Ecotourism: Definitions

By definition, ecotourism is connected with the desire by the traveller to experience nature for nature's sake and is often used interchangeably with the term 'nature tourism'. In her highly acclaimed study on ecotourism, Boo in fact uses the term 'ecotourism' in the book's title, yet frequently refers to the more comprehensive term, 'nature tourism', throughout the text. Ceballos-Lascurain expands the definition by stating that ecotourism is

> tourism that involves travelling to relatively undisturbed or uncontaminated natural areas with the specific object of studying, admiring, and enjoying the scenery and its wild plants and animals, as well as existing cultural aspects found in these areas ... the person who pratices ecotourism has the opportunity of immersing him or herself in nature in a way most people cannot enjoy in their routine, urban existences. This person will eventually acquire a consciousness ... that will convert him into somebody keenly involved in conservation issues (Ceballos-Lascurain, 1988, p. 13).

Ziffer offers a more succinct definition by stating that ecotourism is 'a form of tourism inspired primarily by the natural history of an area, including its indigenous cultures' and usually takes place in rather undeveloped areas of a country (Ziffer, 1989, p. 6). She distinguishes the ecotourism from nature tourism and postulates that the latter is akin to leisure travel in which one happens to participate in outdoor activities. Her approach is not shared by Laarman, who defines nature tourism to include natural history education and recreational aspects (Laarman, 1986). He further breaks down the nature tourist into 'hard' and 'soft' categories in which the former includes biologists, geologists and other scientific specialists. The latter group mixes natural history forays with other activities ranging from 'sun and surf', fishing and shopping to adventure and cultural undertakings.

There are subtle differences between ecotourists and leisure visitors to national parks and reserves. For the leisure visitor, being with friends or family is often the main reason for the outing. Such a visitor – especially a host-country national – might just as easily have gone to a cafe or a movie than to a park. Leisure visitors may contribute more significantly to noise, litter and general park degradation than ecotourists. This tends to be the case in Costa Rica's Poas Volcano National Park, which attracts large numbers of leisure visitors (Boo, 1990). One solution would be to convert the leisure tourist into an enlightened natural-history visitor through conservation education.

This brings us to the conservation, or environmental, aspect of ecotourism. Maintenance of this significant foreign-currency-generating sector depends on preserving flora and fauna as economic assets. With the onset of ecotourism in Latin America a symbiotic relationship has developed between the scientific community, which is interested in saving endangered species, and those interested in maintaining a business venture. Sergio Miranda, director of the Marenco Biological Station (Costa Rica) and owner of the Horizontes Travel Agency, best explained this relationship between conservation and business when he stated that 'Biologists have no money. Money has no environmental awareness' (Whelan, 1987). Conservation for profit is likely to remain a viable solution as long as it is properly managed by both private and public sectors. By exploiting the environment in its natural state the need is reduced for countries such as Costa Rica to rely heavily upon rainforest-destructive activities such as export agriculture or logging. Tourism can fill the economic niche once filled by coffee, bananas or other commodities and contribute to economic diversification.

The situation is trickier in Ecuador, where tourism is hard-pressed to compete with the cash-generating ability of petroleum. To the dismay of conservationists, sections of the ecologically endangered Amazon are being deforested by the petroleum industry. In an era of burdensome foreign debt, Latin American nations are facing grave dilemmas in the policy-making arena. Yet in the 1980s tourism was the second (after petroleum) most important contributor to foreign-currency earnings (Boo, 1990).

This chapter makes two assumptions about ecotourism: (1) ecotourism contributes to economic development; and (2) ecotourism helps to slow the pace of environmental destruction in Latin America. Two questions arise from these assumptions: (1) exactly how much do ecotourists actually contribute to economic development? (2) With ever increasing numbers of visitors to national parks, can ecotourists avoid becoming part of the environmental problem?

ENVIRONMENTAL IMPERATIVE IN LATIN AMERICA

Conservation of Latin America's flora and fauna is considered critical by environmental specialists. Four of Myers' list of the ten most significant global 'hotspot' areas in tropical forests are in South America: the Atlantic Forest (Brazil), Colombian Choco, Western Amazonian Uplands (Brazil, Ecuador, Peru) and Western Ecuador (Myers, 1988). The publicity and impact generated by ecotourism becomes all the

Table 7.1   Countries with the highest numbers of species of selected organisms

Mammals		Birds	
Indonesia	515	Colombia	1 721
Mexico	449	Peru	1 701
Brazil	428	Brazil	1 622
Zaire	409	Indonesia	1 519
China	394	Ecuador	1 447
Peru	361	Venezuela	1 275
Colombia	359	Bolivia	1 250(+/−)
India	350	India	1 200
Uganda	311	Malaysia	1 200(+/−)
Tanzania	310	China	1 195
Amphibians		*Reptiles*	
Brazil	516	Mexico	717
Colombia	407	Australia	686
Ecuador	358	Indonesia	600(+/−)
Mexico	282	Brazil	467
Indonesia	270	India	453
China	265	Colombia	383
Peru	251	Ecuador	345
Zaire	216	Peru	297
USA	205	Malaysia	294
Venezuela	197	New Guinea/Thailand	282*

*Each country has 282 reptile species.

Source: McNeely *et al.* (1990).

more important when one considers the large 'megadiversity of species for the region.

Table 7.1 shows that several Latin American countries rank high among those with the greatest number of species of selected organisms. What is striking is the fact that Mexico ranks in the top five for three of four categories, yet its ecotourism potential is played down in favor of the highly successful 'sand and surf' approach. Ironically Costa Rica is a country in which all tourism tends to be labelled 'eco', yet it does not appear on this species list at all. In fact, of all the Latin American neo-tropical countries, Costa Rica consistently ranks near the bottom in terms of large numbers of species, as Table 7.2, indicates. 'Ecomarketing' is thus becoming more important in attracting nature tourists than the sheer numbers of species.

Seeking alliances with the private and public sector has become

Table 7.2 Latin American countries with the highest numbers of species of selected organisms

Mammals		Birds	
Mexico	449	Colombia	1 721
Brazil	428	Peru	1 701
Peru	361	Brazil	1 622
Colombia	359	Ecuador	1 447
Venezuela	305	Venezuela	1 275
Ecuador	280	Bolivia	1 250(+/−)
Bolivia	267	Mexico	1 010
Argentina	255	Argentina	942
Panama	217	Panama	907
Costa Rica	203	Costa Rica	796
Amphibians		Reptiles	
Brazil	516	Mexico	717
Colombia	407	Brazil	467
Ecuador	358	Colombia	383
Mexico	282	Ecuador	345
Peru	251	Peru	297
Venezuela	197	Venezuela	246
Panama	159	Costa Rica	218
Costa Rica	150	Panama	212
Argentina	130	Argentina/Guatemala	204*
Guyana	100	Bolivia	180

* Argentina and Guatemala each have 204 reptile species.

Source: McNeely *et al.* (1990).

critical to those who seek to preserve the existence of these many tropical species. This is especially true in light of extensive deforestation that occurs throughout Latin America and in Costa Rica in particular. Costa Rica's 50 900 square kilometers have been deforested rapidly since the 1940s and the country has the second highest tropical deforestation rate in Latin America (see Table 7.3).

Enlightenment with regard to the loss of Costa Rica's natural resources has prompted the Costa Rican government to act, so that the country now boasts a superb system of national parks and reserves, as well as several private reserves. These parks serve as the basis for attracting international ecotourists. While agriculture, logging and cattle ranching have not disappeared in Costa Rica, the country now boasts a National Park Service, created in 1970, and parks that cover approximately 11 per cent of its territory (Rovinski, 1991). Creation of

Table 7.3   Deforestation rates for selected Latin American countries
1981–5 (projections)*

Country	Annual deforestation (%)
Paraguay	4.7
Costa Rica	4.0
Haiti	3.8
El Salvador	3.2
Nicaragua	2.7
Ecuador	2.4
Guatemala	2.0
Colombia	1.8
Mexico	1.3
Panama	0.9
Peru	0.4
Brazil	0.4
Venezuela	0.4

* These figures are estimates and are derived from the Food and Agriculture
Organization of the United Nations' *Tropical Forest Resources Assessment
Project*, conducted every 10 years. The 1991 results have yet to be released.

Source: McNeely *et al.* (1990).

parks to preserve flora and fauna is a relatively new phenomenon in
Latin America, and Costa Rica is no exception. Prior to 1968, Costa
Rica only had two national parks and protected areas, Irazu Volcano
National Park and Cabo Blanco Natural Area Reserve. Today it has
29 (Rachowiecki, 1991). In about 20 years this Central American country
has responded to the demands of those who seek to preserve the
natural habitat, yet this process – conducted largely at the national
level – includes moving people off their land to make way for parks.
Compensation offered to the rural population may lead to disputes
and, according to Whelan, many small farmers have not yet been compensated (Whelan, 1991). Two alternatives exist for these people: (1)
they can relocate to cities already suffering from high unemployment,
or (2) they can find alternative sources of income in their rural area.
Such disruption frequently puts the national government at odds with
local-level community advocates.

While ecotourism is viewed as one way to alleviate the revenue
generating problem for those living in areas of biological or geologi-
cal interest, it must be placed in a comprehensive perspective. Ideally
this perspective should include all aspects of managing the ecotourist

trade at the national, regional and local levels. From World Bank estimates, we know that 55 cents on every tourist dollar are usually expatriated from developing countries. The remainder normally stays in the capital city, with very little revenue actually accruing to the rural areas visited by tourists. With this skewed distribution of tourism revenue in mind, anticipation and planning thus become crucial components if ecotourist expansion is going to help develop rural areas.

ECOTOURISM IN A COMPREHENSIVE PERSPECTIVE

The linkage between ecotourism and conservation interests can be harmonious as long as a comprehensive management loop is used and key groups, such as those resident on the borders of national parks, are not excluded from the decision-making and management process. Figure 7.1 contains a general model aimed at making the link between tourism and conservation a solid one in which certain elements of society do not feel left out of the process. It can serve as the basis for structuring ecotourism within the political system. It also underlines the interconnectedness of the various elements. Each element will be discussed in the following sections.

Definition/Redefinition of Needs

Environmental needs

First came the conservationists with their desires to study and preserve flora and fauna. In Ecuador this activity was conducted especially through private groups such as the Fundación Natura and the Charles Darwin Research Center. The former manages the Pasachoa Protected Forest and the latter operates extensive facilities in the Galapagos Islands. In Costa Rica, various groups exist, such as the Organization for Tropical Studies (OTS), founded in 1963 as a consortium of universities in the US and the University of Costa Rica, and the Tropical Research Center (TRC). The former operates La Selva Biological Station and the latter Monteverde Cloud Forest Reserve. With the proliferation of private groups, environmental constituencies were gradually built up in both countries. This resulted in the expansion of each country's national parks. Hence conservation of each country's flora and fauna became a defined priority (Tangley, 1988).

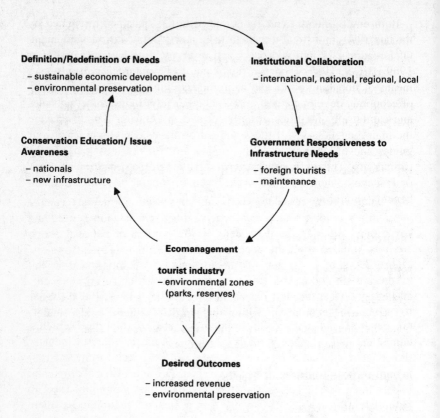

Figure 7.1   Ecotourism/conservation model

Economic needs

While there were always ecotourists in Latin America, prior to the 1970s many tended to be biologists and other scientists. The expansion of ecotourism to include 'soft', or non-expert, nature tourists followed as the travel industry saw an opportunity for increased business through the marketing of nature. Business interests in each country lent support to this environmental priority. Metropolitan Touring, for example, is Ecuador's largest tour agency and has long promoted excursions internationally to the Galapagos. In addition Metropolitan Touring dominates the market for jungle excursions to the Amazon and runs the Flotel Orellana, which is also promoted internationally as one of the few tourist facilities in the Ecuadorian 'Oriente', or Amazon basin (Wilson, 1987).

Both environmental and economic priorities became entrenched by the late 1970s and stood to benefit from newly defined ecodevelopment. Of Ecuador's 12 national parks and reserves, nine were created after 1969 (IUCN, 1985). Tourism thus came to be regarded not only as a means of financing parks and nature areas, but also as a viable source of economic development at all levels of society. Large travel agencies and capital city facilities, usually located in Quito or San José, were the main beneficiaries of these defined priorities. Employment of tour guides and bus drivers was also conducted, for the most part, in the capital city. This is true today as well, although the definition of economic development has been broadened to include a realization that benefits should accrue at the rural level as well.

Institutional Collaboration

National responsiveness

At the national level both Costa Rica and Ecuador have 'tourist incentive laws' designed to encourage general tourism through, for example, tax benefits such as accelerated depreciation on imported vehicles, computers and other items used by those within the tourism industry (hotels, tour operators and so on) (Laarman, 1986). Yet, for the environmental priority to be successfully meshed with tourism, governmental bodies must not make what are perceived at the community level to be unilateral decisions made at the top. If such a situation exists then, for example, poaching of natural resources within the park boundaries may very well continue despite park ranger attempts to stop it. Also, if the level of economic development surrounding the parks stagnates, locals may come to regard the neighboring nature area as an unwelcome nuisance to their community.

National-level responsiveness to local concerns is perhaps one of the most critical elements in maintaining a balance between conserving nature and meeting the needs of residents living near the parks. In his study for the World Resources Institute, Lindberg notes that 'developing an efficient, equitable and sustainable channeling mechanism is difficult and very site-specific' (Lindberg, 1991, p. 25). While balanced ecotourist development may be difficult, the problems are not insurmountable. Policymakers in Latin America can also glean useful information from the way other countries with an older ecotourist tradition handle their problems. Two of the best documented examples to learn from are the Parc des Volcans in Rwanda and Amboseli

National Park in Kenya. Amboseli is, as Lindberg notes, perhaps one of the best examples of 'conservation justified by nature tourism' (Lindberg, 1991, p. 6). Economic analysts calculate the 'visitor attraction' worth of each Amboseli lion to be $27 000 annually and that of one elephant herd to be $610 000 (Lindberg, 1991). While tourism is Kenya's primary foreign currency earner, locals living near the park felt they were ignored by the Kenyan government. To alleviate the problem, the government now provides fiscal incentives to communities by ensuring that local goods, services and local labor are used by the tourism industry whenever possible. Visitors to game lodges are also charged an extra tax that is allocated to the local communities (Olindo, 1991). Rwanda's Parc des Volcans is the home of the mountain gorilla. The park generates approximately $1 million annually from entrance fees alone and now enjoys the support of locals. Two surveys of residents around the park revealed a gradual realization that the park is a benefit locally, regionally and nationally.[1] Longitudinal surveys of area villagers residing near parks in Latin American countries would also be helpful to policymakers in gauging local satisfaction levels vis-à-vis the parks.

For the economic priority to be a success, generation of tourist revenue must be felt at the local level. It must not remain primarily in the capital city. This is especially true in a small country like Costa Rica, where many parks, such as Carara, Irazú, Poas or Manuel Antonio, can be visited in one day without the tourist ever checking out of his/her San José hotel room. Of course, the Galapagos Islands in Ecuador present a different situation. Tourists going to the islands often stop on the mainland long enough to rest in Quito or Guayaquil and then normally proceed to take a cruise ship to the islands. Opportunities for spending money on the mainland are thus limited to overnight stays in either of Ecuador's two largest cities, Guayaquil and Quito.

When analyzing the governmental role in tourist policy, Richter reminds us that the 'problem of control is particularly acute in developing nations where so many possess so little, including political clout' (Richter, 1989, p. 190). Thus national-level policies regarding either conservation or tourism will tend to be influenced by the most well connected private advocates and representatives of influential logging, banana, petroleum or large travel agency interests. The problem of responsiveness to local interests as national policies are formulated is made more acute in Ecuador, with its lower socioeconomic level than Costa Rica's. Ecuador's per capita GNP is placed at $990 (1990 dollars) while Costa Rica's is $1900 (1990 dollars). The literacy level for Ecuador is roughly 86 per cent, while Costa Rica's is 93 per cent (World Bank, 1992). To further aggravate national-level and regional or local tensions in Ecuador, there is the cultural/linguistic gap between Spanish-speaking policymakers and the non-Spanish-speaking indigenous, rural communities often found near nature areas. Costa Rica's rural communities, even in the most remote areas, do not suffer from a high degree of linguistic or cultural dissimilation and are, consequently, better prepared to deal with national, and even international, level leaders in both the private and public sectors.

Grassroots activity

The success of Mauricio Salazar, a Bribri Indian, in publicizing ecotourism at both the national and international levels provides testimony to the level of resourcefulness to be found among Costa Rican rural communities adjacent to nature areas. Salazar heads the Talamanca Association for Ecotourism and Conservation (ATEC) located in the south-eastern Costa Rican town of Puerto Viejo. Using ecotourism as a development vehicle, residents of the area are trying to capitalize on their proximity to Cahuita National Park, the Bribri Indian Reservation and Gandoca-Manzanillo Wildlife Refuge. Salazar is also owner of the private nature reserve, Cabinas Chimuri.

Because of the Caribbean influence on the Atlantic coast, Salazar's knowledge of English affords him the ability to make contact with funding sources at the international level. This Caribbean English connection might also prove useful in creating an alliance between environmental and ecotourist interests in one of Nicaragua's least developed areas, Zelaya Province. According to Ray Hooker, the Nicaraguan National Assembly representative from Zelaya Province, some residents of this rainforested area are concerned about what they consider to be excessive concessions granted to Asian logging interests by the Chamorro government (Hooker, 1992), yet little environmental concern has been voiced at the international level by such groups as Conservation International or the World Wildlife Fund.

While on a recent fund-raising trip to the US sponsored by the Sierra Club, Salazar explained ATEC's philosophy. Put simply, the group wishes to (1) derive benefits for locals who are displaced by national conservation efforts in the area; and (2) slow the sale of private rainforest land to banana companies who will, in turn, deforest it (Salazar, 1992). ATEC works under the assumption that local knowledge needs to be tapped and that a balance must be struck between large tourism investors represented in San José and small ones represented by residents around Puerto Viejo. ATEC organizes locals to give ecotours on bird watching, medicinal plants and local culture and is currently conducting a tour guide training program for 15 locals. The group recognizes that it can offer 'rustic' tours provided with local English-speaking guides. ATEC also offers environmental education on local flora and fauna, pesticide use and problems associated with visitors, such as disposal of plastic garbage. A booklet in English, entitled *Welcome to Coastal Talamanca*, is also published by ATEC.

What ATEC represents is a grassroots, non-profit effort with economic development proposals that are often regarded as 'too small' to be of interest at the national level (Salazar, 1992). Such proposals stress micro enterprise-type development which is ideally suited to locales where larger tourist endeavors are unprofitable. Nevertheless ATEC is well known in national circles and an ATEC member sits on the board of the Eco Institute, a San José-headquartered think tank described in the following section.

Private–public sector alliance

The non-profit Eco Institute of Costa Rica was formed in 1991 and has as its president Maurice Strong. Strong is best known for organizing the 1992 United Nations Conference on Environment and Development, held in Rio de Janeiro. The Institute includes government officials, private developers, community activists, environmentalists and tourist industry representatives. The group is unique to Costa Rica in that, for the first time, both public and private interests from all levels – national and local, large and small – meet to exchange ideas on enhancing sustainable tourist development. On an international scale, the group hopes to have Costa Rica's tourism policy serve as a model for other Latin American countries. The institute hopes to influence government policies, represent community and conservation interests, coordinate appropriate development projects, mitigate negative aspects of tourism, include marginal groups in decision making and profit sharing, and improve the tourism profile of Central America (Eco Institute of Costa Rica, 1991).

This group is consciously trying to preserve the natural environment through the 'controlled use of tourism'. It represents an important effort to achieve needed collaboration among various interests and levels in order to avoid having Costa Rica become an 'environmental theme park' (ibid.). Eco Institute members are undoubtedly reminded of Mexico's sun and surf tourism policy and the creation of Miami beach-style hotels lining Aculpulco and Puerta Vallarta shores. While such hotels may generate revenue, they certainly do not mesh well with environmentalists' interests. Evans-Pritchard, Eco Institute's director, notes that one goal of the group is to encourage planning so that most of the country is not sold to foreigners (Evans-Pritchard, 1992). This is a very real concern. Ironically the opposite would appear to be the case if one views investment video tapes distributed by the Costa Rican government. These tapes aimed at American investors clearly reveal that the Costa Rican government still wants to attract large-scale hotel chains to build along pristine beaches, despite its attention to ecotourism.

Public–private ventures also exist in Ecuador, where the Fundación Ecuatoriana de Promoción Turística (FEPROTUR) was established as a public–private collaborative effort to plan and promote tourism. What appears at first glance to be a national tourism board comprised of tourist industry and government representatives, could end up being dominated by the country's largest travel agency, Metropolitan Touring. Should this happen, small-scale efforts originating in communities near nature areas may find their voices drawned out by an agency with offices throughout Ecuador and the USA. Nevertheless FEPROTUR benefits from USAID financial assistance in its efforts. Metropolitan Touring was also instrumental in establishing the Ecuadorian Foundation for Conservation and Sustainable Development (FECODES). This non-profit organization is devoted to research, environmental education and the preservation of natural resources. A scientific station is planned and a strategy of developing 'safe tourism patterns' will be encouraged (Garcia, 1991).

Another public–private endeavor is the Ecuadorian Tourism Corporation (ETC) which helped draft a new protection plan for the Galapagos Islands. A victim of its own success, the Galapagos has seen the number of tourists increase from 25 000 in 1981 to approximately 60 000 in 1989 (Smith, 1990–1). With the introduction of non-native species observed on the islands, as well as pollution stemming from 'tourist overload', the ETC urged strict controls on economic activities within the Galapagos. A long-range goal is to welcome only educational tourism, rather than leisure tourism, to the islands.

Despite various efforts at public–private collaboration, Laarman reminds us that 'in neither Costa Rica nor Ecuador does there appear to be a strong working relationship between the government and the private sector in the tourist industry' (Laarman, 1986, p. 16). This dilemma is likely caused in part by heavy Latin American government central-ization in which the private sector played little or no formal role in mechanisms such as policy boards. Rather private-sector influence tended traditionally to arise in informal, one-on-one relations between a busi-ness, especially a family-run one, and government officials. Thus bringing together public and private representatives may not result in immedi-ate and well coordinated proposals that might be hoped for by ob-servers in the US.

Governmental Responsiveness to Infrastructure Needs

Infrastructure needs include those both in the nature parks and in the surrounding community. In a survey conducted by the World Wildlife Fund, ecotourists to Costa Rican parks were asked how their visit could be improved. A majority of respondents cited more technical informa-tion, guide books, promotional materials, maps, transportation and signs (Boo, 1990, 45). While it exists, such material is inadequate for a country that is trying to make itself the center of ecotourism in Latin America. Information and maps are often printed in Spanish only and, while park rangers can be extremely helpful, few are bilingual.

Ecotourists are known to be less demanding of creature comforts and even expect some degree of primitive infrastructure. For example, the narrow estuary at the entrance to Manuel Antonio National Park does not appear to deter tourists. Getting one's feet wet becomes part of the nature trip. However even the hardiest of ecotourists cannot come in steady or greater numbers if roads are inadequate or seasonally im-passable. Likewise poor communications and lack of continuous elec-trical supply can also prevent ecotourism from becoming a serious alternative source of income for locals. Lefever points out that, in the case of Tortuguero, Costa Rica, round-the-clock electricity was not achieved until 1986, while the village's first – and only – telephone was not installed until 1972 (Lefever, 1992). While nearby Tortuguero National Park awaits tourists anxious to see the highly publicized green and leatherback turtles nesting on the beach, the main obstacle re-mains getting to the park.

Following the earthquake of April 1991 the famous Jungle Train, which linked the capital to the Caribbean coastal city of Limon, was destroyed. Damaged tracks have yet to be repaired and serve as a vivid reminder to ecotourist advocates that sustainable ecotourist de-velopment is not as simple as it sounds. For ecotourism to work, govern-mental outlays for building roads, installing electricity and other amenities in and around national parks must be realistically assessed.

Ecomanagement

Managing the tourists as well as the flora and fauna is a large undertaking. Will success and high visitor rates to fragile and underfunded national parks damage the very ecosystem they were designed to protect? How many tourists are too many? Park carrying capacity needs to be calculated and potential damage to flora and fauna assessed. Boo reminds us that such knowledge is currently lacking in many Latin American parks and that environmental damage is usually assessed through casual observation, rather than through scientific investigation.

One of the advantages of ecotourism versus the sun and surf variety is that ecotourists are less demanding of high-quality or luxurious accommodation. The small local hotel or pension will often do just fine for such a traveller, as will the small, local restaurant. The many small hotels/pensions adjacent to the Monteverde Cloud Forest Preserve in Costa Rica attest to the fact that tourists are willing to stay in very modest, but clean, lodgings. However, while ecotourists are a hardy bunch, too many of them can overwhelm understaffed parks, causing trail degradation, litter problems and general depreciation of the facility. Let us not forget that their proliferation may in turn drive the very animals they came to see farther into the rain forest. Heavily 'promoted' animals such as the three-toed sloth in Manuel Antonio National Park (Costa Rica) or spider monkeys in Carara Biological Reserve (Costa Rica) are not always visible to the ecotourist, as this author readily discovered.

Lack of attention to general park maintenance can result in negative conditions which may provoke a downturn of the tourist 'life cycle'. This means that nature travel will continue to increase as it is currently doing in both Ecuador and Costa Rica, but should fall off as these destinations become overcrowded (Lindberg, 1991; Choy, 1992). As more tourists visit an area, it risks being labelled 'overrated' which drives off naturalists who will then search for a more pristine location for their next trip. Fickle behavior on the part of tourists is well known and must be factored into any development plan. Of course, as many Costa Ricans are quick to point out, coffee and banana prices are not faring so well either, fluctuating downwards.

User fees as revenue

One way to curb excessive visitor numbers to parks is through raising user fees. We are reminded that the high user fee of $180 in Parc des Volcans, Rwanda enables tourists a glimpse of mountain gorillas for visits of up to three days. Through high user fees, park management can collect more money from fewer people. Because of the obvious disparity in disposable income between foreign tourists and their national counterparts, sliding-scale user fees are in effect for Ecuador and Costa Rica.

While Ecuador collects a substantial $80 from foreign tourists visiting the Galapagos, Costa Rican park fees are still quite low for foreigners, falling in the $0.75–$1 range (Rachowiecki, 1991, 1992). Costa Rican policy currently reflects a fear that raising fees would drive tourists away from what government officials believe is an already expensive destination for North American tourists, who account for most of that country's visitors (Evans-Pritchard, 1992). However user fees for private parks such as Monteverde reflect the belief that visitor numbers need to be controlled while revenue is maintained. For this reason the preserve imposes a $10 user fee in addition to the $10 entrance fee for each foreign visitor travelling with an organized tour group.

User fees revenue generated from highly successful parks such as the Galapagos tend to be much greater than those less of popular parks, such as Pichincha or Cotopaxi. Of the 75 per cent of respondents to a World Wildlife Fund survey who visited Ecuadorian parks, 90 per cent visited no other Ecuadorian park than the Galapagos Islands (Boo, 1990). A portion of the Galapagos fees, totalling some $560 000 annually, then go to support Ecuador's 14 other parks which together only account for $40 000 in fees (Lindberg, 1991). While seemingly unfavorable to the Galapagos, this system permits funding of other important, but less visited, areas of environmental interest in Ecuador.

The problem of Ecuador's lopsided notoriety of having but one park, the Galapagos, can be alleviated through increased promotion of tourism to mainland Ecuador. In particular, foreign ecotourist excursion groups might be persuaded to alter their 'Galapagos only' approach and include other natural parks in Ecuador as well. According to Garcia, director of the Ecotourism Department for Metropolitan Touring, the company has, for example, initiated an extensive new Amazon excursion in the Aguarico River Region (Garcia, 1991).

In addition to user fees, highly frequented parks might generate added revenue through small, on-site restaurant and gift shop concessions. Few such facilities exist in either Costa Rica or Ecuador largely because such endeavors are feared to be unprofitable. Poas Volcano Park, popular among Costa Rican tourists, is one of the few parks able to support such facilities.

International financial assistance

A host of conservation organizations work to preserve Latin America's endangered areas. 'Debt for Nature Swaps' in Costa Rica and Ecuador are well known and worldwide environmental groups are busy working to raise money to purchase more land for park use. Ecuador's Fundación Natura, with assistance from the World Wildlife Fund, is currently involved in such a debt for nature swap which focuses on Sangay National Park, Yasuni National Park and Cotocachi-Cayapas Reserve (McNeely *et al.*, 1990).

Costa Rican efforts at obtaining financial assistance have been very successful and garnered more publicity valuable to ecotourism than similar efforts in Ecuador. Its closer proximity to the United States, pleasant lifestyle and politically stable government attracts not only tourists, but also scientists and conservation organizations. Monteverde Cloud Forest Preserve is one example of good ecomanagement that appears to have achieved an adequate balance between conserving the environment, handling tourism and obtaining adequate funds. Visitors to the preserve increased from 300 in 1973, one year after its creation, to 15 000 in 1989. Rovinski notes that the preserve also increased in size from 2000 to 10 000 hectares by 1990 (Rovinski, 1991). Acquiring more land permits greater leeway in designing park carrying capacities and enables rainforest fauna greater mobility because they are not confined to areas subject to heavy tourism. Some land problems caused by squatters near the preserve were alleviated when the Monteverde Conservation League, created in 1986, conducted a successful fundraising effort and obtained the support of the World Wildlife Fund (WWF). With WWF assistance, the League created a program to sell 'honorary deeds' to the preserve at $25 an acre. These deeds are, in fact, tax-deductible donations which League environmentalists use to buy out squatters who still benefit from Costa Rica's lax homestead laws. More than $360 000 was raised in this effort and 14 000 acres were preserved as forest (Dwyer, 1988).

Buying more land for forest preservation is an expensive undertaking and instances abound of cash-poor countries such as Costa Rica benefiting from private foreign conservation assistance. Guanacaste National Park, established in 1989, also took advantage of a large grant from the John D. and Catherine T. MacArthur Foundation to buy land from local farmers. The Guanacaste land purchase falls under the administration of the Fundación Neotropica, a non-governmental organization that works closely with the government to create a

national conservation plan (Cahn and Cahn, 1987). However credit
for generation of international publicity for Guanacaste National Park
goes to Daniel Janzen, a University of Pennsylvania biology professor,
who has acquired a Harrison Ford image akin to the adventurous professor in 'Raiders of the Lost Ark'. This image has enabled Janzen to
tell the Guanacaste story not only to scientific journals, but also to
Time and *Newsweek*. Such publicity is invaluable for Guanacaste's
fundraising efforts and for ecotourist development of the region.

The nuts and bolts of ecomanagement for tourism and the national
park systems in Latin America really come down to the issue of money.
Trained personnel exist who in turn can train others, so that lack of
expertise is not a major problem in most Latin American countries,
but building more park visitor centers, printing materials, and improving ranger training and salaries all require funding. How to raise and
allocate it thus becomes a crucial aspect of ecomanagement. International efforts serve to complement government means such as collecting special taxes destined in part for park management. For example,
Costa Rican legislation specifies that a portion of certain fiscal stamps
required for municipal level legal documents, passports, initial automobile registration and operating licenses for establishments serving
liquor must go into a Conservation Fund (McNeely *et al.*, 1990). Despite these efforts, Costa Rica's large national park system – the drawing
card for its ecotourist industry – is maintained on a meager budget of
around $1 million annually (Laarman, 1986).

Conservation Education/Awareness

Both private groups and the government recognize that conservation
education is a vital component of maintaining a proper balance between ecotourism and the environment. Much of this education effort
is naturally aimed at Costa Ricans or Ecuadorians and is designed to
instill an appreciation of the flora and fauna of their own countries.

Today's environmentalists, such as Janzen, hope to build a long-
term or permanent education component into parks such as Guanacaste,
which is designed to be a functioning part of the school system and
ecology and natural history are actually taught in the park. It is hoped
that thousands of schoolchildren will benefit from the program. Janzen
reminds us that it is these very children who will be the future park
managers, mayors and businesspeople (Allen, 1988). The rationale is
simple: it will pay to have these future decision-makers on the side of
conservation.

Conservation education is varied and derives from many sources. In Ecuador the Fundación Natura seeks to improve conservation education in the Pasochoa Forest Reserve, which it manages, by providing educational material to park visitors. Since 80 per cent of park visitors are Ecuadorian, the local population stands to benefit from this effort (Boo, 1990). In general, however, printed material is often in short supply and/or in Spanish only. Of five Costa Rican parks visited by this author in 1991, only in the privately owned Monteverde Park was material available in both Spanish and English. None was provided at Carara or Irazu Volcano, while a map/brochure in Spanish only was provided at Manuel Antonio National Park.

Such material should be regarded as possessing a dual benefit. When acquired by foreign ecotourists it can (1) increase knowledge and appreciation of the specific flora and fauna of a given country; and (2) act as a 'publicity pieces' that is carried back to the ecotourist's home country. The first will help to create a positive experience for the ecotourist and encourage that individual to recommend the trip to others. For the second, word of mouth would be reinforced by the printed material, which would take on the role of advertising. Park management should reassess the cost of producing such material with these benefits in mind.

Desired Outcomes

The ecotourist–environmental collaboration is today just beginning to be refined. It owes its viability to the fact that each can serve the needs of the other. The Costa Rican Tourist Board (ICT) identified nature tourism as one of five tourism types to be developed: (1) nature tourism, (2) adventure tourism, (3) sun and surf tourism, (4) cruise ship tourism, and (5) convention/business tourism. However defining an ecotourist so that he/she can be exploited by the travel industry is not as simple as merely making categories. Most travel experts agree that travellers often 'cross over' from one category to the next within the same trip (Ziffer, 1989). This means that creation of an 'environmentally conscious' image for a country can have a highly desirable spillover effect. The cruise ship passenger visiting Carara Biological Reserve or the business traveller taking a day trip to Manuel Antonio Park become ecotourists by default if their primary objective for that day is to see and learn about nature contained in a given park. This image is currently winning much publicity for Costa Rica, both at home and abroad.

On the other hand, apart from the Galapagos Islands, Ecuador is still lacking in overall ecological image as an ecotourist destination. Perhaps the positive contribution of conservationists and biologists in the 1960s and 1970s which played such an important role in putting Costa Rica on the tourist map should become a major focus in the development of Ecuador's mainland ecotourist trade. Once mapped out by ecologists and biologists, publicity for the nature area under study usually follows close on the heels of these scientific adventurers. Journalists, after all, love an adventure story for their columns.

Government and businesspersons, both large and small, have been quick to jump on the ecotourist bandwagon in countries like Costa Rica.[2] Small success stories, such as the Monteverde Craft Shop founded as a cooperative endeavor in 1982, abound. The 'coop', Cooperativo de Artesanos de Santa Elena y Monteverde, now has 70 members and annual sales totaling approximately $50 000 (Boo, 1990). In addition, there is the for-profit nature area, Rara Avis, located at the edge of Braulio Carrillo National Park (Costa Rica) that, according to Rovinski, contributes some $80 000 to the surrounding community of Horquetas. This makes ecotourism one of the most importance sources of income and employment for the community (Rovinski, 1991).

Financial success stories resulting from nature tourism at the local level can certainly foster a more harmonious relationship between locals, park officials, scientists and the government. This makes the task of conservation a little easier and can create 'green' allies in the community when the political need arises. Given the ever-present threat of deforestation, especially by banana interests in Costa Rica, the need to unite becomes very pertinent. For ecotourism to become a viable, long-term and sustainable contributor to both the national and local economies of a nation, it must be recognized, not as an economic panacea, but as one more link in the economic diversification game.

Notes

1. The survey of residents living near Rwanda's Parc des Volcans produced the following results.

National benefit	Percentage of respondents	
	1979	*1984*
Yes	65	85
No	11	5

Regional benefit

Yes	39	81
No	50	11

Personal/local benefit

Yes	26	49
No	72	50

Source: Lindberg (1991, p. 26).

2. It is useful to note that the purpose of national parks and reserves is, first and foremost, the preservation of flora and fauna. Blower reminds us that developing countries that are short of foreign currency may come to consider these areas for their economic value. When this happens, the fear arises that decision makers and planners may pursue more profitable land use ventures in the future, should the tourist value not live up to expectations (Blower, 1984).

References

ALLEN, WILLIAM H. (1988) 'Biocultural restoration of a tropical forest', *Bioscience*, vol. 38, no. 3, pp. 156–61.

BLOWER, JOHN (1984) 'National Parks for Developing Countries', in J.A. McNeely and K.R. Miller (eds), *National Parks, Conservation, and Development: The Role of Protected Areas in Sustaining Society* (Washington, DC: Smithsonian Institution Press).

BOO, ELIZABETH (1990) *Ecotourism: The Potentials and Pitfalls*, vols I and II (Washington, DC: World Wildlife Fund).

CAHN, PATRICIA and ROBERT CAHN (1987) 'Costa Rica: Coast of Riches', *National Parks*, vol. 67 (September–October) pp. 18–20.

CEBALLOS-LASCURAIN, HECTOR (1988) 'The Future of Ecotourism', *Mexico Journal*, 17 January, pp. 13–14.

CHOY, DEXTER J.L. (1992) 'Life Cycle Models for Pacific Island Destinations', *Journal of Travel Research*, vol. 30, no. 3, pp. 26–31.

DWYER, VICTOR (1988) 'Cheap conservation at $25 an acre', *Maclean's*, vol. 101, no. 15, p. 52.

ECO INSTITUTE OF COSTA RICA (1991) 'Costa Rica Think Tank Starts First Sustainable Tourism Initiative', press release, November.

EUROPA WORLD YEAR BOOK/I (1992) (London: Europa Publications Ltd).

EVANS-PRITCHARD, DIEDRE (1992) interview conducted 17 August.

GARCIA, MARCO (1991) 'Ecotourism Development Project of Metropolitan Touring in the Ecuadorian Amazon', paper presented at the 1991 World Congress on Adventure Travel and Ecotourism held on 28–31 August Colorado Springs, CO.

HOOKER, RAY (1992) personal communication, 17 August.

INTERNATIONAL UNION FOR CONSERVATION OF NATURE AND NATURAL RESOURCES (IUCN) (1985) *United Nations List of National*

Parks and Protected Areas (Gland, Switzerland: IUCN).

LAARMAN, JAN G. (1986) 'Nature-Oriented Tourism in Costa Rica and Ecuador: Diagnosis of Research Needs and Project Opportunities', FPEI Working Paper (Raleigh, NC: North Carolina State University).

LEFEVER, HARRY (1992) *Turtle Bogue: Afro-Caribbean Life and Culture in a Costa Rican Village* (Selingsgrove, PA: Susquehanna University Press).

LINDBERG, KREG (1991) *Policies For Maximizing Nature Tourism's Ecological And Economic Benefits* (Washington, DC: World Resources Institute).

McNEELY, J.A., K.R. MILLER, W.V. REID, R.A. MITTERMEIER and T.B. WERNER (1990) *Conserving the World's Biological Diversity* (Gland, Switzerland: IUCN).

MYERS, N. (1988) 'Threatened biotas: "hotspots" in tropical forests', *Environmentalist*, vol. 8, no. 3, pp. 1–20.

OLINDO, PEREZ (1991) 'The Old Man of Nature Tourism: Kenya', in Tensie Whelan (ed.), *Nature Tourism: Managing for the Environment* (Washington, DC: Island Press).

RACHOWIECKI, ROB (1991) *Costa Rica* (Berkeley, CA: Lonely Planet Publications).

RACHOWIECKI, ROB (1992) *Ecuador and the Galapagos Islands* (Berkeley, CA: Lonely Planet Publications).

RICHTER, LINDA K. (1989) *The Politics of Tourism in Asia* (Honolulu: University of Hawaii Press).

ROVINSKI, YANINA (1991) 'Private Reserves, Parks, and Ecotourism in Costa Rica', in Tensie Whelan (ed.), *Nature Tourism: Managing for the Environment* (Washington, DC: Island Press).

SALAZAR, MAURICIO (1992) interview conducted 13 May.

SMITH, GERI (1990–1) 'A New Species of Tourist', *Americas*, vol. 42, no. 6, pp. 17–20.

TANGLEY, LAURA (1988) 'Studying (and saving) the tropics', *Bioscience*, vol. 38 (June), pp. 375–85.

WHELAN, TENSIE (1987) 'Conservation Means $$ in "Nature Tourism"', *The Tico Times*, 23 October, p. 11.

WHELAN, TENSIE (1991) 'Ecotourism and its Role in Sustainable Development', in Tensie Whelan (ed.), *Nature Tourism: Managing for the Environment* (Washington, DC: Island Press).

WILSON, MYSTIE (1987) 'Nature Oriented Tourism in Ecuador: Assessment of Industry Structure and Development Needs', FPEI Working Paper No. 20 (Raleigh, NC: North Carolina State University).

WORLD BANK (1992) *World Development Report 1992: Development and the Environment* (New York: Oxford University Press).

WORLD COMMISSION ON ENVIRONMENT AND DEVELOPMENT (1987) *Our Common Future* (New York: Oxford University Press).

WORLD TOURISM ORGANIZATION (1989) *Yearbook of Tourism Statistics/I & II* (Madrid: World Tourism Organization).

ZIFFER, KAREN A. (1989) 'Ecotourism: The Uneasy Alliance', Working Papers (Washington, DC: Conservation International).

Part IV

Political Policy

8 Beyond the Party List: Electoral Reform in Venezuela

José Molina

In 1984, pressure for state reform became quite strong in Venezuela. One of the main goals of this movement towards reform was the modification of the electoral system. The objective was to increase the power of selection and control by the citizens over their representatives, *vis-à-vis* the parties. Venezuela had, for the election of all legislative institutions (the two chambers of Congress, state legislative assemblies and municipal councils), a system of closed list proportional representation (Molina, 1986a, p. 25, 1986b, pp. 163–70). Under this system the voter chose a party list but could not alter the rank order of the candidates. Thus the voters decided only how many seats each party would hold, but not which individuals would receive them. It was a system conducive to party accountability, but not to individual accountability of the representatives to the voters. The goal of the movement for electoral reform was personalized voting and individual accountability as a way to increase responsiveness. It was thought that closed list voting was an important factor in the low level of responsiveness and accountability of Venezuelan politicians in general.

The increasingly strong urban neighborhood associations, a score of intellectuals and a sizeable number of politicians joined forces to call for electoral reform. When President Lusinchi established a multi-party Presidential Committee for State Reform in December 1984, modification of the electoral rules was one of its main assignments, along with the process of decentralization, undoubtedly linked to the former, as will be seen. From that time onwards the debate on electoral reform proliferated. There were scores of panels, seminars and debates on the subject. The Supreme Electoral Council presented a document to Congress analyzing the pros and cons of the proposed alternatives to the existing system (plurality in single-member districts, preference voting and German-style personalized proportional representation) (Consejo Supremo Electoral, 1987). The Presidential Committee for

165

State Reform organized several meetings with the political parties and the social organizations involved, looking for a consensus. However this was not yet reached at the time Congress began discussions on the matter. Acción Democrática (the largest party), having defended preferential voting, became a supporter of single-member plurality, particularly at the local level. The MAS (Movement Towards Socialism) supported preferential voting within proportional representation; and COPEI (the Christian Democrats, Venezuela's second largest party) put forward a bill that proposed adopting the German system of personalized proportional representation. The bill presented by Acción Democrática, with the proposal to switch to single-member plurality for local elections, was approved by the Lower Chamber, but rejected narrowly in the Senate by the votes of COPEI, MAS and one independent. After that, the parties reached a compromise, and Congress passed a reform of the Electoral Act in September of 1989. The new Act maintained the previous system for the election of the Senate (pure list proportional representation without preference voting), adopted the German-style personalized proportional representation for the lower house of Congress and for the state legislative assemblies, and preference voting with panachage for local elections. The new system for both the Lower Chamber of Congress and the legislative assemblies takes effect in December 1993. Local elections were held using preference voting with panachage in December 1989. In addition to these modifications aimed at improving accountability, there were other innovations made in 1988 and 1989 affecting the system of registration, proportionality, frequency of local and state level elections, and the direct election of mayors and governors, the latter as the centerpiece of the process of decentralization and refurbishing of the Venezuelan federal system.

This chapter will describe the reforms of 1988 and 1989 and suggest their probable consequences for the Venezuelan political system. It will also evaluate their fitness in terms of fulfilling their stated objective of increasing accountability. In the case of preference voting for local elections, the assessment will be made on the basis of its performance in December 1989.

PERSONALIZED PROPORTIONAL REPRESENTATION

This system has its origins in Germany, where it has been used for the election of members of the Bundestag since 1949 (Sasse, 1979,

p. 83).[1] The German model can be described briefly as a system of proportional representation that incorporates, secondarily, single-member constituencies, in order to obtain a personal link between a single representative and his constituency, in the single-member seats (Nohlen, 1981, p. 519, 1984, pp. 147–52; Neuber and Akalin, 1986; Kaase, 1984).[2]

This chapter will describe the system as it has been adopted in Venezuela, as well as considering the effects it is likely to have, once it enters into operation in December 1993, for the Lower Chamber of Congress and the legislative assemblies.

Personalized Proportional Representation in Venezuela

For the purposes of describing the system, the Chamber of Deputies will be used as a model. However it should be kept in mind that the system will also be applied to the legislative assemblies where constituency magnitude (M) is usually greater,[3] but where there are no compensatory additional members allocated nationwide.

For the elections in the Lower Chamber of Congress there are 23 constituencies.[4] The number of seats for each of these is proportional to their population, except that the federal territory elects one deputy in any case, and no state may have less than two seats. The total population of each constituency is divided by a quota, which is set at 0.55 per cent of the population of the country. The number resulting from this division is the number of seats each constituency has for this first round allocation of seats. If in this calculation there is a remainder larger than half the quota, another seat is given to the constituency. This procedure leads to a total number of seats very close to 182,[5] and an average magnitude of eight. The additional seats allocated at the national level increase the total members of the Lower Chamber to around 200.

In those constituencies with a seat magnitude (M) of three or more, the reform states that half of the seats must be elected in single-member districts by plurality. If M is an uneven number, then the number of single-member districts to be drawn is M divided by two, plus one. The single-member districts are to be drawn by the Supreme Electoral Council at least nine months before the election date, keeping them within the boundaries of each constituency. The districts must be drawn in such a way that their population does not vary more than 15 per cent in either direction from the figure obtained by dividing the total population of the whole constituency by the number of single-member districts.

Each party will propose a slate of candidates for the whole constituency. This list may have as many candidates as four times the number of seats of the constituency.[6] In addition each party can nominate one candidate for each of the single-member districts. These candidates may or may not appear in the general party list for the constituency; in Germany they usually do. Voters have two votes. They can vote for a party ticket and also for one of the candidates in the single-member district where they are registered. They can vote for the list of one party and for the single district candidate of another. The lists are closed lists without preference voting or panachage. In this way the Venezuelan system is similar to its German model.

Once the votes are counted, and the winners of the single-member districts known, the proportional allocation of seats takes place. Unlike the use of Germany, this is done at the constituency level. On the basis of the list vote of each party, the seats are distributed by the D'Hondt formula. All the seats of the constituency are distributed in this way. The seats corresponding to each party are first given to the single-member district winners of that party; if the party still has a right to more seats, these are given to the candidates nominated on the list according to numerical order. As in Germany, if any party wins more single district seats than proportional mandates, it keeps the extra seats. The elected deputies also have substitutes. These are the non-elected candidates from the list, in a number equal to three times the number of seats gained by the organization, and in the order established by the party list.[7]

In the way described above, the number of seats won by each organization in the various federal entities, and the occupants thereof, will be determined. To compensate for the distortion of proportionality that characterizes the D'Hondt formula in medium-sized constituencies, Venezuela has a system of additional seats distributed at national level. This was maintained, with a slight modification that will be dealt with later.

Political Consequences of Personalized Proportional Representation in Venezuela

On the power of selection and control by the citizens over their representatives

The system is not suitable for achieving the main goal of the electoral reform, which is to increase significantly the power of selection of the elector *vis-à-vis* the party list, and also the accountability of the representatives. This is because, in this type of system, the voter is not able to modify the nominations presented by the parties. As in a pure list system, the voter will decide how many seats a party will hold, but the names of those occupying them will depend almost completely on the party's internal nomination procedure. This is obviously true of the closed lists which control half of the seats. But it is also true of the single-member districts. Certainly the voter could split his vote, which, while it may hurt the overall chances of the party that does not receive the list vote, does not modify its list order. The German experience shows that very few people (10 per cent) split their votes (Nohlen, 1984, p. 149).

It is possible that the single-district vote may result in the election of party candidates who were not on the party list, or that ranked very low on it, so that they would not have been elected under the previous pure closed-list system. However the parties may avoid this nuisance by locating their high-ranking list candidates in districts where the odds are more favorable. In fact the German experience again shows that this tends to happen, and that the single-member seats do not lead to the modification by the electorate of the nomination wishes of the party. One can expect, therefore, that the number of representatives elected in single-member districts that would not have also received a seat on the party list will be minimal. This means that the probable number of displacements will be low. Displacement occurs when a candidate is elected who would not have won on the basis of the party list order. In the case of personalized proportional representation, displacement takes place when an elected single-member district candidate was not among the party list nominees who would have been elected if the party had not won any single district in the constituency (Katz, 1986, p. 97).[8] Our hypothesis, to be tested when the system is first applied in 1993, is that the displacements, taken as a percentage of the total seats elected in the country, will be lower than those that occur at local level with panachage in 1989. If this hypothesis holds true then it would follow that the latter increases the selection power of the voter and candidate accountability more than the former in Venezuela; and thus would be more adequate to attain the main goal of the electoral reform process.

The rise of the constituency-minded representative

Personalized proportional representation is likely to lead to a new relationship between those elected in single-member districts and their constituents. It may result in the development of a type of constituency-minded politician, similar to that common in countries using single-member districts as the basis of their electoral system. This may be the most positive aspect of the new system. However the fact that re-election will continue to depend heavily on the closed list system may hinder this development, as will the Venezuelan tradition of representatives being more dedicated to general issues than to attending the specific problems of their constituents.

On the party structure

The new system may encourage party decentralization. This could occur if the single-member district becomes the main focus of attention for the electorate, and if the candidates for them are chosen locally. Otherwise the effect on the structure of parties will be minimal. Of course the situation may be different for each organization.

On proportionality

The system is likely to lower the proportionality of the Venezuelan electoral system (Molina, 1986). Given the homogeneity of the partisan distribution of votes within each federal entity that has characterized the country, it is very likely that the overall winner in the constituency will gain more single-member districts than the proportional seats it would have a right to. If this cumulates in favor of one or two parties it may give rise to a significant increase in the advantage that the previous system already accorded the main parties. This is particularly true for the state legislatures where there is no compensatory system of additional members, as there is at the national level. Even here, the compensatory effect of the additional seats will be dampened by the increased distortion of proportionality at the state level.

Also the system is vulnerable to a practice that, should it occur, would greatly affect the proportionality and even the legitimacy of the system (Rey, 1986). A party might put up a list but not formally support any single-member district candidates. At the same time an electoral group managed by the party could nominate for the single-member seats persons associated with it but who are not card-carrying members. In this situation the single-member seats won by that electoral group would not be subtracted from the mandates attained through the list vote. The party would thus fool the system and obtain a very large bonus.

Even if the second of the two situations mentioned never happens, the first is enough to give reason to fear an increase in disproportionality.

Such an increase could affect even the second largest party, and could facilitate manufactured majorities in Congress, at a time when public opinion is demanding greater control over the president.

Increased concentration of the vote

It has been suggested that the concentration of the votes in favor of the two main parties, which is characteristic of Germany despite its high proportionality, has been greatly influenced by the single-member districts (Taagepera and Shugart, 1989a, p. 55). This can be attributed to the psychological effect of plurality in single-member districts (Duverger, 1957) as it affects the list vote (Taagepera and Shugart, 1989a, p. 55), leading voters progressively to abandon parties that do not have a real chance of winning the single-seat election.

Shugart considers that, in Venezuela, personalized proportional representation will not lead to a transfer of the psychological effect from the single-member districts to the list vote; and that there will be more split voting than is usual in Germany (Shugart, 1991). The reason for this difference is that, in Germany, there is a parliamentary system, whereas Venezuela has a presidential one. According to this author, in Germany:

> If voters came to favor one of the large parties for the sake of what these parties could offer as district representatives, there would be little incentive to give the list ballot to another party, since the ability of the party preferred at the district level to form a government would be weakened by widespread ticket splitting. In Venezuela's presidential system, on the other hand, the incentives stemming from government formation will not be operative. Many voters may see good reason to maximize their own representation by voting for different parties, especially since the presidential system will allow candidates in the districts to tailor their messages for their districts, including openly seeking the support of voters who would give their list vote to another party (Shugart, 1991).

Shugart's point is interesting. However most of Venezuelan voters are not, up to now, split voters. Most of them vote the same party for president as for the legislative organs. Furthermore Venezuela has undergone a process of polarization of both the presidential and the parliamentary vote. The effective number of elective parties (Taagepera and Shugart, 1989b, p. 79) for the first democratic election was 2.94;

it rose in 1963 to 5.00, continuing to rise in 1968 to 6.25, and then dropped sharply to 3.44 in 1973, 3.12 in 1978, 3.03 in 1983 and 3.44 in 1988. A factor in this process of concentration has been the fact that the list vote for parliamentary elections is simultaneous with that of the presidency. The fact that the presidential election is the predominant one and the main focus of attention has not only made this plurality election a two-party contest, but has also transferred the concentration of the presidential vote to the congressional list vote. The concentration process that has occurred in the simultaneous presidential and parliamentary elections means that the Venezuelan voter has transferred the two-party concentration of the plurality dominant election to the proportional representation election, which is seen as subordinate. This is not only likely to occur again but, more precisely, to become strengthened, if the single-member district becomes the main focus of attention in the parliamentary elections. In fact the major parties will strongly advocate this. It is important to remember that congressional elections will continue to be held concurrently with that of the president.

On electoral procedure

The system is easy to manage. The only complication may appear in determining the area of the single-member districts. Gerrymandering is always a possibility in this type of system. However, as the single-member districts are not crucial for the distribution of seats, this temptation will not be as great as it is in plurality or majority systems. The problem may still appear if the voters come to regard the single-member district as the most important of their two parliamentary votes. This is particularly true if it tends to pull the list vote, or to become the touchstone of success or failure for politicians.

PANACHAGE PREFERENCE VOTING

Most of the European countries that have adopted proportional representation, and some in Latin America such as Peru and Brazil, give the voters the opportunity to indicate preferences for one or several of the list nominees. The degree of influence by the voter as to which of the candidates will occupy the seats varies according to the modality used (Katz, 1986; Molina, 1986b). There are two basic types of preference voting: closed or open list. *In the closed list type the voter casts preferences only for the candidates of one list*; this is a categorical preference ballot (Rae, 1971, p. 17). *In the open list, also known as panachage, the voter may cast preferences for candidates of any of the competing lists, up to the number of selections he is allowed* (Katz, 1986). Following Rae's classification, this is an ordinal preference ballot (1971, p. 17). In this section we will describe and consider the political consequences of the open list preference voting system used in Venezuela for the election of local council members in December 1989.

Panachage Preference Voting in Venezuelan Local Elections

In 1989, Venezuela elected 1963 councillors for 269 municipal councils. Each municipality was considered to be a constituency, with the number of councillors varying from five to 25 according to the population. The average magnitude (M) of these constituencies was seven. Nomination was by lists presented by parties or electoral groups for each municipality. The candidates were rank ordered by the party, and could total as many as three times the number of seats, where these were seven or less. When the number of seats was greater than seven, the number of candidates in each list could not exceed a maximum equal to the total number of seats plus 15.

Voters could cast either a straight-list vote by marking a box placed at the top of each party list, or a preference vote by selecting up to as many candidates as there were seats in the particular municipal council. If the voter decided to vote for individual candidates he could choose these from the various lists (panachage). The total number of votes obtained by each list was equal to the number of straight-list votes multiplied by the number of seats, plus the number of preference votes received by its candidates. On the basis of this total, seats were distributed among the lists by the D'Hondt formula.

Once it was determined how many seats were won by each party, these were then allocated to the candidates. For this allocation, both the straight-list votes and the individual votes were taken into account in a peculiarly Venezuelan way. The seats attained by the party were divided between the two modalities of voting in proportion to their contribution to the total list vote. Thus some were allocated according to the list order, and others according to the number of personal votes received by the nominees. This meant that, if the list supplied 60 per cent of the party vote, then 60 per cent of the seats would be allocated to candidates in the order of nomination. The other 40 per cent would be allocated to the rest of the nominees on the basis of personal votes received. The distribution of seats between the straight-list votes and the preference votes was determined using the formula of the natural quota and largest remainders (Consejo Supremo Electoral, 1989). The rationale behind this procedure was that it was up to the voters of each party to decide how many of its seats would be allocated according to the list rank order, and how many on preference voting.

The nominees that were not elected were considered to be deputies of those holding the mandates, and could stand in for them in their absence. The deputies substituted for the councillors elected on the list vote according to their place on the list; and substituted for those elected on preference votes in a rank order determined by their individual votes. For preference voting Katz has worked out an indicator similar to the threshold of exclusion for parties (Taagepera, 1990). This preference vote threshold of exclusion is defined by Katz as:

> the minimum number of voters whose concerted support for a single candidate would be required in order to elect that individual rather than a candidate of the party's choice, defined here to be those candidates who would be elected if no explicit preference votes were cast, assuming all other voters cast simple party ballots (Katz, 1986, p. 93).

According to this definition, the preference-voting threshold of exclusion for the system used in Venezuela in 1989 would be equivalent to dividing the party vote (V) by twice the number of elected candidates (e) attained by the party, and then adding one to the result. This means that at least one preference vote councillor would be elected from a party list when the number of preference votes received by one or more of its candidates was superior by at least one vote to the total votes of the party divided by twice the number of mandates gained:

$$\frac{V}{2e} + 1$$

This system was implemented at a time when public opinion favored personalized voting. However, as it was passed by Congress only three months before the election, the publicity surrounding the system, both institutional and partisan, was rather limited. The parties were not helpful in campaigning for the preference vote of their individual candidates; instead they sought the full list vote. As a result, just a few candidates undertook rather sketchy personal campaigns, and there was a general lack of information among the voters with respect to the proposals and characteristics of the individual candidates. Thus there was on the one hand an electorate disposed towards personal voting, and, on the other, an electoral campaign that did not do much in this sense.

As for the election day voting procedure itself, voting was smooth. The percentage of void ballots was 7.3 per cent (estimated).[9] Void ballots for the previous local elections on closed and blocked lists were 4.09 per cent in 1979 and 4.36 per cent in 1984. For the simultaneous 1989 election of governors, void ballots were 4.4 per cent. Given the lack of information for this first election with preference voting, the increase is not alarming.

Problems occurred in the process of counting the votes. Precinct Electoral Committees were overwhelmed by the task of counting preference votes, and as a consequence an unusual number of mistakes and appeals occurred. This experience has strengthened the position of those who propose the use of counting machines.

Political Consequences of Panachage Preference Voting in Venezuela

Prior to the adoption of this system and its trial run in 1989, the debate focused on two points: firstly, whether this new system was capable of increasing the voters' power of selection and control *vis-à-vis* the parties; and secondly, its effect on the consolidation of party factions. We will deal with both of these aspects with respect to the 1989 election results. A third area will be also dealt with: the effect of the system on the partisan orientation of the vote, to see whether, given the opportunity, Venezuelan voters cross party lines or, on the contrary, tend to remain loyal to one organization.

Effects on the power of selection and control by the electorate

We will analyze the extent to which the system was used by the voters, as a sign of its acceptance. The impact it had on the election of preference vote councillors will also be studied, in order to assess its effectiveness, according to the objective formulated. Finally the capability of the system to modify party lists will be evaluated: that is, whether, it provides the voters with an instrument that allows them to decide on their own the names of those that will occupy the seats gained by any given party.

In countries having optional preference voting (Katz, 1986, p. 88), the percentage of use is variable, but tends, after several elections, to be over a quarter of the voters. Preference voting has been reported to have reached 30 per cent in Italy (Seton-Watson, 1983, p. 115); 50 per cent in Denmark (Norby, 1979, p. 53) and Belgium (Lakeman, 1974, p. 104); 42 per cent in Luxembourg (Kintzelle, 1979, p. 187); and James reports extensive use of preference voting in Bavaria (1988, p. 35). In the case of Venezuela, expectations were rather low for this first time. The most optimistic predicted a preference vote of around 20 per cent.

For estimating the percentage of preference voting, the number of void votes, calculated on the basis on the percentage given earlier, was subtracted from the total turnout. The result was the number of valid votes. The official number of straight-list votes was subtracted from this number. The resulting figure represents the estimated number of preference vote ballots, from which the percentage of preference voting was calculated. According to this procedure, preference voting was estimated at 34.4 per cent.[10] That so many voters took advantage of preference voting was highly satisfactory. This is particularly so in view of the fact that the conditions under which the system was tested were not favorable, with the single exception of a public opinion climate in favor of personal voting. It is this latter which may account for the rather high percentage of preference voting, despite the very low level of information available and the almost non-existent campaigning for personal votes.

In order to evaluate the effectiveness of the system, it is not enough to know that it was used by a sizeable portion of the electorate. It is necessary to determine whether any councillors at all were elected by preference votes rather than by the party lists. As was stated earlier, the system was designed so that the percentage of councillors elected by personal vote would be proportional to the preference votes of each party *vis-à-vis* its straight-list votes. This proportion was not to be the same as that between straight-list ballots and preference vote ballots, because it seemed likely that, as indeed happened, a number of voters would not use all the preference votes which they were allowed, so diminishing the effect of personal voting *vis-à-vis* straight-list voting.[11] Also, as the distribution was on a party-by-party basis, the weight of the nominal voting would be attenuated by the effect characteristic of small constituencies. For a party electing five or six councillors, the proportional distribution of seats between the straight-list vote and the preference vote tends to be adequate. However, in the case of small parties that would usually obtain only one seat in the council, preference votes had to contribute over 50 per cent of the party vote in order to get that councillor elected on the basis of individual votes.

Out of 1963 elected local councillors, 494 (25 per cent) were elected by preference vote.[12] This result confirms that the system is able to fulfil its original objective: to give the public the opportunity to elect representatives by personal vote, according to the degree to which the voters use this opportunity.

As important as knowing that the system is able to elect councillors by preference voting, is to know whether, and to what extent, it is able to bring about the displacement of one party nominee by another on the same basis: that is, the displacement of a candidate who would have been elected on the basis of a pure list system by another placed lower in the list but who received more preference votes. For the Venezuelan debate, which focused on the overwhelming party control over political and social life, it was of paramount importance that the system chosen prove to be capable of modifying the will of the party bureaucracy as expressed in the list order. From the official information made available by the Supreme Electoral Council, it was found that, in 295 cases, displacements occurred.[13] This represents 60 per cent of the 494 councillors elected by preference voting and 15 per cent of all the council seats elected in 1989.

Preference voting and party unity

After only one election, and one in which the system was implemented in a hurried manner without time to be fully understood by all the actors, it is not possible to determine with any degree of precision what its future effects would have been with respect to the unity and organization of the parties, had the system been continued. (In February 1992, Congress rescinded this reform in favor of a different system that will be referred to later.) However it is possible to put forward some hypotheses about the probable consequences.

By personalizing the vote, preference voting provides an alternative to internal struggles in the rise and maintenance of electoral leadership. Electoral leadership could grow out of popular support, rather than developing inside the party structure. It is very likely that these electoral leaders would later use their popular support for achieving party leadership as well. In this sense preference voting would probably bring about a decrease in the phenomenon described by Duverger as 'oligarquization' (1957, p. 181), opening the door to new and external entries to the party leadership. By giving personal electoral support to the councillors, it would have watered down their dependence on the party bureaucracy, and given more autonomy to the party councillors *vis-à-vis* their particular party.

It has been pointed out that preferential voting is likely to strain party unity (Katz, 1986, p. 101). This is because it creates a favorable habitat for party factions as, even if their candidates are relegated to the bottom of the list, they can still count on their electoral appeal, provided the internal system for party nomination allows the proportional representation of tendencies in the lists. However, before condemning the system for this probable consequence, it is germane to look at what happens right now within the Venezuelan parties. In the three main parties, very deeply entrenched factions and organized groups already exist. What may change now, and for the moment only at local level, is that the electorate will have a say in a process that before occurred behind closed doors. The competition among party candidates for the popular vote can scarcely be more intense than it now is for the support of the party bosses, and in any case will give to the minorities a better and more democratic chance of reaching public office. Katz is right in suggesting that this system, even if it consolidates the factions, will diminish the chances of a party split (Katz, 1986, p. 102). It is likely that this would have been the case in Venezuela as well.

The partisan orientation of the vote

The former electoral system allowed only partisan voting. It is also probable that this system contributed to the development of a strong partisan orientation of the vote (Torres, 1984, p. 63) and a view of the electoral process as party-centered. This being the case, one could expect this partisan orientation of the vote to persist, even when the possibility exists for departing from this. Thus it is also to be expected that most of the voters, even when using the preference vote, will remain within the limits of one party. This first preference voting election gives us the opportunity to find out to what degree the Venezuelan voter is party- or individual-oriented. Party-oriented voters are defined here as those voting for the straight party list, or for individual candidates nominated by one party only (no panachage). Individual-oriented voters are those voting for candidates nominated by two or more parties.

It has already been stated that 70 per cent of the voters supported a full party list. In a study of preference vote ballots, made at the time of counting, and organized by this researcher in collaboration with the Fundación Consejo Supremo Electoral, 2628 ballots were analyzed. These came from 63 electoral precincts, located in three cities: Caracas, Barquisimeto and Maracaibo (Fundación Consejo Supremo Electoral and Dirección de Estadísticas y Encuestas del Consejo Supremo Electoral, 1990). Of the 2628 ballots, 53 per cent contained votes for candidates of only one party. This suggests that half of the voters that cast preference votes were party-oriented. Thus one should add a further 17 per cent to the 66 per cent that cast straight-list votes. Overall, 83 per cent of the valid votes in the municipal elections were party-oriented. Thus the evidence suggests that preference voting in 1989 did not markedly weaken the partisan orientation of Venezuelan political life (Blais, 1991, p. 249).

REFORMS ON PROPORTIONALITY, ELECTORAL REGISTER AND DIRECT ELECTION OF GOVERNORS AND MAYORS

The Reform on Proportionality

For the election of the two chambers of the Venezuelan Congress, a first round distribution of seats is made, using the D'Hondt formula. As was pointed out earlier, in the Chamber of Deputies there are 23 constituencies with an average M of eight. In the Senate, there are 22 constituencies (21 states and the Federal District), each of which elects two senators.

To improve the degree of proportionality in Venezuela, additional compensatory seats are allocated to those parties whose percentage of seats is under their percentage of votes. The total valid votes are divided by the overall number of seats allocated at constituency level, thus determining the national quota for members of the Chamber of Deputies and for Senators; then the national vote of each party is divided by these quotas, and the results are compared with the number of seats arrived at in the first distribution. Parties get additional compensatory seats to make up the difference. In the case of the Chamber of Deputies a maximum of four compensatory seats was set, now increased to five. In the case of the Senate the limit was two compensatory seats, now increased to three. The reform was operative for the 1988 election and had a practical effect, because the third party would have obtained one deputy and one senator less under the old system. This modification tends to improve proportionality, albeit slightly, especially in favor of medium-sized parties.

Direct Election of Governors and Mayors

Beginning in 1989, Venezuelans now elect their state governors and mayors directly. Prior to this, governors were appointed by the president, and local governments were run by a council with legislative and executive functions. Both governors and mayors are elected by plurality in a one-round election. Party alliances are permitted and played an important part in the 1989 elections (Molina, 1989a; Cortés and Mosquera, 1990). For both mayors and governors, re-election is permitted for the following term only. The first direct elections for the 20 governors and 269 mayors were held on 3 December 1989.

The electoral reform replaced the previous five-year term with three-year terms for both state and local elected offices. Nationally elected officials continue to serve five-year terms. It is germane to mention two consequences of this reform: firstly, it has been a decisive step towards decentralization. Governors and mayors, from the very beginning, have sought more resources and powers, in order to be able to fulfil voter expectations and face re-election under favorable conditions. Secondly, direct election of governors has brought the opposition to power in nine of the 20 states, among them some of the more important both politically and economically (Molina, 1989a). Two of the states were carried by parties other than Acción Democrática and COPEI.

The New System for the Electoral Register

Before the electoral reform of 1989, Venezuela had a citizen application electoral register (Powell, 1980, p. 10; Molina, 1989b, p. 21). Application was legally compulsory but dependent on the voter's initiative. The 1989 Electoral Act called for registration to be automatic, based on the information provided by the citizen when applying for his national identity card. As each citizen becomes eligible, he should automatically be included in the register by the Supreme Electoral Council. The duty to register personally still remains for those that change addresses, those that were not eligible for legal reasons and later became so (for example, the military), those that have failed to vote in two consecutive national elections,[14] and foreigners eligible for voting in local elections. However the reform passed in February

1992 left it to the Supreme Electoral Council to decide when the new registration system will become operational; until that time the former pre-1989 citizen application system will be used.

CONCLUSION

It would not seem to be possible to retract the steps that have been taken towards going beyond the pure party list system, that is towards personalized voting. However the search for a particular system that fits the needs and wishes of the political actors involved is far from over. The debate, both inside and outside Congress, has continued, and the reforms already passed should still be regarded as transitional. In fact panachage preference voting for local elections has already been replaced by a system in which two-thirds of the seats will be elected by single-member plurality, and the rest allocated proportionally by the D'Hondt formula. On applying this formula, all parties will lose as many quotients, from the top downwards, as single-member districts won. The total vote of each party will be the sum of the votes obtained by its single-member district candidates. The seats allocated by the D'Hondt formula will be for the single-member district candidates of that party, not elected by plurality, that received the highest number of votes. The parties may also nominate a supplementary slate of candidates to fall back on should they win in the proportional distribution a number of seats higher than the number of single-member districts. This system will be applied for the first time in the 1992 local elections.

Personalized proportional representation is still waiting for its debut, scheduled for 1993. it is likely to encourage the elected candidates to link their activities to the specific issues that are relevant for their constituencies, and to dedicate more time to the individual problems of their voters. However its effect on accountability and responsiveness will be dampened by the safeguard that the closed list gives to the politicians.

Panachage preference voting was implemented for only one election, that of 1989. The system was approved only three months before the election, information on its workings was scarce and there were no campaigns for the preferential vote by individual candidates to any significant degree. Despite all of this, the system proved capable of giving voters an instrument actually to personalize their selection, and to decide, above and beyond the order presented by the party, who would take the seats won. The possibility is not to be discounted that panachage preference voting may be turned to again in the future. This is particularly likely if the new system should result in a large decrease in proportionality, as it may well do, thus harming not only minor parties but also those ranking second and third.

It would likewise seem that there is no going back on the issue of decentralization. The process that began with the direct election of governors and mayors has continued on through an increased participation in the budget and the devolution of some powers held by the national government. A generalized feeling of satisfaction exists with respect to these reforms up to the present.

With respect to automatic registration, the situation is not particularly bright. In fact there is no sign that the organizational change needed on the level of the Supreme Electoral Council and the Ministry of the Interior are taken place. Consequently it does not seem likely that the Supreme Electoral Council will decide to put it into operation in the short term, at least not for the next local, state or national elections.

Notes

The author thanks Diehter Nohlen and Matthew Shugart for their comments on a previous version of the chapter, and Ms Janeth Hernández, who, as a graduate student in Political Science, collaborated in collecting and collating the data for this chapter. The author also acknowledges the support of the Supreme Electoral Council in supplying the documents needed through the Division of General Information and its Secretary General, and in helping to carry out, through its Foundation and the Direction of Statistics, the polling day survey referred to in this chapter.

1. Taagepera and Shugart (1989a, p. 56) prefer to call it a 'compensatory member system'. This chapter follows the traditional name, 'personalized proportional representation'.
2. The Mexican electoral system also combines, for the lower chamber of Congress, proportional representation for 200 seats with single member plurality for the other 300, but in a framework that is clearly majoritary (Barquin, 1987).
3. Average M for the legislative assemblies for the 1988 elections was 16 (20 states).
4. Comprising 21 states, the Federal District, and one federal territory. Until 1991 there were 20 states and two federal territories; but at that time one of the territories was granted state status by Congress.
5. The number of deputies elected in the constituencies has been, for the

last four elections, 182 in 1983 and 88; and 183 in 1973 and 1978.

6. In a federal territory the party list can nominate only three candidates: a primary candidate and two substitutes.

7. In the case of the state legislatures, all the non-elected candidates can replace those elected in the order in which they appear in the list.

8. For a similar purpose Katz uses as indicator of the impact of preference or personalized voting the percentage of incumbent defeats due to preferential voting, which he calls 'intrapartisan defeats' due to preference votes (Katz, 1986, p. 97). This indicator of the effect of personalized or preferential voting is useful for international comparisons, particularly when some of the countries in the analysis do not use rank ordered party lists. But when, as in Venezuela, there is a rank ordered party list, the concept of displacement seems a better indicator of the effect of personalized or preferential voting because it refers, not only to incumbent defeats, but to the total number of cases in which the winning candidates would have not been elected without preferential or personalized voting.

9. The percentage of void ballots has been estimated from a large sample of tally records submitted to the Supreme Electoral Council by the precinct poll workers. The sample covers 64 per cent of the ballots cast in the election. The total number of ballots cast was 4 156 333, of which the sample covers 2 665 646.

10. The information on turnout and the number of straight ballots was taken from an official publication by the Statistics and Surveys Division of the Supreme Electoral Council (Dirección de Estadísticas y Encuestas del Consejo Supremo Electoral, 1991). This division of the Supreme Electoral Council, in its calculation of preference vote ballots, assumed that the percentage of void ballots was equal to that obtained in the simultaneous elections for state governors (4.4 per cent), whose ballots were easier to handle by the voters. This procedure under-estimates void ballots and therefore over-estimates preference voting, which is why they estimate preference voting at 36 per cent, while this chapter estimates it at 34.4 per cent.

11. On polling day, during the process of counting, an analysis was made of a sample of preference vote ballots. For four municipalities (Libertador in the Federal District; Baruta and Sucre in Miranda State, and Iribarren in Lara State), information is available about the number of preferences used by a sample of 1557 voters. Out of 23 775 preferences that could have been cast in the 1577 ballots that were examined, only 14 827 (62 per cent) had actually been used. Therefore 38 per cent of the preferences allowed were wasted, reducing the weight of those votes vis-à-vis straight-list votes. These data are calculated from the information given out by Fundación Consejo Supremo Electoral y Dirección de Estadísticas y Encuestas del Consejo Supremo Electoral (1990).

12. This calculation is based on information on councillors elected by preference voting made available by the Dirección General de Información Electoral and the Dirección de Estadísticas y Encuestas del Consejo Supremo Electoral (1991). This information was checked against the electoral results, where differences appeared.

13. Displacements were determined on the basis of the official records submitted by the Municipal Electoral Committees, taking into account the modifications that resulted from appeals to the Supreme Electoral Council.
14. These will be deleted automatically from the electoral register.

References

BARQUIN, M. (1987) *La Reforma Electoral de 1986–1987 en México. Retrospectiva y Análisis* (San José de Costa Rica: CAPEL).

BLAIS, A. (1991) 'The Debate over Electoral Systems', *International Political Science Review*, 12, pp. 239–60.

CONSEJO SUPREMO ELECTORAL (1987) *Informe para el Congreso Nacional* (Caracas: Consejo Supremo Electoral).

CONSEJO SUPREMO ELECTORAL (1989) *Totalización, Adjudicacíon y Proclamación de Gobernadores, Alcaldes y Concejales Elecciones 1989* (Caracas: Consejo Supremo Electoral).

CORTÉS, J. and J. MOSQUERA (1991) 'Las Alianzas Electorales en las Elecciones de Alcaldes 1989', *Cuestiones Políticas*, 8, pp. 85–102.

DIRECCIÓN DE ESTADÍSTICAS Y ENCUESTAS DEL CONSEJO SUPREMO ELECTORAL (1991) *Resultados Electorales de Concejales* (Caracas: Consejo Supremo Electoral).

DUVERGER, M. (1957) *Los Partidos Políticos* (México DF: Fondo de Cultura Económica).

FUNDACIÓN CONSEJO SUPREMO ELECTORAL & DIRECCIÓN DE ESTADÍSTICAS Y ENCUESTAS DEL CONSEJO SUPREMO ELECTORAL (1990) *'Estudio de Opinión Elecciones 3 de diciembre de 1989 Area Metropolitana de Caracas, Lara y Zulia'*, unpublished paper.

JAMES, P. (1988) 'The Bavarian Electoral System', *Electoral Studies*, 7, pp. 33–9.

KAASE, M. (1984) 'Personalized Proportional Representation: The "Model" of the West German Electoral System", in A. Lijphart and B. Grofman (eds), *Choosing and Electoral System* (New York: Praeger) pp. 155–64.

KATZ, R. (1986) 'Intraparty Preference Voting', in B. Groffman and A. Lijphart (eds), *Electoral Laws and Their Political Consequences* (New York: Agathon Press) pp. 85–103.

KINTZELLE, G. (1979) 'Luxembourg', in G. Hand, J. Georgel and C. Sasse (eds), *European Electoral Systems Handbook* (London: Butterworth) pp. 170–92.

LAKEMAN, E. (1974) *How Democracies Vote* (London: Faber & Faber).

MOLINA, J. (1986a) 'La Reforma del Sistema Electoral Venezolano', in F. Guzmán (ed.), *La Reforma del Sistema Electoral Venezolano* (Caracas: Consejo Supremo Electoral) pp. 25–41.

MOLINA, J. (1986b) 'La Reforma Electoral Municipal', in M. Magallanes (ed.), *Reformas Electorales y Partidos Políticos* (Caracas: Consejo Supremo Electoral) pp. 159–98.

MOLINA, J. (1989a) 'Venezuela: Elecciones Estatales y Municipales, 3 de Diciembre de 1989', *Boletín Electoral Latinoamericano*, 2, pp. 50–5.

MOLINA, J. (1989b) *La Participatión Electoral en Venezuela* (San José de Costa Rica: CAPEL).

NEUBER, M. and O. AKALIN (1986) *Derecho Electoral* (Colonia: Inter Naciones).

NOHLEN, D. (1981) *Sistemas Electorales del Mundo* (Madrid: Centro de Estudios Constitucionales).

NOHLEN, D. (1984) 'Alemania Federal', in Consejo Supremo Electoral (ed.), *Simposio Sistemas Electorales Comparados* (Caracas: Consejo Supremo Electoral) pp. 145–73.

NORBY, L. (1979) 'Denmark', in G. Hand, J. Georgel and C. Hasse (eds), *European Electoral Systems Handbook* (London: Butterworth) pp. 29–57.

POWELL, G.B. Jr. (1980) 'Voting Turnout in Thirty Democracies: Partisan, Legal and Socio-Economic Influences', in R. Rose (ed.), *Electoral Participation* (London: Sage) pp. 5–34.

RAE, D. (1971) *The Political Consequences of Electoral Laws* (New Haven: Yale University Press).

REY, J.C. (1986) 'Reformas del Sistema Electoral Venezolano', in M. Magallanes (ed.), *Reformas Electorales y Partidos Políticos* (Caracas: Consejo Supremo Electoral) pp. 119–58.

SASSE, C. (1979) 'Germany', in G. Hand, J. Georgel and C. Sasse (eds), *European Electoral Systems Handbook* (London: Butterworth) pp. 58–86.

SETON-WATSON, C. (1983) 'Italy', in V. Bogdanor and D. Butler (eds), *Democracy and Elections* (Cambridge: Cambridge University Press) pp. 110–21.

SHUGART, M. (1991) 'Leaders, Rank and File and Constituents: Electoral Reform in Colombia and Venezuela', unpublished paper, forthcoming in *Electoral Studies*.

TAAGEPERA, R. and M. SHUGART (1989a) 'Designing Electoral Systems', *Electoral Studies*, 8, pp. 49–58.

TAAGEPERA, R. and M. SHUGART (1989b) *Seats and Votes* (New Haven: Yale University Press).

TORRES, A. (1984) 'Venezuela', in Consejo Supremo Electoral (ed.), *Simposio Sistemas Electorales Comparados* (Caracas: Consejo Supreme Electoral) pp. 49–67.

9 Contagion of Democracy in Latin America: The Case of Paraguay

Mikael Bostrom

INTRODUCTION

More than a decade has elapsed since a wave of military returns to barracks started in Latin America. This political process has given birth to hundreds of academic books and articles on transition to, and consolidation of, democracy in the region. However, although the process has been regional, in the sense that a dozen regime changes of the same kind have taken place within a short timeframe in one specific region of the world, this aspect has remained unresearched. The proximity in time and place of the transitions has made several scholars within this field address the question of whether these regime changes are linked to one another in some way. Concepts used to describe these linkages between the separate political processes include 'snowballing' (Huntington, 1991), 'diffusion' (Diamond, 1991) and 'contagion' (Rouquié, 1989; Welch, 1987). Surprisingly enough, however, none has tried to make an empirical study of these effects. This chapter is an attempt at approaching the issue of linkages between the individual transitions from authoritarian rule in Latin America during the last 15 years. It will be made, firstly, by discussing a framework for analysis of the spread of democracy in Latin America and, secondly, by applying this framework to the case of Paraguay.

A FRAMEWORK FOR ANALYSIS

Political Contagion in the Literature on Transition to Democracy

One reason why the regional aspect of democratization in Latin America has remained unexplored seems to be that scholars share the view that it is difficult to clarify empirically (O'Donnell, 1986, p. 16; Morlino, 1987, p. 58). Moreover the dominating theoretical view in the recent literature is that the political transitions in the Latin American countries have been endogenous processes and that external factors have played only a marginal or secondary role (O'Donnell and Schmitter, 1986, p. 18; Whitehead, 1986, p. 4; Baloyra, 1987, p. 297; Pastor, 1989, p. 141). Accordingly most empirical studies have dealt with carefully identified political actors playing a transition game on domestic arenas that have no, or only a few, doors open to let in international influences. An unfortunate consequence of this perspective is the neglect of political influences across national boundaries within Latin America.

As already mentioned, the lack of empirical explorations of diffusion and contagion effects does not mean, however, that scholars are unaware of them. Welch (1987, p. 201) argues that the 'contagion factor' has been important in the Latin America democratization process, emphasizing the influence on the neighboring states of the Brazilian political opening in the late 1970s. In the Latin American part of the Diamond, Lipset and Linz four-volume study of democratization in the third world, Diamond and Linz (1989, p. 48) even suggest that these effects have been especially potent in Latin America, pointing to the impact of the Cuban revolution, the Brazilian coup of 1964 and, more importantly, of 'the overall context of political trends in the region as a salient influence for or against democracy'. The 'current regional context of "democratic contagion"', they claim, appears to have had an impact on the survival of democracy in Peru, the return of democracy in Chile and the inauguration of democracy in Paraguay. However among the case-studies in the same volume only Waisman (1989, p. 98) deals at some length with this issue, suggesting that what he interchangeably calls demonstration and diffusion effects have played a historical role in the cyclical political development of Argentina.

These are just a few examples of the cursory way of dealing with the regional factor in the literature on democratization in Latin America. Thus when looking for a framework for analysis of the spread of democracy this literature is of little help. The more general transition literature, especially that which includes in its analyses the East European 'snowball' of regime changes as well, gives more clues. Although the concepts related to this aspect of democratization are seldom defined clearly in this literature, three different types of external influences can be identified: promotion of democracy, demonstration effects, and contagion effects. Diffusion seems to be used as a concept that summarizes all these types of effects.[1]

Promotion of democracy means the democratic nations', mostly the great powers', deliberate efforts at spreading their form of government to other nations. It can be made through, for example, imposition, as in the historic cases of West Germany and Japan, or through the use of more subtle means, such as symbolic expressions of support for democratic forces in authoritarian nations. By 'demonstration effect' is most often meant the long-term, diffuse and unintentional effect the attractiveness of democracy has on authoritarian societies throughout the world (Di Palma, 1990, p. 185; Whitehead, 1990, p. 21). Finally, contagion effects are the more short-term effects of democratization in the country on the surrounding region.[2] The term contagion is used to describe the pace of the process and the proximity in place of the units influenced by this effect. Contagion effect can be both intentional and unintentional. It means that the contagion of democracy to one particular country may, for example, include a neighboring government's attempts at promotion of democracy as well as the indirect impact, in the form of sheer encouragement or political learning, of that latter country on the former. In this chapter it is the contagion effect that will be focused upon.

The Linkage Politics Approach

Thus, with the help of the transition literature, the process in question can be separated from other forms of political diffusion. To develop the analytic framework further, however, other theoretical sources must be used. One relevant and fruitful theoretical background is the attempt to bridge the studies of comparative and international politics by studying linkage politics (Rosenau, 1969). Rosenau considers a linkage approach is made necessary by, for example, the absence of tools to explain the wave of coups d'état in Africa during the 1960s (Rosenau, 1969, p. 6). His argument for suspecting international – national linkages in these cases is the same as in the cases of democratization in Latin America and Eastern Europe, namely the similarity of the events as well as their proximity in time and place. What, according to Rosenau, is lacking is not studies of 'the power of example' but a theory that tells us under what conditions such a process is likely.[3]

There are a number of concepts of the linkage approach which are useful for this study. Firstly, Rosenau (1969, p. 45) defines a linkage as 'any recurrent sequence of behavior that originates in one system and is reacted to in another'. The focus of this study is the wave of transitions to democracy in Latin America, not one particular regime change, although one case is used to illuminate the contagion phenomenon. In other words, it is the recurrence of events and processes this study is aimed at.

Secondly, the stages of a linkage explored in this study are environmental outputs and polity inputs. The former is a sequence of behavior which is initiated in the external environment, whereas the latter is a sequence of behavior within a polity, the impulse for which, originates in the external environment. Thirdly, these outputs and inputs can be of a direct or indirect type. Those that are designed to cause responses in other systems (such as foreign policy) are direct policy or environmental outputs and inputs, whereas those which bring about processes of perception or emulation (such as elections and coups d'état) are indirect outputs and inputs (Rosenau, 1969, p. 46).

In the literature on the transition to democracy in Latin America the discussion of the role of external factors has mostly dealt with direct outputs and inputs, that is the US attempts to export democracy and the effects of that effort in the Latin American countries (Whitehead, 1986; Wiarda, 1986; Lowenthal, 1991), the policy of international political organizations and other international bodies (Angell, 1989; Whitehead, 1986) as well as the influence of exiles (Angell, 1989). As already mentioned, few studies have discussed the role of the democratizing neighbors in the domestic political process of a particular country. The focus of this chapter is both on direct and indirect outputs and on inputs in the form of intentional and unintentional transfers of the democratic message across national boundaries. In contrast to most of the recent studies of the impact of external factors on democratization, the focus is shifted from relations between the advanced Western and Third World countries to the relations within a Third World region.

Fourthly, Rosenau (1969, p. 46) also differentiates between three types of linkage processes. The two opposite types are the penetrative and the reactive processes. Applied to a context of democratization, the former corresponds to what is called 'promotion of democracy' in the transition literature, since Rosenau defines it as a political process in which members of another polity participate directly (for example, the activities of an occupying army). The latter describes a sequence of behavior which is a response to activities initiated in the environment, without the direct participation of members of other polities. The third type, the emulative process, is a special form of the reactive type. It is a linkage process in which the input is not only a response to, but also takes the same form as, the output. According to Rosenau, this type corresponds to what is usually labeled demonstration or diffusion effects. Using the concepts of the transition literature, however, it corresponds to contagion effects as well.

Fifthly, Rosenau (1969, pp. 60–3) subdivides the concept of environment into six categories: two geographically defined (the contiguous and the regional) and four functionally defined sub-environments (the Cold War, the racial, the resource and the organizational). This subdivision of the concept of environment has great merits since it facilitates a systematic investigation of the sources of linkage processes. Scholars who study the role of external factors in the various Latin American transition games have, as already noted, concentrated on the Cold War (that is, the impact of the worldwide competition between the two superpowers), the resource (the economic dependency effects) and, to a lesser degree, the organizational sub-environments (the role of OAS, EC and so on). Since the purpose of this study is to explore the regional spread of democracy by using a case study of Paraguay, the focus is on the contiguous and regional sub-environments of this particular country.

The contiguous environment refers to 'any cluster of polities that border geographically upon a given polity' (Rosenau, 1969, p. 61). In the Paraguayan case this environment consists of Brazil, Argentina and Bolivia. The concept of regional environment is a more flexible one. Region may be defined subjectively or objectively and the result may differ considerably. In this study the standard definition of Latin America is utilized to identify the regional environment of Paraguay (*SALA* 1988, p. x).[4] Furthermore the historical role of the US as the hegemon in the Western hemisphere justifies the inclusion of this country in the extended regional environment.

Thus to use Rosenau's approach means to place democratization in an international–national linkage context. It means that the usual distinction between external and internal explanatory factors is not made. The process focused upon in this study is an emulative process, or the contagion of democracy from the contiguous and regional environments (which in the Paraguayan case means the immediate neighboring countries and the whole of Latin America, plus the US, respectively) to Paraguay. The outputs and inputs linked in this process may be direct as well as indirect (or intentional as well as unintentional), which implies that the foreign policies of the democratizing neighbors towards Paraguay, as well as pure psychological effects on, for example, opposition activists in Paraguay, should be studied.

Diffusion Theory

The linkage politics approach does not tell anything about where and when emulative political process, such as contagion of democracy, can be expected. Diffusion theory offers some useful elements to fill this gap. The main problem of applying diffusion theory to this study, however, is that the latter is not about the spread of an innovation. Diffusion theory is to a large extent theory about the way innovations are spread and adopted. In Rogers' classic diffusion study he defines an innovation as 'an idea perceived as new by individual' (Rogers, 1962, p. 13). Since democracy comes and goes in Latin America (Bostrom, 1989) and most of the countries have experienced shorter or longer periods of democratic rule, democracy cannot be regarded as an innovation in this part of the world. What may have been spread in Latin America during the 1980s are not the basic ideas and principles of democracy but, rather, the ideas of how to reestablish democratic rule, how to return to the barracks in a dignified way, political strategies and tactics, and even the courage and determination needed to challenge the authoritarian regime.

Most often the observed process of a diffusion study is a process that grows and develops continuously in space and time. An agricultural tool, or a social security law, is 'invented' in one country and, soon, it is imitated and adopted in the neighboring countries. The process can be easily observed and the extension of the diffusion measured. Contagion of democracy is not easily observed and measured because the 'object' that is spread is diffuse, the spread is frequently halted, and the process is extremely complex.

Despite these caveats regarding the applicability of general diffusion theory, some of the generalizations of the theory are relevant for this study. Firstly, according to the theory, intensive and long-term contacts between the units facilitate diffusion (Karvonen, 1981, p. 16). In his study of the impact of demonstration effects on the Argentine postwar policy, Waisman points to this generalization: 'Demonstration effects circulate through cultural channels; the greater the degree of interaction between cultures, the more likely the demonstration effects (Waisman, 1987, p. 233). Therefore, according to Waisman, the effects of the Cuban revolution were directly felt in the rest of Latin America, in spite of structural and institutional differences among the countries of the region. What made the revolution so influential was that the cultural *network* was strong within Latin America.

Secondly, structural similarities between countries facilitate diffusion between them. However gaps between the same countries in terms of international prestige and status, competence, the *level* of development, as well as dependent relationships between the two, may explain the direction of the diffusion – from the more developed to the less developed country (Karvonen, 1981, p. 16; Midlarsky, 1970). It should be emphasized that structural similarities combined with the above-mentioned gaps should not be seen as conditions for diffusion. When the cultural network is strong, structural differences do not need to be obstacles to diffusion. Strong cultural links may result in spatial diffusion patterns being as likely as hierarchical ones (Collier and Messick, 1975).

The third generalization relevant for this study concerns the perceptions of the actors of the diffusion process, or the linkage groups. According to Waisman (1987, pp. 233–4) political events are more likely to bring about what he calls demonstration effects when, firstly, there are elite and other groups in the recipient country who see similarities between the context of the sender country and their own situation and, secondly, the perceived efficacy of the foreign model is high. With regard to the spread of democratization, these linkage groups could be softliners within an authoritarian regime, as well as opposition parties, social movements and the like.

Thus diffusion theory offers some generalizations regarding the conditions for and likelihood of contagion of democracy: intensive and long-term contacts between two nations are conducive to political contagion; structural similarities facilitate emulation; gaps in terms of status and competence as well as assymetry in terms of dependence may explain the direction of a contagion process; and the political elite's perceptions of the relevance and applicability of the foreign model have a great impact on the likelihood of political contagion.

A PRELIMINARY STUDY OF THE CASE OF PARAGUAY

On 3 February 1989, the 35-year rule of General Alfredo Stroessner came to an abrupt end in a violent coup d'état. The leader of the coup, General Andrés Rodríguez, was elected president three months later in national elections which, in a Paraguayan context, were fairly open and honest (LASA, 1989). Without doubt, since the coup Paraguay has witnessed a political process that contains elements that are considered typical for a transition from authoritarian to democratic rule.[5]

For the purpose of this chapter, the important question is to what extent the political change in Paraguay has involved linkage processes. The dramatic events in 1989 occurred at a time when the whole of the contiguous environment and almost the whole of the regional environment had undergone a process of transition from authoritarian rule. Did the transitions in Paraguay's neighboring countries have any impact on the fall of the Stroessner regime? If they had, what are the concrete expressions of such relationships, and to what extent did these transitions next door affect the Paraguayan polity? Did they restrict the opportunities for regime status quo and, instead, enhance the opportunities for establishing democracy in Paraguay?

The case study, aimed at discussing these issues, starts with a brief outline of the basic conditions for linkage processes in Paraguay, built on the generalizations taken from diffusion theory. Going on the assumption that no contagion process can take place without actors of flesh and blood, a tentative analysis of the potential linkage groups is then made. Finally the impact of government level of the regime changes in Paraguay's contiguous and regional environments is discussed. The focus on the governmental level is motivated by the clear character of the Paraguayan transition as a 'transition from above'.

The Conditions for Linkage Processes in Paraguay

Without underestimating the structural differences between the Latin American countries, this region of the world is one where, according to diffusion theory, there should be quite a few opportunities for the emergence of emulative processes. Most importantly the homogeneity with regard to language and culture should pave the way for all kinds of political contagion. Concerning the specific case under study, it is difficult to consider the structural differences between Paraguay and its contiguous environment as obstacles to the contagion of political ideas and strategies. However Paraguay is poorer and less industrialized than Argentina, Brazil and Uruguay, richer (or less poor) than Bolivia, and has a tiny population and area compared with Brazil and Argentina. Furthermore the country has a large guaraní-speaking minority but is, in comparison with both Bolivia and Brazil, more homogenous with regard to race (*mestizos*).

The economic dependence of Paraguay on Brazil and Argentina has, as will be discussed below, been one underlying factor of the democratization in the former. Moreover the gaps in terms of level of development and international status between Paraguay and its two large neighboring countries may be one further explanation of the chronological order of the transitions to democracy of these three cases. However it must be emphasized that in the overall Latin American context there is slight evidence that democratization is spread from more developed and high-status to less developed and low-status countries. The development of the Latin American 'democratic wave' simply does not lend support to that hypothesis (see Boström, 1989).

Paraguay is often seen as an isolated country. This may be true from a global, though not from a regional, perspective. The historical record shows that the cultural and political links at the elite level have been strong between Paraguay and its neighbors. The isolationist policy during the rule of José Gaspar Rodríguez de Francia, 1814–40, was in fact an attempt of the dictator at limiting the power of the landed aristocracy closely linked to Buenos Aires. This isolation, however, ended with the death of Francia and the coming to power of Carlos Antonio López in 1841. During the latter part of his rule (1841–62) Paraguay experienced a penetration by foreign, mostly West European, states in the shape of invited *técnicos* who constructed ships, shipyards, arsenals, railroads and telegraph systems, opened up mines, offered medical and educational services and so on (Williams, 1977). In Rosenau's terms, the rapid economic modernization of Paraguay was to a great extent a result of a penetrative process. The disastrous effect of this penetration, however, was a massive militarization which made Francisco Solano López (Carlos Antonio's son and successor) dream of a greater Paraguay. Thus the foreign-led modernization was one important factor behind the war with the 'Triple Alliance' (Argentina, Brazil and Uruguay) from 1864 to 1870 (Williams, 1977, p. 256).

During a 20-year period subsequent to the war, penetrative processes continued to shape the Paraguayan polity. Brazilian troops occupied the country for six years after the war and the constitution of 1870 was written under the tutelage of the conqueror. Furthermore Brazil played a major role up to 1890 in the abundance of elections, coups and plots following the war (Abente, 1988, p. 76; Roett, 1989, p. 126). Shortly after the turn of the century, Brazil was replaced by Argentina as the most important external force in Paraguayan political life (Abente, 1988, p. 74). After the Second World War, Brazil resumed much of its former status as the most powerful neighbor, whereas the US rose as the undisputed hegemon of the Western Hemisphere and, consequently, became the most influential non-Latin-American force in Paraguayan politics.

Paraguay's historical record shows how strongly interwoven the country has been in a cultural, political and economic network of the Southern Cone. As already noted, according to diffusion theory such networks facilitate the spread of innovations. The regional democratization during the last 15 years is not exactly a case of the spread of an innovation, but the intensive and long-term contacts between Paraguay and its neighbors may also have facilitated the spread of ideas and strategies for bringing about the end of an authoritarian regime.

The Potential Linkage Groups: Regime Members

The national political system under Stroessner has been characterized as a modern form of *caudillismo*. Generally the central feature of such a system is said to be personal rule maintained by a loyal personal following, which is retained by rewards of wealth or the power of patronage (Hicks, 1971, p. 99; Lezcano, 1989, pp. 14–15). In the Paraguayan case, the core of this following was the military officers who stood closest to Stroessner and who were granted 'unusual opportunities for self-enrichment' (Hicks, 1971, p. 99). The means of self-enrichment were, to a large extent, corruption, as well as the control and handling of the large-scale traffic in contraband items and, in the last decades, drugs (Miranda, 1990, pp. 114–16). Therefore in order to preserve the system the military had incentives to maintain a low public profile and not to draw international attention to itself (Hicks, 1971, p. 100).

Why, then, did General Rodríguez, the man who before the coup was depicted as 'the nation's major smuggler' (Williams, 1987, p. 27),[6] challenge the whole system by not only ousting the caudillo, but by paving the way for a transition to democracy? Assuredly among many officers there was widespread dissatisfaction with the rumors about President Stroessner's son, Gustavo,[7] and unease that future restructuring of the army would lead to forced retirements (Roett and Sacks 1991, p. 131; Sandgren, 1988, p. 7). There was also a real threat against General Rodríguez's position as commander of the powerful First Army Corps (Lezcano, 1989, pp. 30–1; Roett and Sacks, 1991, p. 131). These were internal problems for the military, however, which should have been possible to solve through a military coup d'état that replaced Stroessner and his clique. Why did Rodríguez take the political change one step further?

It is clear that one of the frequently mentioned conditions for a political transition, a split within the regime, had existed for a long time in Paraguay. The stability of the Stroessner regime, which rested on a tripartite alliance between the government, the armed forces and the ruling party, was increasingly threatened by divisions within the two latter branches. Factionalism within the ruling Colorado Party dates back to the 1940s, but was intensified after the 1954 seizure of the presidency by Alfredo Stroessner (Hicks, 1971, p. 93). A dissident faction known as the Movimiento Popular Colorado (MOPOCO) – formed shortly after Stroessner's inauguration – was even forced into exile in 1959. During the 1980s the Colorados split on several occasions. First, in 1984, the question of loyalty to President Stroessner gave rise to a division between the *militantes* (who stood closest to Stroessner) and the *tradicionalistas*. The latter group was uncomfortable with, on the one hand, the government's loss of domestic support and, on the other, and more importantly for this study, the regime's growing international isolation (Nickson, 1988, p. 248). They tried to attain (perhaps mainly for continued self-enrichment) the separation of the party from Stroessner, but they also wanted political liberalization and even cautious democratization (Sandgren, 1988, p. 5).

A second split came in 1985, when a faction led by a member of the Junta de Gobierno (Carlos Romero Pereira) criticized the Colorado Party for widespread corruption and lack of political ethics. The group (the *éticos*) was the first within the Colorados which, since 1959, publicly called for a civilian successor to Stroessner. The regime responded by banning the group, which Stroessner himself called deserters (Abente, 1989, p. 34; Nickson, 1988, p. 250). Several other factions of the Colorado Party emerged in the mid-1980s (Abente, 1989, pp. 34–5; Nickson, 1988, pp. 248–50; Sandgren, 1988, pp. 15–16). The main division, however, was the one between the hardline *militantes* and the softline *tradicionalistas*.[8] At the Colorado Party convention in 1987 the split was displayed openly and violently. The latter group was prevented by the police from entering the convention, leaving the former in total control of the party leadership (Abente, 1989, p. 35; Roett and Sacks, 1991, p. 129).

Although most officers supported the *tradicionalistas* (Abente, 1989, p. 38) it seems obvious that the split within the Colorado Party was mirrored by a corresponding division within the armed forces.[9] Lezcano (1990a, pp. 7–8) suggests that economic interests linked General Rodríguez to the modernizing group within the economic elite rather than to the Stroessner family. This is a plausible explanation for Rodríguez showing sympathy for the *tradicionalistas* before the coup (LASA, 1989, p. 40; Roett, 1989, p. 137). However it does not explain why Rodríguez chose democratization as a means to satisfy his economic self-interests. His support for the *democraticos* in the on-going dispute within the Colorado Party suggests that he continues to encourage democratization (Keesing's, 37118). Thus General Rodríguez has supported the more democratic wing of the Colorado Party before as well as after the coup. What made him change from Stroessner's closest ally to a supporter (although uncommitted) of democratic tran-sition? Was the call of the Colorado and military softliners for politi-cal changes in a democratic direction a sign of linkage processes?

The Potential Linkage Groups: The Opposition

One conclusion in the transition literature is that cracks within the regime and loss of legitimacy are necessary but not sufficient condi-tions for regime breakdown. There also needs to be an organized alternative that can 'present a real choice for isolated individuals' (Przeworski, 1986, p. 52). Alternatives to Stroessner rule were organ-ized within the ruling bloc (*tradicionalistas*, *éticos*) though these were not really presented to the people before the coup d'état. It may be questioned whether these alternatives were real choices for the citizens but, nevertheless, they won the comparatively democratic elections in May 1989. There were, however, other more radical alternatives or-ganized by the opposition, which had already been presented to the people prior to the coup. What was the role of this growing opposi-tion in the pre-coup period?

At least five opposition groups which grew in strength during the 1980s should be discussed in the Paraguayan context: the opposition parties, the Catholic Church, the trade unions, the student movements and the peasant movements. The important issue here is to what ex-tent these forces influenced the Rodríguez faction and to what extent their growing strength was a result of linkage processes.

The Opposition Parties

The political parties under Stroessner were divided simply – those that participated in the regular elections and those that did not (Roett, 1989, p. 134). Legalized factions of the Liberal Party took part in every election from 1963, when Stroessner decided to tolerate a token opposition. Following its legalization in the mid-1960s, the Febrerista Party (PFR) decided to participate in the 1968 and 1973 national elec-tions, but withdrew in 1977 when it became clear that Stroessner would be re-elected in the 1978 elections (Nickson, 1988, p. 244). Consequently, during the last 16 years under Stroessner, a few loyal opposition parties were represented in the Paraguayan Congress. From 1968 up to the coup, they were even guaranteed one-third of the seats as a result of the peculiar electoral law (McDonald and Ruhl, 1989, p. 71).

The participating parties (in the last three elections under Stroessner, the Partido Liberal and the Partido Liberal Radical) never functioned as a direct opposition to the government and the Colorado Party, but served almost solely to 'create a domestic and international image of a legislature with opposition representation' (McDonald and Ruhl, 1989, p. 71).[10] Much more important as opposition and pressure groups were the illegal and extra-parliamentary political parties. Three of these joined, in 1978, with the exiled MOPOCO faction of the Colorados to form an opposition alliance, the Acuerdo Nacional (the National Accord – AN). One of the member parties of this alliance was the legal Febrerista Party. The other two were not officially recognized: the Partido Liberal Radical Auténtico (PLRA) and the small Partido Demócrata Cristiano (PDC).

The political goals of the AN were outlined in a 14-point declaration in which the restoration of democracy, the release of political prisoners, the independence of the courts, a new electoral law and the lifting of the 25-year-old state of siege was demanded (Nickson, 1988, pp. 244–5; SIJAU, 1986, p. 293). Obviously the alliance became an annoyance to the regime. It frequently attempted to destroy the coalition, through, for instance, the expelling in 1982 of Domingo Laíno, the leader of PLRA and also the main leader of the AN and, after his return in 1987, repeated arrests of him as well as other PLRA leaders (Keesing's, 36688). The alliance survived, however, and was (in spite of police harassment) the first opposition group in decades which managed to organize public opposition meetings and demonstrations, some of them attended by tens of thousands of people (Keesing's, 35887).

It is difficult, however, to estimate to what degree the AN influenced the softliners within the regime (*tradicionalistas*, the Rodríguez faction) and, thus, contributed to their decision to topple Stroessner and initiate a transition.[11] According to an opinion poll in 1986, 47 per cent of the respondents had never heard of the Acuerdo Nacional (Morínigo and Silvero, 1986, p. 137). This result indicates that AN's mobilizing effect was low among the Paraguayan people and, consequently, that it, in itself, was hardly regarded by either the softliners or the hardliners as presenting a serious challenge to the regime.

Social Movements

The impact of the opposition parties may be more fairly judged if it is seen in a broader perspective. The Catholic Church and the peasant, labor and student movements constituted, together with the political parties, a growing opposition front which the regime could not neglect. These groups also joined in various umbrella organizations, such as the Coordinadora Nacional por Elecciones Libres (AN together with labor and student organizations), the Movimiento Democrático Paraguayo (led by the recently elected Mayor of Asunción, Carlos Filizzola) and Encuentro Permanente de Organizaciones Sociales (Abente, 1989, p. 31; Sandgren, 1988, p. 61).

After a period of fairly moderate criticism, the Catholic Church, through the Conferencia Episcopal Paraguaya (CEP), began in the early 1980s to show growing discontent at the regime by, for example, openly criticizing the level of corruption and the spread of smuggling (Keesing's, 33458), by publicly supporting the peasants' demands for land, by making plans for social action among the poor, and by proposing, in 1986, a national dialogue between the government, the opposition parties and private business (Carter, 1991, pp. 77–86; Nickson, 1988, p. 246). Moreover the CEP issues the weekly bulletin, *El Sendero*, which during the last Stroessner years was the main opposition paper, and owns Radio Cáritas, the main opposition radio station after the government had closed down Radio Ñandutí in January 1987 (Carter, 1991, p. 83; Sandgren, 1988, p. 20). In the final years of the Stroessner rule, the Church began to act even more openly and directly against the regime through, for example, demonstrations, open support for political prisoners (Sandgren, 1988, p. 21) and the boycott, in 1988, of Stroessner's last reinauguration ceremony (Carter, 1991, p. 94; Keesing's, 36688).

Although the trade-union movement in Paraguay was (and remains) extremely small and weak, it also formed a part of the growing opposition to the Stroessner regime.[12] In 1985 a breakaway group within the official and Stroessner-controlled trade-union body, Confederación Paraguaya de Trabajadores (CPT), formed the Movimiento Intersindical de Trabajadores (MIT), which was soon recognized by international trade union organizations (Nickson, 1988, p. 247). The independent labor movement may have reached its most important role in the political process through its contacts and negotiations with the frustrated business community. Sandgren (1988, p. 28) suggests that MIT, through these contacts, gained a semi-legal status that increased its freedom of action. The erosion of the business community's support for the

Stroessner regime was a result of the economic recession that followed the completion of the Itaipú project.[13] Stroessner's development model, they thought, was too state-centered and even 'anti-industrial' (LASA, 1989, p. 42).[14] In this context of a growing economic crisis that could lead to widespread social unrest, private business considered it necessary to negotiate with an independent representative of the workers (Sandgren, 1988, p. 28).

Land scarcity and the extremely unequal land distribution made the peasant movements more and more discontented during the 1980s. This discontent laid the basis for the emergence of at least four larger rural organizations, more or less tied to political parties, the Church or the trade unions (Sandgren, 1988, pp. 24–6). Occupation of land became a frequently used means to draw attention to the peasants' precarious situation. The largest of these organizations, the Movimiento Campesino Paraguayo (MCP), demanded a popular dialogue that included a much more radical reform program than the Church's corresponding national dialogue (Nickson, 1988, p. 256).

In April 1987 an independent student organization was formed by some 6000 students who had broken away two years earlier from the official Federación Universitaria del Paraguay (FUP). The new organization, Federación de Estudiantes Universitarios del Paraguay (FEUP), called for the independence of students from the government, the political parties, the Church and so on. It also recommended the active participation of students in the nation's policy process (Sandgren, 1988, p. 30). In spite of the regime's heavy repression, FEUP successfully mobilized students at Paraguay's two universities and soon became the largest of the two student organizations.

In sum, the opposition to the Stroessner regime spoke with louder voices and became better organized during the 1980s. Through street demonstrations, land occupations, strikes, media protests and so on, the opposition attempted to force the government to open up the authoritarian system. As already noted, the government was not insensitive. It reacted to the growing opposition with, on the one hand, increased violence and repression, but also, on the other, with small acts of liberalization. In December 1984 it permitted the return from exile of several MOPOCO politicians (Keesing's, 33457) and in April 1987 the main opposition leader, the exiled Domingo Laíno, was allowed to return. The same month it lifted the state of siege which had been in force, almost continuously, since 1947. Furthermore it began to authorize some demonstrations and meetings organized by the opposition parties as well as to give way to some of the rural land occupations. In May 1987 – to mention the most dramatic case – the government eventually accepted 4000 peasants' demands for access to foreign-owned land in the Alto Paraná region after police and army forces had encircled them for months (Americas Watch Committee, 1988, pp. 27–31).

In spite of these government concessions, many observers point to the weakness of the opposition groups and their insignificant role in the transition (Roett, 1989, pp. 135–6; Lezcano, 1989, pp. 50–1). Indeed Stroessner was not overthrown by these groups. On the contrary, the transition in Paraguay is a clear example of a 'transition from above' (Simón, 1989, p. 9). Nevertheless the role of the opposition during the pre-coup period should not be underestimated. As already mentioned, the Paraguayan *caudillismo* system under Stroessner was to a great extent built on smuggling and corruption (in other words, crime), which meant that the regime members had incentives to keep a low public and international profile. When, in the 1980s, the opposition groups became more vocal and better organized the basic structure of the regime became more and more visible both domestically and, perhaps more importantly, internationally. This, in turn, isolated the regime even further and aggravated the antagonisms within its three branches – the government, the armed forces and the Colorado Party. The important question is why the opposition dared to speak louder and act more intensively in the 1980s. Were the political parties and social movements encouraged and supported by corresponding groups or even governments in the contiguous and regional environment? In other words, did these opposition organizations function as linkage groups through which the regional democratic wave could spread?

Much more research is needed to map and analyze the role of the opposition parties and movements as linkage groups in the transition process. Little is known, for example, about the extent to which the neighboring regime changes functioned as sources of political learning for the Paraguayan political actors (Bermeo, 1992, p. 283). Therefore the impact of international–national linkages on the behavior of the opposition will only be touched upon briefly in the concluding section of this chapter. In the following section the focus is on the regime's external relations, which are particularly significant in a case of 'transition from above'.

The Regime's Relations with the Contiguous Environment

It has already been noted that the political history of Paraguay has been, to a large extent, conditioned by the behavior of two of the three contiguous neighbors, Brazil and Argentina, whereas contact with Bolivia was almost non-existent from the war between the two countries in 1932–5 (the Chaco War) up to the fall of Stroessner. Obviously the shifts from military to civilian and democratic rule in Argentina (1983) and Brazil (1985) had a direct impact on the political–diplomatic relations between Asunción and the governments of these two countries. Moreover, and even more important, the regime shifts in these countries, as well as Uruguay, paved the way for an integration process in the Southern Cone from which the Stroessner regime was excluded. The bilateral economic relations, however, seem to have suffered much less from the regime changes in Buenos Aires and Brasilia.

Relations with Argentina

The return to democracy in Argentina led to a far-reaching change in Buenos Aires's policy towards Paraguay: from military and political cooperation to a policy characterized by concern over the Stroessner dictatorship (Lezcano, 1990b, pp. 379). Immediately after his inauguration, President Alfonsín made it clear that he would prefer a change of political regime in Asunción.[15] Several diplomatic and political disputes contributed to the deterioration in relations between the two countries. These reached an all-time low in August 1987 when Buenos Aires sent for the Argentine ambassador to Paraguay and did not allow him return to Asunción until three months later (Keesing's, 35888; Bouvier, 1990, p. 258; Lezcano, 1990b, p. 380).

The deterioration in diplomatic relations was, to a large extent, caused by the support of the respective side for opposition forces in the neighboring country. Stroessner hosted Argentine officers who were accused of being involved in the 'dirty war', while Alfonsín offered the exiled political parties and factions plenty of room for demonstrations and other political actions against the Stroessner regime (Keesing's, 34417; Masi, 1990, p. 23; Lezcano, 1990b, pp. 379–80; Bouvier, 1990, p. 258). On a lower regime level the relations were not that bad. Some state governors, such as the present president of Argentina, Carlos Menem, maintained good relations with Stroessner and paid regular visits to Asunción (Abente, 1988, p. 89; Masi, 1990, p. 23; Yopo, 1990, pp. 132–3). Obviously, however, Menem travelled to Paraguay as a leader of the Perónist Party, which Stroessner supported, rather than as a representative for Argentina.[16]

To use Masi's (1990, p. 15) terms, Alfonsín's behavior was one important factor that led to the erosion of the policy of 'benign isolation' (*aislamiento benévolo*). It has already been noted that this low-profile policy was necessary in order for the regime to maintain an economic system partly built on crime, while, at the same time, receiving international economic, financial and military aid.[17] As long as domestic stability was guaranteed and the true character of the regime was fairly unknown internationally, this policy worked very well. However the civilian and democratic government of Argentina pursued a policy that made the true character of the Stroessner regime more visible through, on the one hand, its open condemnation, even in international fora, of the regime's human rights violations (Masi, 1990, p. 23) and, on the other, its support for the exiled opposition. Thus, Alfonsín contributed greatly to a *political* isolation of Paraguay that was not benign (Masi, 1990, p. 22).

The deteriorated bilateral relations did not result in any direct economic costs for the Stroessner regime. Although in the 1980s Argentina had long been surpassed by Brazil as Paraguay's most important trading and financial partner, it received in 1986 15.1 per cent of Paraguay's exports and accounted for 14.3 per cent of Paraguay's imports (UN, 1987, p. 678). These figures indicate that economic sanctions from the Alfonsín government would have hurt the Paraguayan economy. However, according to Masi (1990, p. 23), Alfonsín never attempted to punish Stroessner by using the economic weapon.

Relations with Brazil

In contrast to the case of Argentina, the civilian takeover in Brazil in 1985 did not result in any radical change of policy vis-à-vis Paraguay. Brazil's profitable economic relations with Paraguay made the Sarney government much less willing to criticize Stroessner. It is possible that, in Brasilia, the transition to democracy in Paraguay was even regarded as unfavorable to Brazilian self-interests (Masi, 1990, pp. 23–4). Brasilia suspected that a political opening would arouse Paraguayan demands for renegotiations of the Itaipú Treaty, as well as various trade agreements. The suspicion was justified, as such demands were included in the programs of most of the opposition groups, for example the Acuerdo Nacional (SIJAU, 1986, p. 295; Abente, 1988, p. 92).[18]

Nevertheless some small changes in Brazil's policy can be detected: growing irritation over the illegal trade to and from the Brazilian free port of Paranaguá, culminating in the removal of the Paraguayan consul in the city; attempts by President Sarney to avoid official meetings with Stroessner; the termination of Brazilian assistance in the persecution of the Paraguayan opposition; and the appointment of a civilian as Brazil's ambassador to Asunción (Bouvier, 1990, pp. 258–9; Lezcano, 1990b, pp. 381–2). These political and diplomatic measures were small signals that the Brazilian government no longer supported the Stroessner regime unconditionally.

The Integration of the Southern Cone

Most observers of Paraguayan politics agree that the democratization of the two big neighbors had an indirect impact that was more important than the direct impulses from these political changes. The basis of that indirect relationship was laid when the Brazilian–Argentine relations shifted from a zero-sum to a variable-sum game (Abente, 1988, pp. 87–8).[19] This means that the democratic governments of the two countries seem to have realized that they had mutual economic and political interests in the region and that economic cooperation would help to consolidate democracy at home (Keesing's, 34157; Manzetti, 1990, p. 109). The Brazilian–Argentine economic integration pact was formalized in November 1985 in the Act of Iguazú. Some two years later, in February 1988, the Act of Alvorada sanctioned the adherence of Uruguay to the pact.

Although the economic results of the integration process in the Southern Cone have not been impressive (Manzetti, 1990), its emergence radically affected Paraguay's traditional policy and status within the region. Furthermore the declaration that the integration process should involve only democratic nations made Paraguay's participation under Stroessner impossible. Thus the integration of the contiguous environment altered the prerequisites for the traditional 'pendular' policy of Paraguay *vis-à-vis* its two huge neighbors (Simón, 1990, p. 350).[20] Asunción could no longer derive political advantage from a zero-sum foreign policy game between Argentina and Brazil. This eroded even further the 'benign isolation' and exacerbated a political isolation of an unfavorable kind (Abente, 1988, p. 88; Masi, 1990, p. 22).

The Regime's Relations with the Regional Environment

Paraguay may be a deviant case in the Latin American context because of its extreme economic and political dependence on the contiguous environment, Brazil and Argentina. Seen from a linkage perspective, this means that the recent political changes in the rest of

Latin America have only had indirect effects on the Paraguayan polity. However since, for obvious reasons, the relations with the hegemon of the Western hemisphere, the US, cannot be neglected, Washington's response to the regional democratic wave must be explored. This response is probably the most significant *indirect* effect of the democratization in Paraguay's regional environment.

Relations with the United States

It is no exaggeration to claim that the ties between Palacio de López and the White House during the first two decades of Stroessner rule were formed exclusively out of a Cold War rationale. From the point of view of the US it was evident that 'while the dictatorial nature of the government was recognized, it was always perceived as a lesser evil than the threat (or potential threat) of communism and, therefore, was always rationalized in one way or another' (Abente, 1988, p. 86). In concrete terms, this US policy meant large sums of economic and military aid, which, in the 1962–5 period, amounted to around 5 per cent of Paraguay's GDP (Abente, 1988, p. 84). In return, Washington got one of its most loyal partners in the international political arena (Mora, 1990, p. 80).

These cordial relations remained until the introduction in 1977 of President Carter's human-rights policy. The overall success of this policy is unclear. In the case of Paraguay, however, it seems evident that it had a far-reaching impact on the nation's relations with the US: US economic and military aid decreased dramatically; military advisers were temporarily withdrawn; and US diplomatic protests were frequent (Mora, 1990, p. 84). Moreover, since the Stroessner regime was not totally insensitive to these steps, one cannot conclude that Carter's policy had no intended effects. The government's decision to release about one thousand political prisoners in 1977–8 indicates this sensitivity (Abente, 1988, p. 90; Mora, 1990, p. 84).

In spite of these steps, Carter's human rights policy did not overthrow Stroessner, or any other Latin American dictator. Instead the wave of democracy in the region coincided with conservative rule in Washington. As for the policy towards Asunción, the change of US presidents in 1981 meant a return to the 'silent diplomacy' of the pre-Carter period. From the mid-1980s, however, once again the relations between the two countries deteriorated considerably and the silent diplomacy was replaced by open criticism (Masi, 1990, p. 18). The main concern that the US had with the Stroessner regime may have been the regime's involvement in the narcotics trade.[21] However US pressures on Asunción to take measures against this illegal trade were combined with hard pressures for a political opening and respect for human rights. Washington may have concluded that these issues could not be detached from the question of drug trafficking. From the point of view of the linkage approach, it is important to ask whether Washington also thought that it was not possible for them to neglect these issues in the case of Paraguay, at the same time as a wave of democracy was sweeping over almost the whole of the continent.

During the last years of Stroessner rule, the abovementioned concerns made the tensions between the US and Paraguay grow steadily: President Reagan declared in 1985 that Paraguay, together with Chile, Nicaragua and Cuba, were the only remaining dictatorships of Latin America; the US embassy in Asunción became 'a friendly gathering place for the opposition' (Abente, 1988, p. 90); the government of Paraguay threatened to declare the US ambassador, Clyde Taylor, *persona non grata* and even tear-gassed a party attended by him; Washington withdrew Paraguay from the list of countries under the generalized system of trade preferences and threatened to withdraw it from the list of recipients of anti-drug aid; and the Stroessner government, of course, responded on several occasions by charging the US with violating the non-intervention principle (Keesing's, 35194; Abente, 1988, pp. 90–1; Masi, 1990, pp. 18–21; Mora, 1990, pp. 84–8; Roett, 1989, pp. 132–3; Yopo, 1990, pp. 137–41).

It is difficult to assess to what extent the US policy affected the political process in Paraguay. On the one hand, the release of prisoners and the lifting of the state of siege may have been direct results of US pressure. On the other hand, in spite of the threats, US economic, military and anti-drug aid continued to flow into the country (Bouvier, 1990, pp. 263–6; Masi, 1990, pp. 20–1). This indicates that the greatest US influence may have been of an indirect kind, canalized through the embassy's open support for opposition forces such as the PLRA. A necessary condition for this support was that the opposition parties eliminate anti-US rhetoric, which, consequently, deprived the regime of a key source of good relations with the US. In turn, these changes in the rules of Paraguay's political game were partly a result of the obsolescence of Cold War ideology. More importantly for this study, however, it was also a result of the democratization of Paraguay's neighbors (Abente, 1988, p. 93). Thus, within a regional political context totally different from the 1960s and 1970s, Washington could do nothing but welcome the struggle for democracy in Paraguay.

CONCLUSIONS: INTERNATIONAL–NATIONAL LINKAGES AND DEMOCRATIC TRANSITION IN PARAGUAY

The linkage politics approach draws attention to political processes that may be penetrative, reactive or emulative. In the case of democratization in Paraguay it is evident that the process has emulative characteristics. Since the overthrow of Stroessner, the sequence of behavior has taken a form that is similar to the processes which, in the neighboring countries, have recently led to political democracy. This points to a political change that is, to a great extent, a result of environmental outputs. Consequently the contagion effect should be seriously taken into account in order to present as complete as possible an explanation of the liberalization and democratization in Paraguay.

Since the countries of Latin America in general and the Southern Cone in particular form a strong cultural network, the probability for political contagion within these regions is comparatively high. Paraguay is, furthermore, economically tied to its contiguous environment, making it even more likely in this specific case that radical political changes in the latter have significant effects on the internal political process. In order for political processes and events in one country to have effects in a neighboring one, however, there must be linkage groups transmitting these effects. In this study the roles of some potential linkage groups have been discussed. It was concluded that the opposition parties and social movements, through their loud protests, made the criminal character of the regime visible, both domestically and internationally. This eroded the low-profile policy of the regime that was necessary to uphold the *caudillismo* system. More research is needed to assess the impact of international–national linkages on the behavior of the opposition forces. Here it can only be concluded that the democratization in the neighboring countries widened the political space for the opposition forces, such as the illegal political party PLRA, which gained support from the highest political levels, both in Argentina and Brazil (Keesing's, 34418; Abente, 1988, pp. 88–9; Masi, 1990, note 22).

It was also concluded that the wave of democracy in the environment had an essential indirect effect on the opposition forces. Because of the changes in US and Brazilian policies towards the Stroessner regime – caused by the democratic wave – the opposition groups could, in the last years of Stroessner rule, eliminate their anti-Brazilian and anti-US rhetoric (Abente, 1988, pp. 92–3). Thus the opposition grasped the significance of the political changes in the contiguous and regional environments and, to use Abente's words, 'turned them to its own advantage' in the form of foreign support (Abente, 1988, p. 92).

The conclusions about the impact of government-level linkages on the domestic political processes are less tentative. It has been shown how detrimental the democratizations in the contiguous and regional environments were for Asunción's relations with the surrounding world. Most importantly the political transitions in Argentina and Brazil paved the way for an integration process between the South American giants and, consequently, undermined Paraguay's traditional balancing policy vis-à-vis the two. Moreover the wave of democracy in the region made it impossible for the US administration to uphold a trustworthy policy towards Paraguay without emphasizing the demand for a democratic opening.

These changes in the Stroessner government's relations with the contiguous and regional environments help explain why the political change in Paraguay did not end with the coup d'état in February 1989. The coup coalition under the leadership of General Rodríguez realized that the overthrow of Stroessner would certainly solve the military's institutional problems and, in the short run, the succession crisis, but would not suffice either to break the regime's unfavorable isolation or to silence the opposition. What was needed in a period of regional transition from authoritarian rule was to emulate the environment and start a Paraguayan democratization. The Rodríguez government's haste in holding national elections (1 May 1989) and eagerness to improve relations with the neighboring countries and the US, as well as to participate in the integration of the Southern Cone strengthen this conclusion.[22]

The transition from authoritarian rule in Paraguay is only one part of a regional political process which started in the late 1970s. Therefore, to explain this transition, Paraguay must be placed in a regional context. The domestic economic crisis, the succession crisis, the splits within the regime and the social mobilization are important internal factors which were all linked to the political transformations in Paraguay's environment. To study these linkages is to give a better understanding for the Stroessner rule ending in 1989 and being replaced by a liberalizing and democratizing regime. Thus case studies based on a linkage approach broaden the understanding of individual cases of transitions to democracy at the same time as they demystify the political phenomenon so often mentioned in the literature – the contagion of democracy in Latin America.

Notes

1. See Diamond (1991) and Giuseppe Di Palma's chapter on democracy by diffusion in Di Palma (1990).
2. Huntington (1991, p. 16) uses the concept of 'snowballing' to describe contagion of democracy.
3. Unfortunately Rosenau has not developed a linkage theory that can tell us under what conditions linkage processes can be expected. However his 'typological skeleton' (Rosenau, 1969, p. 16) can be used as a tool that helps to study such processes systematically. Hypotheses on the conditions for linkage processes can be found in theories of diffusion (see below).
4. *SALA* bases its definition on the countries' self-identification of their region. However the same definition can be reached by using quantitative criteria. In a statistical analysis of the global institutional network during 1950–80, Nierop (1989) concludes that Western Europe and Latin America are the oldest and tightest clusters of IGO members. On average, a Latin American republic shared 47 IGO memberships with another Latin American republic in 1980. The Latin American cluster corresponds to SALA's standard definition of the region.
5. A transition involves liberalization as well as democratization. The former means the extension of the human and civil rights considered necessary for a liberal democracy, whereas the latter means the extension and effectuation of the rules and procedures which guarantee the principle of citizenship (see O'Donnell and Schmitter, 1986, pp. 7–8). According to the LASA observation group (LASA, 1989, p. 46), the liberalization immediately after the coup against Stroessner was obvious, including a marked decrease in human rights violations and the establishment of a 'remarkable degree of freedom of the press, speech, and assembly' (LASA, 1989, p. 46). The democratization was more problematic: the lifting of the ban against party activity did not include communist parties; the ruling Colorado Party totally controlled the electoral machinery in the 1989 elections; electoral fraud was systematic and widespread; the electoral law which guarantees the majority party two-thirds of the parliamentary seats remained intact. However great steps towards political democracy were taken when municipal elections were held in May 1991, and elections to a constituent assembly in December 1991.
6. See Roett and Sacks (1991, pp. 133–4) for details about Rodríguez's involvement in smuggling and drug-trafficking.
7. The rumor was that the *militantes* planned to appoint Gustavo Stroessner (promoted an air force colonel on 31 December 1988) as Alfredo Stroessner's successor (Lezcano, 1989, p. 30; Miranda, 1990, p. 130; Nickson, 1988, p. 258; Roett and Sacks, 1991, p. 130).
8. See Abente (1989, pp. 33–40) and Lezcano (1990a, pp. 6–10) for insightful analyses of this split and its consequences. Abente (1989, p. 35) claims that the hardliner v. softliner description of the split is only relatively true because of the *tradicionalistas'* ambivalent attitude towards liberalization.
9. This was quite self-evident since membership of the Colorado Party was

mandatory for officers (see Lezcano, 1989, pp. 10–11).

10. The weak support for the loyal opposition parties became evident in the elections after the coup. PLR received 1.1 per cent of the vote in the congressional elections, whereas PL won only 0.4 per cent.

11. The AN gained support from the *éticos*, which in April 1988 signed a document, together with the PLRA, in which they demanded a transition to democracy led by a provisional Colorado–PLRA government (Keesing's, 36687).

12. According to Sandgren (1988, p. 28) only 2 per cent of the working population were members of trade unions before the coup. CPT had 17 000 members, whereas MIT had 3000.

13. The Itaipú hydro-electric plant – one of the world's largest plants – is on the Paraguayan–Brazilian border (the River Paraná). The joint Paraguayan–Brazilian project to build the plant (which was finished in 1982) resulted in a period of rapid economic growth in Paraguay.

14. According to Masi (1990, p. 8) the traditional authoritarian character of the Stroessner regime hindered a sweeping capitalist development and, therefore, the regime provoked its own breakdown.

15. Alfonsín held several meetings with Domingo Laíno during the latter's exile in Argentina. He also acted openly to try to obtain the release of political prisoners, for example, the MOPOCO leader González Casabianca (Keesing's, 34418; Yopo, 1990, p. 130; see also Masi, 1990, note 18).

16. Menem was heavily criticized by the *renovadores* faction within the Perónist party for his visits to Paraguay. This perhaps made Menem less prone to show sympathy for the Stroessner regime during the presidential election campaign which coincided with Stroessner's last months in power (Abente, 1988, p. 89).

17. Simón (1990, p. 233) calls this low profile policy *albanización sudamericana*. Although this term hints at the meaning of Stroessner's policy, a comparison with the almost total isolation of communist Albania is not relevant.

18. In the AN program of April 1984 it is stated that 'The government should make a revision of the Itaipú treaty . . . since the clauses currently in force regarding prices – and other issues – adversely affect the interests of Paraguay' (SIJAU, 1986, p. 295).

19. A prerequisite for the economic integration seems to have been a change in Brazilian foreign policy doctrine which was in part based on an old geopolitical tradition (Abente, 1988, pp. 78–9). This policy frightened Brazil's neighbors and made them suspect that cooperative efforts of Brasilia had expansionist motives (see Ferris, 1981, p. 158). Obviously this was one important source of friction between Brazil and Argentina.

20. See Birch (1990) for an analysis of the pendular policy.

21. The appointment in 1985 of an expert on drug trafficking (Clyde Taylor) as ambassador to Asunción shows the US concern with this issue.

22. On 26 March 1991, Paraguay became a member of the Mercado Común del Cono Sur, or Mercosur (the Common Market of the Southern Cone) when it, together with Argentina, Brazil and Uruguay, signed the Act of Asunción.

References

ABENTE, D. (1988) 'Constraints and Opportunities: Prospects for Democratization in Paraguay', *Journal of Interamerican Studies and World Affairs*, vol. 30, no. 1.

ABENTE, D. (1989) *Stronismo, Post-Stronismo, and the Prospects for Democratization in Paraguay*, Working paper no. 119, The Helen Kellog Institute for International Studies, University of Notre Dame, Notre Dame.

AMERICAS WATCH COMMITTEE (1988) *Paraguay: Repression in the Countryside* (New York: Americas Watch, May).

ANGELL, A. (1989) 'La cooperación internacional en apoyo de la democracia política en America Latina: El caso de Chile', *Foro Internacional*, vol. XXX, no. 2.

BALOYRA, E. (ed.) (1987) *Comparing New Democracies: Transition and Consolidation in Mediterranean Europe and the Southern Cone* (Boulder and London: Westview Press).

BERMEO, N. (1992) 'Democracy and the Lessons of Dictatorship', *Comparative Politics*, vol. 24, no. 3.

BIRCH, M. (1990) 'La politica pendular: politica de desarollo del Paraguay en la post guerra', in J.L. Simón (ed.) (1990).

BOSTROM, M. (1989) 'Political Waves in Latin America, 1940–1988', *Ibero Americana: Nordic Journal of Latin American Studies*, vol. XIX, no. 1.

BOUVIER, V. (1990) 'Cambios en el ambiente internacional', in J.L. Simón (ed.) (1990).

CARTER, M. (1991) 'The Role of the Paraguayan Catholic Church in the Downfall of the Stroessner Regime', *Journal of Interamerican Studies and World Affairs*, vol. 32, no. 4.

COLLIER, D. and R. MESSICK (1975) 'Prerequisites versus Diffusion: Testing Alternative Explanations of Social Security Adoption', *American Political Science Review*, vol. 69, no. 4.

DIAMOND, L. (1991) 'Ripe for Difussion: International and Domestic Factors in the Global Trend Toward Democracy', paper presented at the meeting of the International Studies Association, Vancouver, 1991.

DIAMOND, L. and J. LINZ (1989) 'Introduction: Politics, Society, and Democracy in Latin America', in L. Diamond *et al.* (eds).

DIAMOND, L., J. LINZ and S.M. LIPSET (eds) (1989) *Democracy in Developing Countries: Latin America* (Boulder: Lynne Rienner).

DI PALMA, G. (1990) *To Craft Democracies: An Essay on Democratic Transition* (Berkeley/Los Angeles: University of California Press).

FERRIS, E. (1981) 'The Andean Pact and the Amazon Treaty: Reflections of Changing Latin American Relations', *Journal of Interamerican Studies and World Affairs*, vol. 23, no. 2.

HICKS, F. (1971) 'Interpersonal Relationships and Caudillismo in Paraguay', *Journal of Interamerican Studies and World Affairs*, vol. 13, no. 1.

HUNTINGTON, S.P. (1991) 'Democracy's Third Wave', *Journal of Democracy*, vol. 2, no. 2.

KARVONEN, L. (1981) *'Med vårt västra grannland som förebild': en undersökning av policydiffusion från Sverige till Finland* (Åbo: Åbo Akademi Forskningsinstitut).

Keesing's Contemporary Archives/Record of World Events (1985–90) vols 31–6 (London: Longman).

LATIN AMERICAN STUDIES ASSOCIATION (LASA) (1989) 'The May 1 1989 Elections in Paraguay: Toward a New Era of Democracy?', Report by International Commission of the LASA to Observe the Paraguayan Elections, *LASA Forum*, vol. XX, no. 3.

LEZCANO, C.M. (1989) *The Military Regime of Alfredo Stroessner: Armed Forces and Politics in Paraguay (1954–1988)*, Grupo de Ciencias Sociales (GCS), Red Series, document no. 1, Asunción.

LEZCANO, C.M. (1990a) *Las fuerzas armadas y el proceso de transicion a la democracia en el Paraguay*, Grupo de Ciencias Sociales (GCS), Serie roja, Documento de Trabajo, no. 5, Asunción.

LEZCANO, C.M. (1990b) 'Relaciones exteriores del Paraguay y percepciones de amenaza: La política pendular del régimen de Stroessner y las perspectivas de cambios después del golpe de febrero de 1989', in J.L. Simón (ed.) (1990).

LOWENTHAL, A. (ed.) (1991) *Exporting Democracy: The United States and Latin America, Themes and Issues* (Baltimore: Johns Hopkins University Press).

MANZETTI, L. (1990) 'Argentine–Brazilian Economic Integration: An Early Appraisal', *Latin American Research Review*, vol. XXV, no. 3.

MASI, F. (1990) 'Relaciones internacionales del Paraguay: con Stroessner y sin Stroessner', paper presented at the conference, 'The Transition to Democracy in Paraguay: Problems and Prospects', The Helen Kellog Institute for International Studies, University of Notre Dame, 7–9 December.

McDONALD, R. and M. RUHL (1989) *Party Politics and Elections in Latin America* (Boulder: Westview Press).

MIDLARSKY, M. (1970) 'Mathematical Models of Instability and a Theory of Diffusion', *International Studies Quarterly*, vol. 14, no. 1.

MIRANDA, C. (1990) *The Stroessner Era: Authoritarian Rule in Paraguay* (Boulder: Westview Press).

MORA, F. (1990) 'Relaciones Estados Unidos–Paraguay: Conflicto y Cooperación', *Perspectiva Internacional Paraguaya*, vol. II, no. 3.

MORÍNIGO, J. and I. SILVERO (1986) *Opiniones y actitudes en el Paraguay: Resultados de una encuesta de opinión* (Asunción: Fundación Friedrich Naumann Universidad Católica Nuestra Señora de la Asunción).

MORLINO, L. (1987) 'Democratic Establishments: A Dimensional Analysis', in E. Baloyra (ed.).

NICKSON, A. (1988) 'Tyranny and Longevity: Stroessner's Paraguay', *Third World Quarterly*, vol. 10, no. 1.

NIEROP, T. (1989) 'Macro-regions and the Global Institutional Network, 1950–1980', *Political Geography Quarterly*, vol. 8, no. 1.

O'DONNELL, G. (1986) 'Introduction to the Latin American Cases', in G. O'Donnell *et al.* (eds).

O'DONNELL, G. and P. SCHMITTER (1986) 'Tentative Conclusions about Uncertain Democracies', in G. O'Donnell *et al.* (eds).

O'DONNELL, G., P. SCHMITTER and L. WHITEHEAD (eds) (1986) *Transitions from Authoritarian Rule: Prospects for Democracy* (Baltimore and London: Johns Hopkins University Press).

PASTOR, R.A. (ed.) (1989) *Democracy in the Americas: Stopping the Pendulum* (New York and London: Holmes & Meier).

PRZEWORSKI, A. (1986) 'Some Problems in the Study of the Transition to

Democracy', in G. O'Donnell *et al.* (eds).

ROETT, R. (1989) 'Paraguay after Stroessner', *Foreign Affairs*, spring.

ROETT, R. and R.S. SACKS (1991) *Paraguay: The Personalist Legacy* (Boulder: Westview Press).

ROGERS, E. (1962) *Diffusion of Innovations* (New York: The Free Press of Glencoe).

ROSENAU, J.N. (ed.) (1969) *Linkage Politics: Essays on the Convergence of National and International Systems* (New York: The Free Press).

ROUQUIÉ, A. (1989) *The Military and the State in Latin America* (Berkeley: University of California Press).

SANDGREN, C. (1988) *Paraguay – en landrapport* ('Paraguay – a country study') (Stockholm: SIDA (Swedish International Development Agency).

SIJAU (Secretario Internacional de Juristas por la Amnistía en Uruguay) (1986) *Paraguay: Un desafío a la responsibilidad internacional* (Montevideo: Ediciones de la Banda Oriental/SIJADEP).

SIMÓN, J.L. (1989) *El Paraguay después de Stroessner: De la transición incompleta a la democracia?* (Asunción: Centro Paraguayo de Estudios Sociológicos (Cuadernos de discusión)).

SIMÓN, J.L. (1990) 'Una política exterior de automarginamiento: El Paraguay en la crisis terminal del autoritarismo de Stroessner y América Latina en la década de los ochenta', in J.L. Simón (ed.) (1990).

SIMÓN, J.L. (ed.) (1990) *Política exterior y relaciones internacionales del Paraguay contemporáneo* (Asunción: Centro Paraguayo de Estudios Sociológicos (Serie relaciones internacionales, vol. 1)).

Statistical Abstract of Latin America (SALA) (1988) (Los Angeles: UCLA Latin American Center Publications, University of California).

UNITED NATIONS (1987) *International Trade Statistics Yearbook 1987.*

WAISMAN, C.H. (1987) *Reversal of Development in Argentina: Postwar Counterrevolutionary Policies and Their Structural Consequences* (Princeton: Princeton University Press).

WAISMAN, C.H. (1989) 'Argentina: Autarkic Industrialization and Illegitimacy', in L. Diamond *et al.* (eds).

WELCH, C. (1987) *No Farewell to Arms? Military Disengagement from Politics in Africa and Latin America* (Boulder: Westview Press).

WHITEHEAD, L. (1986) 'International Aspects of Democratization', in G. O'Donnell *et al.* (eds).

WHITEHEAD, L. (1990) 'International Support for Democratization', paper presented at the ECPR joint sessions of workshops, Bochum, West Germany, 2–7 April.

WIARDA, H. (1986) 'Can Democracy be Exported? The Quest for Democracy in US–Latin American Policy', in K. Middlebrook and C. Rico (eds), *The United States and Latin America in the 1980s: Contending Perspectives on a Decade of Crisis* (Pittsburgh: University of Pittsburgh Press).

WILLIAMS, J.H. (1977) 'Foreign Técnicos and the Modernization of Paraguay, 1840–1870', *Journal of Interamerican Studies and World Affairs*, vol. 19, no. 2.

WILLIAMS, J.H. (1987) 'Paraguay's Stroessner: Losing Control?', *Current History*, January.

YOPO, M. (1990) 'La politica exterior del Paraguay: continuidad y cambio en el aislamiento', in J.L. Simón (ed.) (1990).

10 Post-Marxism, the Left and Democracy in Latin America

Ronald H. Chilcote

Marxism today is in a period of crisis, provoking a rethinking of its premises and usefulness but also leading some left theorists to search for a new understanding as they move on to a 'post-Marxist terrain'. The present chapter explores the implications of this crisis and the turning of some intellectuals away from Marxism in their retreat from analysis of class and class struggle in Latin America. The intent is not only to invite dialogue on this question, but to challenge the premises of the new thinking. One might begin by asking to what extent Latin American intellectuals exiled in Europe were associated with the thought of Gramsci, Poulantzas, Althusser and others. Did Eurocommunism of the late 1970s influence their thinking? What was the impact of dictatorship and repression upon the new thinking as discussion moved from rural and urban guerrilla warfare to issues of political culture, pluralist democracy and reformism? What was the significance of the split in the communist movement since the 1960s, especially among currents that sought collaborative political arrangements and alliances with social democratic and liberal currents? What has happened to the political parties as they came to dominate the democratic openings, thereby obscuring the mass popular movements that emerged to challenge the dictatorships? How does a class analysis relate to mass popular movements (feminist, ecological, grassroots and so on)? What is the situation of the labor movement and its traditional ties to the state (especially in Argentina, Brazil and Mexico), its struggle for autonomy and its participation in the electoral process? To what extent have the advances of capitalism worldwide and the reorganization of capital and labor in Latin America had their consequences for the new thinking? Have these changes (including a declining standard of living) undermined the revolutionary commitment of intellectuals tied to the state-financed universities? As regimes moved from dictatorship to democracy, to what extent were state institutions and class forces structurally retained, and what has been the impact on post-Marxist thinking? What is the state of the current search for a 'new left' now that some intellectuals see the working class in decline and the traditional left parties in disarray?

The notion of post-Marxism has appeared in recent theoretical literature as the latest of many 'post' formulations of an evolution toward a new society. These formulations imply a transition from the contradictions of the bourgeois order, the class struggle and the dilemmas of capitalism to a newly emerging order devoid of ideology and conflict. Daniel Bell foreshadowed this trend with his advocacy of an 'end of ideology' (1960), while his thesis of the 'postindustrial society' (1976) envisioned better living standards and a closing of the gap between social classes through mass education, mass production and more consumption. Other 'post' formulations have referred to society as 'post-bourgeois', 'posteconomic', 'postcivilized', 'postmaterialist' and 'postmodern' society (see Frankel, 1987, for discussion and criticism of these 'post' forms; and Jameson, 1984 and 1989, for the view that they are idealistic manifestations in defense of capitalism). However radical criticisms of these conservative and liberal views have not deterred some left theorists from also moving beyond capitalism. The anticapitalist and utopian socialism of Rudolf Bahro (1984) and André Gorz (1980), for example, provide a basis for their search for a more egalitarian and democratic world. Fred Block (1987) sees the state as comprising less traditional hierarchies, a postindustrial 'debureaucratization' dependent on a renewal of citizen participation in the regulation of social life. Samuel Bowles and Herbert Gintis (1986) seek a radical democratic synthesis in their advocacy of postliberalism, and argue that neither liberalism nor Marxism has given priority to democracy. Their postliberalism seeks the expansion of personal rights through traditional forms of representative democracy and industrial liberty while ensuring innovative and democratically accountable economic freedoms. Becker *et al.* (1987) attempt to move beyond neo-imperialist and dependency explanations of capitalist underdevelopment in their conceptualization of postimperialism. They see the coalescing of dominant class elements across national boundaries, the integration of diverse national interests on a new international basis and the rise of a transnational bourgeoisie as an alternative to a deterministic understanding of imperialism and to dependency orthodoxy. Ernesto Laclau and Chantal Mouffe (1985) move toward a 'post-Marxist terrain' in their call for a new politics based on a project of radical democracy (see Chilcote, 1988, for a full discussion of these 'post' forms).

Laclau, an Argentine social scientist now residing and teaching in England, is renowned for his attack (1971) on André Gunder Frank's thesis (1966) of capitalist development of underdevelopment in Latin America. He criticized Frank for stressing capitalist relations of exchange and circulation of commodities rather than production as Marx had emphasized in *Capital*. This essential point proved to be an early step in the process of reassessing theories of underdevelopment and dependency in the light of Marxism (many of the debates over these questions are found in *Latin American Perspectives (LAP)*, especially in issues no. 1 (1974), no. 11 (1976) and nos 30–31 (1981). In the present period, however, Laclau and Mouffe attempt to move beyond a Marxist analysis in what Ellen Meiksins Wood has characterized as their retreat from a class analysis and declassing of the socialist project. A number of propositions, synthesized from Wood (186, PP. 3–4), characterize the new direction: post-Marxism argues that the working class has not evolved into a revolutionary movement; economic class interests are relatively autonomous from ideology and politics; the working class holds no basic position within socialism; a political force may form out of 'popular' political and ideological elements, independent from class ties so that feminist, ecological, peace and other forces become effective in a changing society; a socialist movement may evolve independent of class; the objectives of socialism transcend class interests; and the struggle for socialism comprises a plurality of resistances to inequality and oppression.

The roots of the post-Marxist thinking may be found in Eurocommunist and Eurosocialist developments of the 1970s and 1980s. Fernando Claudín, a Spanish Marxist, writes (1978) about Eurocommunism in terms of historical conjunctures, the last being the economic crisis of overproduction, recession and democratic transitions in Southern Europe during the mid-1970s when the international workers movement failed to move the capitalist crisis to a socialist transition. At the time, the French and Italian communist parties agreed that, while socialism would constitute a higher phase of democracy, small and medium agrarian and industrial producers could participate in the building of socialism; they believed that the democratization of the state must increasingly provide a role for local and regional government, for a plurality of parties, and for freedom and autonomy of trade unions (Claudín, 1978, pp. 65–6). Nicos Poulantzas, a Greek Marxist who lived many years in exile in Paris, applied a class analysis to a structural theory of the state in his comparative study (1976) of the democratic openings made possible by the crisis and fall of the dictatorships in Spain, Portugal and Greece. In particular, the revolutionary period in Portugal during 1974 and 1975 may have influenced him to abandon a Marxist–Leninist position that emphasized dual power so that workers and popular forces who had built their revolutionary base outside the state apparatuses could confront state power; instead these forces might turn to the possibility of a bloodless revolution through penetration and occupation of key state apparatuses. The argument that struggle within the state apparatuses was necessary to disrupt the balance of forces and allow for a socialist transition was expressed in his later work (1978) and may have inspired some left intellectuals in the early 1980s to move beyond structured interpretations and evolve theory within a post-Marxist terrain.

The post-Marxism of Laclau and Mouffe reflects intellectual thinking that has accompanied political discourse on social democracy and democratic socialism within countries where socialist parties have come to power (especially France and Italy, Spain, Portugal and Greece since the mid-1970s). This discourse has focused on the transition to socialism, the necessity of blocs of left–center political forces to ensure a political majority within a fragmented multiparty setting, popular reforms to mitigate demands of the popular classes (workers and peasants) and tolerance to promote and develop the forces of production in the present capitalist stage. The realities of mainstream politics appear to have obscured the revolutionary rhetoric so that terms like class struggle, working class, dictatorship of the proletariat, and even Marxism itself are dropped from left dialogue.

What distinguishes Marxism from the new thinking is the traditional view that the working class is essential for its revolutionary potential because of its structural position as the class that produces capital. In excising classes from a socialist perspective, the post-Marxists avoid analysis of the exploitative relations between capital and labor as central to the accumulation and reproduction of capitalism as a mode of production. Further the emphasis on politics and ideology as autonomous from economics undermines the attention to political economy which has been of interest to classical and contemporary Marxists. Debate on the nature of the capitalist mode of production no longer appears as important. Consequently classes and class struggle are displaced by an emphasis on political pluralism, political organizations and interest groups. Analysis of the state may stress differences between the power bloc and the people while overlooking opposition between capital and labor. There may also be a tendency to focus on a single or a few political institutions; the segmenting of political forces may limit prospects for a societal overview. Political movements attempting to penetrate the mainstream may be isolated; populist strategies designed to challenge the establishment may be diffused and weakened by the separation of particular interests.

Laclau and Mouffe are explicit in their denunciation of Marxism: 'it is no longer possible to maintain the conception of subjectivity and classes elaborated by Marxism, nor its vision of the historical course of capitalist development' (1985, p. 4). Their ideas relate especially to the crisis of left intellectuals. On the one hand, there is the rise and decline of French structuralism once so dominantly represented in the work of Louis Althusser (see especially the useful analysis of Hirsh, 1981). On the other hand, the English experience reflects the moderation of a Marxist position among some intellectuals through such journals as *Marxism Today* (the theoretical journal of British Eurocommunism), *New Socialist* and *The New Statesman* and their withdrawal from some basic socialist positions. Ralph Miliband (1985) calls them 'the new revisionists' and Ellen Meiksins Wood (1986) labels them 'the new true socialists'. Their ranks include Gareth Steadman Jones of the History Workshop group at Oxford, and Paul Hirst and Barry Hindess who recanted their earlier orthodox interpretation of mode of production. While these intellectuals differ in many respects, they appear to agree that the primacy of organized labor should be repudiated because the working class in capitalist countries has failed to live up to its revolutionary expectations and the model of struggle should now incorporate a multitude of interests emanating from various strata, groups and social movements.

Historically the defection of left intellectuals from a Marxist discourse in the US has been part of a cyclical phenomenon dating from events since the Russian Revolution, the appearance of communist, socialist and Trotskyist groups of intellectuals and the shift of many of them to the right toward social democratic and neo-conservative tendencies as they were affected by the Stalinist purges of 1934–6, the rise of McCarthyism during the early 1950s and the impact of advanced capitalism. Alexander Bloom (1986), Terry Cooney (1986) and Alan Wald (1987) provide a portrayal of this left and its maverick commitments since the 1930s, while Russell Jacoby (1987) compares a 'classical' generation of intellectuals, born at the turn of the century, with a 'transitional' generation, born around 1915 to 1920, and then with a generation of the post-1940s which sought refuge in the universities and lost its role as 'public intellectuals'. Accounts by Gitlin (1987), Isserman (1987) and Miller (1987) do well in delineating the rise and decline of the new left since the late 1960s.

I became interested in these developments a few years ago during a sabbatical leave in Portugal, where I assessed the literature on the Portuguese revolutionary experience of 1974–5, about which I am at present writing. These events caught the interests of left intellectuals at a historical conjuncture similar to the workers and students' uprising in France in 1968, the victory of socialist Salvador Allende in 1970 and the Beijing demonstrations of 1989. With the exception of those who remained loyal to the Partido Comunista Português (PCP), which continues today to adhere to its Stalinist foundations, I was especially struck by the demise of the Portuguese left and the broad retreat of intellectuals from a Marxist discourse. While the dictatorship of nearly half a century had not tolerated such a discourse, socialism clearly became the focus after the coup of 25 April 1974, and a transition to socialism was anticipated, if not in the ardor of the revolutionary moments, in the writing of the 1976 constitution. Visits to Madrid and Barcelona, Athens, Paris and London during my year abroad brought awareness of changes in left intellectual thinking.

Table 10.1 juxtaposes recent Marxist thinking with its non-Marxist counterpart so that the former would include works on imperialism and dependency, in particular the notions of sub-imperialism in Marini (1978) and the new dependency in Santos (1970) with attention to class and class struggle, and the latter thinking would include most of the work on dependency, from the *desarrollista*, or developmental approach in Furtado (1964) to the associated dependent capitalism of Cardoso (1972). The aforementioned issues of *LAP* present these views. Emanating from and in response to the dependency debates have been the works on the mode of production (see Foster-Carter, 1978; Ruccio and Simon, 1986, for an overview), some of it represented in the journal *Latin American Perspectives* (Rodrigues, 1980; Rojas, 1980; Sindico, 1980) and on internationalization of capital (Howe, 1981; Barkin, 1981). A counterpart of these perspectives would be such radical proposals as the New International Economic Order (NIEO), a third world policy prescription to correct inequalities between wealthy and poor nations. Mainstream social science approaches to understanding the military dictatorships and authoritarian rule that have persisted in Latin America since the 1960s include conceptions of traditional corporatism and societal corporatism (Schmitter, 1974); bureaucratic authoritarianism (O'Donnell, 1973, 1988); and the transition from authoritarian rule to social democracy (O'Donnell, Schmitter and Whitehead, 1986). These approaches were analyzed and criticized in *LAP*, issue 58 (Summer 1988). The

Table 10.1   Comparison of Marxist and non-Marxist trends in Latin America

Innovated revisionist and Marxist trends	*Innovated non-Marxist or anti-Marxist trends*
Imperialism and dependency with class and class struggle (Santos; Marini)	Dependency and institutional analysis: Desarrollismo (Prebisch) and associated dependent capitalism (Cardoso)
Internationalization of capital and modes of production (Montoya; Rodrigues; Royas; Sindico)	New International Economic Order
State in Instrumental and Structural formulations; state and national security (Alves)	Corporatism and bureaucratic authoritarianism (Schmitter; O'Donnell)
Transition to democratic and revolutionary socialism (Harris; Burbach and Núñez; Fagen, Deere and Coraggio)	Post-Marxism, pluralism and the retreat from class (Laclau and Mouffe)

Marxist literature has focused more explicitly on the state in its instrumental and structural forms, for example on the role of the national security state (Alves, 1985). Finally the Marxist interpretation has examined the question of democracy in terms of a transition to democratic and revolutionary socialisms (see Harris, 1988), especially in the case of third world revolutions (see the essays in Fagen, Deere and Coraggio, 1986) and of Nicaragua in particular (Burbach and Núñez, 1987). Thinking about the socialist transition dominates debate on the left over the prospects for revolution, especially in the Caribbean and Central America. The debate incorporates the issue of democracy, leading, on the one hand, to ideas on the way to strengthen and deepen socialism within Marxism and, on the other, to post-Marxism and the abandonment of many Marxist principles.

The following six sections relate the questions raised at the outset; these sections deal with the impact of external intellectual influences upon Latin America; the consequences of repressive periods upon cultural production; changes in the intellectual community brought about by the advances and reorganizations of world capitalism; the persistence of the traditional state institutions and class forces in the transition to democratic rule; the role of formal representative democracy, manifested through political parties in constraining mass popular movements; and the position of the left parties on the reorganization of capital.

REVISIONS OF MARXIST POLITICAL THOUGHT

The crisis of Marxist political thought in Latin America dates back a decade. Tomás Vasconi (1990) notes the differences in the rhetoric of the 1970s, in which revolution and socialism were stressed, from that of the 1980s, in which democracy and socialism became the dominant discourse. He identifies one source of dialogue around the question of democracy as taking place at the 1978 meetings in San José, Costa Rica, of the Consejo Latinamericano de Ciencias Sociales and, for another, he cites a paper by Laclau on hegemony and popular alternatives in Latin America, presented in a seminar at Morelia, Mexico, during 1980 (this changing discourse is also traced by Lechner, 1985a, 1985b and criticized by Cueva, 1984).

The roots of the crisis, however, are at least partially attributable to external intellectual influences. Exiles in Europe influenced the substance of the left discourse in Latin America, and it useful to identify the connections while acknowledging that the debate in Latin America differs from that in Europe, just as the debate in England differs from that in France and in Italy or Portugal and Spain (a point emphasized in correspondence from Michael Lowy, Paris, 27 January and 2 May 1987). Eurocommunist developments and the break of the traditional communist parties from Stalinism provided an opening for a coalition of left forces, most notably in Italy. This also led to splits within the movement, especially in France and Spain. During the 1960s the Sino–Soviet dispute resulted in a serious division within the Partido Comunista Brasileiro (PCB) as well as the Portuguese PCP. In each case the dissident offshoot splintered into a multitude of groups oriented toward a revolutionary outcome influenced by Albanian, Chinese or Cuban experiences. Within Brazil from 1968 to 1972 many of these groups joined the urban armed struggle but ultimately succumbed to the ruthless and overwhelming repression of police and security forces. Many intellectuals who had associated with these groups fled to Western Europe, where the structuralist influence of Althusser and Poulantzas was dominant in left circles. They also joined a wave of intellectuals inspired by the thought of Antonio Gramsci. Latin Americans exiled in Lisbon, Madrid and Paris were able to observe the fall of the dictatorships in Southern Europe and contemplate the democratic openings and the pragmatic maneuverings of the socialist and communist parties in their pursuit of Marxist theory and practice. Once they returned home, many of them turned to practical politics and the prospects for democracy. In the case of Brazil, for example, before the 1964 military coup

Leonel Brizola had followed in a populist–nationalist tradition, but later associated with the Socialist International, especially after his return to Brazil in the early 1980s, when he became governor of the state of Rio de Janeiro.

PERIODS OF REPRESSION AND THE IMPACT ON CULTURAL PRODUCTION AND INTELLECTUAL THINKING

Prior to the democratic openings, structural Marxism had been assimilated by the left in Latin America (see Harris, 1979, for a useful overview). The influence of Althusser and Poulantzas was visible (see Portantiero, 1974, for an early example, and Cardoso, 1982) and the work of Gramsci was popular (Coutinho, 1981). Vasconi believes that Gramsci was consistently Marxist in his thinking, in contrast to the way Portantiero and other Latin Americans used his thought in advocating new directions for socialism. However leftist parties and labor organizations had also been shaken by systematic repression and internal disorganization. Dialogue began to shift from issues of rural and urban guerrilla warfare to political culture, pluralist democracy and reformism. At stake were traditional leftist conceptions of the revolution and the need to destroy the bourgeois state, the impossibility of capitalism in the periphery and the role of popular mobilization and democracy (see, for example, the works by Coutinho, 1979; Kondor, 1980; and Weffort, 1984, along with the essays by Cardoso, Sousa and Weffort in Stepan, 1989, pp. 299–394).

In his summary of recent debate within the 'renovation of the left' in Latin America, Robert Barros (1986) identifies three prominent views. The first sees the reinstitutionalization of democratic forms as only a tactical objective for the working class, a step in facilitating the formation of a revolutionary movement with real participatory, not formal, democracy as its basis. Barros criticizes this 'orthodox' tendency because it appears to disguise authoritarian Marxism as democracy with answers to all fundamental questions: 'Inevitably, the discourse of "formal" and "real" democracy turns out to be a cover for an authoritarian Marxism whose real concepts are objective interests, vanguard party, political revolution, and dictatorship of the proletariat' (1986, p. 57). A second current envisages democracy without socialism. It disregards traditional left issues such as the concern for capitalism and imperialism and the struggle for equality. Inherent in this view is the hope that formal or representative democracy can lead to a higher form of democracy. Barros criticizes these views for failing to examine objective constraints and strategies that might lead to a different democracy (citing Landi, 1981, and Delich, 1983). A third position, the radical democratic alternative to bourgeois democracy, argues that a political recomposition must move away from traditional left concerns, including a 'secularization' of Marxism (Moulian, 1981b); abandonment of predetermined lines of thinking (Portantiero, 1981); and deemphasis of the role of the working class (Nun, 1981). Gramscian themes of hegemony and national populism pervade this discourse, which looks to alternative forms of culture, organization and struggle in the building of a plurality of social opposition against domination and institutionalized hierarchies; the implementation of democratic practices and institutions will lead to the formation of a broad popular–democratic movement (see Flisfisch, 1983, and Moulian, 1983, for reflections on this possibility). Barros believes that these theorists (for example, Aricó, 1980; Nun, 1984; Portantiero and Ipola, 1981) are not relating to their real situations: 'we are left with the contours of a normative conception of democracy, but no attempt to ground possibilities for its realization . . . this position obscures the tension between its project and fragile bases of postauthoritarian democratic compromises' (Barros 1986, p. 66).

Particularly interesting is the case of Chile where, under the Allende regime, socialism was to evolve in a peaceful way, only to be toppled by a military dictatorship, resulting in the repressive aftermath and struggle for a democratic opening in which leftist intellectuals have sought a theory of 'socialist renovation'. Manuel Antonio Garretón has analyzed this as a process of the left distancing itself from the traditional political model by stripping away the orthodoxy of the Marxist–Leninist tradition so that the economic structure is not determinant in all social transformations, a scientific conception of human political action is abandoned, and a specific class is no longer identified with or finds its expression in a vanguard or party. Furthermore the conception of socialism need not be deduced from a concrete classical model of socialism, nor must there be an instrumental view of democracy or a reduction of nation–class–party to a particular political action. Garretón argues that the core of Marxism–Leninism is crumbling

because the very elements of the theory have withered away and lost their internal and logical consistency. This is the product of the material, social, and cultural transformations in contemporary society. The emergence of the tertiary sector of the economy, technological

change, the declining importance of the working class in the overall make-up of the labor force, the explosion of demands, and the
proliferation of social actors overrunning the world of labor, the
growing complexity and heterogeneity of society ... make it impossible for the socialist project to base itself entirely on one
social class (1989, p. 21).

In my own work on Brazilian intellectuals (Chilcote, 1985a, 1985b) I
draw upon examples that illustrate the vacuum of the repressive military period. Florestán Fernandes, a political sociologist who lost his
chair during the 1960s, has referred to intellectuals of this period as
'the lost generation', while Sergio Miceli linked cultural production
to 'state mechanisms' and 'markets of capital goods', implying that
the state provides resources and disseminates cultural ideology when
culture is subject to the pressures of state policy and the structures of
power. An expansion of capitalism and the alienating influences of
foreign culture accompanied the repression; part of the growth involved
new research centers, close ties between the universities and government to ensure adequate funding, and a structuring of academic intellectuals along lines of specialization in response to government planning
and priorities.

THE ADVANCES AND REORGANIZATION OF CAPITALISM AND THE IMPACT ON INTELLECTUALS

The internationalization of capital has affected relations of production
in the advanced capitalist nations as well as in Latin America. Vasconi
associates the question of democracy with consensus and peaceful pacts
or compromises that define the limits of capitalism within which social
movements function to achieve necessary cooperation and maintain
political and economic stability. Under previous dictatorships, discourse
of intellectuals looked at opposition, antagonisms and violence. He
notes that, while parliamentary struggles, strikes and other disruptions
may ensue, they do not necessarily imply a rupture of society so that
the so-called 'transition to socialism' envisaged by some intellectuals
appears within the capitalist mode of production as something similar
to the emergence of capitalism within feudal society. A real socialist
transition necessitates the expropriation of the private means of production, whereas a *transición pactada*, or compromised transition, does
not lead to socialism. Thus constraints appear in the struggles for democ-

racy and socialism: the insertion of the national political economies into the world order; the disarticulation of the internal productive apparatus because of its subordination to the international system; the concentration of property and wealth; the impoverishment of the popular and exploited classes; and the continuing military presence. These constraints reflect the complexity of society and its classes and the role of the working class in the construction of a democratic order and socialism. In a similar vein, James Petras (1988) argues that leftist intellectuals turned neo-liberal have adapted to the needs of capital while rejecting the class content and program of labor unions and left parties. Class analysis of the Latin American political economy has been obscured by attention, first to fascist categories of corporatism in order to emphasize interest groups within the authoritarian capitalist state, and, second, to Weberian categories of bureaucratic authority. Recent intellectual currents, he believes, have deemphasized the centrality of class struggle and reified the state as autonomous, stripping it of any class content. He attributes the undermining of the leftist commitment to the dependence of intellectuals on research centers that rely on funding from foreign private foundations and government aid agencies. During the repressive period while the universities and public institutions were under siege these centers became oases of research and critical analysis. The result has been the formation of a generation of 'institutional' intellectuals in contrast to the 'organic' or independent intellectuals of a generation ago, and the best hope for the coming decade will be the defection of intellectuals of the new generation who choose 'to reconstitute themselves through organic ties to the popular movements'.

THE CONTINUITY OF STATE AND CLASS IN THE DEMOCRATIC OPENING

If during the period of dictatorship the state became stronger – not only though its national security apparatuses of surveillance, control and propaganda, but also through its ties to the financial, industrial and commercial fractions of the bourgeoisie and through its institutional arrangements that ensure credits and concessions to domestic and foreign capital – then we must ask to what extent these state ties remain after the fall of the dictatorships. In the democratic openings and the indirect representative parliamentary rule which normally characterize such change, it is clear that military rulers are replaced by a new regime. Obviously, if there is no overthrow of the capitalist state, its continuity is assured in the democratic opening. In these periods the political agenda does not include the possibility of a transition to socialism. Only in the Portuguese case during 1974–5 was the socialist transition part of the political discourse, but in no other situation, including cases where socialists have come to power (France, Greece and Spain) has a socialist transition been seriously considered, and this has been particularly evident in Latin America where emerging democratic forces hesitate to manifest positions of socialism in confrontational ways that could provoke military intervention. In such circumstances it is important to note the continued activity of intelligence services, national security policy and military personnel in the agencies of the state.

It can be argued, especially in the Southern Cone (Argentina, Brazil and Uruguay) that there is continuity of state and ruling class interests, even where, in the rise of the opposition prior to the transition from authoritarian rule, the bourgeoisie splits, with commercial and comprador factions aligning with the old regime and elements of the domestic industrial bourgeoisie aligning with the opposition, as occurred in Brazil (see Pereira, 1984). The point is underscored by Petras:

> these political changes have not in the least changed the nature of the state but rather have led to changes at the level of government and regime . . . the military, police, and judicial officials have remained in place, with the same controls over 'security,' with the same values and ideologies and without having been brought to justice for their terrorist behavior . . . the same class linkages that defined the state before the changes continue under the new regimes (1988, p. 9).

Cardoso (1982) recognizes the state as the continuing regulatory force of the new society but suggests 'a new paradigm of democracy' in which

> the state represents class domination in this paradigm, but it is not reduced to that . . . Because the state has turned into a producer-state and has sheltered an entrepreneurial bureaucracy, 'society's' struggle becomes *ipso facto* a struggle 'within the state'. In addition, the state intervenes in capital competition and formation through its regulatory functions. Nor can the regulation of citizenship be reduced to defining who can vote when and about what (1986–7, p. 28).

Cardoso seems to be acknowledging that the process of transformation and democracy takes place within as well as outside the state, as suggested by Poulantzas in his later work. Finally he acknowledges that the search for the new democracy can be cast 'in a post-Marxist light that would not deny the prevalence of class conflict' (1986–7, p. 41).

POLITICAL PARTIES AND FORMAL DEMOCRACY VERSUS MASS POPULAR MOVEMENTS AND THE PROSPECTS FOR PARTICIPATORY DEMOCRACY

In the transition from dictatorship, political instability and economic crisis usually characterize the period of democratic opening. Popular movements emerge: for example, Brazil during the late 1970s and early 1980s was marked by labor-organized strikes and thousands of neighborhood groups and ecclesiastic base communities that mobilized millions of supporters. The importance of these movements diminished, however, as the political parties organized. The problem here relates to the limitations of bourgeois democracy, the constraints on direct forms of participation and the need, perceived by compromised politicians and intellectuals, to ensure political stability through the parliamentary system.

Recent academic analysis explicitly emphasizes the role of representative, indirect, bourgeois democracy in Latin America. A radical critique of this position appears in a *LAP* issue on democracy and class struggle (Summer, 1988), including an exposé by Arthur MacEwan (1988) of the essays edited by O'Donnell, Schmitter and Whitehead (1986). Jorge Nef (1988) also reviews this work alongside another collection of essays on the same subject edited by Drake and Silva (1986). He demonstrates that their debate about democratization shares many of the basic conceptual and normative assumptions of the 'developmentalism' of two decades ago. He questions whether the 'restricted' democracy manifested in these works is really democratic, and he concludes that it is neither congruent with the practice of democracy in the region, nor does it allow for the possibility of a popular revolutionary democracy.

While the agenda of many Latin American intellectuals may preclude a popular revolutionary democracy, it does not necessarily limit the possibility of socialism (see Barros, 1986, for theoretical lines of a socialism constructed along authoritarian or democratic lines). Cardoso has suggested above that class struggle can evolve within and outside the capitalist state, but it is also evident, given his role as a congressional leader, that democratization must be associated with political parties which seek to represent civil society. Evans notes in the case of Brazil that, if socializing the means of production and decentralization of politics are important, 'the left must not maintain a single-minded perspective of capturing the state apparatus'. He believes that the democratic transition provides space for new leftist parties such as the workers Partido Trabalhista (PT) of Brazil, and that it allows weak social movements to become powerful forces even if the parties ultimately predominate (1986–7, p. 17).

Finally Ronaldo Munck (1990) recasts the debate in terms of what transition is feasible, given the demise of the dictatorships and the process of demilitarization. He identifies an old left that has learned nothing in the past 20 years and a new left that has yet to find its direction in the new democracies. He agrees with Norberto Bobbio that democratic socialism must incorporate the bourgeois–liberal conception of individual rights. He argues that only a fully egalitarian socialist expression of democracy can lead to resolution of social and economic problems in Latin America. Clearly this is the direction of most Argentine leftist thinkers whose search for answers to major political questions must take into account the current crisis of their country (see, for example, the essays edited by José Nun and Juan Carlos Portantiero, 1987, and the issues of the Buenos Aires quarterly, *Plural*).

Toward the end of his essay, Vasconi reinforces and deepens the argument by reaffirming that democracy must be thought of, not as an ideological cultural fact, nor as a politico–institutional phenomenon, but as an integral question that also touches the base of society, the productive forces and the development of the social relations of production. Thus democracy, socialism and revolution are inseparable.

THE LEFT POLITICAL PARTIES AND THE LABOR MOVEMENT IN THE REORGANIZATION OF CAPITAL AND SOCIALISM

The redemocratization of much of Latin America has permitted a revival of leftist party politics and labor unions, but the parameters of political discourse have been limited by the crippling external and internal debts, galloping inflation, high unemployment and other problems. The military regimes used the state to facilitate arrangements of domestic and foreign capital and promote, with some success, export economies. For example, Brazil experienced years of trade surpluses and a competitive international position for some industrial and agricultural products; and Chile pushed new agricultural export industries that competed favorably in international markets. The internationalization of portions of these economies came at a high social cost, including lower real wages and a regressive distribution of income, along with dislocation of segments of the labor force, unemployment and impoverishment of a large portion of the population. Peter Winn has related these conditions to the alarming observation that 'socialism has gone out of fashion in the Southern Cone' although he concedes that in Chile, where 'few leftists talk of socialism', the prospects for the left are the brightest (1989, p. 882).

While these and other reasons may have obscured socialism and Marxism in the Southern Cone, revolutionary socialism and democratic socialism have not faded altogether in Latin America. Fidel Castro has made it clear that Cuba is proud of its tradition of revolutionary socialism and that, although Cuba maintains close relations with the Soviet Union, the country will seek an independent course. While *glasnost* and *perestroika* are scarcely mentioned in the official Cuban press, the themes of democracy, revolution and socialism appear in academic journals. While echoing the official position, these writings nevertheless strive to relate to the discourse elsewhere in Latin America. Dilla (1987), for example, argues that Cuba has the only socialist democracy based on a dictatorship of the proletariat, and he justifies this proposition through a review of the history of democratic forms in Cuba since the turn of the century and, in particular, in the period since 1959. He argues that forms of participatory democracy emerged in the 1970s through the constitution and *poder popular*, or popular power. My brief visit to Havana in December 1987 confirmed the desire and willingness of most Cuban intellectuals to participate in open dialogue (see Hitchens, 1988, for similar impressions). At the same time the Cuban arts include a prolific and engaging literature, creative cinema and vanguard art.

The Nicaraguan revolution also inspired a new theoretical discourse, as Roger Burbach and Orlando Núñez remind us in their plea to develop a new vision: 'To deal with this challenge the revolutionary movements in the Americas need a new political agenda. We need to rethink our old ideas, to understand the limits of the established socialist societies, and above all, to incorporate the needs and aspirations of ordinary people into our political programs' (1987, p. 2). They find their agenda in the Sandinista experience, its advocacy of national liberation and participatory democracy, flexibility in defining the revolutionary process, internal debate and experimentation in the evolution of new forms. In view of the crisis of orthodox Marxism they see an opportunity to enrich contemporary Marxist thought and argue that the impetus for change comes not only from the working class or a peasant–worker alliance, but also from a third force of middle-class intellectuals, progressive Christians, the urban poor, the petty bourgeoisie, and ethnic and social movements. This enthusiasm was shared by many of the collaborators in the provocative and exploratory essays in Fagen, Deere and Coraggio (1986) which emphasize the Nicaraguan revolutionary experience.

Doug Brown (1990) critically examines the Sandinista contribution, offers a more pessimistic assessment and argues that Nicaragua experienced one of the first socialist revolutions to ground its political strategy on what the American left currently refers to as a discourse of rights and in this process it sought to develop a democratic hegemony while avoiding the economic determinism of Leninist strategies. He draws upon Laclau and Mouffe to distinguish between authoritarian and democratic hegemony and concludes that Nicaragua's experience with a rights strategy and the objective of democratic hegemony posed serious problems, given the fragile mix of progressive forces and the economic crisis. He feels that the Sandinista strategy was more appropriate for advanced capitalist nations.

It is appropriate to conclude this chapter with reference to the comprehensive, stimulating essay by Enrique Dussel (1990) who has systematically examined the original manuscripts and various editions of Marx's work. He argues that revision of Marxist thought dates back to 1932 with the publication of the previously unknown *Economic and Philosophical Manuscripts of 1844* and to 1939 with the publication for the first time of the *Grundrisse*. The ensuing debate has sought alternatives to the extreme economic determination that characterized interpretation and assessment of Marx's thinking at that time. Dussel believes that we can now transcend the first 100 years of debate after Marx's death (1883) to rediscover the foundations of his scientific thinking that permit a critique not only of capitalism but of socialism as well. Thus, rather than dwelling upon the post-Marxism of the present moment, we need to return to Marx in order to comprehend his method and his categories, his theory and practice. The question of dependence serves as a point of departure for this endeavor.

This appeal for a return to Marx is refreshing but not necessarily unique among Latin American thinkers (see for example, Echeverría,

1986; Cueva, 1987). Likewise the effort to discover in revolutionary Nicaragua a revitalization of Marxist theory is indicative of an evolution of new Marxist conceptions in light of contemporary conditions. That there is something to learn from the Cuban revolutionary experience also is a promising prospect. The defection of some intellectuals from Marxism and the attempt of others to recast their thought in the post-Marxism of the present era are but symptoms of the current crisis of Marxism, socialism and democracy. As I have attempted to demonstrate, the crisis is also a reflection of changing conditions within capitalism and democracy.

Note

This chapter is an updated and revised version of my essay, 'Post-Marxism: The Retreat from Class in Latin America', in *Latin American Perspectives*, 17 (Spring 1990) 3–24.

References

ALVES, MARIA HELENA MOREIRA (1985) *State and Opposition in Military Brazil* (Austin: University of Texas Press).

ARICÓ, JOSÉ (1980) 'Mariátegui y la formación del Partido Socialista del Perú', *Socialismo y Participación*, vol. 11, pp. 139–67.

BAHRO, RUDOLF (1984) *From Red to Green* (London: Verso).

BARKIN, DAVID (1981) 'Internationalization of Capital: An Alternative Agenda', *Latin American Perspectives*, vol. 8 (summer and fall), pp. 156–61.

BARROS, ROBERT (1986) 'The Left and Democracy: Recent Debates in Latin America', *Telos*, no. 68 (Summer), pp. 49–70.

BECKER, DAVID G., JEFF FRIEDEN, SAYRE P. SCHATZ and RICHARD L. SKLAR (1987) *Postimperialism, International Capitalism and Development in the Late Twentieth Century* (Boulder: Lynne Rienner Publishers).

BELL, DANIEL (1960) *The End of Ideology* (Glencoe: Free Press).

BELL, DANIEL (1976) *The Coming of Post-Industrial Society* (Harmondsworth: Penguin).

BLOCK, FRED (1987) *Revising State Theory: Essays in Politics and Postindustrialism* (Philadelphia: Temple University Press).

BLOOM, ALEXANDER (1986) *Prodigal Sons: The New York Intellectuals and their World* (Oxford University Press).

BOWLES, SAMUEL and HERBERT GINTIS (1986) *Democracy and Capitalism: Property, Community, and the Contradictions of Modern Social Thought* (New York: Basic Books).

BROWN, DOUG (1990) 'Sandinismo and the Problem of Democratic

Hegemony', *Latin American Perspectives*, vol. 17 (spring), pp. 39–61.

BURBACH, ROGER and ORLANDO NÚÑEZ (1987) *Fire in the Americas: Forging a Revolution Agenda* (London: Verso).

CARDOSO, FERNANDO HENRIQUE (1972) 'Dependency and Development in Latin America', *New Left Review*, no. 74 (July–August) pp. 83–95.

CARDOSO, FERNANDO HENRIQUE (1982) 'Poulantzas e os partidos do Brasil', *Novos Estudos CEBRAP*, vol. 1, no. 2, pp. 3–7.

CARDOSO, FERNANDO HENRIQUE (1986–7) 'Democracy in Latin America', *Politics and Society*, vol. 15, no. 1, pp. 23–41.

CHILCOTE, RONALD H. (1985a) 'A crise da vida intelectual', *Lua Nova*, vol. 2 (July–September), pp. 82–6.

CHILCOTE, RONALD H. (1985b) 'Reflections on Brazilian Thought and the Crisis of the Intellectual', *Luso-Brazilian Review*, vol. 22 (winter), pp. 111–21.

CHILCOTE, RONALD H. (1988) 'Capitalist and Socialist Perspectives in the Search for a Class Theory of the State and Democracy' paper presented to a Conference, 'Comparative Politics: Research Perspectives for the Next Twenty Years', New York: City University Graduate School; and *Comparative Politics*, 7–9 September. Published as 'The Search for a Class Theory of the State and Democracy', in Dankwart Rustow and Kenneth Erickson (eds), *Comparative Political Dynamics* (New York: Harper Collins, 1991), pp. 75–97.

CHILCOTE, RONALD H. (1990) 'Post-Marxism: The Retreat from Class in Latin America', *Latin American Perspectives*, vol. 17 (spring), pp. 3–24.

CLAUDÍN, FERNANDO (1978) *Eurocommunism and Socialism* (London: NLE).

COONEY, TERRY A. (1986) *The Rise of the New York Intellectuals: Partisan Review and its Circle* (Madison: University of Wisconsin Press).

COUTINHO, CARLOS NELSON (1979) 'A democracia como valor universal', *Encontros com a Civilizaçao Brasileira*, no. 9 (March), pp. 33–47.

COUTINHO, CARLOS NELSON (1981) *Gramsci* (Porto Alegre: L & PM Editores).

CUEVA AGUSTÍN (1984) 'El fetichismo de la hegemonia y el imperialismo', *Cuadernos Políticos*, no. 39 (January–March), pp. 31–9.

CUEVA AGUSTÍN (1987) *La teoria marxista: categorias de base y problemas actuales* (Mexico: Planeta).

DELICH, FRANCISCO (1983) 'La construcción social de la legitimidad política en processos de transición ala democracia (1)', *Crítica y Utopia*, vol. 9, pp. 39–42.

DILLA, HAROLDO (1987) 'Democracia y poder revolucionario en Cuba', *Cuadernos de Nuestra América*, vol. 4 (January–June), pp. 55–75.

DRAKE, PAUL and EDUCARDO SILVA (eds) (1986) *Elections and Democratization in Latin America, 1980–1985* (San Diego: Center for US–Mexican Studies, Institute of the Americas, University of California).

DUSSEL, ENRIQUE (1990) 'Marx's Economic Manuscripts of 1861–63 and the "Concept" of Dependency', *Latin American Research Review*, vol. 17 (spring), pp. 62–101.

ECHEVERRÍA, BOLÍVAR (1986) *El discurso crítico de Marx* (Mexico: Ediciones Era).

EVANS, PETER (1986–7) 'Three Views of Regime Change and Party Organization in Brazil: An Introduction', *Politics and Society*, vol. 15, no. 1, pp. 2–21.

FAGEN, RICHARD R., CARMEN DIANA DEERE and JOSÉ LUIS CORAGGIO (eds) (1986) *Transition and Development* (New York: Monthly Review Press).

FLISFISCH, ANGEL (1983) 'El surgimiento de una nueva ideologia democrática en América Latina', *Crítica y Utopia*, vol. 9, pp. 11–29.

FOSTER-CARTER, AIDEN (1978) 'The Modes of Production Controversy', *New Left Review*, no. 107 (January–February), pp. 47–77.

FRANK, ANDRÉ GUNDER (1966) 'The Development of Underdevelopment', *Monthly Review*, vol. 18 (September), pp. 17–31.

FRANKEL, BORIS (1987) *The Post-Industrial Utopians* (Madison: University of Wisconsin Press).

FURTADO, CELSO (1964) *Development and Underdevelopment* (Berkeley: University of California Press).

GARRETÓN, MANUEL ANTONIO (1989) 'The Ideas of Socialist Renovation in Chile', *Rethinking Marxism*, vol. 2 (Summer), pp. 8–39.

GITLIN, TODD (1987) *The Sixties: Years of Hope, Days of Rage* (New York: Bantam), pp. 513.

GORZ, ANDRÉ (1980) *Farewell to the Working Class* (London: Pluto Press).

HARRIS, RICHARD L. (1979) 'The Influence of Marxist Structuralism on the Latin American Left', *Insurgent Sociologist*, vol. 9 (summer), pp. 62–73.

HARRIS, RICHARD L. (1988) 'Marxism and the Transition to Socialism in Latin America', *Latin American Perspectives*, vol. 15 (winter), pp. 7–54.

HIRSH, ARTHUR (1981) *The French New Left: An Intellectual History from Sartre to Gorz* (Boston: South End Press).

HITCHENS, CHRISTOPHER (1988) 'Minority Report', *Nation*, no. 246 (23 January), p. 79.

HOWE, GARY NIGEL (1981) 'Dependency Theory, Imperialism and the Production of Surplus Value on a World Scale', *Latin American Perspectives*, vol. 8 (summer–fall), pp. 82–102.

IPOLA, EMILIO DE and JUAN CARLOS PORTANTIERO (1984) 'Crisis social y pacto democrático', *Punto de Vista*, no. 21 (August), pp. 13–20.

ISSERMAN, MAURICE (1987) *If I Had a Hammer . . . The Death of the Old Left and the Birth of the New Left* (New York: Basic Books).

JACOBY, RUSSELL (1987) *The Last Intellectuals: American Culture in the Age of Academe* (New York: Basic Books), p. 290.

JAMESON, FREDRIC (1984) 'Postmodernism, or the Cultural Logic of Late Capitalism', *New Left Review*, no. 146 (July–August), pp. 53–92.

JAMESON, FREDRIC (1989) 'Marxism and Postmodernism', *New Left Review*, no. 176 (July–August), pp. 31–67.

KONDOR, LEONDRO (1980) *A democracia e os comunistas no Brasil* (Rio de Janeiro: Graal).

LACLAU, ERNESTO (1971) 'Feudalism and Capitalism in Latin America', *New Left Review*, vol. 67 (May–June), pp. 19–38.

LACLAU, ERNESTO (1980) 'Tesis acerca de la forma hegemónica de la política', paper presented to the seminar, 'Hegemonia y Alternatives Populares en América Latina', Morelia, Mexico; cited by Vasconi (1990).

LACLAU, ERNESTO and CHANTAL MOUFFE (1985) *Hegemony and Socialist Strategy: Towards a Radical Democratic Politics* (London: Verso).

LANDI, OSCAR (1981) *Crisis y lenguajes políticos* (Buenos Aires: Estudios CEDES 4), no. 4, Centro de Estudios de Estado y Sociedad). See his initial essay, 'Sobre lenguajes, identidades y ciudadanías políticas', pp. 11–42.

LECHNER, NORBERT (ed.) (1982) *Que significa hacer política?* (Lima: Centro de Estudios y Promoción del Desarrollo (DESCO). See his introductory essay with the same title on pp. 15–36.

LECHNER, NORBERT (1985a) 'De la revolución a la democracia. El debate intelectual en América del Sur', *Opciones*, no. 6 (May–August), pp. 57–72.

LECHNER, NORBERT (1985b) 'Pacto social: nos procesos de democratizaçao, la experiência latino-americana'. *Novos Estudos CEBRAP*, no. 13 (October), pp. 29–44.

LECHNER, NORBERT (1986) 'La democratización en una cultura posmoderna', *Leviatán*, nos 23–4 (spring–summer), pp. 179–87.

MacEVAN, ARTHUR (1988) 'Transitions from Authoritarian Rule: A Review Essay', *Latin American Perspectives*, vol. 15 (summer), pp. 115–30.

MARINI, RUY MAURO (1978) 'World Capitalist Accumulation and Sub-Imperialism', *Two Thirds*, vol. 1 (fall), pp. 29–39.

MILIBAND, RALPH (1985) 'The New Revisionists in Britain', *New Left Review*, no. 150 March–April), pp. 5–26.

MILLER, JAMES (1987) *'Democracy is in the Streets': From Port Huron to the Siege of Chicago* (New York: Simon & Schuster).

MOULIAN, TOMÁS (1981a) 'Crítica a la crítica marxista de las democracias burguesas', in Henry Pease García (ed.), *América Latina 80: democracia y movimiento popular* (Lima: DESCO), pp. 45–56.

MOULIAN, TOMÁS (1981b) 'Por un marxismo secularizado', *Chile–América*, nos 72–3, pp. 100–104; reprinted in his *Democracia y socialismo en Chile* (Santiago: FLACSO, 1983), pp. 223–32.

MOULIAN, TOMÁS (1983) 'Una reflexión sobre intelectuales y política', in *Democracia y socialismo en Chile* (Santiago: FLACSO), pp. 7–19.

MUNCK, RONALDÓ (1990) 'Farewell to Socialism? A Commentary on Recent Debates', *Latin American Perspectives*, vol. 17 (Spring), pp. 113–21.

NEF, JORGE (1988) 'The Trend toward Democratization and Redemocratization in Latin America: Shadow and Substance', *Latin American Research Review*, vol. 23, no. 3, pp. 131–53.

NUN, JOSÉ (1981) 'La rebellión del coro', *Nexos*, no. 146, pp. 19–26.

NUN, JOSÉ (1983) 'El otro reducionismo', *Zona Abierta*, no. 28.

NUN, JOSÉ (1984) 'Democracia y socialismo: etapas o níveles?' in Fundación Pablo Iglesias, *Caminos de la democracia* (Madrid: Editorial Iglesias), pp. 249–61.

NUN, JOSÉ (1986) 'Elements for a Theory of Democracy: Gramsci and Common Sense', *Boundary 2*, vol. 14 (spring), pp. 197–229.

NUN, JOSÉ and JUAN CARLOS PORTANTIERO (eds) (1987) *Ensayos sobre la transición democrática en la Argentina* (Buenos Aires: Puntosur Editores).

O'DONNELL, GUILLERMO (1973) *Modernism and Bureaucratic-Auth-*

oritarianism: Studies in South American Politics (Berkeley: Politics of Modernization Series (9), Institute of International Studies).

O'DONNELL, GUILLERMO (1988) *Bureaucratic Authoritarianism: Argentina 1966–1973 in Comparative Perspective* (Berkeley: University of California Press).

O'DONNELL, GUILLERMO, PHILIPPE C. SCHMITTER and LAURENCE WHITEHEAD (eds) (1986) *Transitions from Authoritarian Rule: Prospects for Democracy* (Baltimore: Johns Hopkins University Press). Citations from volume on Southern Europe.

PEREIRA, LUIZ CARLOS BRESSER (1984) *Development and Crisis in Brazil, 1930–1983* (Boulder: Westview Press).

PETRAS, JAMES (1988) 'The State, Regime, and the Democratization Muddle', *LASA Forum*, vol. 18 (winter), pp. 9–12; see also 'The Metamorphosis of Latin America's Intellectuals', *Latin American Perspectives*, vol. 17 (spring 1990), pp. 102–12.

PORTANTIERO, JUAN CARLOS (1974) 'Dominant Classes and Political Crisis', *Latin American Perspectives*, vol. 1 (Fall), pp. 93–120.

PORTANTIERO, JUAN CARLOS (1981) 'Lo nacional-popular y la alternativa democrática en América Latina', in Henry Pease García *et al.* (eds), *América Latina 80: democracia y movimento popular* (Lima: Centro de Estudios y Promoción del Desarrollo (DESCO), pp. 217–40.

PORTANTIERO, JUAN CARLOS and EMILIO DE IPOLA (1981) 'Lo nacional-popular y los populismos realmente existentes', *Nueva Sociedad*, vol. 4, pp. 7–18.

POULANTZAS, NICOS (1976) *Crisis of the Dictatorship: Portugal, Greece, Spain* (London: NLB).

POULANTZAS, NICOS (1978) *State, Power, Socialism* (London: NLB).

RODRIGUES, O. GUSTAVO (1980) 'Original Accumulation, Capitalism, and Precapitalist Agriculture in Bolivia', *Latin American Perspectives*, vol. 7 (fall), pp. 67–82.

ROJAS, ANTONIO (1980) 'Land and Labor in the Articulation of the Peasant Economy with the Hacienda', *Latin American Perspectives*, vol. 7 (Fall), pp. 67–82.

RUCCIO, DAVID F. and LAWRENCE H. SIMON (1986) 'Methodological Aspects of a Marxian Approach to Development: An Analysis of the Modes of Production School', *World Development*, vol. 14 (February), pp. 211–22.

SANTOS, THEOTÓNIO DOS (1970) 'The Structure of Dependence', *American Economic Review*, vol. 60 (May), pp. 231–6.

SCHMITTER, PHILLIPPE C. (1974) 'Still the Century of Corporatism?' *Review of Politics*, vol. 36 (January), pp. 85–131.

SINDICO, DOMENICO, E. (1980) 'Modernization in Nineteenth-Century Sugar Haciendas: The Case of Morelos (from Formal to Real Subsumption of Labor to Capital', *Latin American Perspectives*, vol. 7 (fall), pp. 83–99.

STEPAN, ALFRED (ed.) (1989) *Democratizing Brazil: Problems of Transition and Consolidation* (New York: Oxford University Press).

VASCONI, TOMAS (1990) 'Post-Marxism, the Left, and Democracy', *Latin American Perspectives*, vol. 17 (Spring), pp. 25–38.

WALD, ALAN M. (1987) *The New York Intellectuals: The Rise and Decline of the Anti-Stalinist Left from the 1930s to the 1980s* (Chapel Hill:
University of North Carolina Press).

WEFFORT, FRANCISCO (1984) *Por que democracia?* (São Paulo: Editora
Brasiliense).

WINN, PETER (1989) 'Socialism Fades out of Fashion', *The Nation*, vol.
248, 26 June, pp. 882–6.

WOOD, ELLEN MEIKSINS (1986) *The Retreat from Class: A New 'True'
Socialism* (London: Verso).

11 The Legacy of Authoritarianism in Democratic Brazil*

Paulo Sérgio Pinheiro

After the collapse of Latin American dictatorships in the 1980s, the major challenge facing the incoming political regimes was to exercise the state monopoly of physical violence within the limits of legality. In these brief notes we shall try to develop some preliminary remarks concerning the control of arbitrary practices by state agencies and of illegal violence in interpersonal relations or crime during political transitions and under democratic governments that emerged from them after the end of dictatorships. We would like to demonstrate that in some cases these governments were not able to ensure one of the basic cornerstones of democracy, the control of illegal violence, or to explain the processes and mechanisms that led to this situation.

Special attention will be given to the legacy of authoritarianism and we will try to answer questions such as the following: after the political transition, what elements in the pattern of violence are a true legacy of dictatorship? Which elements could be explained by the reproduction of a traditional structure of domination and power? Which aspects of the pattern are reinforced by authoritarian governments? In many societies, like Brazil, where power relations have been traditionally characterized by illegality and by arbitrary power to which the majority of the population has been forced to submit, authoritarian practices are not affected by political change and by free and competitive elections alone. The legacy in many political transitions is the persistence of an extremely high level of illegal violence and of violent conflict, without the intervention of the judiciary system in society.

TRANSITION OR FALSE PACIFICATION?

Transition: passage, change, from one place or state or act or set of circumstances to another. When political oppression ceases, those who

237

have lived under a dictatorship or an authoritarian regime have no doubt that many changes occur. As political freedom is restored, elections are held, power alternation returns. But democracy is not guaranteed. This is especially so because political transitions do not question the transformations of the state with regard to its relationship with the popular classes in its most crucial aspect, *l'encadrement, la normalisation*.[1] As in the period that followed the eighteenth-century revolutions, now democracy exists only as a 'constitutive idea'[2] which should be built. However it would be impossible to deny that the return to democratic organization constitutes in itself an important barrier to an arbitrary state power, opening better perspectives for popular resistance actions for the strengthening of legal self-defense mechanisms.[3]

The phenomenon of political transitions, as described by José Álvaro Moisés, Philippe Schmitter, Guillermo O'Donnell, Thomas Skidmore, Alfred Stepan and Abraham Lowenthal, have called our attention to the continuity of illegal state violence even after political dissent ceased to be considered a crime. The return to the 'formality' of democracy at the last phase of political transition does not imply that from there on democracy is established. The rule of law, understood as the effective guarantees of the basic rights for the majority of the population, as was the case after other political transitions in the Brazilian history, is again a mere ritualistic reference. The shortcomings that affect the judiciary system do not guarantee the access of the majority of the population to the legal rights that have been reconquered and even enlarged by the new 1988 constitution.

A transition process conceived as limited to the institutions of political representation could make believe that the explicit war in power relations that prevailed during dictatorship was being suspended and that, after the end of dictatorship, the relations between social classes would lead to a return to political citizenship (even if only nominally for the majority of the population). Political transitions theories in most cases locate power relations in the system of political representation without giving emphasis to the social movements of the civil society: those very movements that, during resistance to dictatorship, were able to call into question the conditions in which the state exercised its monopoly of violence. But, as we know, this pacification of violence during the political transition is an illusion, if we take into account Michel Foucault's premise that power relations in the present society are essentially based on relations of strength:

And if it is true that politics ends war, to try to impose peace in civil society, it is not to suspend the effects of war or to neutralize the desequilibria that manifested themselves in the last battle, but to reintroduce perpetually these relations of force, through a kind of silent war, in the institutions and in the economic inequalities, in the language and even in the body of the individuals.[4]

The political transition is just an episode in this very war.

Civilian governments that emerge from political transition, after a period of mobilization of political dissent and criticism of the practices of dictatorship, have enormous difficulty in transforming the language of law that would allow normalization and control to replace repression. Prison and all the 'political technologies' of the exercise of power are affected. On the contrary, during the process of democratization, under the new civilian governments, those illegal practices are frequently reinforced, as the policies of public security put into practice after 1983 by the state governments show. To fight crime, for instance, governments continue to broaden and strengthen the instruments of violence – suspension of the 'Fleury law' for first-time criminals who were allowed to answer charges while on bail, hardening of judiciary practice with respect to the concession of parole, disregard for the law as regards the carrying out of prison sentences on the grounds that the language of the law is too lenient. In countries with an authoritarian tradition, like Brazil – where there was never any break with the *ancien régime* – the apparent pacification of political transitions, that comes after the benevolent traits of the last days of a dictatorship and the euphoria of the first moments of the new civilian governments hides the real limitations of the democratization of power. We must try to unveil those masks, identify those limitations that are historically reproduced and aggravated as times goes by.

AUTONOMY AND DISSIMULATION OF THE REPRESSIVE APPARATUSES

The access to government from the former groups of opposition to the dictatorship does not mean the reform of violence: the election of representatives from democratic political parties through free and competitive elections does not eliminate the previous illegality of state violence, nor affect the substantial autonomy in the functioning of police apparatuses. These are not a thing, or a neutral structure.[5] The repressive state apparatuses in Brazil are impregnated by arbitrary power and terror. The new democratic governments elected during political transitions have dealt with police apparatuses as if they were neutral apparatuses to serve democracy, thus underestimating the authoritarian legacy in their practices. During transitions, the dismissals of police personnel and the reform of state apparatuses are maintained inside the limits imposed by the force relations that have made transition possible.[6] The simple presence of José Sarney, head of the new civilian government, in 1985, a former dignitary of all the military governments, as vice-president and then president (after the death of Tancredo Neves who, because of his illness, was never able to take the oath as president), chosen through indirect election by the National Congress, is an evident sign of that continuity. The state officials who practiced torture or those who served illegal repression continue in their state jobs, thanks to the political amnesty.

The possibilities of transformation of the organization of state apparatuses (especially those in charge of violence) are very faint or almost non-existent during political transition. In fact a *régime d'exception* continues in place, as a parallel state network, in the sense suggested by Nicos Poulantzas: *network* because it permeates the several state branches and apparatuses; *parallel* because it functions behind the external appearances of state apparatuses that disguise it; *state* because it is generally para-public, constituting a permanent resource for the ruling groups to assure and protect their power.[7]

Thus, instead of transition, there is a strong continuity at the level of the *dispositives disciplinaires* (as Michel Foucault would say) which are present in the functioning of several institutions of control, and at the level of the apparatuses themselves, thus resulting in continuity in the practices and in the structure of the apparatuses. As Guillermo O'Donnell has indicated,[8] the political transition of the authoritarian regime is not necessarily a democratic transition: it does not affect hierarchy in society, the illegality of state violence, or the control of the autonomy of repressive apparatuses enlarged during dictatorship. In the Brazilian case this situation is aggravated because the constitution of 1988 has confirmed the organization of the repressive apparatuses as defined during the military dictatorship. In this domain, there is no transition but instead full continuity, and what is most revealing is that those very instruments were not conceived by the dictatorship: the military governments simply used – in a more systematic and intense way – the *institutions of violence* such as torture, commonly employed during constitutional periods.

In Brazil the political transition barely affects the conditions of repression, which have, as always, the role of enforcing hierarchy, essential to the reproduction of power relations. The case of human rights protection is crucial to understanding this kinship between illegal patterns of violence and political transition. In spite of the resistance during the dictatorship and the last phase of transition, under the elected state governments, those rights were initially presented for the protection of political dissent and afterwards enlarged for all society, especially the poor and miserable (the more than 60 million Brazilians classified statistically as miserable, non-citizens who survive with a family income of less than US$60 a month) the preferred target for illegal violence.

These deadlocks of political transition in Brazil indicate that the autonomy of repressive apparatuses and the practices of illegal violence have survived at levels not present in other transitions in Latin America or European countries, such as Spain or Greece. Torture, the systematic extra-legal execution of criminal suspects and other practices of the *pedagogy of fear*, routinely applied to the popular classes – residence invasions, sweeps, beatings, kidnappings, murders of rural labor leaders, – are tolerated. The official discourse displays a rhetorical indignation which is not translated into any concrete action, impunity being assured to illegal violence, those practices, which during the military dictatorship usually aroused protests, marches and demonstrations – because the victims were mostly from the white middle classes and bourgeoisie. At present, as during other *normal* democratic periods, as the victims of the very same practices are from the popular classes and common (mostly petty) criminals, those methods previously repudiated are fully accepted and tolerated.

The fight against crime, for instance, follows the same illegal lines of the periods before dictatorship, aggravated by such innovations of the dictatorship as the militarization of police patrol (confirmed by the democratic Constitution of 1988). The Brazilian state has never renounced any of its practices in the field of illegal repression – from the rubber truncheon at the beginning of the century to the parrots's perch and electric shocks of the military governments. The democratic governments after the transition were not able to modify this situation because they thought that this coercion, illegal or not legal, could be affected by political change at the formal centers of power through elections. However this change would only be possible if the relations of violence were located where they effectively take place, for instance prisons or police precincts overcoming the dissimulation that usually covers them: as Pierre Bourdieu has said, 'the specific character of every relation of force is to disguise itself as such, and to acquire all its force only because it is so disguised'.[9] There is only a real democracy in the control of violence when society succeeds in imposing transparency upon disguise: an operation, an about-face, which no traditional liberal discourse on public security of democratic politics in Brazil is in any condition to carry out. Authoritarianism goes hand in hand with dissimulation.

The democratization of government does not lead automatically to the hegemony of the principles of democracy in the functioning of the repressive apparatuses. Political reform at the level of discourse or political ideology cannot magically transform power relationships because these are not on the political scene, but far away from our sight, in the extremities, in the micro contexts, where concrete relations between classes occur. The behavior of the agents in the state apparatuses is not synchronized with the timing of the political opening: for instance, 18 inmates suffocated to death on carnival Sunday, 5 February 1989, murdered by asphyxiation in a cell measuring 3 meters by 5 in which 51 people were put at a police precinct in São Paulo.[10] Moreover, if the conception of power is displaced from the political institutions to specific cultural practices, it is very difficult to develop a general theory of power, a theory of transition that could encompass change or continuity at the micro political level. Who makes real justice in daily life is not only the judge, but the prison officers; who assures security is not the police forces considered in their legal definition or broad strategies, but policemen on the streets or in police precincts. What is decisive to the imposition of democracy on the repressive apparatus is the monitoring, the control of their action. But it is now clear that dissimulation and *a régime d'exception* would not survive if they could not count upon support and legitimacy in society itself, as we will see towards the end of this chapter.

GROSS HUMAN RIGHTS VIOLATIONS AND THE RULE OF LAW

One of the characteristics of the Brazilian case is the extraordinary longevity of authoritarian culture and practices, independently, as we have already stressed, of the transformations of the political regime and the complexity of society. The past seems to have a decisive weight in the present.[11] As the novelist Elizabeth Hardwick, who visited Brazil in the middle 1970s, during the Geisel dictatorship, puts it: 'The centuries seem to inhabit each moment; the diamonds at Minas, the slave ships, Dom Pedro in his summer palace at Petropolis, the liberal tradition, the terrorists, the police, Vargas, Kubitschek, the Jesuits. All exist in a continuous present – a consciousness overcrowded and given to fatigue'.[12]

The *circuits of power* – to use the expression of Sewart R. Clegg – that have prevailed in Brazil in the twentieth century require the negation of the guarantees of law to the majority: the political transition is a soft event that does not affect the hard system of exploitation. The philosopher Gerard Lebrun, commenting on the work of Brazilian sociologist Florestan Fernandes, called attention to the fact that there never was in Brazil a rupture with the *ancien régime*. Colonial absolutism has simply been transformed into the absolutism of the ruling groups; a complete asymmetry between ruler and dominated has survived the abolition of slavery: 'The civilian order is transformed, but in so unequal, unarticulated and ambiguous a way that he has much of the "slave" in potential and much less as a citizen'.[13] It is a kind of authoritarian power syndrome described by Primo Levi: 'a distorted view of the world, dogmatic arrogance, the need for adulation, convulsive clinging to the levers of command, and contempt for the law',[14] especially the disdain for the law. In Brazil the law never served the poor, miserable, indigent, black or mulatto; throughout the entire Republican period since 1889, there was little difference between arbitrary extra-legal power and the rule of law, understood here, not as class power, but as the contradictory possibilities of imposing effective inhibitions against the exercise of direct unmediated force.[15] Philippe Schmitter, in a 1988 interview, observed that 'there is not in all the world a country with democratic institutions where there is so widespread a violation of its own law'.[16] Unlike other countries, where the bourgeois revolutions of the eighteenth century gave birth to institutions able to control or overcome abuse by the rulers, in Brazil the law has mostly served as the expression of domination without offering any of the basic guarantees to the majority of the population. Here, as in the metaphor of Alain Rouquié, we are confronted by an authentic *trompe l'oeil culture* where 'the false windows of juridical universalism cover the particularism of personal relations of force'.[17]

In spite of the continuous sophistication of the *violence douce* in many social and ideological controls, these have never affected the *violence ouverte*. The refinements of torture and lynching survive today within all the refinements of democratic institutions and controls. In any case, it must be clear that the *violence symbolique* is only effective through the permanent threat and the legal (or illegal) use of actual violence: in the sense indicated by Alf Lüdtke, that 'the different forms of symbolic violence for the dominated always include the experience as well as anticipation of physical violence "from above". So *violence douce*, which masks itself in the way it works, should not be perceived as the more modern rational opposite of physical force; on the contrary, it works only by the permanent presence of *violence brute* which it symbolises'.[18]

It would probably be of value to return to the discussion of the formation of the state monopoly of physical violence. We have learned with Norbert Elias that the establishment of military and police monopoly within the limits of the state in general leads to the creation of what he terms 'pacified spaces', where the recourse to violence occurs as an exception.[19] But in Brazilian society violence continues to be the rule, not the exception. Physical coercion is a daily threat to the majority of the population. The Brazilian case shows that gross human-rights violations may persist after democratic opening, free and competitive elections and constitutional reform. Torture is systematically administered in every police precinct throughout the country, independently of the socioeconomic level of each state. We may even formulate the paradox that the daily number of those common criminals or suspects tortured by the police is many times larger than the number of all those tortured for political reasons during the 20 years of dictatorship. Last year there were even four cases of torture of soldiers in military barracks. From 1981 to 1989 the Corregedoria de Policia Civil, in São Paulo, registered 259 cases of accusation of torture involving 580 policeman (of whom 383 were found not guilty). Physical abuse and illegalities continue to go unpunished in every prison in the country, with a very large degree of support from society (100 000 prisoners crowded into) prisons meant to hold half that number. In São Paulo, more than 3500 prisoners, roughly 8 per cent of the state prison population, are detained in filthy overcrowded police precinct pens.

Violent death is common, and a substantial proportion of such deaths continue, even after the end of the military regime, to be attributed to death squads – as in the states of Pernambuco, Espírito Santo and Rio de Janeiro– and to vigilante groups and '*justiceiros*' (gunmen). In the periphery of the big cities there are estimated to be more than 200 extermination groups, in most cases financed by the local communities and by commerce owners. In the city of São Paulo between January and August 1990, 300 people were murdered by '*justiceiros*'. In at least 15 Brazilian states these death squads are the main cause of the violent death of children and adolescents. The register of the Comissão Pastoral da Terra shows, since 1964, 1501 killings in rural conflicts, two thirds of them in the 1980s, decade of the political transition. But only 14 cases have been brought before the courts.

The highest world level of deaths in police conflict among democratic countries continues to be that of São Paulo. The number of 599 deaths of suspects and criminals in 1989 is almost equivalent to the average number of killings in police conflicts in the whole of the USA, with a population ten times and police forces four times larger. Between 1979 and 1989, as José de Souza Martins had demonstrated,[20] there were 272 lynchings of common criminals and criminal suspects: of these, 136 occurred during the civilian government (1985–9). And the most worrying detail is that 131 cases occurred in São Paulo, the most developed state of the federation. In view of these data, we may state that there is not a democratic regime in the world that presents, alongside high levels of criminality (Brazil is the world champion of homicides in relation to its population – 104 per 100 000 of the population, 370 a day), these levels of human-rights violations and impunity.

With these records, Brazil is ranked second, immediately after Colombia, in the number of human-rights monitors murdered in 1989, according to Americas Watch. During the political transition many human rights groups fought for the extension of the guarantees of the rule of law to the poor, miserable, indigent, black classes. This transfer from the defense of human rights for the former dissent minority under dictatorship – based on a broad coalition of sympathies and support in society – to the defense of human rights for the majority of the population enters into conflict with the power structure. The enlarged application of those rights threatens (or seems to threaten, in the perception of middle and ruling classes) the institutionalization of the rules of domination,[21] offering some risks to the systems of hierarchy that had historically prevailed in Brazilian society, ensuring the asymmetry between the dominant classes and the subordinated groups.

THE LEGACY OF AUTHORITARIANISM

If we state that there is this continuity during political transition, there must exist some legacy of this authoritarianism. Questions arise when we begin to ask ourselves what are the components of this legacy. In this legacy, there are many elements of the authoritarian structure of the previous dictatorship, still present in the institutional, legal and administrative framework – what was called at the beginning of the Sarney government (1985–90) 'the authoritarian rabble' (*o entulho autoritário*). Hence the laws of exception, the 1967 constitution written by the military government, and all the Institutional Acts issued and that in fact prevailed throughout the period of the first civilian government until the new constitution of 1988 was written. The first civilian government was not able to dismantle the authoritarian structures, despite of the willingness of several members of National Congress to do so.

This was not a novelty: a similar process took place after the collapse of the Estado Novo (1945) until the constitution of 1946 was written, the 'authoritarian rabble' of the previous dictatorship also prevailed. This allowed the provisional government of Jose Linhares (1945–6) and the Dutra presidency in its early years (1946–50) to use extensively the 'laws of exception', for instance to repress strikes and to control the labor movement. But this is the most visible aspect of the legacy: there are other aspects of the legacy more remote, less visible yet still alive, such as the survival of the labor legislation dating from the Estado Novo (1937–45).

The ambiguity which was expressed in the two faces – authoritarian and democratic – of the different Vargas governments (1930–37; 1937–45; 1950–54) allowed the ruling classes to adopt in their relations with the popular classes, as the political scientist Michel Debrun has demonstrated, strategies of 'compromise' (*conciliação*) and of *demobilizing authoritarianism.*[22] Debrun's concept of *political and ideological archetypes*, 'models of the global perception of society, articulated with certain practices that may be found in diverse historical periods',[23] seems to us more and more appropriate and also an inducement to further study. This helps us to understand that the authoritarian legacy, at the ideological level and at the level of social practices, is extremely flexible and capable of being transformed.

It is very difficult to identify any transition in this area because here the changes are much slower than the ones at the level of juridical changes in the political regimes and institutions. Instead of transitions we have a formidable continuity which means that, though we may have changes at the political institutional level, political culture will not be affected. At the level of culture and of ideology, reproduction of the components of the legacy restrict the possibilities of transformation, or at least they do not occur at the speed of political reform. It is very complex to put into practice, for instance, projects to reform political culture, and attempts to do so in Brazil have all failed. A good example of this elsewhere is the fate of several attempts at 'denazification' carried out in European countries and which were examined by John Herz.[24] This author demonstrates that the obstacles and difficulties for the transformations in the political culture to follow those of the political transition.

To confront the problem of relations between democracy and the control of illegal violence we must identify the components of the pattern of violence which constitute a real legacy of dictatorship, and to indicate which components may be explained as consequences of the reproduction of the traditional structure of domination and power, taking into consideration that some components are just reinforced by authoritarian governments. To comprehend more fully these components it is necessary to evaluate the transition processes beyond the limits of the state and of the political institutions. Since Foucault we have known that the intercrossing of power relations with knowledge and body (pointing to the question of physical violence) is not located in a single institution or in a single power apparatus, that is, the state.[25] The emphasis of the analysis of transitions on political institutions, while ignoring illegal violence, contributes to reinforcing the tolerance towards arbitrary power, while at the same time it succeeds in dissimulating its mechanisms.[26] It is precisely in those mechanisms of power that no transition takes place.

Illegal practices are intensified by impunity and the dissimulation of illegal violence. For instance, in the state governments elected during the last years of the political transition from dictatorship (1982) and during the first civilian federal government (1985), the newly democratic administrations soon abandoned any real effort to enforce the demands for effective reforms in judicial and police institutions.

A '*RÉGIME D'EXCEPTION*' UNDER THE CONSTITUTION

Throughout the period of the Republic in Brazil, the repressive practices of state apparatuses and of the ruling classes were characterized by a very high level of illegality, independently of the existence or otherwise of constitutional guarantees. For the poor people, the miserable, that have always constituted the majority of the population, we may speak of a continued '*régime d'exception*' that has survived under every form of political regime, constitutional or authoritarian.

In such a regime the illegality to which the popular classes, the *torturable classes*, as Graham Greene says, are submitted is much greater than that normally present in law enforcement or in police practices. This regime is independent of the political regime *stricto sensu*, of the constitutional regime: any of the so-called democratic transitions, either after the dictatorship of the Estado Novo, or the several military governments, from 1964 to 1985, have affected substantially this *régime d'exception* (under a constitutional regime – an expression that was brought to our attention by the observations of a Dutch worker in Brazil regarding the limitations of the application of the constitution in 1925.[27] The description of that regime – constructed in opposition to the constitution, which has always been considered an obstacle to be overcome, not respected – presented by that worker, Joh de Bruin, who lived for 18 years in Brazil, a member of the *Allgemeiner Arbeiterverein* (General Union of Workers, a social-democratic association founded in 1892) seems to prevail until the present day: 'the constitution promises much freedom to us, workers, but ... as time goes by, many laws have been written that conflict with the constitutional text, which in consequence has no value at all'.[28] Every act of defensive violence is countered by the employers and by the police through physical violence.[29]

During the periods of constitutional democracy, 1934–7 or 1946–64 – even if the existence of a constitution meant legal guarantees to the majority of the population – a *régime d'exception* was disguised because physical repression was compensated for by other, well-hidden, mechanisms of social control. The conditions of exploitation in the workplace were somewhat improved, salaries at certain moments even increased and a welfare policy was launched, through social security laws and institutions. However in periods of effective authoritarianism – such as that of the First Republic (1889–1930), when there were some weak initiatives of social policy of legalized authoritarianism, as well as during the Estado Novo dictatorship (1937–45) and from 1964 to 1985 – this diguise disappears: the need to adjust the contradictions inside the ruling groups demands the intensification of political repression to establish control over the popular classes without any mobilization or participation, and the frontiers between political repression and common repression come down. The specialized apparatuses for this repression continue to act, without limitation, completely instrumentalized by the ruling classes. In turn, this authoritarianism reveals in its practice what in the democratic periods is disguised: the real character of authoritarian repression and the profile of illegal physical violence.

'SOCIALLY ROOTED' AUTHORITARIANISM

These observations with reference to developments in civil society and in the state after the end of the military dictatorship show a structural kind of resistance that demands research beyond the political system *stricto sensu*. It was reasonable to expect, taking into consideration the historical evolution of Brazil, that the modification of the political regime would not imply the dismantling of that resistance, because these authoritarian structures are not dependent on the political regime. It seems to us that the authoritarian governments were so successful for so long because they had simply played, with strong social support, on certain decisive authoritarian elements present in Brazilian political culture. To understand these resistances we believe that the approach must be displaced from the political institutions to the micro dimensions of power, to the micro scenes of concrete interactions, especially the violent ones, to the micro despotism that survived the authoritarianism of dictatorships. In the Brazilian case, a *socially rooted* authoritarianism persists which precedes and survives the authoritarian political regimes and is independent of political periodization. The inspiration for this expression comes from Guillermo O'Donnell, in his observation that, perhaps because authoritarianism is so 'socially' implanted in Brazil, the state apparatus was and, especially, has appeared, so powerful and decisive, and was so overwhelmingly present on the national scene.[30] This authoritarianism seems to be inscribed in the great authoritarian continuity which characterizes Brazilian society (and its political culture). It depends directly on the hierarchical systems built by the ruling classes and regularly reproduced with the help of the instruments of political oppression and the ideological control over the majority of population.

This *socially rooted* authoritarianism has sources more profound than the legacy of dictatorship. Usually the political analyses of authoritarianism are not successful in dealing with this *socially rooted* authoritarianism because power relations are not only present in macro political institutions. If, in the transition, the relations of power between the ruling classes change – especially in the scope of representation – the asymmetrical power relations in society are not affected. We are thus obliged to analyze the transition through the micro practices of power, untouched by transition. In order to do so we must register and reconstitute the concrete interventions of the agents in the micro contexts where the relation of power occurs, shifting our attention from the political scene and the organs of formal representation.

This violence which is so present in personal interactions in society, has its origins in previous practices, such as those that were established during the colonial regime and slavery. In Brazilian society, a system of values operates that includes violence as legitimate and even as an imperative, being effective and frequently orienting the behavior of many sectors in social life.[31] For this, an important contributing element must have been the fact that Brazil, as Florestan Fernandes has pointed out in his reflections on violence, is

> an extreme historic case of coexistence between a highly unequal and rigid regime of social classes including a high concentration of institutionalized and organic violence at the 'top' . . . of institutionalized violence among those at the 'bottom' with a strong crystallization of 'anomic' and inorganic violence of the poor and oppressed population, abandoned by the civil order constituted to protect and unite, if possible, the members of the privileged strata or, later, the upper and middle classes, and practically blind to the fate of the dispossessed.[32]

To understand the ways socially rooted authoritarianism is built – since those remote historical origins – and is reproduced, it would be essential to reconstitute the network of micro despotisms in the most diverse social contexts: violence in the family, racial discrimination, child abuse, violence against women, 'vigilantes', lynchings. Authoritarian patterns may also be found in the acts of 'petty authorities' that were reinforced and developed during dictatorship. From industry to the reception desks of residential buildings (formerly controlled by the political police through the building superintendents, who were obliged to send in forms with details on each person living there) those petty authorities have adapted to some micro contexts the pattern of oppression diffused by macro power.[33] The '*você sabe com quem está falando?*', ('do you know to whom you are speaking?') syndrome has been spread in every social interlocution.[34] The myth of racial democracy remains very powerful, functioning as a highly efficient disguise for a large spectrum of micro despotisms against the black and mulatto population. It was never necessary in Brazil to institutionalize a legal *apartheid* because, in addition to social and economic discrimination, those petty authorities and the 'você sabe com quem está falando?' syndrome always has a role in containing black and poor people in civil society. Black and poor children grow up inside the barriers of those micro despotisms imposed by white and dominant society. Together with the several forms of illegal violence, the *violence douce* of prejudice and discrimination are important elements of socially rooted authoritarianism.

If this authoritarianism were someday to be less dissimulated, certain possibilities could be open for the reform of violence. In fact, if there should be a real effort to overcome the immense social and economic inequalities – Brazil is today a country with the biggest concentration of poor in the West and in the Southern Hemisphere – there could be some chance of a true democratization. But democracy will be effective only when the process of dismantling this complex network of micro despotism, to which the popular classes in Brazil are historically submitted, is under way. At present, despite the sufferings of the majority of miserable and poor and some level of organization and resistance in civil society, there are no signs of this process on the horizon.

Notes and References

* A previous version of this paper was presented at the XVth World Congress of the International Political Science Association, 21–25 July 1991, Buenos Aires, Argentina. The present version benefitted from presentations at: Law School, New York University; Latin American Studies, Brown University; Dept of Political Science, New School for Social Research, New York; Institute of Latin American and Iberian Studies and Center for the Study of Human Rights, Columbia University, from January to February 1992, when I was teaching at the School of International Affairs, Columbia University.

1. Nicos Poulantzas, *O Estado, o Poder, o Socialismo* (Rio de Janeiro: Graal, 1981), p. 181.
2. Agnes Heller, 'On Formal Democracy', in John Keane (ed.), *Civil Society and the State* (London: Verso, 1988), p. 136.
3. Nicos Poulantzas, op. cit., p. 82.
4. Michel Foucault, *Microfísica do Poder* (Rio de Janeiro: Graal, 1979), p. 176.
5. Nicos Poulantzas, *A Crise das Ditaduras* (Rio de Janeiro: Paz e Terra, 1978), p. 73.
6. Nicos Poulantzas, *A Crise das Ditaduras*, p. 77.
7. Nicos Poulantzas, *A Crise das Ditaduras*, p. 79.
8. Guillermo O'Donnell, 'Transições, continuidades e alguns paradoxos', in Fábio Wanderley Reis and Guillermo O'Donnell, *A Democracia no Brasil. Dilemas e Perspectivas* (São Paulo: Vértice, 1988), p. 43–4. See also Alfred Stepan (ed). *Democratizando o Brasil* (São Paulo: Paz e Terra, 1988), especially, the contributions: Maria do Carmo Campello de Souza 'A Nova República Brasileira'; Thomas Skidmore 'A lenta via brasileira para a democratização', and the masterly contribution from A. Stepan, 'As prerrogativas militares nos regimes pós-autoritários: Brasil, Argentina, Uruguai e Espanha'.
9. See Jean Baudrillard, *Simulations* (New York: Semiotexte, 1983), p. 27.
10. Americas Watch, 'Brazil – Notorious Jail Operating Again in São Paulo', *News from Americas Watch*, vol. 10, (October 1989), pp. 1–3.

11. Gerard Lebrun, 'O Brasil de Florestan Fernandes', in Maria Angela D'Incao (ed.) *O Saber Militante* (Rio de Janeiro: Paz e Terra, 1987), p. 268.
12. Elizabeth Hardwick, 'Sad Brazil', in *Bartleby in Manhattan and other Essays* (London: Weidenfeld and Nicolson, 1983), p. 216.
13. F. Fernandez, quoted in G. Lebrun, op. cit., p. 267.
14. Primo Levi, *The Drowned and the Saved* (New York: Summit, 1990), p. 67.
15. E.P. Thompson, 'The Rule of Law', in *Whigs and Hunters* (Harmondsworth: Penguin, 1977), pp. 264–5. See also Eugene Genovese, *A Terra Prometida (Jordan, Roll)* (Rio de Janeiro: Paz e Terra, 1988), especially 'A função hegemônica do direito', pp. 48–76.
16. Philippe Schmitter, 'Condenados à Democracia', *Jornal do Brasil*, 10 July 1988, Caderno Especial, p. 10.
17. Alain Rouquié, *Amérique Latine* (Paris: Seuil, 1987), p. 113.
18. Alf Lüdtke, 'The State and Social Domination in Eighteenth and Nineteenth-Century Prussia', in Samuel Raphael (ed.), *People's History and Socialist Theory* (London: Blackwell, 1981). See also the extended version of the same text, 'The role of state violence in the period of transition to industrial capitalism: the example of Prussia from 1815 to 1848', in Alf Lüdtke, *Social History*, vol. 4, no. 2 (May 1979), pp. 175–221. See also Pierre Bourdieu, 'Les modes de domination', *Actes de la Recherche en Sciences Sociales*, vol. 2–3 (June 1976), pp. 122–132, to distinguish 'violence douce' or 'violence symbolique' and 'violence ouverte'.
19. Norbert Elias, 'Violence and Civilization', in Keane, op. cit., pp. 177–98.
20. José de Souza Martins, 'Linchamentos: a vida por um fio', *Travessia: Revista do Migrante* (São Paulo: Centro de Estudos Migratórios) vol. II, no. 4, (March–April), pp. 21–7.
21. Henri Laborit, *'La Nouvelle Grille'* (10/18) (Paris: Union Générale D'editions, 1974), p. 184.
22. Michel Debrun, *A Conciliação e outras Estratégias* (São Paulo: Brasiliense, 1983), p. 33.
23. M. Debrun, op. cit. p. 134.
24. John Herz, (ed.), *From Dictatorship to Democracy* (Westport: Greenwood Press, 1982). See especially 'Denazification and Related Policies', pp. 15–38.
25. Hubert Dreyfus and Paul Rabinow, *Michel Foucault, un parcours philosophique* (Paris: Gallimard, 1984), p. 167.
26. Michel Foucault, *Histoire de la Sexualité* (Paris: Gallimard, 1976), p. 113, cited in Dreyfus and Rabinow, op. cit., p. 195.
27. Joh de Bruin, 'Rapport over die arbeidens verhoridingen in Brasilien' (translated from Dutch, 'Relatório sobre a situação operária no Brasil'), São Paulo, manuscript, p. 24, Archives Albert Thomas, ABIT, from which parts were published in Paulo Sérgio Pinheiro and M. Michael Hall, *A Classe Operária no Brasil, Documentos, 1889–1930, v.II* (São Paulo: Paz e Terra, 1983). I used this expression in P.S. Pinheiro, *Repressão e Insurreição (Communistas, Tenentes e Violência do Estado no Brasil, 1922–1935).* (dissertation, University of São Paulo, 1987), pp. 238–78; and in P.S. Pinheiro, *Estratégias da Ilusão. A Revolução Mundial e o*

Brasil (1922–1935) (São Paulo: Companhia das Letras) 1991.
28. Joh de Bruin, op. cit.
29. The expression 'defensive violence' is from Herbert Marcuse, Jurgen Habermas, *et al.*, *Conversaciones con Herbert Marcuse* (Barcelona: Gedisa, 1980), p. 173.
30. Guillermo O'Donnell, 'E eu com isso? Notas sobre a sociabilidade política na Argentina e no Brasil', in *Contrapontos, Autoritarismo e Democratização* (São Paulo: Vértice, 1986), p. 141; about micro despotisms, 'Democracia en la Argentina: micro y macro', in Oscar Oszlak (ed.), *Proceso, crisis y transición democrática* (Buenos Aires: Centro Editorial de América Latina, 1984), passim. I presented the suggestion of 'socially existing authoritarianism' (later, reading O'Donnell, *socially rooted* authoritarianism) in my post-doctorate dissertation, *Insurreição e repressão (Communistas, Tenentes e a Violência do Estado)* (São Paulo: FFLCH, 1987), passim and later, in a presentation in the Symposium, 'Dificuldades da redemocratização no Brasil', Seminário Século XXI, UNICAMP, Campinas, São Paulo, 7 July 1988, coordinated by Luciano Martins. See also P.S. Pinheiro, 'Violence de l'état et Dissidence Politique (le cas du Brésil, 1920–1935)', in Colloque sur le Crime Politique, International Association for the History of Crime and Criminal Justice, 2–3 June 1989, Paris; P.S. Pinheiro, 'Autoritarismo depois da ditadura', *Tempo e Presença*, São Paulo, October 1989, pp. 4–5. On micro despotisms in Brazil, see P.S. Pinheiro and Emir Sader, 'O controle da polícia no processo de transição democrática no Brasil', *Temas IMESC*, São Paulo, vol. 2, no. 2 (1985), pp. 77–95; Maria Célia Paoli, 'Violência e Espaço Civil', in Maria Célia Paoli *et al.*, *A Violência Brasileira* (São Paulo: Brasiliense, 1982), pp. 45–56.
31. Maria Sylvia de Carvalho Franco, *Homens Livres na Sociedade Escravocata* (São Paulo: Ática, 1969), pp. 55–7.
32. F. Fernandes, A *Ditadura em Questão* (São Paulo: TAQ, 1982), p. 45.
33. The preceding sentences draw on 'Continuidade Autoritária e Construção da Democracia', a thematical project of the Center for the Studies of Violence, University of São Paulo, coordinated by Paulo Sérgio Pinheiro and Sérgio Adorno, September 1990, mimeo.
34. Roberto Da Matta, *Carnavois, malandros e herois* (Rio de Janeiro: Zalvar, 1978).

Part V

Constitutional Policy

12 From Coparticipation to Coalition: The Problems of Presidentialism in the Uruguayan Case, 1984–90

María Ester Mancebo

This chapter deals with the effects of presidentialism on the creation of coalitions in Uruguay. It studies the negotiations carried on by the elected presidents, J.M. Sanguinetti and L.A. Lacalle, in 1984–5 and 1989–90, respectively, to form their first cabinets with ministers representing the Colorado Party (CP) and Blanco Party (BP).[1] The results of those negotiations were the agreements called 'National Intonation' and 'National Coinciding'.

The comparative analysis, based on structured interviews with politicians belonging to all main political fractions and secondary data (electoral results, survey data), demonstrates that the two alliances were not coalitions in the strict sense but were indicative of a cooperative relation between those parties. Apart from the specific – and important – characteristics of each of the two junctures, there were some constant factors that promoted both agreements while others exercised a brake-like influence upon them. The elected presidents – worried about the problem of ruling democratically without controlling a majority of parliamentary seats – played a central role in the negotiation process, but they met all the difficulties of forming coalitions in a presidentialist regime and dealing with fractionalized parties in a fragmented party system.

The first section of the chapter describes the negotiations that preceded the 'National Intonation' and 'National Coinciding' agreements. The second section compares them as interparty agreements. The third and fourth sections present the factors that prompted and hindered the formation of true coalitions. Finally the conclusion points out the importance of the institutional arrangements in the power-sharing and coalition-forming processes that took place in Uruguay in the recent transition to and consolidation of the democratic regime.

THE BIRTH OF THE 'NATIONAL INTONATION' AND 'NATIONAL COINCIDING' AGREEMENTS

The Uruguayan national election of November 1984 marked the end of the 11-year period of authoritarian rule. The CP emerged as the leading party with 41 per cent of the vote and 42 per cent of the seats in the 130-seat legislature. The BP obtained 35 per cent of the vote and 35 per cent of the seats, the Broad Front (BF) 21 per cent of the vote and 21 per cent of the seats and the Civic Union (CU) 2 per cent of the vote and 2 per cent of the seats.

During the electoral campaign most of the politicians made reference to the idea of 'national unity' in their speeches, showing that the political elites were willing to work for pluralism, a principle that had been widely accepted in the Uruguayan polity until the late 1960s. Furthermore 'national unity' seemed to be the indispensable formula to avoid another coup and, specifically, the seizure of power by the military. Political parties seemed to be ready to cooperate in the building of a new democratic order. In this context the negotiations to create a 'national unity government' started immediately after the elections and continued until the end of February 1985. They were carried on at the highest political level, through a series of meetings that the elected President Sanguinetti had with the main leaders of the opposition, Wilson Ferreira Aldunate (BP), Líber Seregni (BF) and Juan Vicente Chiarino (CU).

Sanguinetti played a central role in the elaboration of the concrete proposal to create a national unity government. In his view a multi-party cabinet should be the culmination of the agreements reached on policies by the main political parties – not the starting-point of them – and the first necessary step was to continue with the successful dialogue established among them in the last phase of the authoritarian rule. Formally none of the principal parties of the opposition were excluded from the negotiations, since the proposal was made to the BP, the BF[2] and the CU. However, in practice, Sanguinetti's strategy soon made it clear that it would be very difficult for the non-traditional parties to come to a political agreement: 'We will try to create a national unity government. First we will have to agree on what has to be done. If we come to a consensus on this regard, I do not exclude the possibility of forming a cabinet with members from other parties . . . from the BP and the BF . . .' (Sanguinetti, *Búsqueda*, 29 November 1984). From the very beginning of the negotiations the CU adopted a favorable attitude towards Sanguinetti's proposal, but the main parties of the opposition, the BP and the BF, tended to reject it.[3]

When, by the end of January, they did so explicitly,[4] Sanguinetti responded with the suggestion of incorporating in his cabinet outstanding non-Colorado citizens who would act on personal grounds. The term 'government of National Unity' was then replaced by 'National Intonation'.

Finally the cabinet was formed by six Colorados, two Blancos and one Civic. The Blanco ministers did not represent their party, though. That meant that the BP and the CU would not stand as jointly responsible for the government's actions, but would play the role of opposition. By contrast, the BP, BF and CU wanted to participate in the boards of the Entes,[5] because they thought they could develop useful practice and, simultaneously, control the government at that level of the administration. It appeared that in the negotiations of 1984–5 the CP focused on retaining this majority in the Entes as much as the BP did on securing a stable legislative majority in 1989–90. Finally Sanguinetti retained the majority of votes in the boards and offered 13 positions to the BP and six to the BF.[6] This was of great importance because it was the first time in history that the left entered the boards of the Entes and shared power at such a high level of the administration.

The national elections held in November 1989 changed the pattern of distribution of power in the Uruguayan restored democracy. The BP won, with 39 per cent of the popular vote and 40 per cent of the seat share in the general assembly. It was followed by the CP with 30 per cent of the vote and 30 per cent of the seats, the BF with 21 per cent and 22 per cent, respectively, and the New Space (NS)[7] with 9 per cent and 8 per cent. Indeed,

> Considering their previous share of the electorate . . . the net winner of the election was the left. On the one hand, though divided into two alliances – or perhaps partly thanks to this division – the whole of the left obtained as many votes as the Colorados at the national level. On the other hand, the BF won the local election in Montevideo . . . something less than a provincial governor, since Uruguay is a unitary state, but more than just a city mayor. Both results were absolute firsts in Uruguayan political history (González-Gillespie, 1990, pp. 44–5).

The formation of interparty coalitions capable of sustaining government majorities had been a central issue of the campaign. In particular, Lacalle made it a core of his platform and, as a result, in the summer of 1989–90 he devoted most of his efforts to it. In his view, the 'European-style coalition' would make the decision-making process easier and therefore contribute to the realization of two important objectives: the efficiency of the government and the implementation of changes that the country could not continue putting off.

Throughout the negotiations Lacalle stated the accordance of this formula with Uruguayan constitutional arrangements: he noted the coalition could be based on the revival of the Council of Ministers,[8] and suggested the idea of parliamentary approval of individual ministers. Because the elected president was not interested in the integration of the BF or NS in the coalition, his offer was made to the defeated fractions of the BP (MNR and PLP) and to the CP, and he resorted to diverse mechanisms to pressure these potential allies to accept his offer. At the beginning of January, Lacalle used data from a public opinion poll[9] that showed that a majority of people interviewed in Montevideo was in favor of a coalition government. He then made the posts usually held in the Entes by the opposition conditional upon their acceptance of his proposal. Finally, at the end of February, he declared that he would reject the Colorados' plan to appoint as ministers technicians who would not represent the CP and announced his desire to form a Blanco cabinet instead.

In reply to this strategy, Lacalle received immediate but conditional support from the BP and a compromise to cooperate from the CP. This was the 'National Coinciding':[10] four of the president's cabinet appointees were Colorados and eight of them were Blancos,[11] and the executive could count on a relatively stable legislative majority made up of 69 of the 99 representatives and 22 of the 31 senators.

THE 'NATIONAL INTONATION' AND 'NATIONAL COINCIDING' AS INTERPARTY AGREEMENTS

The 'National Intonation' was not what Sanguinetti looked forward to in the 'national unity government', nor was the 'National Coinciding' the 'European-style coalition' Lacalle sought. However both experiences were openings towards biparty alliances that can be analyzed from a comparative perspective.

The Actors' Positions

From 1984 to 1989, the players' individual traits varied: in the first negotiation Sanguinetti and the CP acted as sender, whereas in the second one Lacalle and the BP played that role; Wilson and his party functioned as receiver in 1984–5 while Pacheco–Batlle–Sanguinetti[12] and the CP did so in 1989–90. On the other hand, the sender's and receiver's positions were constant in both processes because they were determined by the electoral results. Sanguinetti and Lacalle promoted their cooperative initiatives with firm political will in their role of 'elected president', a role that involved a high degree of legitimacy and the responsibility of forming the cabinet. As future presidents they were expected to generate the political resources to rule effectively and democratically.[13]

As receivers, Wilson and Pacheco–Batlle–Sanguinetti gave priority to interests of their parties that had been defeated in the recent elections. Besides they had to undertake the hard task of aggregation of internal interests throughout the negotiation processes. As sender that job was easier for the CP in 1984 than for the BP in 1989, while as receiver the CP in 1989 met more difficulties in conciliating internal differences than the BP did in 1984. This fact shows that those difficulties were associated with the internal situation of each party in both junctures and not with the position as sender or receiver in the negotiation. In addition it indicates the existence of a paradox: even though both parties dealt with more problems in 1989 than in 1984, at the moment of its creation the 'National Coinciding' was a stronger alliance than the 'National Intonation'.

In accordance with the described positions, the actors made their different bets and evaluated the costs and benefits of reaching a certain agreement. The sender aimed at establishing the coresponsibility of both traditional parties in government because that alliance provided the political resources for a good administration. In terms of decision-making theory, the pact meant for the CP in March 1985 and BP in 1990 a high concentration of benefits, with costs that were distributed between the two traditional parties. In contrast, the receiver wanted to get an advantageous position in the political system, and felt that the alliance burdened it with a great responsibility for unknown – and doubtful – electoral profit. In other words, the alliance meant to accept asymmetrically distributed costs and benefits. However it is important to state that the CP and BP were both trying to avoid the risk of political blockade, were looking forward to achieving a stable democracy[14] and were willing to leave aside their particular interests, if necessary. That made the 'National Intonation' and 'National Coinciding' possible.

The Negotiation

The negotiation started immediately after the national elections, in December 1984 and December 1989. That early start revealed the importance and urgency assigned to the subject by the sender. In fact the deadline for the conversations was 1 March (1985 and 1990) because on that day Sanguinetti's and Lacalle's cabinets had to be formed. Indeed by setting previous deadlines Lacalle tried harder than Sanguinetti to obtain the receiver's final answer sooner, but he failed to achieve a fluent process with this pressure method.[15]

Both elected presidents defined some non-negotiable areas. They reserved the principal positions of the economic administration for their own political fraction. Lacalle also kept the Ministry of Foreign Relations, Defense and Interior for the Herrerismo. Paradoxically, in 1989–90, Lacalle seemed to look for a deeper alliance than Sanguinetti had in 1984–5, but was ready to distribute fewer political goods. Yet, taken by itself, this simple numerical indicator is misleading. It has to be considered in connection with the strategy chosen by each elected president: in public, Sanguinetti appeared to be more flexible (only one non-negotiable area) and finally he ceded two ministries to the Blancos; Lacalle appeared more rigid (four non-negotiable areas) but he offered all the other ministries to the Colorados, who accepted four of them at the end of the negotiations.

Two factors can explain this difference. First, in the summer of 1984–5 the CP gave Sanguinetti its complete backing, with a highly cohesive attitude,[16] and the BP was unified under Wilson's leadership. On the contrary, in 1989–90, Lacalle had to negotiate with two factions of his own party (MNR and PLP) and three of the CP; that is, he had to discuss with five players, each of them standing for its own interests and goals. For that reason, he kept those ministries that dealt with subjects of uttermost importance for his faction. Second, Sanguinetti presented his proposal under the enchantment of the democratic transition and he did not dare to threaten the prevailing spirit of 'national unity'. The 1989 elections initiated a period of democratic consolidation that enabled Lacalle to assume a pragmatic and more rigid position.

The economic policy to be followed by the new administration was a keystone of both agreements. According to Wilson, 'There are two possible roads for the parties of the opposition: they can try to impose the economic policy they consider correct or they can allow the government to carry on his and let the facts prove who was right. We prefer the second solution' (*Búsqueda*, 2 July 1985). The addressee not only argued that policy hindered its integration to the cabinet but also questioned – on ideological, not technical, grounds – the appointments made by the elected president to the economic administration. It should be noted that in the negotiations preceding the 'National Intonation' the CP showed a high degree of consensus on the economic policy,[17] but that topic was a real Gordian knot for the unity of the BP as sender because the liberal orientation sustained by the Herrerismo was hard to conciliate with the interventionist one defended by the other fractions. These internal problems were used by the CP to justify its refusal to enter the coalition.

Apart from these similarities, the structure of the negotiation showed differential traits in both experiences. The first difference refers to the unity of the party that had won the elections. With his 'strategy of concentric circles' Lacalle made explicit that his initiative was directed to the other factions of the BP[18] in the first place, and then to the CP. It is clear that Lacalle had to secure the support of his own party unlike Sanguinetti who had been backed by a completely united CP.

The second differential characteristic was the early and clear exclusion of the left from the negotiation that preceded the 'National Coinciding'. In fact, that exclusion diminished the uncertainty about the selection of the principal players and can be explained in relation to the peculiarities of each juncture. In 1984–5 all political actors were concerned about the success of the transition of democracy. Moreover, the CP and the BF had been allies in the pact celebrated with the military to regulate the end of the authoritarian government[19] and in consequence the left had to be included as a player in the negotiation.[20] On the contrary, in 1989–90, the BF and the NS were not qualified as players: they did not receive a concrete offer to join the cabinet, which left them with no internal decisions on the subject to be made.

The third difference in the structure of the negotiation refers to the nature of the proposed agreement. Lacalle's 'European-style coalition' meant a deeper compromise than Sanguinetti's 'national unity government'. It could even been said that the former was more articulated than the latter, because Lacalle delimitated the menu of alternative pacts precisely: the coalition with the NS was useless because it did not provide the executive with a parliamentary majority and the one with the BF was discarded because of the ideological distance between the leftist coalition and the BP.

Fourth, the two elected presidents exhibited different patterns of distribution of benefits to the potential allies: Sanguinetti did not make the distribution of positions in the boards of the Entes conditional upon the pact, whereas Lacalle announced that, if the CP did not agree to conform to the coalition, it would not be represented in the Entes.

In sum, there is little doubt that on both occasions the sender was able to give shape to the negotiation as he set the bases of the discussion – when, who, what, how – but this does not mean that he had a complete command of the game. On the one hand, he could not change the rules set by the political structures[21] – presidentialist regime, constitutional norms on the status of the cabinet, past experiences of interparty agreements – and, on the other, he did not control the receiver, who deliberated upon the proposal freely. There were few 'senior players' involved in the decision-making process, but the political agreement reached cannot be analyzed as a purely rational decision resulting from an exact estimation of costs and benefits on the part of those few actors. On the contrary, those senior players had to take into consideration the dominant views in their respective parties on the alliance and consider public opinion's reactions to it.

The Alternatives and the Result

In decision-making processes the involved actors do not always take into account all possible alternative solutions to a problem. Neither do they always follow the principle of optimization of the results, and they often work for the realization of their goals instead (Mena, 1989, p. 120).

What were the effective alternatives considered by the actors in the periods that preceded the 'National Intonation' and 'National Coinciding'? In 1984–5 the Colorados preferred a multi-party agreement of medium strength that would provide the government with the political resources to solve the problems of the transition to democracy. The second possible option was to come to a medium-strength agreement with the BP exclusively, which would guarantee an important degree of stability to the government. The third and fourth options were, respectively, to reach a weak compromise with all important parties or with the BP alone. It is important to note that the Colorado leaders thought of establishing a party government but the difficulties of the transition led them to concentrate on diverse options for an interparty pact. They never considered the formation of a true coalition, though.

In the negotiation process developed in the summer of 1989–90, the sender conceived three alternatives. They were, in order of preference, a strong, medium and weak biparty alliance. The 'European-style coalition' was presented by Lacalle as the optimum way to avoid the political deadlock resulting from the lack of legislative majorities. Unlike the previous experience, these three options did not include an alliance with either of the two leftist parties, the BF or NS. Moreover the idea of setting up a party government was used as part of the strategy to put pressure on the CP, but it was far from being a privileged goal.

All told, this list of preferences shows that in both negotiations the agreement between both traditional parties was specially favored. The Colorados' search for a biparty alliance in 1984–5 probably had a positive effect when they considered the idea as receiver in 1989–90. Following in this line of thought it can be said that these negotiations contributed significantly to a learning process of cooperative behavior between both traditional parties. Thus the 'National Intonation' and 'National Coinciding' were certainly indicative of the existence of a cooperative biparty relation, but they were not coalitions in the strict sense, especially because of the type of representation the electorally defeated party had in the government: there were two Blanco ministers, Iglesias and Ugarte, in Sanguinetti's cabinet, but they did not represent the BP. Lacalle wanted Colorado politicians in his cabinet and he resisted the 'Ugarte experience' – that is, the appointment as secretary of state of a technician without important militant activity in his party – but he had to accept an ambiguous representation, that was neither personal nor political, on the part of the Colorados. Furthermore, the agreements reached by the two traditional parties were highly-undefined. The documents written by the CONAPRO[22] in 1984 and the 'Bases of Agreement'[23] prepared by the Herrerismo in 1989 could have been taken as 'foundation-stones' of both pacts, but they were not. Even though those documents proved to be useful in the definition of consensus areas they were far from being the base of an accorded program.

Besides, in 1985 Wilson Ferreira Aldunate defended the Blancos' right to play the role of opposition. In 1990 Colorado Senator Americo Ricaldoni did so for his own party. That is, neither of the two addressees resigned the right to act as 'responsible opposition'. This approach was incompatible with the existence of a true coalition.

Finally, neither Sanguinetti's nor Lacalle's cabinets received an explicit approval in parliament. Such an idea was suggested by the Herrerismo as sender but it was not discussed by the political elites.[24]

Leaving aside the formal aspects, the 'National Intonation' and 'National Coinciding' showed that they were not true coalitions in the practice of government. Sanguinetti's frequent use of the president's veto power can be taken as an indicator of the absence of a legislative coalition he could rely on. A second indicator is that in both administrations each bill or governmental initiative required a hard and slow negotiating process, features that were also associated with the lack of leadership in Congress: during the 'National Intonation', Wilson was a key reference for all his party but he was not a member of parliament; during the 'National Coinciding' the CP was divided into four factions that responded to four different leaders,[25] three of whom were not members of parliament. To make matters worse, one of them – Millor – headed the Colorado internal opposition to the 'National Coinciding'.

The 'National Intonation' and 'National Coinciding' were not coalitions, but were they new versions of the traditional Uruguayan 'coparticipation'? The answer to this question is not simple because, even though the term has often been used as opposed to 'party government', it has had different meanings. Most of these meanings were born in association with the different forms of coparticipation that have existed in Uruguayan history: by the end of the nineteenth century, 'coparticipation' referred to the agreement between both traditional parties according to which the BP ran certain regions in the interior of the country while the CP controlled the national government; in the 1930s 'coparticipation' mainly took place at the Entes, where the parties of the opposition obtained a share of the seats on their boards.

To present the history of the coparticipation would be to exceed the scope of this chapter.[26] Yet it is worth noting that 'coparticipation' has never led the parties of the opposition to assume full responsibility for government; it has coexisted with party government and it has been a useful mechanism to exercise democratic control. From this point of view, the 'National Intonation' and 'National Coinciding' kept 'coparticipation' alive. The 'National Intonation' allowed an inclusive coparticipation because the BF was represented in the Entes, whereas the 'National Coinciding' led to a restrictive coparticipation: 'restrictive' because the parties that were not part of the 'National Coinciding' were excluded from the boards of the Entes; 'coparticipation' because the Colorados' participation in the boards of the Entes assumed the traditional format and the Colorado leaders declared that the CP was neither government nor opposition.

Finally, even if the coalition had been formed, coparticipation could have existed: they are not contrary institutions because they allow parties to share power at different levels.

FACTORS THAT PROMOTED THE INTERPARTY AGREEMENTS

The comparative analysis of the 'National Intonation' and 'National Coinciding' shows that there were some *constant* factors that helped forward both interparty alliances: the role of the elected president, the problem of governability of the country and the traditional cooperation between the CP and BP.

Both elected presidents had a central role in the creation of the 'National Intonation' and 'National Coinciding'. On the one hand, Sanguinetti and Lacalle defined the interparty alliance as a prior instrument that would contribute decisively to the realization of their objectives: to Sanguinetti it would bring political peace to a society that was certainly challenged at the institutional level; to Lacalle the pact would help to pass the socioeconomic reforms the country needed. On the other hand, the future presidents had a central role in the definition of the strategy to follow throughout the talks, and they carried on the negotiations with firm political will, unifying their respective parties behind their idea.

The future presidents' high degree of involvement in the negotiations[27] can be explained on the basis of their leadership: in the period of the negotiations Sanguinetti and Lacalle were medium-strength leaders[28] in their parties and enjoyed the popular legitimacy coming from the recent elections. However the variable that best explains that involvement is the presidential regime itself. As González and Gillespie note,

In at least partially consolidated polyarchies, the institutional position of the president conveys a mix of resources and pressures that is by definition unique. He has material means, institutional resources, personal legitimacy, and, when lacking parliamentary support, arguments that provide him with a ready-to-use rationalization for his potential anti-system behavior (1990, p. 36).

Because of the great powers associated with their future office, Sanguinetti and Lacalle themselves were expected to form their cabinets, with the positive and negative results for the presidency and the political system this type of appointment might introduce:

A presidential cabinet is less likely than its parliamentary counterpart to contain strong and independent-minded members. The officers of a president's cabinet hold their posts purely at the sufferance of their chief; if dismissed, they are out of public life altogether (Linz, 1990, p. 63).

A second constant factor to be taken into consideration is the problem of governability that is derived from the complex relation between participation, demands and institutions, and has risen in contemporary developed and underdeveloped societies, with particular features in each of them.[29] Uruguayan political elites showed a great preoccupation with governability in the talks of 1984–5 and 1989–90, though the source of the worry changed from the first to the second experience.

At the end of the authoritarian rule the problem of governability was associated with the success of the transition to democracy and, for that reason, Wilson Ferreira Aldunate presented his 'governability theory'[30] as the necessary mechanism to preserve democracy through the control of excessive demands and pressures on the new administration. In the period of consolidation of democracy initiated by Lacalle, the elected authorities wanted to avoid the political deadlock that could result from the lack of parliamentary majorities and, as a result, the problem of governability focused on the drawbacks of the Uruguayan political system, particularly the presidential form of government and electoral law.

In the light of the literature on the subject it is possible to distinguish two different versions of the problem: in the period that preceded the 'National Intonation' the term 'governability' was directly linked to the risks of a coup while in the negotiations towards the 'National Coinciding' it was associated with the diminished capacity of the state to implement public policies. Putting aside those differences, there can be no doubts about the fact that the political elites' preoccupation with this problem made them seek a new pattern of political cooperation in both occasions.

The third factor that promoted the pacts was the 'coparticipation' between both traditional parties. Different interpretations of its importance in Uruguayan history have been presented, and some of them appear to be contradictory: Pareja and Pérez (1990) think that coparticipation has had an enormous significance for Uruguayan democracy because it introduced pluralism at diverse institutional levels, while González and Gillespie (1990) consider that Uruguayan democratic governments have always been party governments, whatever the level of 'coparticipación' that may have existed.

Putting aside these different approaches on the *institutional* relevance of 'coparticipation', there is no doubt that it has been important from the point of view of *political culture*: it has given traditional parties multiple chances to practice cooperative behavior and has helped them develop a consociational political style. In particular, in 1984–5 and 1989–90, 'coparticipation' provided a solid cultural base for the formation of biparty alliances. Apart from these *constant* factors that urged both interparty agreements, there were some *specific* ones: that is, factors that were present in one juncture but not in the other.

In the case of the 'National Intonation' it is important to consider that, after 11 years of authoritarian rule, the government elected in November 1984 faced a variety of grave institutional and economic problems. Therefore the decision-making process that preceded the 'National Intonation' occurred in a situation of crisis that the actors tried to overcome with a strong spirit of 'national unity'.[31] In this respect, the CONAPRO was a fundamental antecedent of the 'National Intonation' because it created a suitable environment for the political elites to practice the art of negotiation and show to the public their desire to reach compromises. Besides, the CONAPRO was a serious attempt to find consensus areas within which future authorities could work towards finding national solutions to the problems of the country. In effect the CONAPRO was a 'policy game' that led to the formulation of policies and influenced the development of the 'decision game' (which led to senior-players' decisions) played in the summer of 1984–5 (Allison and Halperín, p. 232).

The Uruguayan elections of November 1989 marked the end of the transition to democracy and the beginning of the process of its consolidation.[32] The risks of military insubordination, ideological polarization and extreme social conflict had not disappeared but were no longer acute. In particular, the nature of the threat to democracy diverged from the one experienced in 1985 because it did not come from the military but from the political system itself: 'Efficiency is the main problem of the Uruguayan political system. The question is how to give the government the chance to rule' (Sturla, *La Democracia*, 28 September 1990).

Most of the leaders learned about the so-called 'political blockade' during Sanguinetti's term of office. From the point of view of the political scene in which decision-making processes occurred, the 'National Coinciding' was born in a 'reflexive situation': the threat to democratic stability had not ended, the involved actors were not surprised by the situation and they were able to take their time in reading those solutions that fitted their medium- and long-term goals.

In fact, during Sanguinetti's term in office, the problems of Uruguayan political institutions caught the attention of the intellectual and political elites. That could be seen in the debate over the 'Political Reform' that started in 1986 and focused on two main aspects: the character of the reform – that is, whether it should be constitutional, electoral or 'reform without reform' (reform in political practices – and the most suitable form of government – quasi-presidentialism,[33] pure presidentialism, pure parliamentarism or quasi-parliamentarism.

With regard to the first point, it is important to take into account that, according to the survey answered by a representative sample of the members of the legislature in 1987,[34] 90 per cent of the senators and representatives thought that the political reform should include a reform of the constitution. Furthermore, by the beginning of 1988, important sectors of the opposition elaborated a proposal for constitutional reform that would establish a quasi-parliamentary regime.[35] The CP reacted against this scheme, defending the existing presidentialism and introducing the idea of a majoritarian government through the suppression of proportional representation. Thus the debate on political reform showed there were two opposed models of democracy in the country: the opposition was in favor of a 'consensual' government, whereas the CP looked to a 'majoritarian' one.[36]

To sum up, this debate over political reform helped to identify the problems of Uruguayan quasi-presidentialism.[37] During the electoral campaign of 1989 there were constant references to them, specially on the part of Lacalle's faction that had been against the 1987–8 negotiations to reform the political system. Therefore that consciousness[38] of the importance of the institutional setting had a significant effect on the creation of the 'National Coinciding' – while it had not been a relevant factor in the negotiations towards the 'National Intonation' – and led the political elites to think about different alternatives to build legislative majorities.[39] Moreover the leaders of the traditional parties were particularly impressed by the growing fragmentation of the party system:[40] a two-party system until 1971, a 'two and a half' format after the appearance of the BF in the elections held in that year, and moderate pluralism – with four relevant actors – from 1984 onward (González, 1988). In a private interview, an important Herrerista leader expressed the opinion that

What gives cohesion to the 'National Coinciding' is the consciousness that not only the BP government but also the traditional Uruguayan party system is at risk . . . If Lacalle fails to make a good government we do not have any guarantee that the next President will be Colorado or Blanco (12 September 1990).

FACTORS THAT HINDERED THE FORMATION OF STRONG BIPARTY AGREEMENTS

Any explanation of the failure of these two attempts to create strong party alliances in Uruguay should first consider the importance of the institutional setting, and specifically the impact of the presidential form of government. Indeed presidentialism imposes serious obstacles to the formation of true coalitions because the invitation to be part of the government is not at all attractive for the parties of the opposition, since they can obtain little profit from it: 'If things go well they do not receive much of the political credit but if things go wrong as a result of actions they do not control, they may have to take part of the blame' (González-Gillespie, 1990, p. 34). Besides, in presidential regimes elections assume a zero-sum character[41] and are held on fixed dates. Winners and losers were clearly defined in November 1984 and 1989 and that definition was valid for the entire presidential term of office. This fact led political actors to establish temporal limits to the potential agreements at the very beginning of the negotiation process: Sanguinetti spoke of a 'three-year period of national unity government', while Lacalle offered the Colorados the possibility of setting the time limit for the coalition.

A third characteristic of presidentialism that hindered the formation of true coalitions is the power and plebiscitarian legitimacy of the president. In fact, Sanguinetti and Lacalle wanted to rely on the parliamentary traits of Uruguayan quasi-presidentialism and keep the central role of the president simultaneously. That was an extremely difficult goal to achieve because

A president is not a *primus inter pares* a prime minister is, and cannot be replaced because of disagreements on policies, whatever their intensity [only by impeachment] . . . The institutional position of a president thus necessarily implies that the minority partners in a governing coalition have to participate in a subordinate position that is politically damaging for them, and that they lend political capital without any guarantee (González-Gillespie, 1990, pp. 34–5).

The dual legitimacy that characterizes presidential regimes also hampered the formation of enduring and strong alliances because legislators felt the voters expected them to defend the electoral platforms to the last consequences. As a Blanco legislator put it:

> To come to an agreement on those controversial matters would weaken the political system because the people who voted for Lacalle or Pereyra could not understand they abandoned their original proposal on those matters (MNR Senator, 1990).

In sum, presidentialism set structural difficulties to the formation of interparty alliances in the summer of 1984–5 and 1989–90. The form of government stands out as the *constant* obstacle that hindered coalitions, but there are other variable factors that have to be included in a complete explanation.

With regards to the *variable* factors it is important to consider, in the case of the 'National Intonation', the impact of the Naval Club Pact that regulated the transition from authoritarian government and also put an end to the unity among the parties that opposed to the military. The Blancos felt that the electoral result would have been completely different if Wilson Ferreira Aldunate had been able to run as a candidate, and in turn the Blanco leaders developed a speech characterized by democratic radicalism that placed the party in a dual position. On the one hand the BP presented itself as the main defender of democratic institutions; on the other the BP charged the left and the Colorados with betrayal and, as a result, it declared that compromise with them was not possible. This second stance would finally become predominant:

> The BP will give freedom back to the unfairly persecuted and victims of the military justice. To do all this, to give the country the unity and peace it needs and to provide the people with confidence in the institutions, I do not want the government to be looked at from the opposite sidewalk . . . I have often been asked to state that the BP opposes violence and I refuse to do so. Ours is a party that resorts to violence whenever it is necessary to preserve liberty (Wilson, *Búsqueda*, 28 February 1985).

Moreover, after the 1989 elections, there was a widespread perception that the CP would rule for the rest of the century: it enjoyed the image of a predominant party;[42] it appeared to be united, coherent and made up of politicians with great experience; in particular, the Colorado leaders tended to think that during Sanguinetti's administration the CP would prove to have a command of the art of ruling the state and, as a result, its position as predominant party would be consolidated:

> We [CP] are now in the government, we have applied our policies for three years and we are going to apply them for at least twelve more years, that is until the year 2000 . . . By the year 2001 people may change their opinion and choose another government and another policy (Colorado Senator, J. Batlle, *Cuadernos de Marcha*, January, 1988).

This certainly did not help negotiations to reach an interparty agreement. By contrast, in 1989–90 the BP recognized it had less experience in government than the CP, had to demonstrate that it could rule the country and, in consequence, looked forward to the agreement with the CP.

Finally, a third variable factor that held back the creation of a solid alliance was the cultural base of the CP.[43] Most important Colorado leaders believe in the practice of party government, in which the majority implements its political platform, the minority controls and the citizenship judges the governmental performance in the next election. Some Colorados even questioned the historical coparticipation: 'The experience of sharing responsibility in the different areas of coparticipation was too expensive for the country. Because of it Uruguay suffered from a stalemate in the sixties' (outstanding Colorado economist, interview, 16 August 1990).

In the case of the 'National Coinciding', the factionalization[44] of the parties held back the creation of Lacalle's 'European-style coalition', a factor that had not worked as a brake in the 'National Intonation'. In the summer of 1989–90 the CP showed a high level of internal conflict and was divided into four rival factions[45] that did not recognize a common leader and carried on separate decision-making processes with regard to the BP's offer. One of those four factions – Cruzada 94 – did not enter into the 'National Coinciding', and another one – Foro – had virtually left it by mid-1991. The BP was divided into four main factions, and the Herrerismo found a completely loyal ally in Renovación y Victoria (RV) but not in PLP and MNR, for different reasons: the former suffered a serious leadership crisis and could not offer significant support to the government; the latter held political views that were quite distant from the president's with regard to such important issues as economic policy, the role of the state and the so-called 'reform of the state'. Thus the division in the BP had an ideological basis, though there were also 'methodological' differences: the leaders belonging to the Herrerismo found it very difficult to understand the internal direct democracy practiced in MNR in taking important decisions.

In conclusions, in 1989–90 both traditional parties were highly factionalized and that affected the creation of a strong biparty agreement. On top of that, even though Uruguayan leaders were acquainted with the creation of pacts, they had no prior experience in the formation of true coalitions, which was a significant handicap to the 'National Coinciding'. It could be said that the past learning process of cooperative behavior was not strong enough to overcome the obstacles referred to, because the importance of political agreements has not always been recognized and legitimatized by leaders in public.

CONCLUSION

As soon as the CP won the elections held in November 1984, Sanguinetti emphasized two central ideas: the need to form a 'national unity government' and the convenience of making the CONAPRO a permanent institution. Both ideas were quite vague, but they certainly showed that the CP evaluated that its responsibility as party government was incremented by the uncertainty of the democratic transition. In that juncture Lacalle opposed the BP's promise to cooperate with the Colorados' government, but the Herrerista faction finally accepted the decision of the Blanco majority led by Wilson to secure the governability of the restored democracy. Five years later, in 1989, Lacalle defended the formation of a coalition in the strict sense so as to count on a working legislative majority.

The comparative analysis of the 'National Intonation' and 'National Coinciding' highlighted the distance between the interparty alliance the elected presidents and their parties sought and the one they finally reached. Sanguinetti and Lacalle had to accept the cooperation the parties in the opposition were ready to offer – even though that cooperation did not come up to their high expectations – because its rejection could open the way to an early politico–institutional stalemate.

The second conclusion of this chapter is that, in the period 1984–90, Uruguayan political elites were certainly willing to cooperate to restore and consolidate democracy. On both occasions the Colorado and

Blanco leaders looked for a new pattern of cooperation that would supersede the historical 'coparticipation', but they failed to do so at the institutional level: even though 'coparticipation' adopted some new, differential traits, it kept its traditional format, it was not transformed into a coalition, and it did not coexist with a true coalition. However, as 'coparticipation' was part of Uruguayan political culture, it certainly promoted the biparty alliances of 1984–5 and 1989–90, because elites were used to transforming conflict into dissensus.

The third conclusion is that, at the time of its creation, the 'National Coinciding' was a stronger alliance than the 'National Intonation', even though both traditional parties dealt with more internal problems in 1989 than in 1984. The explanation for this apparent paradox should take into account the valuable experience gained by the elites with the 'National Intonation' and their increasing preoccupation with the so-called 'political blockade'.

Finally this chapter assumes that the institutional arrangements shape the entire political process and, specifically, that they have significant effects on the power-sharing processes. In this, this case-study provides empirical data on the implications of presidentialism for the formation of coalitions in Uruguayan recent history. The party system showed a growing degree of fragmentation and fractionalization, and both Sanguinetti and Lacalle were quite explicit about the importance they assigned to the building of a solid biparty alliance that would give them an absolute majority of parliamentary seats. In spite of all these favorable conditions, the electorally defeated parties played the role of opposition and did not become part of the government. The constant and variable factors that promoted the alliances were not strong enough to make political actors go beyond the structural constraints imposed on coalitions by presidentialism.

Notes

1. These parties are usually called 'traditional parties, because their origins go back to 1836: that is, to the immediate post-independence years. They won about 90 per cent of the vote until the mid-1960s.
2. Well-known politicians belonging to the BF were considered as possible ministers – Juan Young as minister of health and José D'Elía as minister of labor and social security.
3. With regard to this matter there was no unanimity in the BP. The larger factions, Por la Patria (PLP) and Movimiento Nacional de Rocha (MNR), thought the BP did not have to compromise with the government, but

the Unión Nacional y Herrerista, led by Dardo Ortiz, was favorable to the Blancos' integration into Sanguinetti's Cabinet. In particular, it is interesting to note that in 1984 Lacalle was against sharing the responsibility of the executive branch and was doubtful about cooperation in the legislative branch.

4. The way in which the rejection was made was not the origin of the risk underlined by Linz, though: 'The public rejection of an olive branch publicly proffered could harden positions on both sides and lead to more, rather than less, antagonism and polarization' (Linz, 1990, p. 60).

5. The 'Entes Autónomos' are decentralized public agencies that were created in the 1930s and 1940s.

6. These appointments were not easy to make as the internal fractions aimed at having a representation that would be proportional to their votes (for example, of the 13 positions obtained by the BP, four were for PLP, four for MNR, three for the Consejo Nacional Herrerista (CNH) and two for independent Blanco technicians).

7. When the BF broke down at the beginning of 1989, the moderate wing became known as 'New Space' (the former Colorado faction 'Lista 99', Christian Democrats, and CU) and the radical wing (Communist, Socialist and other small radical factions) kept the original name 'BF'.

8. The Council of Ministers was created in the Constitution of 1934, and maintained in the Constitutions of 1942 and 1966, but it was never an important institution of governmental practice.

9. A total of 676 telephonic interviews were carried out on 6 and 7 February 1990 by EQUIPOS Consultores.

10. Lacalle had used the term 'Coinciding' in December 1989 in reference to the agreement he meant to promote between labor unions and business organizations.

11. Five of these eight secretaries belonged to the president's faction, Herrerismo: Defense, Economy and Finance, Interior, Foreign Relations, Social Security and Labor.

12. These were the leaders of the main Colorado factions.

13. As Allison says, 'Positions define what the players can do and what they should do. Those positions determine the advantages and handicaps that the actors can use in the different games, but they also determine their obligations (1988, p. 240).

14. In fact this goal was shared by the majority of the social and political actors, not just by the traditional parties.

15. In Linz's terms it could be said that Lacalle suffered from one of the perils of presidentialism: 'His awareness of the time limits facing him and the program to which his name is tied cannot help but affect his political style. Anxiety about policy discontinuities and the character of possible successors encourages what Albert Hirschman has called "the wish of vouloir conclure". This exaggerated sense of urgency on the part of the president may lead to ill-conceived policy initiatives, overly hasty stabs at implementation, unwarranted anger at the lawful opposition, and a host of other evils' (1990, p. 66).

16. The CP backed Sanguinetti up, but did not participate actively in the negotiations. In fact, some of its leaders, such as Jorge Batlle, adopted a

distant attitude towards the initiative because of their philosophical adhesion to the majority principle.

17. This consensus was maintained during Sanguinetti's term of office.
18. Movimiento Nacional de Rocha, Movimiento Renovación y Victoria y Por la Patria.
19. The 'Naval Club Pact' resulted from the talks the CP, BF and CU celebrated with the military in July 1984. As Wilson Ferreira Aldunate was in prison the BP refused to take part in the negotiations and denounced the pact as treason to the unity of the opposition. In Gillespie's words: '[With the Naval Club Pact] the military succeeded in dividing the dangerous coalition that had opposed them since the beginning of 1984' (Gillespie, 1987, p. 463).
20. As a 'junior player', not as 'senior player', though.
21. According to L.E. González, 'political structures include (a) institutional features (in the political sense, e.g., whether the system is unitary of federal), and (b) purely political features (e.g., the ideological background of elites) of the polity. These features become "political structures" only if they have already been institutionalized in the sociological sense of the word. Hence they involve by definition observable regularities in the behavior and expectations of political actors' (1990, p. 1).
22. In the period September 1984–February 1985 the social and political organizations that opposed the military rule debated upon the most important issues of the forthcoming democracy – economic policy, education, health, etc. That institution was called 'CONAPRO' (Concertación Nacional Programática).
23. Document elaborated by the Herrerismo that was handed in to the Colorado leaders Pacheco, Tarigo and Batlle on 22 January 1990. It was organized in nine chapters focused on the issues that should be the base of the alliance.
24. In fact, from a legal point of view that approval was not needed because according to the constitution the ministers are to be appointed and dismissed by the president.
25. Batlle, Sanguinetti, Pacheco, Millor.
26. In fact, a comprehensive history of the Uruguayan coparticipation has not yet been written.
27. According to Rico, the variable 'degree of presidential involvement' is fundamental in bureaucratic–organizational theory and has rarely been analyzed (1987, p. 12).
28. Pareja points out that in Uruguay presidents show a particular style of leadership because Uruguayans do not trust leaders who 'overflow' the frontiers of parties (1990, p. 71).
29. See Sartori (1987); Huntington, Crozier and Watanuki (1975); Bobbio (1985). In relation to the Uruguayan case, see Filgueira (1985); González (1986).
30. As soon as Wilson was liberated (30 November 1984) he announced his 'governability theory', according to which the BP would cooperate with the CP so that it could stabilize the democractic regime and rule the country effectively.
31. With regard to the contexts of decision-making processes, see Rico (1987).
32. An alternative starting point of the consolidation process could be the

referendum held on 16 April 1989 on the Ley de Caducidad (Statute of Limitations) that had been passed in December 1986 granting effective immunity to all those accused of past violations of human rights.

33. This term is used by Luis E. González to characterize the Uruguayan system: 'Under democratic governments Uruguay has been essentially a quasi-presidential system; "quasi" points out to the colegiado times and to the secondary traits typical of parliamentary systems it has exhibited – some of which still remain' (1988, p. 40).

34. EQUIPOS Consultores carried on this survey in the Uruguayan legislature in 1987 and in the Argentinian one in 1988.

35. According to the cited survey, 76 per cent and 87 per cent of the legislators from the BP and BF, respectively, considered that a quasi-parliamentarism or mixed regime was the best form of government for the country, while 80 per cent of the Colorados expressed their favorable opinion on presidentialism.

36. The 'majoritarian' model of democracy emphasizes that majorities should govern and minorities should oppose, whereas the 'consensus' model looks to consensus instead of opposition and inclusion instead of exclusion (Lijphart, 1984).

37. In this respect, Uruguay is not an exception because, as Nohlen points out, '[In Latin America the discussions over the political reform have had] indirect effects ... they have created a greater consciousness on the functional deficiencies of the existing system and on the way the political actors' behaviour affects that system' (1989, p. 32).

38. 'Any proposal to change the political system implies that the political actors not only accept new rules of the game but are ready to transform their political habits and their own consciousness as well (Sturla, *La Democracia*, 31 August 1990).

39. By mid-1990, the president's faction proposed to modify the electoral system on the basis of the principle of majoritarian representation. So did Sanguinetti's faction in 1991.

40. 'Fragmentation refers to the number of relevant parties of the system and/or to that number somehow "weighted" according to the size of the parties' (González, 1988).

41. 'Perhaps the most important implication of presidentialism is that it introduces a strong element of zero-sum game into democratic politics with rules that tend towards a "winner takes all" outcome' (Linz, 1986, p. 13).

42. See González (1990).

43. Pareja (1989) introduced the term, 'Jacobin matrix', in reference to the Colorados' political culture.

44. 'Fractionalization thus appears as a result of the double simultaneous vote and proportional representation. These do not play the same role, however: the DSV is the active principle fostering fractionalization, and PR is the facilitating condition – because by making more prizes available it diminishes the expected costs of actual competition' (González, 1990, p. 20).

45. These factions and their respective leaders were: Cruzada 94 (Millor), Unión Colorada y Batllista (Pacheco Areco), Foro Batllista (Sanguinetti) and Batllismo Radical (Batlle).

References

AGUIAR, CÉSAR (1991) 'Elecciones uruguayas 1989. Un paréntesis en la predictibilidad del sistema, político? (Y una real oportunidad para sus élites), in *Propuestas políticas, comportamientos electorales y perspectivas de gobierno en el cono sur* (Montevideo: Mastergraf).

ALLISON, G. and M. HALPERÍN (1985) 'Política burocrática: un paradigma y algunas implicaciones de política', in *Estados Unidos: perspectiva latinoamerica* (Mexico: CIDE).

ALLISON, GRAHAM (1988) *La esencia de la decisión. Análisis explicativo de la crisis de los misiles en Cuba* (Buenos Aires: GEL).

BOBBIO, NORBERTO (1985) *El futuro de la democracia* (España: Plaza y Janes Editores).

CAPLOW, THEODORE (1974) *Dos contra uno: Teoría de coaliciones en las Tríadas* (Madrid: Alianza Editorial).

COLOMER, JOSEP (1990) *El arte de la manipulación política* (Barcelona: Ed. Anagrama).

COCCHI, ANGEL (comp.) (1988) *Reforma electoral y voluntad política* (Montevideo: FESUR-EBO).

DUVERGER, MAURICE (1970) *Instituciones políticas y Derecho constitucional* (España: Ed. Ariel).

EQUIPOS CONSULTORES ASOCIADOS (1987) 'Informe sobre las actitudes de las élites políticas frente a la Reforma Política', Montevideo.

FERNÁNDEZ BAEZA, MARIO (1987) 'Presidencialismo, parlamentarismo y semipresidencialismo. Tres tesis sobre un sistema de gobierno para Chile', *Cuadernos del CLAEH*, no. 43 (Montevideo: CLAEH).

FILGUEIRA, CARLOS (1985) 'Mediación política y apertura democrática en el Uruguay', in Ch. Gillespie, L. Goodman, J. Rial and P. Winn, *Uruguay y la democracia* (Montevideo: TII, EBO).

GILLESPIE, CHARLES (1987) 'Party strategies and redemocratization: theoretical and comparative perspectives on the Uruguayan case', PhD diss., Yale University.

GILLESPIE, CHARLES (1988) 'La transición uruguaya desde el gobierno tecnocrático-militar colegiado', in G.O'Donnell *et al.*, *Tansiciones desde un gobierno autoritario* (Buenos Aires: Paidós).

GILLESPIE, CHARLES and L.E. GONZÁLEZ (1989) 'Uruguay: The survival of old and autonomous institutions', in Larry Diamond, Juan Linz and Seymour Lipset (eds), *Democracy in Developing Countries*, vol. IV (Latin America) (Boulder: Lynne Rienner Publishers, EEUU).

GONZÁLEZ, LUIS E. (1986a) 'Los partidos políticos y la redemocratización en el Uruguay', in *Cuadernos del CLAEH*, no. 37 (Montevideo: CLAEH).

GONZÁLEZ, LUIS E. (1986b) 'Legislación electoral, partidos y gobernabilidad', in D. Nohlen and J. Rial, *Reforma electoral. Posible, deseable?* (Montevideo: Ed. Banda Oriental).

GONZÁLEZ, LUIS E. (1988) 'Political structures and the prospects for democracy in Uruguay', PhD diss, Yale University.

GONZÁLEZ, LUIS E. (1990) 'Electoral law and party systems: the Uruguayan case' (Montevideo).

GONZÁLEZ, L.E. and C. GILLESPIE (1990) 'Presidentialism and democratic stability in Uruguay' (Montevideo).

HUNTINGTON, S., M. CROZIER and J. WATANUKI (1975) *The crisis of democracy. Report on the gobernability of democracies to the Trilateral Commission* (New York University Press).

LINZ, JUAN (1986) *Democracy: Presidential or Parliamentary. Does it make a difference?* (Yale University, EEUU).

LINZ, JUAN (1990) 'The perils of presidentialism', *Journal of Democracy* (Washington, DC), vol. I, no. 1 (Winter).

LIJPHART, AREND (1984) *Democracies. Patterns of majoritarian and consensus government in 21 countries* (Yale University Press).

LIJPHART, AREND (1989) *Democracia en las Sociedades Plurales. Una investigación comparativa* (Buenos Aires: GEL).

LUJÁN, CARLOS (1990) 'Cambio de régimen y política internacional. El caso uruguayo', Tesis de Maestría (Buenos Aires: FLACSO).

MENA, CARLOS K. (1989) *Toma de decisiones y políticas. Algunas aplicaciones a la política exterior* (Buenos Aires: GEL).

MIERES, PABLO (1985) 'Concertación en Uruguay. Expectativas elevadas y consensos escasos', in *Cuadernos del CLAEH*, no. 36 (Montevideo: CLAEH).

MIERES, PABLO (1987) 'Partidos políticos y cuerpo electoral. Las elecciones de 1984', *Cuadernos del CLAEH*, no. 44 (Montevideo: CLAEH).

MIERES, PABLO (1988) *Cómo votan los uruguayos? Las elecciones de 1984* (Montevideo: CLAEH-EBO).

NOHLEN, DIETER (1989) 'Más democracia en América Latina? Democratización y consolidación de la democracia en una perspectiva comparada', *Estudios Sociales*, no. 59 (Santiago).

NOHLEN, D. AND J. RIAL (comp.) (1986) *Reforma electoral. Posible, deseable?* (Montevideo: FESUR-EBO).

PAREJA, CARLOS (1984) 'Las instancias de concertación', *Cuadernos del CLAEH*, no. 32 (Montevideo: CLAEH).

PAREJA, CARLOS (1988) 'Asignaturas pendientes en el debate de la reforma política', *Cuadernos del CLAEH*, no. 47 (Montevideo: CLAEH).

PAREJA, CARLOS (1989a) 'Polifonía y Jacobinismo en la política uruguaya (I)', *Cuadernos del CLAEH*, no. 49 (Montevideo: CLAEH).

PAREJA, CARLOS (1989b) 'Polifonía y Jacobinismo en la política uruguaya (II), *Cuadernos del CLAEH*, no. 51 (Montevideo: CLAEH).

PAREJA, CARLOS (1990a) 'Parlamentarismo, presidencialismo y gobierno de coalición' (Montevideo: CLAEH).

PAREJA, CARLOS (1990b) 'Los partidos uruguayos y el "señor presidente": un matrimonio mal avenido', *Cuadernos del CLAEH*, no. 55 (Montevideo: CLAEH).

PAREJA, C. and R. PÉREZ (1990) 'Coaliciones: otra lógica política', *Relaciones*, no. 70 (Montevideo).

PEIXOTO, MARTÍN (1987) 'El debate político en el Uruguay', *Cuadernos del CLAEH*, no. 43 (Montevideo: CLAEH).

PEIXOTO, MARTÍN (1988) 'Parlamentarismo y presidencialismo, dónde están las diferencias?', *Cuadernos del CLAEH*, no. 52 (Montevideo: CLAEH).

PÉREZ, ROMEO (1987) 'Parlamentarismo como alternativa? El caso de Uruguay', *Cuadernos del CLAEH*, no. 43 (Montevideo: CLAEH).

PÉREZ, ROMEO (1989a) 'El sistema de gobierno uruguayo. Su caracterización y posibilidades de cambio' (Montevideo: CLAEH).

PÉREZ, ROMEO (1989b) 'Cuatro antagonismos sucesivos. La concreta instauración de la democracia uruguaya', *Revista de Ciencia Política*, no. 2 (Montevideo: FCU-Instituto de Ciencia Política).

RAMA, GERMÁN (1989) *La democracia en Uruguay. Una perspectiva de interpretación* (Montevideo: Ed. Arca).

RICO, CARLOS (1987) 'El método y el caos: buscando una tipología de áreas temáticas en la elaboración de la política exterior de los Estados Unidos', *CIDE*.

SARTORI, GIOVANNI (1987) *Teoría de la democracia* (Madrid: Alianza Universidad).

13 Chile and the Prosecution of Military Officials for Human Rights Violations: A Comparative Approach

Allan Metz

This chapter will study the position of the democratically elected government of Patricio Aylwin in Chile on the human-rights issue and the prosecution of military officials for human rights violations committed during the regime of Augusto Pinochet from September 1973 to March 1990. The experiences of other Southern Cone nations (Argentina and Uruguay) will be discussed within the context of the Chilean case. While a detailed analysis of the handling of rights abuses in Argentina and Uruguay[1] is not possible here, given the complexity and duration of that issue (particularly in Argentina), their experiences clearly influenced the Chilean approach to this problem, with which Chile is still struggling and which, to a large extent, will influence the course of its political and it is hoped, democratic future.

Starting in December 1983, when former Argentine President Raúl Alfonsín formed a commission to investigate human-rights crimes committed by the military regimes which preceded him and ordered the conviction of military officials most responsible, a number of countries have attempted to bring to justice those guilty of human-rights violations. Such efforts have largely failed. In some nations which previously were under military dictatorship, like Uruguay, guilty military officials maintained their positions and effectively prevented their theoretical civilian superiors from taking decisive action in prosecuting military officials for past human-rights abuses.

Only in Argentina had such efforts succeeded, despite a number of military rebellions which compelled Alfonsín to grant concessions to the military. This allowed him to continue to govern by proclaiming an end to military prosecutions ('punto final', or 'final point'). Public documentation and acknowledgement of human-rights violations during the military governments of 1976 to 1983 were contained in *Nunca mas*, published in 1984, and also in the public-court proceedings of nine military officials who had served in the first three military governments which ruled Argentina after the March 1976 coup. Following a fair trial, five junta officials were convicted and sentenced to prison. However President Carlos Saúl Menem, Alfonsín's successor, pardoned most military officials and eventually all of them (including General Carlos Guillermo Suárez Mason) who were still facing punishment.[2] Yet, despite all these difficulties, according to America Watch's Juan Méndez (who is also an Argentine lawyer and an ex-prisoner of the military), Argentina achieved both 'truth and partial justice'.[3]

Chile returned to its century-and-a-half democratic tradition of elected civilian governments after almost 17 years of the military dictatorship of General Augusto Pinochet. The 11 March 1990 inauguration of President Patricio Aylwin Azócar, following a convincing electoral victory over two conservative candidates in December 1989, made the respected leader of the centrist Christian Democratic Party head of state. The new administration's priorities, formally listed in the new president's 21 May 1990 speech to the first legislative session, included clarification of human-rights violations which occurred during the Pinochet era.[4]

The Aylwin government, however, has had considerable difficulty with this issue, owing to resistance from the civilian right and the military. By the end of 1990, the administration had made little progress in resolving the crucial questions of dealing with human rights abuses and consolidating civilian control over the armed forces. The deadlock regarding these issues is a direct legacy of the authoritarian Pinochet period. In 1988, the democratic opposition took the chance that they could defeat Pinochet at his own political game and won the 5 October plebiscite, whose purpose was to continue his power.[5] However, by agreeing to play by Pinochet's political rules (that is, participating in the plebiscite), the opposition agreed to both his schedule for a transition to civilian government and a constitutional system designed to curb civilian authority.

The most irksome legacy of the Pinochet period is the legislature's undemocratic nature. In spite of an electoral and districting system designed to benefit conservative parties, Aylwin's coalition gained an absolute majority in both congressional houses. But since the 1980 Constitution allowed the Pinochet regime to designate nine of 47 senators, the right has a sufficient advantage in the Senate to obstruct any legislation by the ruling coalition, including that on human rights and prosecuting human-rights violators.[6] And so the administration must seek the support of either the moderate National Renovation Party or the more conservative pro-Pinochet Democratic Independent Union. Conservative legislative leaders have demonstrated their skills at such negotiation and look ahead to the 1994 elections, although they share the general political consensus that democracy should be preserved.

Thus the human rights question is one sphere in which the conservatives have successfully impeded the Aylwin administration. From 1973 to 1978, over 660 prisoners in armed forces custody disappeared, thousands suffered torture and hundreds were executed or killed in supposed armed conflict. In the ensuing years, additional thousands more were abused and some were killed by the military. The democratic opposition has long advocated bringing those culpable to justice and public opinion polls indicate that most Chileans support this approach on human rights.[7] The families of those killed, who have disappeared or have been jailed from 1973 to 1990 have been a more insistent voice for justice. While these families, who are supported by both the Roman Catholic Church and leftist parties, possess little political power, they do constitute a strident and highly visible symbol of a moral commitment the government had promised to satisfy. In May 1990 the justice minister offered a series of laws which would have allowed the investigation of human-rights cases, eliminated the death penalty, moderated the draconian security laws and transferred most civilian offenses from military-court jurisdiction. Since then, however, the potential effectiveness of the legislation had been severely limited by congressional conservatives, who were able to tie proposals for judicial reform to the controversial question of 'political prisoners'.

In March 1990, when Aylwin assumed power, almost 400 people were imprisoned on charges or suspicion of 'political crimes', ranging from secret border crossings to assassination. The administration granted pardons to 45 'prisoners of conscience' and put on trial those who allegedly carried out acts of violence. This, however, drew criticism from the prisoners, a number of whom were involved in armed revolutionary organizations, who conducted a hunger strike to demand liberty for all 'prisoners of democracy'. Congressional conservatives were firmly against releasing these accused terrorists and opposed legislation which would lessen their sentences. Conservative opinion was reinforced by a number of violent acts, including an assassination attempt on General Gustavo Leigh, an ex-air-force commander and part of the original ruling junta. Acts of terrorism from both extremes of the political spectrum continued into 1991, which led to growing insecurity and lessened the euphoria following Chile's return to democracy.

Aylwin, however, was resolved to clarify and investigate past viol-ations through the Commission on Truth and Reconciliation, led by lawyer Raúl Rettig,[8] an 81-year-old former senator who once served as chairman of the Chilean Bar Association.[9] The commission was instructed to gather testimony from victims and witnesses, issue a re-port and recommend action. Right-wing parties did not participate, contending that the commission also should have investigated govern-ment violations during the administration of socialist President Salva-dor Allende, who was overthrown and died in the 1973 coup which brought on the Pinochet period. However Aylwin, describing past abuses committed during this period as 'a still-open wound in the nation's soul', believed that to simply ignore them 'would be to prolong a constant source of pain, divisions, hatred and violence'.[10]

In absolute secrecy, the commission gathered testimony from hun-dreds of people and accepted thousands of cases. An amnesty law passed in 1978 does not allow the judiciary to investigate incidents prior to 1978 and the constitution prevents the government from hold-ing a referendum on the issue of amnesty. Thus Aylwin's only alterna-tive may be to make formal acknowledgement of past violations and to secure compensation for victims' families. In attempting to strike a balance between justice and reconciliation, Aylwin is also hampered by another authoritarian legacy, an entrenched conservative judiciary. During the Pinochet period, the Supreme Court unquestioningly ac-cepted the Pinochet government's legitimacy and did not hold the armed forces responsible for repressive actions. In the last year of his rule, Pinochet granted large bonuses to retiring members and named nine new justices to life terms. This practically ensured that the court would oppose reform of the judiciary and attempts to reopen human-rights cases, as clearly demonstrated when the court was faced with its first major challenge to the 1978 amnesty law. In August 1990 the Su-preme Court unanimously sustained the 1978 law, which protected members of the security forces from being prosecuted for violations. The attorneys who disputed the law on behalf of 60 missing prisoners contended that closing the cases without investigation violated funda-mental rights contained in the 1980 constitution. The justices ruled that, since the amnesty law preceded the constitution, the court could not change it. The court also rejected the idea that the law was in violation of the Geneva Conventions by indicating that there was no 'state of internal armed conflict' in Chile.[11] This logic contradicted prior court decisions, which frequently rationalized repressive military acts on the basis that a condition of 'internal war' had existed following the 1973 coup.

The greatest barrier, however, to securing justice and building democracy is the continuing power and autonomy of the military. Pinochet ensured that future presidents would have little control over the armed forces by, for example, revoking the president's right to appoint and remove commanders from the army, navy, air force and national police, and incorporating the intelligence service within the army, which effectively shields clandestine activities from civilian control. For the democratic opposition, however, the most irksome legacy of the years of military government is Pinochet himself and the continued potential threat he poses to Chilean democracy.[12] Despite these difficulties, it may be said that the Aylwin government has more than held its own so far. Aylwin, however, faced his most serious problem in March 1991, with the release of the Rettig Commission Report on human-rights violations.[3]

As previously noted, Aylwin shortly after taking office appointed a Truth and Reconciliation Commission. As the name implied, the commission did not view its authority as including the attainment of justice. Rather, according to human-rights activist Aryeh Neier, the inability of the state to prosecute those who committed abuses during the Pinochet period, including the former dictator himself, was construed as pursuing virtue, that is, reconciliation. The members of the commission reached the conclusion that securing justice was beyond their mandate and that they would attempt to attain what was feasible, based in part on a careful analysis of the Argentine and Uruguayan experiences. Regarding Uruguay, a national referendum held in April 1989 sustained a 1986 law by which the military was given amnesty for violations occurring under military rule from 1973 to 1985. A factor in the outcome, though it is difficult to determine exactly to what degree, was the fear that overturning the amnesty would precipitate another coup by the armed forces. The instability produced by military rebellions in nearby Argentina undoubtedly reinforced that concern in Uruguay. Consequently the state has not officially acknowledged the crimes committed by the military governments (in contrast to Chile and Argentina), which involved the organized torture of thousands, and no one has been placed on trial for these violations. The Uruguayan situation also promotes the mistaken potion that a popular referendum constitutes a proper way to determine issues of justice.

As for Chile, in summary, the problem of attaining justice is complicated by the constitutional system arranged by Pinochet, which did allow for a peaceful transition to power of a civilian-elected government. This system, however, does not give the civilian president control over the military: Pinochet was guaranteed his position as commander of the army. Moreover it grants the military the power to appoint certain Senate members, maintains military jurisdiction over many cases which should be handled by the civilian judiciary, and forbids reform of the Supreme Court. As a consequence, the amnesty law decreed in 1978 by Pinochet and sustained by the Supreme Court remains in effect, which prohibits prosecutions for those who committed human-rights abuses following the 1973 coup and the years during which Pinochet was consolidating power. In contrast, following Alfonsín's assumption of office, the Supreme Court was overhauled and the decree law passed by the military leaders to pardon their own abuses was overturned by the judiciary and the Congress. Finally, in an extra-constitutional obstacle, Pinochet publicly warned that, if any members of the military were threatened with prosecution by the government, there would be an end to the state of law.

The Truth and Reconciliation Commission, which included noteworthy human rights advocates like Jaime Castillo and José Zalaquett, both forced into exile by Pinochet, was charged by President Aylwin with the task of presenting 'the most complete picture of the most serious violations of human rights committed' during the period of military rule from 11 September 1973 to 11 March 1990. The commission could make recommendations for compensation to the victims and legal and administrative measures to avoid a repetition of widespread human-rights crimes. The commission's power, however, did not include any indication of individual responsibility for those violations. 'This is the line that cannot crossed by Chile's democratic government', according to Neier.

There is a consensus within the international human-rights movement that, while both truth and justice are needed to handle past violations on the scale of those which took place in Chile, truth is the higher priority. In other words, the government should acknowledge and reveal the violations committed by military officials. On the other hand, although truth is a higher priority than justice, it would be pretentious to assume that 'reconciliation' which satisfies Pinochet and the armed forces is an acceptable substitute. The commission will fulfil truth and justice if its report makes it clear that justice cannot be served in Chile only because that the civilian government does not have the power to accomplish the task. Thus rights activists urged the government to make every attempt to control the military's power in order that, at least for the future, justice may be served.[14]

The Rettig Report was delivered by the commission to Aylwin on 8 February 1991 and, although it was not released until 4 March, much controversy and anticipation preceded it.[15] The report totally disproved two myths: one, that the 'internal war' carried out by the military was justified and that, unlike their Argentine counterparts, the Chilean military had succeeded in openly winning it. The report also traced ultimate responsibility to Pinochet for only he, as both president and commander-in-chief, could have stopped the illegal actions of the 'DINA', Dirección de Inteligencia Nacional, which formed the basis of his government's repressive system.[16]

The six-volume, 2000-page report confirmed 2279 killings during the Pinochet regime (that is, from 11 September 1973 to 11 March 1990). Only 164 cases (one in 14) were described as victims of 'acts of violence' (for example, armed conflict). Only 132 (one in 17) of those killed were part of the armed or security forces. These statistics contradict the junta's rationale of a 'state of internal war' which it frequently invoked to justify the 1973 coup and subsequent measures. Of the 2115 deaths the report attributed to human-rights violations, 2025 were linked to agents of the state. And it should be noted that, of all civilians killed, 46 per cent had no political affiliations.

The report also suggested that the DINA had originated before the 1973 coup and operated at first as an 'illicit association' with the encouragement of the armed forces high command. Pinochet could have disbanded it as early as 1974, but did not do so until 1977. The report was also highly critical of the Chilean judicial system, which 'did not act with sufficient energy [and] granted the agents of repression a growing certainty of impunity for their criminal actions'. As expected, President Aylwin announced reparations for victims of past repression, such as a pension for relatives, special procedures for declaring the missing dead and other related measures. To respond quickly to possible future human-rights violations, the president also announced the establishment of an office of *defensor del pueblo* (ombudsman). Less anticipated was Aylwin's call for the judiciary to disregard the 1978 amnesty law and act on the testimony presented in the report. The president stated that the amnesty law 'cannot be an obstacle [for the courts to] fulfil their duty and conduct exhaustive investigations'.

With the disclosures of the Rettig Commission Report, the immediate reaction of human-rights groups was that Pinochet should resign as commander of the army. However the 'council of generals', following a meeting with Pinochet, defiantly announced their 'unrestricted loyalty' to Pinochet. Retired air-force general Gustavo Leigh, one of the early members of the junta, stated his full acceptance of responsibility for the role the air force had played. He did, however, attempt to deflect some of the blame away by noting that the DINA was created by the junta, but later only obeyed the commands of Pinochet. Leigh also attempted to excuse the courts by maintaining that justice 'ran up against a grave inconvenience: it had no means to investigate, it had no way of getting to the bottom of things, it had no cooperation [from] the armed forces and the police'. The judiciary made a semi-apology. The acting supreme-court president, Rafael Retamal, stated, concerning human rights, that 'it is possible that I may have made some mistakes; I tried not to make any, and I ask forgiveness for having made mistakes'.[17]

The military's response, in contrast, was hardly apologetic. Refusing to take any responsibility for human-rights violations and other related abuses, it defiantly challenged the Rettig Report. Earlier on the day of the release of the report, 4 March, all four armed forces commanders met President Aylwin in the National Security Council to elicit their reaction to the report. After a tense session, Pinochet delivered on national television a categorical point-by-point rejection of the commission's findings. 'The report shows a twisted view of reality . . . the accusations are totally false, and worse yet, are offensive to the army's immaculate honor', according to Pinochet, who maintained his firm conviction that the coup and the repression which followed were justified. 'The Rettig Report ignores the communist threat and the leftist terrorism that went on here between 1970 and 1990 . . . we fulfilled our duty and saved Chile from communism', Pinochet stated in reference to the coup against Allende.[18] Senate president Gabriel Valdez noted that, while he had not expected Pinochet to issue a public apology, he had hoped for at least an acknowledgement of 'excesses and occurrences that caused the society pain and divided the nation. There is nothing that justifies the atrocities that occurred here, but at some point we have to reconcile. We can't spend our lives blaming each other for what happened, but it seems like the idea of reconciliation is not in the armed forces' vocabulary.'

Those in the military who have supported Chile's return to democracy and attempts at reconciliation have received sharp right-wing criticism. For example, air force commander General Fernando Matthei was labelled a traitor by the rightist Unión Demócrata Independiente. The report has emboldened others to speak out, however. For example, the president of the Association of Physicians publicly apologized for those members who collaborated with the armed forces in committing torture. Victim's relatives could take the report's findings and try to prosecute those responsible. This will prove to be very difficult, however, owing to the fact that the judiciary has many Pinochet appointees, and to the 1978 amnesty law, which pardoned the military. The judiciary is most frequently cited as one of the major barriers to genuine reconciliation in Chile. While the Aylwin administration has expressed its wish to reform the judiciary, it has made little headway. However, according to Sola Sierra, president of the Relatives of the Disappeared Committee: 'Without judicial reform, it will be difficult to carry out justice and reach a national reconciliation, but we have to make an attempt. It is not revenge we want, but simply justice in order to assure that such things never happen again in Chile'.

Human-rights groups' criticisms of the report are based on Aylwin's decision not to include the names of those who committed abuses. In an article which appeared in the bimonthly publication *Punto Final*, families of the victims declared that the 'report does not speak the whole truth. It gives the names of those who died and tells how they died. But the names of the assassins, the human rights violators, are not included'. How was it possible that preference was given to 'the assassins, rather than to the families and human rights organizations'?[19] Juan Méndez of Americas Watch in Washington DC urged the Aylwin administration to follow up and press for court trials of major rights violations. Méndez stated that the 'report will only increase expectations for justice. We believe that the government has the responsibility to do this'.[20] And Rosemarie Bornand, an attorney with the Vicaría de las Solidaridad human-rights group, claimed the report would not lead to justice for the victims: 'There will probably never be justice for a single human rights crime committed under Pinochet. . . . Our democracy is just too weak and the barriers to justice are too high'.[21]

Despite pressure from human-rights groups and his supporters to place those who committed rights violations on trial, President Aylwin has promised not to conduct a 'witch hunt' against the military. According to an unnamed diplomat, few in Chile would support widespread trials of members of the armed forces. Aylwin also did not wish to repeat the Argentine experience of military mutinies following trials of army officers on charges of human-rights abuses.[22] Similarly he wanted to forestall provoking Chile's powerful armed forces by refusing to commit his administration to prosecuting the military officers who allegedly committed rights abuses.[23] Aylwin expressed his hope that the report, with its public acknowledgement of the truth, would bring the issue of human-rights violations committed during the Pinochet period to a close.[24]

In sum, the Rettig Report was the Aylwin government's response

> to two strong and conflicting demands – the call by victims and opponents of the dictatorship for some sort of process in which the military is called to account for the excesses of the Pinochet years, and insistence by leaders (particularly Pinochet) of the armed forces that they will not stand for Nuremberg-style trials. It is an attempt to reconcile Chile with its past. But it also brings back painful memories, heightening bitter divisions.[25]

Such divisions were reflected, for example, in a series of murders of right-wing political figures in March 1991, allegedly by leftist guerrilla groups, which culminated in the murder on 1 April 1991 of rightist senator Jaime Guzmán, a close associate of the Pinochet regime. This incident led Aylwin to adopt a conciliatory stance toward the military, reflecting a sudden change of position. Only weeks before, administration officials, including the president, rejected all notions of plots and conspiracies. However, following the Guzmán murder, the government's response was the establishment of a high-level intelligence agency, the allocation of an additional US$10 million to the police budget, and also an increase for the Carabineros (militarized police) to deal with the terrorist threat. This decision was taken by the government's security commission, with the well-publicized involvement of the chief of the national defense staff, army General Luis Henríquez.

General Henríquez offered the army's interpretation of the country's political situation: 'Within subversive war there are several phases, one of which is propaganda action, and another that of selective terrorism – which is what we are experiencing now'. Henríquez emphasized that there were no members of the military in the new antiterrorist committee and added that the armed forces could assist in the antiterrorist campaign by furnishing information on terrorist activities. Taken together with Pinochet's speech critical of the Rettig Report, the fact that the army viewed Chile as being in the midst of a 'phase of subversive war' was not very reassuring since its perception of an internal state of war, condemned by the report but supported by Pinochet, was the rationale for the 1973 coup. Nor was there much reassurance in the suggestion that the military would again consult its old intelligence files to assist the police in the new antiterrorist campaign.[26]

And so, while the purpose of the Rettig report was to achieve reconciliation in Chile following 20 years of animosity and violence,[27] the political climate surrounding its publication had been anything but reconciliatory. Pinochet, still in charge of the army, once attempted to disband the commission and defiantly promised that no military officials would be allowed to go on trial for abuses which occurred during his rule. The commission received little, if any, cooperation from the armed forces during the course of its nearly one year investigation. And Pinochet had already demonstrated his willingness to exercise power, as in December 1990, when he placed the army on a state of high alert when the government started secret negotiations for his retirement,[28] which under the present constitution will not be required until 1998.[29] Thus, while the release of the Rettig Report was a positive step regarding the human-rights issue in Chile, the military's complete rejection of the report signified that reconciliation will not be easily attained in the foreseeable future.[30] However, a step in that direction may already have been taken at a meeting of the Consejo de Seguridad Nacional. Describing the 90-minute session, which included President Aylwin and leaders of the armed forces, as an 'historic meeting', *El Mercurio* reported on 31 March 1991 that it could prove to be decisive in putting a final point ('punto final') or bringing a close to the divisive debate over the issue of human-rights violations, as documented in the Rettig Report. It was noted that a tense atmosphere prevailed leading up to and just prior to the meeting, but that President Aylwin himself defused the issue and eased fears, reflecting his desire to put the human-rights issue, since it had been dealt with in the report, to rest.[31] This position was consistent with Aylwin's earlier pronouncements on the subject. For example, in March 1990, Aylwin declared that the 'moral conscience of the nation demands that the truth be clarified' in a reasonable amount of time; but once that had been achieved, 'the hour of pardon will arrive'.[32] Thus it appears unlikely that any military officials will ever stand trial for rights violations: 'But the Chileans have established the truth about what went wrong. It cannot be an "official" truth, says Mr. Aylwin, but it is "a truth that nobody in good faith can ignore".' And, according to the *Economist*, 'It is much better than nothing.'[33]

SUMMARY

President Aylwin has been depicted as 'a genial, courtly, mild-mannered yet confident figure who avoids confrontation'.[34] His policy on the difficult human-rights issue in Chile demonstrates this inclination in his attempt to seek a 'middle way' in relation to the handling of the human-rights issue and prosecution of military officials in Argentina and Uruguay. Argentina began the process of bringing to trial top military officials in 1983, which culminated in their conviction in 1985, an end to further prosecutions in 1987 (*punto final*) and, finally, in a reversal of previous policy, President Menem issued pardons to lower-level convicted members of the military in 1989 and a more controversial general pardon and release of imprisoned high-ranking military officials in late December 1990. In contrast, although the state had tried, Uruguay never placed its military officials on trial for human-rights violations and conducted a national referendum in 1989 which confirmed this policy. Aylwin wished to take Chile on a middle course between the Argentine and Uruguayan experiences. He did not wish for trials of military officials, as in Argentina, but, on the other hand, he wanted to go beyond Uruguay's 'hands off' policy and lack of official state acknowledgement of prior rights violations. In other words, on the issue of human rights and the prosecution of military officials for rights violations, the Aylwin administration had the

> experiences of Argentina and Uruguay to learn from. In Argentina, the government's decision to prosecute human rights abusers sparked a military rebellion and only a handful of cases were ever tried. In Uruguay, Army officers' refusal to give evidence in court led to a showdown with the ... civilian government and an eventual blanket amnesty.

This amnesty, granted by the then President Julio Sanguinetti, exempted military officials from human rights prosecutions. The current Uruguayan president, Luis Alberto Lacalle, tends to view the human rights issue as closed, although the unresolved tensions engendered by military rule from 1972 to 1985 still remain.[35]

According to an unnamed member of the Concertación alliance that forms Chile's democratic government: 'Our process will be less dramatically conflictive than the others [that is, Argentina and Uruguay] ... We are committed to justice, but to quick justice'. And Aylwin himself was anxious not to allow the human-rights question to fester, as it had in Argentina. He stated that 'Chile's spiritual health ... demands that we find ways of accomplishing this moral clean-up in a reasonable period.'[36] Hence Chile opted for the 'middle way', a position discussed by Tom Wicker of the *New York Times*: 'Can Chile find a "middle way" on human rights – a means of establishing and insuring respect for those rights without self-defeating retribution against those who violated them in the past?' This constitutes a key issue facing the Aylwin government, which recognizes that it has little choice other than to attempt a middle way, owing to, as noted earlier, the Chilean constitution, which allowed Pinochet to influence the judiciary, the senate and other constitutional bodies with the potential to obstruct Aylwin's legislative initiatives. Moreover Pinochet still controls the army and has vowed that no military officials would be allowed to be prosecuted for human-rights violations under the 1978 amnesty law. Thus Aylwin 'is caught between the rock of General Pinochet's resistance and the hard place of demands for justice and retribution', especially from the victims and relatives of those who suffered during the Pinochet period. The president's solution was the appointment, via executive decree, of the Commission of Truth and Reconciliation, whose task was to find and disclose the facts, but not to attribute blame or to recommend prosecution of individuals, which is a hard distinction to make. The Aylwin administration will not take any further official steps, except for compensating some victims, but individual Chileans could press charges, although essentially in the same judicial system which existed in the Pinochet era. Appointment of the commission took into account the problems faced by the Alfonsín government in Argentina when it attempted to prosecute military human-rights violators. However even a middle way was unsatisfactory for Pinochet, who initially opposed the idea of the commission.

The government's handling of the report constituted a major test for the middle path of balancing human rights and stability, and for democracy in general in Chile. The question is whether enough Chileans concur that justice has been served if the amnesty remains in effect and if little retribution takes place, since many who served in the Allende government have acknowledged their errors, while those who committed past rights abuses have conceded nothing. The government's hope, shared by many political leaders, is that the Chilean public 'will look to the future even at some expense to the whole truth about the past – that they will choose the reconciliation these leaders believe will encourage continuing Chilean democracy'.[37]

PROSPECTS

What are the prospects for reconciliation and the continuance of democracy in Chile? The *New York Times* offered two possibilities, one domestic and the other international – the Roman Catholic Church as a

December 1990, p. A8; 'No Peace in the Dirty War', *Time*, 14 January 1991, p. 52; 'Letting Them Out', *Economist*, 5 January 1991, pp. 34–5; 'Pardoning Mass Murder in Argentina' (editorial), *New York Times*, 3 January 1991, p. A20; and Jacobo Timerman, 'Fear Returns to Argentina', *New York Times*, 5 January 1991, p. 21.

3. Aryeh Neier, 'Watching Rights', *Nation*, vol. 251 (19 November 1990), p. 588.

4. Arturo Valenzuela and Pamela Constable, 'Democracy in Chile', *Current History*, vol. 90, no. 553 (February 1991), p. 53.

5. For additional information on the 5 October 1988 plebiscite, see *Chile, Human Rights & the Plebiscite* (New York: Americas Watch, 1988); Stephen R. Bowers, 'Pinochet's Plebiscite and the Catholics: The Dual Role of the Chilean Church', *World Affairs*, vol. 151 (fall 1988), pp. 51–8; Abraham Santibáñez, *El plebiscito de Pinochet (cazado) en su propia trampa*, 1st ed (Santiago: Editorial Atena, 1988); Nelson Caula, Oscar Bonilla and Hugo Machín, *Chile, la alegría llego* (Uruguay: 1988/9).

6. For a discussion of Pinochet's weighted voting arrangement and the 1989 transition to democracy, see Pamela Constable and Arturo Valenzuela, 'Chile's Return to Democracy', *Foreign Affairs*, vol. 68, no, 5 (winter 1989–90), pp. 169–86.

7. Centro de Estudios Públicos (Santiago), *Estudio social y opinión pública*, Documento de trabajo, no. 136 (August 1990), pp. 49, 67.

8. Valenzuela and Constable, 'Democracy in Chile', p. 55.

9. Eugene Robinson, '2,025 Killings Laid to Pinochet: Commission Details Abuses During 1973–90 Military Repression', *Washington Post*, 5 March 1991, p. A10.

10. República de Chile, Ministerio Secretaría General de la Presidentia, *Discursos del Presidente de la República don Patricio Aylwin Azocar* (Santiago, 1990).

11. 'Suprema declaro constitucional Decreto Ley de Amnistía del 78', *El Mercurio Edición Internacional* (Santiago) 23–9 August 1990, p. 5.

12. Valenzuela and Constable, 'Democracy in Chile', pp. 55–6.

13. Ibid., p. 85.

14. Neier, 'Watching Rights', p. 588.

15. 'Even Unpublished, the Report on Pinochet's Abuses Opens a Can of Worms', *Latin American Weekly Report*, 28 February 1991, p. 1.

16. For more information on DINA and also its Colonia Dignidad, see 'Chile: "Beneficent Society" Brought into the Open', *Latinamerica Press*, vol. 23, no. 9 (14 March 1991), p. 6 and 'Aylwin Receives Rettig Report', *Latin American Monitor – Southern Cone*, March 1991, pp. 872–3.

17. 'Rettig Report Tallies Pinochet's Dead', *Latin American Weekly Report*, 21 March 1991, pp. 2–3. See also 'Chileans Stunned by Rettig Report', *Latin American Regional Reports – Southern Cone*, 25 April 1991, pp. 6–7.

18. More on Pinochet's response to the Rettig report is found in Malcolm Coad, 'Pinochet Criticizes Report on Abuses During His Rule', *Washington Post*, 29 March 1991, p. A17. For an interesting study of Pinochet, see María Dolores Souza and Germán Silva, *Auge y ocaso de Augusto*

conciliator and the US as a reinforcer of Chilean democracy. President Aylwin must 'balance accountability with reconciliation'. On the international front, the US can and should strengthen democracy in Chile through economic policies such as freer trade and investment rules.[38] While the Chilean economy was done well, especially compared with those of other Latin American countries such as Argentina and Mexico, Chile still faced major challenges, such as amending an undemocratic constitution, restoring judicial independence and finding a means to establish accountability for past rights abuses. Chile would best succeed in meeting these political challenges with strong sustained economic growth, which depends on export diversification away from copper and developing new exports. The latter would require access to international markets and investment which could best be achieved with a successful conclusion to the Uruguay Round negotiations on world trade.[39]

The US should make sure that the Chilean military clearly understands that insubordination against civilian government would seriously harm relations between the two countries. The Aylwin administration has continued the economic liberalization policies begun under Pinochet. Most Chilean citizens, however, reject the political repression carried out during that period. Chileans seek official acknowledgement and condemnation of these abuses. Public contrition and prosecution would be more difficult to attain. Prosecution of military officials precipitated armed rebellions in Argentina. Pinochet remains commander of the army, the president constitutionally cannot remove him, and the general has clearly expressed his opposition to the prosecution of military officials. The Roman Catholic Church in Chile could facilitate reconciliation. Its doctrine preaches forgiveness to the sincerely repentant. While judicial punishment of rights violations may prove to be impossible, the church might exercise its 'moral power to demand sincere and public contrition as a precondition for national reconciliation'.[40]

This process appears to have begun under the auspices of the Church. In his Easter message on 31 March 1991, Monseñor Carlos Oviedo, the Archbishop of Santiago, declared that it was Chile's duty to seek understanding and to avoid confrontation, which would lead to 'a new style of democratic dialogue' capable of creating a better balance among the various institutions of government. To this end, the archbishop proclaimed a 'year of reconciliation' to reestablish harmony after so many years of political violence. He indicated that a profound reconciliation was necessary for the sake of the nation's future via political dialogue and understanding. Monseñor Oviedo pledged that the Church would make every effort to enhance and promote 'social peace' and democracy. He wished for President Aylwin to declare 'never again' to human-rights violations while, at the same time, forgiving, in the name of the state, those who had committed these abuses. This simultaneous position of 'never again' and forgiveness had long been that of the Church, the archbishop declared. While acknowledging that achieving this reconciliation would not be easy, Archbishop Oviedo believed that it was essential to promote and stimulate this atmosphere of reconciliation and good will throughout the whole country.[41] This observation was reinforced during a visit to Europe by President Aylwin, which included an audience with Pope John Paul II. On 22 April 1991 the Pope expressed his sadness over the escalation of recent terrorist/political violence in Chile and urged a restoration of 'a climate of peace, dialogue and mutual respect', which would renew hope and strengthen fraternal bonds among all Chileans. The Pope assured Aylwin that the Vatican supported the process of democratization and reconciliation in Chile, as did the Chilean Catholic Church, which provided a good example of 'the mission of the Church in society'.[42]

Following the release of the Rettig Report, and despite the apparent stand-off Aylwin had hoped to avoid between his administration, which supported it, and the military's rejection of it,[43] early indications point to an affirmation of Aylwin's approach to the rights issue both within and outside Chile. Domestically, according to a national survey conducted in late March 1991 by the Centro de Estudios de la Realidad Contemporáneo (CERC), 82.3 per cent of those polled approved of Aylwin's performance as president. The survey also indicated that 65.3 per cent believed Chile was 'moving ahead', 25.6 per cent that it was at a 'standstill' and only 3.9 per cent thought the country was in decline. In other survey findings, 63.8 per cent preferred democracy, as against 15.7 per cent who supported authoritarianism. Regarding Pinochet, 72.2 per cent favored his resignation as army commander while 21.3 per cent believed he should remain in that post.[44] This encouraging domestic opinion was also reinforced at the same time (late March 1991) by a positive response from the US regarding Aylwin's handling of the sensitive human-rights issue. The State Department praised the Aylwin government for its firm stand vis-à-vis the Chilean military over the release of the Rettig Report on human-rights abuses during the Pinochet period. State Department spokesperson David Denny indicated that Aylwin's 'efforts to bring the truth to light about human-rights abuses by certain agents of the Chilean state during the Pinochet dictatorship will help the cause of justice and national reconciliation'.[45]

Notes and References

1. Among the large amount of material on Argentina, the human-ri[ ] sue and the prosecution of military officials for rights abuses, [ ] Argentina, Comisión Nacional sobre la Desaparición de Personas, [ ] *más: informe de la Comisión Nacional sobre la Desaparición de [ ] nas* (Buenos Aires: EUDEBA, 1984), English trans., *Never Ag[ ] Report* (London: Faber, in association with Index on Censorship, [ ] *Definitivamente – nunca más: la otra cara del informe de la CON[ ]* 2nd edn (Buenos Aires: Foro de Estudios sobre la Administrac[ ] Justicia, 1985); Kathryn Lee Crawford, 'Due Obedience and the [ ] of Victims: Argentina's Transition to Democracy', *Human Rights[ ] terly*, vol. 12 (February 1990), pp. 17–52; Jaime Malamud-Goti, [ ] sitional Governments in the Breach: Why Punish State Criminals?', [ ] *Rights Quarterly*, vol. 12 (February 1990), pp. 1–16; Mark J. Osie[ ] Making of Human Rights Policy in Argentina: The Impact of Ide[ ] Interests on a Legal Conflict', *Journal of Latin American Studie[ ]* 18 (May 1986), pp. 135–80; Roger Cohen, 'Alfonsín's Gamble: Arge[ ] Chief's Halt to Army Trials is Risk Taken to Curb Discord; He [ ] Role for a Military Alienated by Prosecution for Killings of L[ ] *Wall Street Journal*, 19 May 1987, pp. 1ff; John Tweedy, Jr, 'T[ ] gentine "Dirty Wars" Trials: The First Latin American Nuremberg?' [ ] *Practitioner: Current Problems; Law and Practice*, vol. 44 (winter [ ] pp. 15–32; José Zalaquete, 'From Dictatorship to Democracy', *N[ ] public*, vol. 193, no. 25 (16 December 1985), pp. 17–21; Patrick La[ ] 'Report on Argentina: The Generals Don't Repent But They'll [ ] Pardon', *Commonweal*, vol. 116, no. 19 (3 November 1989), pp. [ ] and Jaime Malamud-Goti, 'Cry, Argentina', *Nation*, vol. 249, no.[ ] November 1989), pp. 517–18.

   As for Uruguay, see *Uruguay nunca más: informe sobre la vio[ ] a los derechos humanos, 1972–1985* (Montevideo: Servicio Paz y J[ ] Uruguay, 1989); Lawrence Weschler, 'The Great Exception' (Ur[ ] Part 1 – Liberty) *New Yorker*, vol. 65, no. 7 (3 April 1989), pp. [ ] and 'The Great Exception' (Uruguay: Part 2 – Impunity) *New [ ]* vol. 65, no. 8 (10 April 1989), pp. 85–108; Lawrence Weschler ([ ] 10 May 1989, update on Uruguay), *New Yorker*, vol. 65, no. 1[ ] May 1989), pp. 92–3; Cynthia Brown and Robert K. Goldman, [ ] guay – I: Torture, Memory and Justice', *Nation*, vol. 248, no. 1[ ] March 1989), pp. 408–11; Eduardo Galeano, 'Uruguay – II: Sign [ ] Invisible Line', *Nation*, vol. 248, no. 12 (27 March 1989), pp. 41[ ] 'Uruguay Confronts Its Torturers', *U.S. News & World Report*, vol[ ] no. 15 (17 April 1989), pp. 36–7; and Rachel Neild, 'Report from [ ] guay: Forgive & Forget? A Country Confronts its Past', *Common[ ]* 16 June 1989, pp. 358–60.

2. For more on Suárez Masón, see Camille Peri, 'Getting to Know the [ ] of Life & Death', *Mother Jones*, vol. 13, no. 7 (September 1988)[ ] 34–42. On Menem's 29 December 1990 pardon of jailed former mi[ ] leaders (including Suárez Masón), see Eugene Robinson, 'Argentine P[ ] of Jailed Ex-Military Rulers Triggers Protests', *Washington Pos[ ]*

Pinochet: psicohistoria de un liderazgo (Santiago de Chile: Ediciones del Ornitorrinco, 1988).

19. Maureen Meehan, 'Chile: Military Rejects Human Rights Report', *Latinamerica Press*, vol. 23, no. 12 (4 april 1991), pp. 1–2. For more on the reaction of the human rights community, see '"It's Now Known that What We Denounced was True"' (Interview) *Latinamerica Press*, vol. 23, no. 13 (11 April 1991), p. 3.

20. Sam Dillon, 'Chile Blames Military for Killing 1,068 Foes', *Miami Herald*, 5 March 1991, p. A14.

21. Ross Wehner, 'Chile Details Horrors of Pinochet Regime', *San Francisco Chronicle*, 5 March 1991, p. A20.

22. 'Chile Issues a Report Describing 2,000 Slayings Under Pinochet', *New York Times*, 6 March 1991, p. A4.

23. Dillon, 'Chile Blames Military', p. A14.

24. Wehner, 'Chile Details Horrors', p. A20.

25. Robinson, '2,025 Killings', p. A10.

26. 'Army Dismisses the Rettig Report', *Latin American Weekly Report*, 18 April 1991, p. 2. See also 'Right-wing Leader Guzman Murdered: Aylwin Says Terrorists Seek to "Destabilise" Democracy', *Latin American Regional Reports – Southern Cone*, 25 April 1991, p. 6; 'Stability Threatened by Guzman Murder', *Latin American Monitor – Southern Cone*, vol. 3, (April 1991), p. 1; and José Manuel Alvarez, 'Transición democrática chilena rechaza opciones rupturistas', *El Mercurio Edición Internacional* (Santiago) 18–24 April 1991, pp. 1–2.

27. Dillon, 'Chile Blames Military', p. A14.

28. For more detail on the December 1990 army alert, see 'Pinochet Called on Carpet in Chile Army Alert', *New York Times*, 21 December 1990, p. A6.

29. Wehner, 'Chile Details Horrors', p. A20.

30. Meehan, 'Chile', p. 1.

31. 'Una reunión histórica', *El Mercurio International Edition* (Santiago) 28 March–3 April 1991, p. 8.

32. Peter Ford, 'Chile Treads Narrow Rights Path: Public Demand for Punishment is Countered by General's Warning Not to Persecute Military', *Christian Science Monitor*, 19 March 1990, p. 3.

33. 'Chile Post-mortem', *Economist*, 9 March 1991, p. 41.

34. 'Aylwin (Azocar), Patricio', in *Current Biography Yearbook* (New York: H.W. Wilson Company, 1991), p. 44.

35. 'Uruguay: General Admits Military Use of Torture', *Latin American Monitor – Southern Cone* (April 1991), p. 888.

36. Ford, 'Chile Treads', p. 3.

37. Tom Wicker, '"Middle Way" in Chile', *New York Times*, 16 August 1990, p. A25.

38. 'Atrocities and Repentance in Chile' (editorial), *New York Times*, 23 February 1991, p. A24.

39. 'Encouraging Success in Chile' (editorial), *New York Times*, 19 March 1991, p. A22. *Latin American Monitor – Southern Cone* also noted this editorial in its April 1991 issue, p. 885.

40. 'Atrocities and Repentance', p. A24.
41. 'Monseñor Oviedo convoco a "Año de la Reconciliación', *El Mercurio Edición Internacional* (Santiago) 28 March–3 April 1991, p. 5. For more on the role the Church in Chile could play in the process of reconciliation and democratization, see Patricio Dooner, *Iglesia, reconciliación y democracia: (lo que los dirigentes políticos esperan de la Iglesia)*, 1st edn, Libros para la democracia (Santiago: Editorial Andante, 1989).
42. José Manuel Alvarez, 'En bienvenida a Aylwin: llamado del Papa para que cese la violencia en Chile', *El Mercurio Edición Internacional* (Santiago) 18–24 April 1991, p. 1.
43. 'Stability Threatened', *Latin American Monitor*, p. 884.
44. 'Update: Chile: Aylwin Riding High', *Latin American Regional Reports – Southern Cone*, 25 April 1991, p. 5. *Latin American Monitor – Southern Cone* also reported on this survey in its April 1991 issue, p. 885.
45. 'Washington Letter: Chile: Aylwin's Rights Stand Praised', *Latin American Regional Reports – Southern Cone*, 25 April 1991, p. 8.

Part VI

Public Policy Analysis

December 1990, p. A8; 'No Peace in the Dirty War', *Time*, 14 January 1991, p. 52; 'Letting Them Out', *Economist*, 5 January 1991, pp. 34–5; 'Pardoning Mass Murder in Argentina' (editorial), *New York Times*, 3 January 1991, p. A20; and Jacobo Timerman, 'Fear Returns to Argentina', *New York Times*, 5 January 1991, p. 21.

3. Aryeh Neier, 'Watching Rights', *Nation*, vol. 251 (19 November 1990), p. 588.

4. Arturo Valenzuela and Pamela Constable, 'Democracy in Chile', *Current History*, vol. 90, no. 553 (February 1991), p. 53.

5. For additional information on the 5 October 1988 plebiscite, see *Chile, Human Rights & the Plebiscite* (New York: Americas Watch, 1988); Stephen R. Bowers, 'Pinochet's Plebiscite and the Catholics: The Dual Role of the Chilean Church', *World Affairs*, vol. 151 (fall 1988), pp. 51–8; Abraham Santibáñez, *El plebiscito de Pinochet (cazado) en su propia trampa*, 1st ed (Santiago: Editorial Atena, 1988); Nelson Caula, Oscar Bonilla and Hugo Machín, *Chile, la alegría llego* (Uruguay: 1988/9).

6. For a discussion of Pinochet's weighted voting arrangement and the 1989 transition to democracy, see Pamela Constable and Arturo Valenzuela, 'Chile's Return to Democracy', *Foreign Affairs*, vol. 68, no, 5 (winter 1989–90), pp. 169–86.

7. Centro de Estudios Públicos (Santiago), *Estudio social y opinión pública*, Documento de trabajo, no. 136 (August 1990), pp. 49, 67.

8. Valenzuela and Constable, 'Democracy in Chile', p. 55.

9. Eugene Robinson, '2,025 Killings Laid to Pinochet: Commission Details Abuses During 1973–90 Military Repression', *Washington Post*, 5 March 1991, p. A10.

10. República de Chile, Ministerio Secretaría General de la Presidentia, *Discursos del Presidente de la República don Patricio Aylwin Azocar* (Santiago, 1990).

11. 'Suprema declaro constitucional Decreto Ley de Amnistía del 78', *El Mercurio Edición Internacional* (Santiago) 23–9 August 1990, p. 5.

12. Valenzuela and Constable, 'Democracy in Chile', pp. 55–6.

13. Ibid., p. 85.

14. Neier, 'Watching Rights', p. 588.

15. 'Even Unpublished, the Report on Pinochet's Abuses Opens a Can of Worms', *Latin American Weekly Report*, 28 February 1991, p. 1.

16. For more information on DINA and also its Colonia Dignidad, see 'Chile: "Beneficent Society" Brought into the Open', *Latinamerica Press*, vol. 23, no. 9 (14 March 1991), p. 6 and 'Aylwin Receives Rettig Report', *Latin American Monitor – Southern Cone*, March 1991, pp. 872–3.

17. 'Rettig Report Tallies Pinochet's Dead', *Latin American Weekly Report*, 21 March 1991, pp. 2–3. See also 'Chileans Stunned by Rettig Report', *Latin American Regional Reports – Southern Cone*, 25 April 1991, pp. 6–7.

18. More on Pinochet's response to the Rettig report is found in Malcolm Coad, 'Pinochet Criticizes Report on Abuses During His Rule', *Washington Post*, 29 March 1991, p. A17. For an interesting study of Pinochet, see María Dolores Souza and Germán Silva, *Auge y ocaso de Augusto*

Notes and References

1. Among the large amount of material on Argentina, the human-rights issue and the prosecution of military officials for rights abuses, see, for Argentina, Comisión Nacional sobre la Desaparición de Personas, *Nunca más: informe de la Comisión Nacional sobre la Desaparición de Personas* (Buenos Aires: EUDEBA, 1984), English trans., *Never Again: A Report* (London: Faber, in association with Index on Censorship, 1986); *Definitivamente – nunca más: la otra cara del informe de la CONADEP*, 2nd edn (Buenos Aires: Foro de Estudios sobre la Administración de Justicia, 1985); Kathryn Lee Crawford, 'Due Obedience and the Rights of Victims: Argentina's Transition to Democracy', *Human Rights Quarterly*, vol. 12 (February 1990), pp. 17–52; Jaime Malamud-Goti, 'Transitional Governments in the Breach: Why Punish State Criminals?', *Human Rights Quarterly*, vol. 12 (February 1990), pp. 1–16; Mark J. Osiel, 'The Making of Human Rights Policy in Argentina: The Impact of Ideas and Interests on a Legal Conflict', *Journal of Latin American Studies*, vol. 18 (May 1986), pp. 135–80; Roger Cohen, 'Alfonsín's Gamble: Argentina's Chief's Halt to Army Trials is Risk Taken to Curb Discord; He Seeks Role for a Military Alienated by Prosecution for Killings of Leftists', *Wall Street Journal*, 19 May 1987, pp. 1ff; John Tweedy, Jr, 'The Argentine "Dirty Wars" Trials: The First Latin American Nuremberg?', *Guild Practitioner: Current Problems; Law and Practice*, vol. 44 (winter 1987), pp. 15–32; José Zalaquete, 'From Dictatorship to Democracy', *New Republic*, vol. 193, no. 25 (16 December 1985), pp. 17–21; Patrick Lacefield, 'Report on Argentina: The Generals Don't Repent But They'll Take a Pardon', *Commonweal*, vol. 116, no. 19 (3 November 1989), pp. 583–4; and Jaime Malamud-Goti, 'Cry, Argentina', *Nation*, vol. 249, no. 15 (6 November 1989), pp. 517–18.

As for Uruguay, see *Uruguay nunca más: informe sobre la violación a los derechos humanos, 1972–1985* (Montevideo: Servicio Paz y Justicia Uruguay, 1989); Lawrence Weschler, 'The Great Exception' (Uruguay: Part 1 – Liberty) *New Yorker*, vol. 65, no. 7 (3 April 1989), pp. 43–85 and 'The Great Exception' (Uruguay: Part 2 – Impunity) *New Yorker* vol. 65, no. 8 (10 April 1989), pp. 85–108; Lawrence Weschler (Letter, 10 May 1989, update on Uruguay), *New Yorker*, vol. 65, no. 14 (22 May 1989), pp. 92–3; Cynthia Brown and Robert K. Goldman, 'Uruguay – I: Torture, Memory and Justice', *Nation*, vol. 248, no. 12 (27 March 1989), pp. 408–11; Eduardo Galeano, 'Uruguay – II: Sign on the Invisible Line', *Nation*, vol. 248, no. 12 (27 March 1989), pp. 411–12; 'Uruguay Confronts Its Torturers', *U.S. News & World Report*, vol. 106, no. 15 (17 April 1989), pp. 36–7; and Rachel Neild, 'Report from Uruguay: Forgive & Forget? A Country Confronts its Past', *Commonweal*, 16 June 1989, pp. 358–60.

2. For more on Suárez Masón, see Camille Peri, 'Getting to Know the Lord of Life & Death', *Mother Jones*, vol. 13, no. 7 (September 1988), pp. 34–42. On Menem's 29 December 1990 pardon of jailed former military leaders (including Suárez Masón), see Eugene Robinson, 'Argentine Pardon of Jailed Ex-Military Rulers Triggers Protests', *Washington Post*, 31

would make every effort to enhance and promote 'social peace' and democracy. He wished for President Aylwin to declare 'never again' to human-rights violations while, at the same time, forgiving, in the name of the state, those who had committed these abuses. This simultaneous position of 'never again' and forgiveness had long been that of the Church, the archbishop declared. While acknowledging that achieving this reconciliation would not be easy, Archbishop Oviedo believed that it was essential to promote and stimulate this atmosphere of reconciliation and good will throughout the whole country.[41] This observation was reinforced during a visit to Europe by President Aylwin, which included an audience with Pope John Paul II. On 22 April 1991 the Pope expressed his sadness over the escalation of recent terrorist/political violence in Chile and urged a restoration of 'a climate of peace, dialogue and mutual respect', which would renew hope and strengthen fraternal bonds among all Chileans. The Pope assured Aylwin that the Vatican supported the process of democratization and reconciliation in Chile, as did the Chilean Catholic Church, which provided a good example of 'the mission of the Church in society'.[42]

Following the release of the Rettig Report, and despite the apparent stand-off Aylwin had hoped to avoid between his administration, which supported it, and the military's rejection of it,[43] early indications point to an affirmation of Aylwin's approach to the rights issue both within and outside Chile. Domestically, according to a national survey conducted in late March 1991 by the Centro de Estudios de la Realidad Contemporáneo (CERC), 82.3 per cent of those polled approved of Aylwin's performance as president. The survey also indicated that 65.3 per cent believed Chile was 'moving ahead', 25.6 per cent that it was at a 'standstill' and only 3.9 per cent thought the country was in decline. In other survey findings, 63.8 per cent preferred democracy, as against 15.7 per cent who supported authoritarianism. Regarding Pinochet, 72.2 per cent favored his resignation as army commander while 21.3 per cent believed he should remain in that post.[44] This encouraging domestic opinion was also reinforced at the same time (late March 1991) by a positive response from the US regarding Aylwin's handling of the sensitive human-rights issue. The State Department praised the Aylwin government for its firm stand vis-à-vis the Chilean military over the release of the Rettig Report on human-rights abuses during the Pinochet period. State Department spokesperson David Denny indicated that Aylwin's 'efforts to bring the truth to light about human-rights abuses by certain agents of the Chilean state during the Pinochet dictatorship will help the cause of justice and national reconciliation'.[45]

conciliator and the US as a reinforcer of Chilean democracy. President Aylwin must 'balance accountability with reconciliation'. On the international front, the US can and should strengthen democracy in Chile through economic policies such as freer trade and investment rules.[38] While the Chilean economy was done well, especially compared with those of other Latin American countries such as Argentina and Mexico, Chile still faced major challenges, such as amending an undemocratic constitution, restoring judicial independence and finding a means to establish accountability for past rights abuses. Chile would best succeed in meeting these political challenges with strong sustained economic growth, which depends on export diversification away from copper and developing new exports. The latter would require access to international markets and investment which could best be achieved with a successful conclusion to the Uruguay Round negotiations on world trade.[39]

The US should make sure that the Chilean military clearly understands that insubordination against civilian government would seriously harm relations between the two countries. The Aylwin administration has continued the economic liberalization policies begun under Pinochet. Most Chilean citizens, however, reject the political repression carried out during that period. Chileans seek official acknowledgement and condemnation of these abuses. Public contrition and prosecution would be more difficult to attain. Prosecution of military officials precipitated armed rebellions in Argentina. Pinochet remains commander of the army, the president constitutionally cannot remove him, and the general has clearly expressed his opposition to the prosecution of military officials. The Roman Catholic Church in Chile could facilitate reconciliation. Its doctrine preaches forgiveness to the sincerely repentant. While judicial punishment of rights violations may prove to be impossible, the church might exercise its 'moral power to demand sincere and public contrition as a precondition for national reconciliation'.[40]

This process appears to have begun under the auspices of the Church. In his Easter message on 31 March 1991, Monseñor Carlos Oviedo, the Archbishop of Santiago, declared that it was Chile's duty to seek understanding and to avoid confrontation, which would lead to 'a new style of democratic dialogue' capable of creating a better balance among the various institutions of government. To this end, the archbishop proclaimed a 'year of reconciliation' to reestablish harmony after so many years of political violence. He indicated that a profound reconciliation was necessary for the sake of the nation's future via political dialogue and understanding. Monseñor Oviedo pledged that the Church

Pinochet: psicohistoria de un liderazgo (Santiago de Chile: Ediciones del Ornitorrinco, 1988).
19. Maureen Meehan, 'Chile: Military Rejects Human Rights Report', *Latinamerica Press*, vol. 23, no. 12 (4 april 1991), pp. 1–2. For more on the reaction of the human rights community, see '"It's Now Known that What We Denounced was True"' (Interview) *Latinamerica Press*, vol. 23, no. 13 (11 April 1991), p. 3.
20. Sam Dillon, 'Chile Blames Military for Killing 1,068 Foes', *Miami Herald*, 5 March 1991, p. A14.
21. Ross Wehner, 'Chile Details Horrors of Pinochet Regime', *San Francisco Chronicle*, 5 March 1991, p. A20.
22. 'Chile Issues a Report Describing 2,000 Slayings Under Pinochet', *New York Times*, 6 March 1991, p. A4.
23. Dillon, 'Chile Blames Military', p. A14.
24. Wehner, 'Chile Details Horrors', p. A20.
25. Robinson, '2,025 Killings', p. A10.
26. 'Army Dismisses the Rettig Report', *Latin American Weekly Report*, 18 April 1991, p. 2. See also 'Right-wing Leader Guzman Murdered: Aylwin Says Terrorists Seek to "Destabilise" Democracy', *Latin American Regional Reports – Southern Cone*, 25 April 1991, p. 6; 'Stability Threatened by Guzman Murder', *Latin American Monitor – Southern Cone*, vol. 3, (April 1991), p. 1; and José Manuel Alvarez, 'Transición democrática chilena rechaza opciones rupturistas', *El Mercurio Edición Internacional* (Santiago) 18–24 April 1991, pp. 1–2.
27. Dillon, 'Chile Blames Military', p. A14.
28. For more detail on the December 1990 army alert, see 'Pinochet Called on Carpet in Chile Army Alert', *New York Times*, 21 December 1990, p. A6.
29. Wehner, 'Chile Details Horrors', p. A20.
30. Meehan, 'Chile', p. 1.
31. 'Una reunión histórica', *El Mercurio International Edition* (Santiago) 28 March–3 April 1991, p. 8.
32. Peter Ford, 'Chile Treads Narrow Rights Path: Public Demand for Punishment is Countered by General's Warning Not to Persecute Military', *Christian Science Monitor*, 19 March 1990, p. 3.
33. 'Chile Post-mortem', *Economist*, 9 March 1991, p. 41.
34. 'Aylwin (Azocar), Patricio', in *Current Biography Yearbook* (New York: H.W. Wilson Company, 1991), p. 44.
35. 'Uruguay: General Admits Military Use of Torture', *Latin American Monitor – Southern Cone* (April 1991), p. 888.
36. Ford, 'Chile Treads', p. 3.
37. Tom Wicker, '"Middle Way" in Chile', *New York Times*, 16 August 1990, p. A25.
38. 'Atrocities and Repentance in Chile' (editorial), *New York Times*, 23 February 1991, p. A24.
39. 'Encouraging Success in Chile' (editorial), *New York Times*, 19 March 1991, p. A22. *Latin American Monitor – Southern Cone* also noted this editorial in its April 1991 issue, p. 885.

40. 'Atrocities and Repentance', p. A24.
41. 'Monseñor Oviedo convoco a "Año de la Reconciliación', *El Mercurio Edición Internacional* (Santiago) 28 March–3 April 1991, p. 5. For more on the role the Church in Chile could play in the process of reconciliation and democratization, see Patricio Dooner, *Iglesia, reconciliación y democracia: (lo que los dirigentes políticos esperan de la Iglesia)*, 1st edn, Libros para la democracia (Santiago: Editorial Andante, 1989).
42. José Manuel Alvarez, 'En bienvenida a Aylwin: llamado del Papa para que cese la violencia en Chile', *El Mercurio Edición Internacional* (Santiago) 18–24 April 1991, p. 1.
43. 'Stability Threatened', *Latin American Monitor*, p. 884.
44. 'Update: Chile: Aylwin Riding High', *Latin American Regional Reports – Southern Cone*, 25 April 1991, p. 5. *Latin American Monitor – Southern Cone* also reported on this survey in its April 1991 issue, p. 885.
45. 'Washington Letter: Chile: Aylwin's Rights Stand Praised', *Latin American Regional Reports – Southern Cone*, 25 April 1991, p. 8.

14 Political Science in Mexico in the Cold War and Post-Cold War Context

Enrique Suárez-Iñiguez

It is not easy to define political science. Political scientists themselves are not in agreement on the definition. Its object of study is not clear. This field has traditionally been concerned with the analysis of (a) the good life; (b) the monopoly of the use of legitimate physical violence; (c) the authoritative allocation of values for a given society; and (d) forms of organization and the exercise of power. It is within this last sphere, perhaps the most generic of all, that we find two positions: the study of power within the state, and how power filters down into society. (Although, in a strict sense, the first is the role of political science and the second of political sociology, even though this is a somewhat artificial division.)

Political science was born with Greek civilization. In ancient Greece and ancient Rome political science had an ethical end: to make better and happier citizens, the so-called 'good life'. Politics and ethics were two parts of the same whole (Plato, Aristotle, Cicero). During the Middle Ages attempts were made to achieve Christian virtues and to with eternal life (Agustine, Aquinas). Machiavelli's most important goal in the discussion of politics was to establish the different ways to attain and preserve power. For this reason some believe political science came into being in the sixteenth century. As an academic discipline we could say that it came into its own during the past century in Europe and the US, and half-way through this century in Mexico. To make a balance of political science requires that these historical considerations be taken into account. In effect, 'Mexico has always been a prodigious country in creating political and social ideas and in the development of political theories and doctrines.'[1] For the purposes of this chapter we will consider political science only as an academic discipline.

As such, according to David Torres Mejía,[2] political science appeared in Mexico in two ways: on the one hand, through research carried out by a group of US professors and, on the other, what was to lead to the establishment of the Escuela de Ciencias Políticas y Sociales (School of Political and Social Sciences) at the UNAM (National University of Mexico). In the US a group of academicians from the functionalist school of thought, who had focused their studies and analysis on Mexico, became well known. These 'Mexicanologists' wrote basic works which, although seldom translated, had considerable impact in Mexico. Perhaps the most outstanding works were Frank Tannenbaum, *Mexico: The Struggle for Peace and Bread* (1953); Robert C. Scott, *Mexican Government in Transition* (1959); Raymond Vernon, *The Dilemma of Mexico's Development* (1963); and Frank Brandenburg, *The Making of Modern Mexico* (1964). These works, supported by a large volume of bibliographic sources and based on empirical data, were optimistic in nature. The Mexican political system was in the process of evolving from authoritarianism toward democracy, while at the same time achieving certain levels of economic development and social justice.[3] Those were the days of the Cold War and the recent triumph of the Cuban Revolution.

On the other hand, at the end of the Second World War, the United Nations tried to establish the idea of a community of nations to avoid a new conflagration, but 'there were not enough specialized agencies to train the citizens who were to represent their countries in international fora and who would establish and direct new institutions that would give consistency and strength to those States recently created or at different stages of development'.[4] With that end in mind, Lucio Medieta y Núñez, at that time director of the Instituto de Investigaciones Sociales at the UNAM, attended a conference on political science sponsored by UNESCO, at which a recommendation to establish departments of social science was presented. When he returned to Mexico he proposed a curriculum, based on the one used at the London School of Economics and Political Science, the Institut d'Etudes Politiques of the University of Paris, and the Ecole de Sciences Politiques at the University of Louvain, to Rector Luis Garrido in order to found the Escuela Nacional de Ciencias Políticas y Sociales in Mexico, and classes began on 25 July 1951.[5]

At first the department was under juridical influence and the professors came from the School of Law. This situation began to change with the arrival in 1957 of Pablo González Casanova as director. González Casanova had won a master's degree in history and completed his doctorate in Sociology at the University of Paris. His training and interest in research led him to give the department a different look. He aimed to set up a team of professors particularly suited to the department, and because there were no sociologists or political scientists at the institution he invited historians and anthropologists to join the other professors already there. He emphasized a knowledge of statistics and drew up a curriculum with common core courses. However he brought together under the same name two disciplines which in reality were different: political science and public administration. This union in turn led to confusion in the definition of Mexican fields of study and for many years subordinated the first field to the second. Political science was seen as a part of public administration rather than a separate academic subject, as was pointed out when the curriculum was redesigned in 1958.[6] During those years the ideological orientation of several critical social sciences was influenced by the Cuban Revolution.

From the moment reforms were made in the curriculum in 1966, little by little political science began to find a place for itself. In 1967 the Division of Graduate Studies was founded and the first 'Escuela' became a 'Facultad' (department) within the university. Under Enrique González Pedrero and Victor Flores Olea political science came into its own, with specialized professors, many of whom were graduates of the independent department. Ties with similar institutions abroad were established. Internationally renowned intellectuals such as Eric Fromm, André Gorz, Roger Garaudi, Eric Hobsbaun, Irving Horowitz, Michael Löwy, Herbert Marcuse, Ernst Mandel, Susan Sontag and others came to teach at the winter sessions, while at the same time graduates of the school went abroad to pursue graduate degrees in political science and sociology, returning to accept professorships in the department. In 1971 a new curriculum appeared on the scene. This was perhaps the best and most polished of all curricula, under which political science and public administration were further separated.[7]

During these years the university began to accept more and more students. Between 1960 and 1983 the number of students in the bachelor's degree program grew at an annual average rate of 12.2 per cent, while the number of students in graduate programs increased 3.8 times between 1970 and 1983. At both levels social and administrative sciences grew at a fast pace – 37.3 per cent at bachelor level, 55 per cent at master level and 45 per cent at PhD level. The total number of students enrolled in the department increased from 384 in 1956 to 1139 in 1966, 2640 in 1971 and 6047 in 1987–8. (Of these students, 848 were studying political science.)

In spite of these statistics, political science still represents only a minimal percentage of higher education in Mexico. At the beginning of the 1985–6 school year only 16 (6.47 per cent) of the 247 universities and institutions of higher learning in Mexico offered a bachelor's degree in this subject. Of a total of 988 078 students enrolled in institutions of higher learning, according to ANUIES (Asociación Nacional de Universidades e Institutos de Educación Superior), only 4892 (0.49 per cent) were enrolled in political science or public administration. In 1985 only 649 students majored in this field. At the graduate level the situation was similar: in 1983 some 30 653 students were enrolled (3.5 per cent of enrollment in BA programs). In 1985–6 only 62 enrolled in a master's program in political science and 19 in the PhD program.[8] In any case the department's growth was impressive, and this influenced its substantive orientation.

Research also received decisive support. Often research centers focusing on specific areas or disciplines were established. At the beginning of the 1970s the Center for Political Studies was founded, where a group of young professors began to carry out research in the field of political science. In 1955 the *Revista Mexicana de Ciencia Política* was established (later on the title changed to *Revista Mexicana de Ciencias Políticas y Sociales*). In 1975 Gastón García Cantú founded *Estudios Políticos*, with articles on political science written by Mexicans. In both journals a significant number of articles on political science appeared.

On the other hand, from 1960 onward another academic group concerned with political research surfaced at the Centro de Relaciones Internacionales at the Colegio de México. Although small in number, this group was influenced by political science in the US and by historians such as Daniel Cosío Villegas, who was their teacher. At the Instituto de Investigaciones Sociales (UNAM), work was also carried out on the Mexican political system. Thus academic political science in Mexico, as occurred in other parts of the world, came into its own at the universities, and the university professors were the main promotors of this field. It is precisely through the analysis of the academic research of these professors that we are able to learn about the progress and orientation of Mexican academic political science.

As indicated above, for quite sometime Mexican authors have been prolific in producing political analyses, but when we use the term 'academic political science' we avoid the mistake that Meyer and

Camacho made when they took into account in their analysis the writings of leaders of political parties or journalists. Even though the division between political science and political sociology is not clearcut, if we consider the former as the study of the form of organization and exercise of power in all spheres (both state and society), then we can rightly speak of a Mexican academic political science. In reality this field has to a large degree followed the evolution of European and North American schools. Thus its main focuses have been Marxist and structural-functionalist. Behavioralism[9] has not been very important in Mexico, and as a resut Easton's classifications of US political science (formal, traditional, behavioralist, and post-behavioralist) are not relevant.

Camacho and Meyer divided Mexican political science into behavioralism, structuralism, Marxism and normative studies. Torres Mejía adopts Klaus von Beyme's classifications (empirica–analytical, critical–dialectal and normative theories). But 'normative' for Meyer and Camacho has an atheoretical content and includes leaders of political parties, literary figures and journalists, whose works in the strict sense cannot be considered political science. While their work can be considered a pioneer study in this field, it has two major flaws. First, in spite of the title, it does not deal with political science, but rather with works related to a variety of writings that are not exclusively academic in nature but deal with journalistic, literary and opinionated works. The other defect is the partiality and bias of their study. In their analysis it seems as though political science in Mexico is carried out only by Americans and professors at the Colegio de México, which is completely false. If one institution deserves to be mentioned as the foremost on the political-science scene in Mexico it would have to be the Facultad de Ciencias Políticas y Sociales at the UNAM, from which many of the most important normative studies, and certainly many of the most important academicians, have emanated. The defects of their professor (Cosió Villegas) are being repeated by his students.[10]

Going back to the classification of the different types of research, one sees that, according to the data from Torres Mejía's sample for the period 1971–85, 38 per cent of the works were empirical–analytical (which term includes functionalism, structuralism, behavioralism and systems analysis) while 46 per cent were dialectical–critical (Marxist analysis of different varieties, which apparently indicates more or less an even share between Marxism and functionalism). But David Torres Mejía himself mentions that his figures should be treated with caution, since his sample only included 172 articles: 'Probably the drop registered in the number of articles written from a Marxist perspective is exaggerated.'[11] When researching works on political theory I discovered that between 1976 and 1987 the most important academic journals only included 166 articles on political theory, of which 84 (50.6 per cent) were on Marxism. The rest sprang from diverse schools of thought. The same phenomenon occurred in bachelors' theses. Until 1986 only 20 of some 2241 theses were on political theory (0.8 per cent), of which nine were on Marxism. Of a total of 667 theses on political science and public administration, until 1988 only eight (1.19 per cent) were on political theory, three of which were on Marxism.[12] If in political theory the percentage of Marxist works is high, in other areas it presumably would be much higher.

Until now Marxism has been the predominant school of thought in social sciences in Mexico. Nevertheless most researchers are not Marxist. How can this be explained? Marxism has played a hegemonic role in teaching and research. There are journals devoted to it; it appears in diverse fora; and it implies political activism. It also has a justifying ideological element which makes it appear 'just'. For a long time this led to a certain fear of expressing points of view which were not Marxist. Fortunately this stigma has changed considerably. With every passing day there are more and more papers on diverse theoretical schools and more and more academic and interdisciplinary journals have been established. Freedom to criticize Marxism is now prevalent, although orthodox Marxists are scandalized. The crisis of Marxism and what has happened in Eastern Europe has accelerated this process and has given its just value to ideologies.

Mexican academic political science came into being in the throes of the Cold War and as a consequence of the measures taken by the United Nations after the Second World War. It was born with the Escuela Nacional de Ciencias Políticas y Sociales at the UNAM in the 1950s and developed further in the 1960s and 1970s, when it housed a group of its own eminent professors and considerable importance was lent to research. In addition diverse journals appeared on the scene or were consolidated. The group from El Colegio de México emerged and a major in political science was offered at the Universidad Metropolitana and at universities in other states. In the 1980s there were some 16 universities in Mexico that offered a BA in political science. By the end of the Cold War, with the collapse of the Berlin

Wall, Mexican academic political science seemed to have found its niche and it is now ready for new horizons. The prospects for the post-Cold-War period are as follows.

Marxism has declined over the past few years, several European nations having not only rejected real socialism, but also the ideology that backed it. A deep restructuring is in order. In spite of this necessity, many Marxists will not be open to this idea: they cannot accept that they were wrong about so many things; deep-rooted biases are hard to get rid of. What does seem to be inevitable is that they will give up the place and the hegemonic role they maintained for many decades, or at least they will share it with other schools of thought. But Marxism should not be underestimated. Its long-standing presence in Mexican social sciences gives it strength to continue in its attempts to explain and transform the world. In Latin America, Marxism is still strong.

Functionalism–structuralism should continue to earn a place in Mexican political science, especially to enable learning more about 'the electoral processes, the impact of norms and laws, the characteristic institutions of the present political administration, and the political class'.[13] In other words, the political system as a whole should be examined by political scientists.

Behavioralism can contribute in a decisive way to understanding phenomena such as public opinion and the behavior of political actors, without their old pretense of value neutrality. What Easton calls the 'post-behavioral stage' founded in the counter-cultural revolution has gained ground in its attempts to study phenomena such as industrialization, sexual and ethical discrimination, poverty, nuclear arms and ecological problems. Both schools of thought require increased methological sophistication with surveys, samplings, statistics and complicated techniques for data collection which, given Mexico's economic crisis, will be difficult to develop.

Another school of thought that could become important in Mexico is what Easton calls 'cognitive political science', that is, the approach which attempts to explain political phenomena through rationality or acceptance of the fact that human beings are rational in their behavior. John Rawls' work, *A Theory of Justice*,[14] is an example of this school of thought, as is the Weberian interpretative method. Eclectic schools of thought that take elements from here and there for their analysis have already gained ground and supposedly will continue to do so. The concepts of 'class struggle', 'ideology', 'hegemony', and 'imperialism' are used less as time goes on, and in their place we find the terms 'populism', 'corporativism', 'authoritarianism', 'bureaucracy', 'elites', 'middle class', 'intellectuals' and 'communication'.

In the near future, there will apparently no longer be a dominant theoretical school of thought in Mexico. Researchers will adopt diverse methods and approaches, replacing the preponderance of ideologies with more scientific research based as much as possible on methods used in the natural sciences. The other trend deserving particular attention is the lack of status of professors, with all the social and economic considerations this concept carries. The economic crisis has considerably affected the educational sector and the low salaries of university professors are a sad example of this. Mexican political scientists also lack funds for research, publications and participation in conferences. If more resources are not made available at the university level the result will be isolation and stagnation. Even now many professors are leaving their positions in the universities to devote their efforts to other fields. Only with true devotion – which requires decent salaries – will Mexican political scientists be able to carry out research and better train university students. Only by recognition of the important role of the universities being recovered will national educational objectives be achieved.

David Torres Mejía claims that the rich Mexican tradition as manifested by Mora, Otero, Molina Enríquez, Lombardo, Vasconcelos or Caso, has not yet been able to 'blend efficiently with the theoretical schools that Mexican university political science has adopted from abroad' (such as functionalism or behavioralism). This claim is not valid. If there is one thing that makes Mexican political science distinctive it is the fact that it has incorporated the thoughts of those authors and those of others from more modern times as basic sources, and has adapted their ideas and interpreted them for Mexico's reality. Nevertheless we still need to integrate them more.

Mexican political science has passed through various stages. In the beginning, the colonial era was the time of Sahagún, Las Casas and Torquemada's writings; then came the historical stage during Independence, the Reform and the Revolution. Some of the most important thinkers during this period were Hidalgo, Morelos, Mora, Juárez, Zarco, Ramírez, Sierra, Molina Enríquez and Luis Cabrera. Next was the post-revolutionary period, with Caso, Lombardo, Vasconcelos, and Silva Herzog, among others, and finally the academic stage that has been considered here: the birth and boom of political-science departments in the universities.

Notes and References

1. Arnaldo Córdova, 'El estudio de la ciencia política', in *La ciencia política en México: estado actual y perspectivas* (Mexico: FCPyS–CECIP, 1986).
2. David Torres Mejía, 'La ciencia política en México', in Francisco José Paoli Bolio (ed.) *Desarrollo y Organización de las Ciencias Sociales en México* (Mexico: Centro de Investigaciones Interdisciplinarias en Humanidades, UNAM–Miguel Angel Porrúa, 1990).
3. Lorenzo Meyer and Manuel Camacho, 'La ciencia política en México. Su desarrollo y estado actual', in L. Meyer, *et al.*, *Ciencias Sociales en México* (Mexico: El Colegio de México, 1979), p. 13.
4. David Torres Mejía, op. cit., p. 150.
5. *Cfr.* Sergio Colmenero and Aurora Tovar, 'Entrevista a Ernesto Enríquez Coyro', primer director de la Escuela Nacional de Ciencias Políticas y Sociales, 1951–1953, *Revista Mexicana de Ciencias Políticas y Sociales*, vol. XXX, no. 115–16 (Jan.–June 1984).
6. 'the school should train students to exercise or advise, to exercise their chosen field *within public administration*' (emphasis added); Leonor Ludlow, 'Documentos: 33 años de historia de la FCPyS', in *Revista Mexicana de Ciencias Políticas y Sociales*, no. 115–116, cited in David Torres Mejía, op. cit., p. 153.
7. In reality the two are joined under the same name: a BA in political sciences and public administration, following the French tradition. At the graduate level they are kept completely separate and the degree is given in political science, following the Anglo-Saxon tradition.
8. Enrique Suárez-Iñiguez, 'La ciencia política en México', in Córdova, Arnaldo, Suréz-Iñiguez, Enrique, *et al.*, *Ciencia Política, Democracia y Elecciones* (Mexico: FCPyS, UNAM, 1989), pp. 69–92; Enrique Suárez-Iñiguez, 'The Role of Political Theory in the Teaching of Political Science in Mexico', in *Teaching Political Science*, vol. 16, no. 4 (Summer 1989), pp. 157–65.
9. David Easton has drawn our attention to the fact that one must be careful not to confuse behaviorism with behavioralism. The first is a school of psychology founded by J.B. Watson, which B.F. Skinner developed further. Behavioralism is a school of thought belonging to political science which sustains that there are uniform characteristics in human behavior that can be confirmed by empirical data. It places emphasis on quantitative and sophisticated methods and in general believes in the neutrality of science: David Easton, 'Political Science in the United States. Past and Present', in *International Political Science Review*, vol. 6, no. 1, pp. 133–52. In spite of this explanation, we find that the general characteristics of behavioralism can also be found in behaviorism.
10. In effect, Daniel Cosío Villegas, in his famous book on *El sistema político mexicano*, points out that in Mexico there is no 'systematic research on national and local political problems and not even a serious and orderly examination of them'. According to him there are no writers 'who seriously examine national problems'. In 1975, in my article, 'Cosío Villegas y la legitimación a través de la crítica', *Estudios Políticos*, vol. I, nos 3–4 (Sept.–Dec., 1975) I maintained that Cosío Villegas' statements were

not true and that they were less the result of ignorance than of ill-will. I cited a list of important contributions that proved he was wrong. Disciples *do* follow the teachings of their professors.

11. David Torres Mejía, op. cit., p. 169.
12. Cf. Enrique Suárez-Iñiguez, 'La ciencia política en México' op. cit., pp. 90–91, and 'The Role of Political Theory in the Teaching of Political Science in Mexico', op. cit., p. 163.
13. Meyer and Camacho, op. cit., p. 45.
14. John Rawls, *A Theory of Justice* (Cambridge, Mass.: Harvard University Press, 1971).

Index

Academic
  political science, 307
  scientific community, 135
Adapting to change, 109
Administration, xvi
Administrative
  costs, 58
  machine, 94
  state model, 127
  structures, 108
Adversarial model, 127
Agencies, xv
Agreements, 16
Agriculture, 145
Aid program, 40
Allende government, 29
Alternatives, xii
Amnesty law, 290
Analysis, public policy, 301
Andean Pact, 20
Argentina, xi, 11, 202, 216
Association, 45
Authoritarian regime, 105
Authoritarianism, 220, 237, 245
Autonomy, 239
Aylwin government, 283

Balance
  environment, 140
  of payments, 14
Banking, 29
Bargaining power, 135
Behavioralism, 307
Biparty agreements, 271
Bolivia, 29, 75, 91, 203, 237
Bureaucratic
  approach, 78
  regime, 105
Bureaucrats, 122
Business, 140

Capitalism, 5, 92, 215, 224
                          205
                    42
                    295

                67

Checks and balances, 4
Chief executive, xiv
Chile, 29, 282
Civil society, 68
Civilian
  government, 295
  rule, 112
Class conflict, 225
Coalition, 257
Cognitive political science, 309
Cold War, 28, 303
Colombia, 31
Communist threat, 289
Comparative
  analysis, 136
  research, 85
Competition, 83
Computer industry, 99
Conservation, 142
  education, 158
Conservative position, xi
Constituency-minded representative, 169
Constitutional
  policy, 255
  provisions, xiv
  rights, xv
Contagion of democracy, 186
Continuity, xiv
Control of politicians, 168
Coparticipation, 257
Corporatism, 126, 220
Corruption, 135
Costa Rica, 152
Cultural production, 222
Customs union, 45

Debt crisis, 42
Decentralization, 62
Decolonization, 28
Defensive alliance, 11
Deforestation, 145
Democracy, 5, 10, 135, 186, 214, 237, 282
  formal, 227
  government, 293
  regime, 107
  transition, 207
Democratization, 187

Dependency, 220
   relation, 21
Developed societies, 122
Developing nations, 12
Development, economic, 140
Dictatorships, 237
Diffusion
   of democracy, 186
   theory, 191
Direct election, 180
Displaced workers, xiv
Dissimulation, 239
Distribution, 64
Due process, xvi
Dynamics, political, 55

Ecomanagement, 148
Economic
   agreements, 16
   boom, 101
   crisis, 200
   dependence, 193
   development, 140
   diversification, 160
   needs, 148
   policies, 26
   policy, xi, 1
   strategy, 36
Ecotourism, 140
Ecotourist–environment collaboration, 159
Ecuador, 30
Education, 56
   ministry, 80
Efficiency, 59, 77
Elderly, 59
Electoral
   procedure, 172
   reform, 165
   register, 179
Electorate signals, 129
Electronics, 91
Employment, xiv, 56
Enforcement, xvi
Entrepreneurship, 109
Environmental
   balance, 140
   needs, 148
   policy, 89
Equal protection, xvi
Equality, 69
Equity, 58
Eurocommunist, 216
European Community, 23

Evaluation, 63
Executive, chief, xiv
Expansion of technology, 132
Expertise signals, 128
Export financing, 26
Expropriation, 29
External tariffs, 27

Factionalism, 196
Financial
   assistance, 157
   organizations, 24
Food policy, 67
Foreign
   enterprises, 27
   investment, 41
Formal democracy, 227
Formal–legal model, 128
Fourth World, 15
Free
   speech, xvi
   trade, 21
Freedom, 4
Functional model, 126

General Confederation of Labor, 9
Glasnost, 229
Goals, xiii
Government structure, xiv
Grassroots activity, 151
Greek civilization, 303
Growth, xiv, 95

Harmonization of policies, 26
Health
   ministry, 80
   preservation, 56
Hierarchical structure, 94
Higher education, 306
Historical progression, 124
Human
   development, 73
   rights, 242, 282
   rights groups, 290

Ideological guerillas, 102
Imperialism, 10, 215
Implementation, 5, 71
Inclusionary regime, 132
Income, 57
Incremental policy, 100
India, 91

Industrial
countries, 13
policy, 137
programming, 26
Industrializing, 76
Inflation, xiv
Infrastructure needs, 148
Innovative institutions, 23
Innovators, 115
Institutional
arrangements, 97, 275
collaboration, 148
weakness, 79
Institutions, xv
Instruments, 98
Integration process, 21
Intellectual thinking, 222
Intellectuals, 224
Interaction models, 136
Interest diversity, 137
International
human rights movement, 287
Political Science Association, xi
system, 28
Internationalization, 220
International–national linkages, 207
Interparty agreements, 267
Investment, 27

Japan, 12
Jobs, xiv
Judiciary, 290
Juridical influence, 304

Labor
movement, 228
unions, 10
Laissez-faire state, 4
Land scarcity, 200
Latin American Free Trade
Association, 21
Left political parties, 228
Leftist terrorism, 289
Left-wing intellectuals, 218
Legality, 237
Legislative assemblies, 165
Legitimacy, 10, 76
Liberal position, xi
Liberalization, 25, 295
Linkage politics, 188
Logging, 145

Macroeconomics, 76
Managers, 115

Market arena, 137
Marxism, 4, 214, 307
Mass movements, 227
Methodology, xi
Mexico, 45, 153, 303
Microelectronic revolution, 95
Military
government, 33
officials, 282
power, 286
regime, 134
Mining, 29
Municipal councils, 165
Municipalization, 84

National
coinciding agreement, 258
intonation, 258
Nationalization, 29
Natural resources, 145
Negotiation, 45, 262
Neo-Liberalism, 6
Neo-Marxism, 6
Networking, 110
Neutral position, xii
Nicaragua, 230
Normative studies, 307
North–South relations, 3

OECD countries, 12
Oil crisis, 7
Oil shock, 32
Ombudsman, 288
Opposition
parties, 199
politics, 197
Optimization, 264
Organizational models, 83

Pacification, 237
Panachage preference voting, 172
Paraguay, 186
Parks, 145
Parliamentary
government, xi
influence, 106
Participation, 84
Participatory democracy, 227
Parties, political, 227
Partisan orientation, 178
Party
list, 165
structure, 170
unity, 177

Payroll taxes, xvi
Peasant movements, 199, 200
Perestroika, 229
Periodization, 94
Peronism, 10
Personalized proportional
  representation, 166
Peru, 29
Phasing of policies, 98
Physicians, 86
Pinochet regime, 283
Policy
  analysis, xvi
  instruments, 24
  linkages, 79
  making, 130
  studies, 20
  Studies Organization, xi
Political
  agreements, 16
  climate, 292
  dynamics, 55
  goals, 198
  parties, 165, 200, 227
  policy, xi, 163
  process, 275
  regimes, 104
  science, 303
  science departments, 310
  sociology, 307
  theory, 308
Political/social environment, 115
Politicians, 123
Popular
  movements, 227
  unity, 29
Population, 71
Post-Cold War, 303
Post-industrialism, 6
Post-Marxism, 214
Poverty, 71, 81
Power, 243
Power sharing, 275
Preference voting, 177
Preferences, 265
Presidential government, xi
Presidentialism, 257
Pressure groups, 198
Primary goods, 13
Private sector, 84
  private–public sector alliance, 152
Privatization, 62, 135
Productivity, 57
Proportional representation, 165

Proportionality, 170
Prosecution, 282
Protectionist attitude, 42
Public policy, 20
  analysis, 301
Public sector, 79

Quito Protocol, 43

Rationality, 69
Reconciliation, 294
Reforms on proportionality, 179
Régime d'exception, 247
Regional
  blocs, 16
  integration, 21
Regulation, 64, 92
Relocating, xv
Reorganization, 228
Representation, 165
Repression, 22
Repressive apparatuses, 239
Research, 306
Responsiveness, xi
  national, 149
Rights, constitutional, xv
Rule of law, 242
Rural organizations, 200

Sandinistas, 230
Sanitation, 56
Science, 130
Sectoral programming, 26
Selection of politicians, 168
Social
  expenditures, 76
  groups, 58
  management, 77
  movements, 199
  policies, 71
  policy, xi, 53
  programs, 81
  sector, 81
  security, 55
Socialism, 215
Socialist ideologies, 8
Socially rooted authoritarianism, 248
Software production, 100
SOS solution, *see* Super-optimum
  solution
Southern Cone, 204
Soviet Union, 12
Species, endangered, 144
Spillover theory, 73

Stability, xi
State authority, 225
State-centered model, 200
Stock market crash, 7
Strategies, 98
Strategy, economic, 36
Stroessner regime, 201
Structural constraints, 113
Structuralism, 307
Structure, government, xiv
Student
  movements, 199
  organizations, 200
Substance, xi
Super-optimum alternative, xii
Super-optimum solution (SOS), xiv
Sustainable development, 141
Systematic analysis, xvi, 302

Tariffs, xiv, 25
Technocratic style, 130
Technoeconomic environment, 115
Technological
  change, xv
  development, 98
Technology, xiv
  policy, xi, 89, 122
Third World, 14, 123
Torture, 290
Tourism, 140
Trade barriers, 39

Trade-union movement, 199
Traditionalism, 196
Training, xv
Transition, 237
Transitional politics, 189
Tripartite alliance, 196
Truth and Reconciliation
  Commission, 287

Underdeveloped societies, 122
Unions, 57
United Nations, 12, 71, 304
United States, 12, 205
Universal coverage, 68
Universities, 310
Uruguay, 257
User fees, 155
Utopia, 15

Venezuela, 34, 165
Vietnam War, 28
Village life model, 126
Voting
  concentration, 171
  process, 132

Welfare state, 3
Western Europe, 12
World Bank, 147
World Health Organization, 71